ASTROLOGICAL

WORKS

OF

THEOPHILUS

OF EDESSA

Translated by EDUARDO J. GRAMAGLIA

Edited with an Introduction by
BENJAMIN N. DYKES, PHD

The Cazimi Press
Minneapolis, Minnesota
2017

Published and printed in the United States of America

by The Cazimi Press
515 5th Street SE #11, Minneapolis, MN 55414

© 2017 by Benjamin N. Dykes, Ph.D.

ISBN-13: 978-1-934586-45-7

ACKNOWLEDGEMENTS

We would like to thank the following friends and colleagues, in alphabetical order: Chris Brennan, Martin Gansten, Thea Girard Marshall, and Charles Obert.

Also available at www.bendykes.com:

 Designed for curious modern astrology students, *Traditional Astrology for Today* explains basic ideas in history, philosophy and counseling, dignities, chart interpretation, and predictive techniques. Non-technical and friendly for modern beginners.

 Dorotheus's *Carmen Astrologicum* is a foundational text for traditional astrology. Originally written written in a lost Greek version, this is a translation of the later Arabic edition. It contains nativities, predictive techniques, aspect and house combinations, and a complete approach to elections or inceptions.

 Leopold of Austria's 13th Century *Compilation* is a good summary and handbook of medieval astronomy and astrology, with astronomical diagrams, defenses of astrology, principles, nativities, questions, elections, and even some instructions for talismans!

 This excellent and popular introduction to predictive techniques by contemporary Turkish astrologer Öner Döşer blends traditional and modern methods, with numerous chart examples.

 The first two volumes of this medieval mundane series, *Astrology of the World*, describe numerous techniques in weather prediction, prices and commodities, eclipses and comets, chorography, ingresses, Saturn-Jupiter conjunctions, and more, translated from Arabic and Latin sources.

Two classic introductions to astrology, by Abū Ma'shar and al-Qabīsī, are translated with commentary in this volume. *Introductions to Traditional Astrology* is an essential reference work for traditional students.

The classic medieval text by Guido Bonatti, the *Book of Astronomy* is now available in paperback reprints. This famous work is a complete guide to basic principles, horary, elections, mundane, and natal astrology.

This first English translation of Hephaistion of Thebes's *Apotelesmatics* Book III contains much fascinating material from the original Dorotheus poem and numerous other electional texts, including rules on thought-interpretation.

The largest compilation of traditional electional material, *Choices & Inceptions: Traditional Electional Astrology* contains works by Sahl, al-Rijāl, al-'Imrānī, and others, beginning with an extensive discussion of elections and questions by Benjamin Dykes.

The famous medieval horary compilation *The Book of the Nine Judges* is now available in translation for the first time! It is the largest traditional horary work available, and the third in the horary series.

The Search of the Heart is the first in the horary series, and focuses on the use of victors (special significators or *almutens*) and the practice of thought-interpretation: divining thoughts and predicting outcomes before the client speaks.

 *The Forty Chapters* is a famous and influential horary work by al-Kindī, and is the second volume of the horary series. Beginning with a general introduction to astrology, al-Kindī covers topics such as war, wealth, travel, pregnancy, marriage, and more.

 The first volume of the *Persian Nativities* series on natal astrology contains *The Book of Aristotle*, an advanced work on nativities and prediction by Māshā'allāh, and a beginner-level work by his student Abū 'Alī al-Khayyāt, *On the Judgments of Nativities*.

 The second volume of *Persian Nativities* features a The second volume of *Persian Nativities* features a shorter, beginner-level work on nativities and prediction by 'Umar al-Tabarī, and a much longer book on nativities by his younger follower, Abū Bakr.

 The third volume of *Persian Nativities* is a translation of Abū Ma'shar 's work on solar revolutions, devoted solely to the Persian annual predictive system. Learn about profections, distributions, *firdariyyāt*, transits, and more!

 Expand your knowledge of traditional astrology, philosophy, and esoteric thought with the *Logos & Light* audio series: downloadable, college-level lectures on MP3 at a fraction of the university cost!

Enjoy these new additions in our magic/esoteric series:

 *Astrological Magic: Basic Rituals & Meditations* is a basic introduction to ritual magic for astrologers. It introduces a magical cosmology and electional rules, and shows how to perform ritual correctly, integrating Tarot and visualizations with rituals for all Elements, Planets, and Signs.

 Available as an MP3 download, *Music of the Elements* was composed especially for *Astrological Magic* by MjDawn, an experienced electronic artist and ritualists. Hear free clips at bendykes.com/music.php!

 *Nights* is a special, 2-disc remastering by MjDawn of the album GAMMA, and is a deep and powerful set of 2 full-disc MP3 soundtracks suitable for meditation or ritual work, especially those in *Astrological Magic*. Hear free clips at bendykes.com/music.php!

 *Aeonian Glow* is a new version of the original ambient work mixed by Steve Roach, redesigned by MjDawn and Vir Unis from the original, pre-mixed files. This MP3 album is entrancing and enchanting: hear free clips at bendykes.com/music.php!

TABLE OF CONTENTS

Table of Figures viii

INTRODUCTION 1

Section 1: Life and works 2

Section 2: The works in this book 19

Section 3: Pingree's hypothesis about Theophilus, Rhetorius, and
Māshā'allāh 36

Section 4: Theophilus's Dorothean source 42

Section 5: Special Vocabulary 44

Section 6: Manuscripts 45

Section 7: Editorial principles 46

LABORS CONCERNING MILITARY INCEPTIONS 49

Chapter 1: Introduction 49

Chapter 2: An inception of war 51

Chapter 3: On the four pivots, configurations, post-ascensions, places,
and degrees of each one 55

Chapter 4: On connection and separation 65

Chapter 5: On triangles 68

Chapter 6: On squares 70

Chapter 7: On diameters 72

Chapter 8: On hexagons 74

Chapter 9: On war, according to Theophilus 74

Chapter 10: If someone wishes to become a tyrant and free himself from
subjection to those in power 76

Chapter 11: If someone (of those making war or those against whom war
is made), sends a herald to the other in order to seek favor or a truce 77

Chapter 12: On tyranny 78

Chapter 13: In what kind of land the war will take place 82

Chapter 14: When there is war 83

Chapter 15: Otherwise, when there is war 84

Chapter 16: Whether the army is large or small 85

Chapter 17: On treachery and betrayal 85

Chapter 18: On war 86

Chapter 19: When they set out moving 86

Chapter 20: On besieged cities 87

Chapter 21: In reference to besieging a city 88

Chapter 22[a]: On besieged cities 88

Chapter 22[b]: On ambush, treachery, and trickery 90

Chapter 23: On military campaigns 91

Chapter 24: The inception of war.. 92

Chapter 25: By Theophilus, on the proposal of a ruler for election........ 92

Chapter 26: On abandoned cities.. 94

Chapter 27: If you are asked whether a city is besieged or not, and—if it is—whether it is taken prisoner or spared............................... 96

Chapter 28: An inception of war.. 97

Chapter 29: If someone wishes to besiege a city, and at the same time find peace.. 99

Chapter 30: A military inception, from which the whole beginning (and reversal) of the war is known 100

Chapter 31: From Zoroaster, by Praxidicus, on expected war or some evil: when it will take place 101

Chapter 32: On undertaking an office or service, how many years and months he continues 102

Chapter 33: On a man who wishes to come to the king and see whether the mighty one fulfills the promises that were made, or not 102

Chapter 34: On kings and powers.. 103

Chapter 35: On war, from Julianus of Laodikaia 103

Chapter 36: Another inquiry on war.. 105

Chapter 37: On the resolution of war 107

Chapter 38: On the turning points of the four seasons............... 108

Chapter 39: On the delivery of letters, from Zoroaster............... 112

Chapter 40: Again, on letters 121

Chapter 41: When it is convenient to send letters 122

THE COLLECTION ON COSMIC INCEPTIONS 123

Chapter 1: Four approaches to ingress charts 123

Chapter 2: The study of the celestial influences of the ruler of the year, such as they are collected from the ancients 125

Chapter 3: On the Lot of the king, from the Sun up to the Moon, and the same from the Midheaven... 128

Chapter 4: On the ruler of the year... 131

Chapter 5: On the month 138

Chapter 6: On the month, according to Nechepsō 140

Chapter 7: On the universal effects of the Nodes........................ 147

Chapter 8: Portents of the New and Full Moons..........................147

APOTELESMATICS **149**

Chapter 1: Introduction...149

Chapter 2: On the winds occurring in the settling of the airs..................154

Chapter 3: On Jupiter..156

Chapter 4: On Mars..157

Chapter 5: On Venus 158

Chapter 6: On Mercury...159

Chapter 7: The influences of the eclipses of the Sun................................160

Chapter 8: On the influence of the eclipses of the Moon.........................162

Chapter 9: On the influence of the five wandering stars and signs,
beginning with Saturn...163

Chapter 10: On Jupiter in the signs...169

Chapter 11: On Mars in the signs..173

Chapter 12: On Venus in the signs 177

Chapter 13: On Mercury in the signs...181

Chapter 14: What each sign and star indicates, and what they rule 185

Chapter 15: What types of thing belong to each star 186

Chapter 16: Also, from metals 186

Chapter 17: What each star is allotted, of animals 187

Chapter 18: The influences of the *paranatellonta* stars in every inception
and question...187

Chapter 19: Different inceptions 193

Chapter 20: On the twelfth-parts 206

Chapter 21: On madmen and epileptics 207

Chapter 22: On robbers 209

Chapter 23: On death...210

Chapter 24: The Lot of the noxious place, from Saturn till Mars (or
alternately, from Mercury) 211

Chapter 25: On the connections and separations of the Moon..............211

Chapter 26: After how long will the influences take place 213

Chapter 27: On knowing whether he lives or has died 214

Chapter 28: On poisoning..214

Chapter 29: In order to know whether a letter is true or false, whether it
was written cunningly, brought by a slave or a free man.....................215

Chapter 30: What does the inquiry indicate? 215

Chapter 31: About what kind of man [is it asked]? 216

ON VARIOUS INCEPTIONS... 218

THE FIRST HOUSE 218

Chapter 1.1: On tropical signs 218

Chapter 1.2: On bicorporeal signs 218

Chapter 1.3: On fixed signs..219

Chapter 1.4: The images of the signs...220

Chapter 1.5: On New and Full Moons 220

Chapter 1.6: On inceptions 221

Chapter 1.7: Otherwise, on inceptions of travel 223

Chapter 1.8: The influence of the ascending and descending Nodes226

Chapter 1.9: On the manner of the inception 227

Chapter 1.10: On the lights 228

Chapter 1.11: On the Sun in the inception.......................................228

Chapter 1.12: On the Moon in the inception....................................229

Chapter 1.13: Examination of the mixture of the stars: what matters someone wishes to inquire about..231

Chapter 1.14: On what someone wishes to ask about.......................234

Chapter 1.15: On the recurrence of the stars 234

Chapter 1.16: About the manner of the inquirer..............................234

Chapter 1.17: Concerning his manner, in another way 235

Chapter 1.18: What we are asked about 235

Chapter 1.19: Of what kind is the inception.....................................236

Chapter 1.20: What is the nature of the inception 236

Chapter 1.21: On inceptional distribution..236

Chapter 1.22: Making conjectures about the inception 237

Chapter 1.23: On the strength of the accomplished effects of the stars and signs 239

Chapter 1.24: On the star ruling the inception.................................240

Chapter 1.25: Of what kind is the inception.....................................241

Chapter 1.26: Whether the matter is helpful or harmful 241

Chapter 1.27: Concerning the character and strength of the inception… 241

Chapter 1.28: On inceptions, in plain language................................242

Chapter 1.29: A synopsis by means of tables....................................245

Chapter 1.30: General instructions...245

THE SECOND HOUSE...246
Chapter 2.1: The second heading … 246
Chapter 2.2: On buying...247
Chapter 2.3: On the finding of lost objects.............248
Chapter 2.4: On legal judgments 249
Chapter 2.7: On runaways 250
Chapter 2.6: On thieves 251
Chapter 2.7: On those we inquire about: whether they are friends or enemies 251
Chapter 2.8: An inception on whether a matter is true or false..........252
THE THIRD HOUSE..253
Chapter 3.1: The third heading 253
THE FOURTH HOUSE 255
Chapter 4.1: The fourth heading 255
THE FIFTH HOUSE 256
Chapter 5.1: The fifth heading 256
Chapter 5.2a: On masculine or feminine births, or about those in the womb...256
Chapter 5.2b: Whether the inception is eminent or not.....................256
Chapter 5.3: When we are asked whether someone will be highly esteemed in his desired pursuits or not 257
Chapter 5.4: Otherwise, whether a woman is pregnant.....................257
Chapter 5.5: Whether the baby is masculine or feminine 259
THE SIXTH HOUSE 261
Chapter 6.1: The six headings of the twelve inceptions....................261
Chapter 6.2: Otherwise, on the sick 262
Chapter 6.3: Another chapter on taking to one's bed, when we know the birth 264
THE SEVENTH HOUSE 266
Chapter 7.1: The seventh heading: on childless hermaphrodites, and which of them is barren...266
Chapter 7.2: On bad luck...266
THE EIGHTH HOUSE 267
Chapter 8.1: Whether the one about whom we ask is a friend or an enemy..267
Chapters 8.2-8.5 267

Chapter 8.6: On the ill-fed degrees by signs, when the Moon comes to them 267

Chapter 8.7: On knowing whether someone lives or has died 268

Chapter 8.8: Otherwise, on those who are dead 269

THE NINTH HOUSE 270

Chapter 9.1: On being abroad 270

Chapter 9.2: Otherwise, on being abroad and returning 271

Chapter 9.3: Another chapter on living abroad 271

Chapter 9.4: On the lord of the ninth place..272

Chapter 9.5: On returning from living abroad 272

Chapter 9.6: When we are asked about vows 273

Chapter 9.7: For the setting up of the cauldron...................................273

Chapter 9.8: On migration from one place to another.........................273

Chapter 9.9: On letters 274

THE TENTH HOUSE..276

Chapter 10.1: On the proposal of a ruler...276

Chapter 10.2: Whether this comes to pass..276

Chapter 10.3: Whether the matter comes to pass or not, and whether it is imminent or delayed..276

Chapter 10.4: On the place pertaining to action 276

APPENDIX A: ARABIC PASSAGES OF THEOPHILUS.......... 277

1. Abū Ma'shar, *Great Introduction* VIII.4 278

2. Al-Rijāl, *Skilled* I.43: Whether the pregnancy will be completed or not 280

3. Al-Rijāl, *Skilled* I.46: If the fetus is male or female...........................281

4. Al-Rijāl, *Skilled* III.17: On imprisonment 282

5. Al-Rijāl, *Skilled* III.22: On the length of the rulership and lives of those in authority..285

6. Al-Rijāl, *Skilled* III.22: On the length of the rulership and lives of those in authority..287

7. Al-Rijāl, *Skilled* VII.11.1: On buying and selling.............................289

8. Al-Rijāl, *Skilled* VII.20.3: On building the foundations of estates and houses...290

9. Sahl, *Nativities* Ch. 2.11: The statement of Theophilus on good fortune and assets 291

10. Sahl, *Nativities* Ch. 3.2: On the abundance and scarcity of siblings... 292

11. Sahl, *Nativities* Ch. 3.4: The benefit of the siblings.........................293

12. Sahl, *Nativities* Ch. 4.1: Introduction to the topic of parents 295

13. Sahl, *Nativities* Ch. 6.2: On chronic illness of the eyesight 296

14. Sahl, *On Times* Ch. 8: On the Times of War 299

BIBLIOGRAPHY: 302

GLOSSARY 306

INDEX 330

Table of Figures

Figure 1: Significators for local tyrant and ruling king (*Labors* Ch. 12)........14

Figure 2: Monthly signs and lords (*Cosmic* Ch. 5, 3-4).....................................24

Figure 3: Possible archetypal assignments, with feminine Saturn 33

Figure 4: Al-Andarzaghar in relation to Sahl, *BA*, and Rhetorius...................40

Figure 5: House significations for an inception of war......................................52

Figure 6: Angles for freeing oneself from a ruler...76

Figure 7: Significators for local tyrant and ruling king......................................78

Figure 8: House significations for election of new ruler....................................93

Figure 9: Abandoned cities 94

Figure 10: House significations for besieging a city...96

Figure 11: House significations for war 98

Figure 12: House significations for war 106

Figure 13: Monthly signs and lords (*Cosmic* Ch. 5, 3-4) 139

Figure 14: The Lot of the month (*Cosmic* Ch. 6, 4-6)...................................141

Figure 15: The Lot of the king (*Cosmic* Ch. 6, 19)...143

Figure 16: Natures of fixed stars: Theophilus 192

Figure 17: Angles for finding lost objects 248

Figure 18: Angles for lawsuits..249

Figure 19: Angles for illness...261

Figure 20: Phases of Moon for buying (Carmen V.44, 48)..............................290

INTRODUCTION

Finding the beginning and end of historical periods in astrology is some-times easier, sometimes harder. For example, Sasanian Persian astrology and its use of Greek-language astrological texts definitely began in the 3rd Centu-ry AD, shortly after the dynasty came to power.[1] In its institutional form it would have come to an end officially in 651 AD, when the last Shah (Yazdi-jird III), was killed. But even then, Persian-language astrology was still influential until the late 700s, when numerous texts were translated into Ar-abic, after which the use of Persian sources dropped off sharply.

The life and works of Theophilus of Edessa (c. 695 – 785 AD) are espe-cially interesting in this context, because he worked as an astrologer and translator, in several languages, during one of the most transformative peri-ods of the Near East between the birth of Muhammad and the Crusades. His first language seems to have been Greek, and he had access to numerous Greek texts, being born in the formerly Greco-Roman or Hellenistic city of Edessa (in modern Syria). Yet he first worked during the more Arab-dominated 'Umayyad Caliphate, which ruled from Damascus, and then later under the more Persian-influenced 'Abbāsid Caliphate, in Baghdad and cen-tral Asia. He was firmly rooted in Greek-language astrology and especially in one of its preeminent texts, the work of Dorotheus of Sidon (1st Century);[2] and yet he was clearly converting natal material into elections or inceptions, as well as into "horary" questions, which played so great a role in later astrol-ogy. So was he the "last" Hellenistic astrologer, or one of the "first" early medieval astrologers? Did he have many colleagues in Edessa who rooted him in the past, or were his professional relationships more with Arab and Persian colleagues, and a focus on the future? And if he was a more transi-tional figure, does this make him more interesting, or less? Below we will explore his biography and see if we can answer these questions.

In this volume I present four of the surviving astrological works of The-ophilus, translated by Eduardo Gramaglia, as well as 14 Arabic passages (translated by me) which illustrate something of his impact—or lack of it—

---

[1] Al-Nadīm, Vol. 2 p. 575.

[2] As of 2017 I have released my own new translation of the Arabic version of Dorotheus, which has some different chapter and sentence numbering than does Pingree's 1976 edi-tion. All references to *Carmen* in my books from here onward, will refer only to my own edition.

on later Arabic-language astrology. The four works are as follows, with a brief description of their contents:

- *Labors Concerning Military Inceptions* (*Labors*). A creative reworking of numerous passages from Dorotheus, put into a military context to answer questions by military strategists and commanders.

- *Collection on Cosmic Inceptions* (*Cosmic*). A mundane work that focuses on Aries (and quarterly) ingresses, some of which is based on Dorotheus and other parts attributed to Nechepsō.

- *Apotelesmatics* (*Apotel.*). A combination of natal and mundane material, much of it from unknown sources but several chapters based on Rhetorius and Ptolemy.

- *On Various Inceptions* (*OVI*). An assortment of elections or inceptions, from a variety of sources.

Section 1: Life and works

Apart from a few anecdotes and historical references, we know little about Theophilus's life; but that is rather typical of many historical astrologers. Nevertheless we do know enough, and especially about his times, to make his situation and life intriguing to the imagination.

But first we must address something uncomfortable, and that is the distorting influence of the scholar David Pingree (1933-2005). Pingree performed great services for the history of astronomy and astrology, and many translations today would likely not exist were it not for him. He was a multi-lingual, experienced pioneer in this whole subject, and we are indebted to him. But for some reason when it came to Theophilus, Pingree's judgment was consistently off the mark, and so we must address that here. I am well aware that I myself have written some howlers in my day, and I hope the reader will forgive my strong tone. Unfortunately, because Pingree claimed so many wrong things about Theophilus for so many decades, and built up such a mythology about the transmission of astrology around him, we could easily be accused of engaging in mere polemics unless we address numerous details. A very tangled skein must be unraveled.

Pingree's interest in Theophilus appears early, such as his claim that "In-do-Iranian astrology" reached 8th-Century Byzantium due to Stephanus (an associate or student of Theophilus), who apparently brought Theophilus's works to Constantinople near the end of Theophilus's life.[3] Over time Pingree began to claim, without evidence, that Theophilus personally intro-duced a copy of Rhetorius to Māshā'allāh.[4] Indeed, in this one statement Pingree condenses two key suppositions together: that (a) Theophilus gave this copy to Māshā'allāh, and (b) that Māshā'allāh himself authored the Ar-abic version of what became the *Book of Aristotle*, which itself has passages from Rhetorius. This connection between Theophilus, Rhetorius, and Māshā'allāh will be examined later, but you can perhaps see what has hap-pened: a cultural transmission of astrology has been distilled down to the actions of one man, with particular books. The very title of Pingree's 2001 article encapsulates this notion about Rhetorius: *From Alexandria to Bagh-dad to Byzantium*.

Likewise, Pingree claimed that Theophilus was "the first" to organize a natal treatise based on the order of the twelve houses or places, rather than stages of life.[5] But how could he possibly know this? Indeed, I will argue later that the source of the *Book of Aristotle*—where this organization does oc-cur—was more likely written by the Persian al-Andarzaghar, who predates Theophilus.

Part of the problem is that Pingree himself was such an institution, and amassed so much information by himself, and from so many languages, that his articles are often dense "data dumps" in which it can take hours to trace out their patterns of evidence, and often enough that evidence turns out to be Pingree himself. As an example, in 2002 (p. 21) Pingree says that The-ophilus expresses a preference for the customs or "way" of Harrān, to that of Edessa—specifically, for "Aristotle, Plato, and mathematics over pious ascet-icism." (This itself is unusual because Platonism is known for pious asceticism.) As proof, he points to his 2001 article (p. 13), which unambigu-

---

[3] See Pingree 1963, p. 243. Pingree suggested several dates for this action by Stephanus, such as 775 (2004, p. 539) and 780 (2001, p. 12). According to Pingree 2004 (pp. 239-40), Stephanus wrote a work on astrological history which focused in particular on the Cali-phates up through al-Mahdī: it is tempting to suppose that he relied on notes by Theophilus to do so, and more work on Stephanus's writings should reveal more.

[4] See for example Pingree 1997, p. 124.

[5] Pingree 1997, p. 125.

ously states, without proof, that Theophilus studied in Harrān, but *not* that he ever expressed this preference. But the citation for *that* refers back to the as-yet unpublished 2002 article! Then in 2004 (p. 545), he again makes this claim about Harrān, citing the 2001 article. This kind of circular self-citation is one reason why the scale of the problem was not really clear to me until I began working on my forthcoming Sahl volume, as well as working with Eduardo Gramaglia on Theophilus. Only with more translations will we be able to say in more detail what is true and what is not.

So, Pingree's articles frequently make great and specific claims for the importance of Theophilus, but they simply do not hold up well under scrutiny. In addition to the Harrān-Edessa statement we might add the claim that Theophilus had a Pahlavi edition of the *Almagest* (no evidence),[6] that he was the first transmitter of Rhetorius (almost certainly wrong, see below), that his work shows a great use of Hephaistion (pretty weak, see below), that it shows the influence of Indian astrology, and indeed Indian military astrology (no evidence),[7] and so on. In his 2004 article (p. 552), after discussing a couple of chapters in *Labors*, he says that while "some of the rest" comes from Greek sources, "much more" comes from lost Pahlavi texts. This is totally, provably wrong: the reader can see in my footnotes that practically everything in *Labors* can be traced back to Dorotheus: as the first person to translate 'Umar's *Carmen* in 1976, Pingree should have known this. But when it came to Theophilus, Pingree consistently lost his sense of perspective.

ಏ   ಏಂ   ಞ

---

[6] See below, where Pingree first is not sure whether it was the Greek or Pahlavi edition, but three years later in an article on Pahlavi-language and Sasanian astrology he insists it was Pahlavi.

[7] A few examples should suffice. Pingree 1976 (1976) says that *Apotelesmatics* Ch. 13 "seems to have been influenced by Indian astrology," and gives two related texts (*Yavanajātaka* Vol. 2, pp. 203-04, and Heph. III.47, **56**); but neither of these lists of correspondences between signs and terrain has any clear relation to Theophilus at all. Pingree 2001 (p. 15) claims that there is some material from Varāhamihira in *Labors*, and points to 1963b (pp. 252-54), which has nothing to do with military astrology. Pingree 2004 (p. 552) claims that *Labors* Ch. 12 is close to the *Bṛhadyātrā* Ch. 9, **6-14**: but the latter has to do with the decans in war, which is not only not the topic of *Labors* Ch. 12, but the closest match is in *Labors* Ch. 30, which is on the houses and uses a different scheme. Similar false matches can be found in Pingree 2004 (p. 552, n. 55, on *Labors* Ch. 2), and 1976 (p. 148, comparing *Labors* Ch. 1.2 [?] with *Bṛhadyātrā* Ch. 2.13).

Let us now introduce some basic details about Theophilus himself and then his times. According to the medieval writer Gregory Bar Hebraeus, Theophilus son of Thomas was born in 695 AD, and died in the summer of 785 AD at age 90, twenty days before his employer, the 'Abbāsid Caliph al-Mahdī (r. 775-785).[8] He was from Edessa, but by his own testimony he lived at some point in Baghdad (obviously after 762 AD),[9] and in his old age he was al-Mahdī's chief (*princeps*) astrologer.[10] But Ibn Khaldun describes him in another, interesting way: as "the Byzantine astrologer of the 'Umayyad period."[11] So despite his working for at least one 'Abbāsid Caliph for many years, at least Ibn Khaldun thought of him essentially as a foreigner, a Roman, and as an earlier, 'Umayyad-era astrologer. So this is something of a puzzle, and should warn us against making too many claims about his importance. There is no doubt that the Theophilus we do have is an interesting man, living in interesting times, and who held a key court position in one of the most dramatic periods in astrology and Islamic history; but his work was highly dependent on previous authors, and it seems he was not used a great deal by later ones.

Now,[12] after the death of Muhammad in 632 AD, the Islamic world was ruled by a series of four Caliphs ("successors") who had personally known him. Under these Caliphs, Muslim armies attacked and subjugated every neighboring land, including those of the Levant (formerly Roman or Byzantine) and central Asia (formerly Sasanian or Persian). But after some civil wars, power finally passed in 661 AD to a distant cousin of Muhammad: Mu'āwiya, the Muslim governor of Syria (conquered in about 637 AD). Mu'āwiya was descended from a man named 'Umayya, hence this new dyn-

---

[8] Hoyland 1997, p. 400; Sezgin, p. 49; al-Qiftī, cited by Cumont in *CCAG* V.1, p. 231 n. 2. There seems to be some confusion over the actual date. Bar Hebraeus says he died 20 days before al-Mahdi, and according to Cumont al-Mahdi died on August 4, 785: this would mean that Theophilus died on July 15 or 16, as Pingree (1976, p. 146) says. But then Cumont also seems to say that Theophilus did (or perhaps others said he did) die on August 15.

[9] *Cosmic* Ch. 1, **7-8**.

[10] Sezgin, p. 49; see also the story below by Bar Hebraeus, and also the testimony of al-Qiftī, cited in Hoyland 2011, p. 6.

[11] Ibn Khaldun Vol. 2, p. 216.

[12] For the general history of what follows, I rely primarily on Kennedy 2004. Later I will also rely on the *Chronicle* (Hoyland 2011).

asty was called the 'Umayyad dynasty.[13] This dynasty was mainly controlled by ethnic Arabs, and ruled primarily from Damascus until the victory of the 'Abbāsids in 750 AD. This was the dynasty in which Theophilus was born, and with which Ibn Khaldun primarily associated him.

This Syria-based Caliphate was centered in the ancient Greco-Roman culture which had been firmly in place for centuries. The native Syrians were wealthy and educated, and their administrative experience must have been invaluable to their new overlords, who had no real background in sophisticated urban life and imperial rule. I would also point out that Egypt had been conquered since the early 640s: this made the civilization of Alexandria and its astrological heritage—such as the work of Rhetorius—available to the 'Umayyads as well.[14]

Islamic expansion and imperialism increased greatly under the 'Umayyads, so that the Persians were conquered by the 650s; and after driving through north Africa, most of Spain was taken by 716, when Theophilus was about 21 years old. By that time as well, the furthest reaches of the Persian realms, bordering on China, were also subdued. It was one of the most remarkable military and political expansions in history.

We do not know where Theophilus was educated, but it could easily have been in Edessa, or in nearby Harrān, which even up until the time of Abū Ma'shar was known as a center of astronomy, astrology, and astrological magic (and for a brief period under the 'Umayyads was even the capital). It is again worth pointing out that the relative unity of the Caliphate, like the relative unity of Byzantine rule, would have made it easy for books to travel back and forth: so if Theophilus was able to get a copy of Greek-language books like Rhetorius's while in Edessa, or Harrān, or even Baghdad, there is no reason why a Persian like al-Andarzaghar couldn't have, as well.

Spiritually, Theophilus was a Chalcedonian Christian,[15] and apparently rather pious, as he devotes ample space in his introductions to Christian de-

---

[13] At least for the first few centuries, dynasties were named after the relative of Muhammad they claimed descent from: thus the 'Abbāsids claimed descent from a relative of his named al-'Abbās.

[14] For example, Principe (pp. 29-30) points out that even in the 8th-9th Centuries it was possible to go to Alexandria to learn things like alchemy: so why not astrology a century before that?

[15] Like others, Pingree claims he was a Maronite Christian (Pingree 2002, p. 21), but according to Hoyland this widespread belief is a confusion originating with Bar Hebraeus (Hoyland 1997, p. 400, n.7; 2011, p. 6, n.7).

fenses of astrology (see below). He had at least one son, Deucalion, to whom he dedicated at least *Labors* and *Apotelesmatics*. What I find interesting is that Deucalion apparently liked "mathematics" but did not know astrology well (*Apotel.* Ch. 1, **2**), and this seems to have been one of the reasons Theophilus was dedicating these works to him—namely, he may have been interested in Deucalion's soul (again, see below).

From works attributed to him as well as the sourcing of his extant astrological works, we know that he had a very good personal library and was a prolific author and translator. He was known as a translator of Greek into Syriac,[16] but also as a translator into Arabic.[17] Unfortunately, very little of those efforts survives, so we cannot say much about them.[18] But he certainly or probably had the following major astrological works, in some form or another, in descending order of certainty:

- Ptolemy: the *Almagest, Handy Tables*, and *Tetrabiblos*. According to Pingree, the *Almagest* is shown by his reference to Timocharis in *Cosmic* (Ch.1, **6**).[19]
- Dorotheus's poem, probably in a Greek prose version that was fuller than what we currently have in the Arabic *Carmen*.[20]
- Rhetorius's *Compendium*, both the fifth book compiled by Rhetorius himself,[21] and the currently untranslated sixth book.[22]

---

[16] Sezgin, p. 49.

[17] Al-Nadīm, p. 587.

[18] Hoyland 1997, p. 400.

[19] Pingree 2002 (p. 21) is more careful and leaves it open as to whether this was a Greek or Pahlavi version; but in 2004 (p. 546), he doubled down and insisted, without evidence or argument, that it was the Pahlavi. (Note that Pingree 2004 is an article on Sasanian astronomy and astrology.)

[20] Pingree (p. 2001, p. 14) speculates that he would have had access to Māshā'allāh's Pahlavi version of Dorotheus as well, though he admits that some of the Dorotheus which Theophilus has knowledge of, is not found in Pahlavi. But since the Pahlavi version does not survive, there is no way Pingree could make this judgment: so he might mean Māshā'allāh's alleged *Arabic* Dorotheus. Nevertheless to me this seems to contradict the notion that Theophilus also read Dorotheus in Greek: why bother with the Pahlavi or Arabic if one already has the Greek? To me this is again a symptom of Pingree's insistence on a historical theory about Māshā'allāh and Theophilus he cannot prove, so various articles shifted the facts back and forth throughout the years.

[21] See Holden's translation (2009).

- Valens's *Anthology* (possibly), as he mentions Critodemus (*Cosmic* Ch. 1, **6**), who is occasionally cited by Valens.[23]
- Some version of the source of Firmicus Maternus on the separations and applications of the Moon: see *Apotel.* Ch. 25, and my citation from *Mathesis* there.
- Some Orphic texts, as *OVI* Ch. 1.2 comes from material which Heeg (p. 62) says is Orphic.
- Hephaistion's *Apotelesmatics* (maybe).[24]

As for astrological works, we can be certain that wrote at least the following:

- *Labors* (in this volume).
- *Cosmic* (surviving portions in this volume).
- *Apotelesmatics* (in this volume).
- *OVI* (surviving portions in this volume).
- An unknown work on nativities (as evidenced in Appendix A).
- An unknown mundane work in which he predicted the length of the Muslim dynasties.[25]
- Possibly a separate work on questions or inceptions (see Appendix A).

---

[22] Forthcoming in a Greek edition by Stephan Heilen. According to Pingree at least, Chs. 35-37 of *Labors* are based on material in this sixth book.

[23] At least, this is the claim of Pingree (2001, p. 16). But Critodemus is also cited by Rhetorius (Chs. 57, 77), so I don't see why it would have to be the original Valens.

[24] See *Labors* Ch. 12, **14**, a slender reed indeed. Pingree (2001, p. 18) also says that Ch. 30 of *Apotel.* (in his numbering, Ch. 29) is from Heph. III.3, but actually it is based on *Tet.* III.8 (Robbins pp. 261-63). Only sentence **1** can be related to Heph. III.3, **3**, but that sentence is based on Ptolemy anyway. So, I have my doubts about Hephaistion.

[25] Ibn Khaldun Vol. II, p. 216. According to Ibn Khaldun, Theophilus said that the Muslim dynasty would last for a full set of great conjunctions (the standardized 960 years), until the conjunctions come back to Scorpio again; and either the dynasty will be less effective, or there will be "new judgments that will make a change of opinion necessary."

The following translations have been attributed to Theophilus, which to me seem like quite the grab-bag of odds and ends, and I suspect that he made more:

- Galen, *On the method of maintaining good health*, into Syriac.[26] Hunain b. Ishaq reports that the translation was poor.[27]
- Homer, the *Iliad*[28] (or two pseudo-Homeric works),[29] into Syriac.[30]
- Aristotle, *Sophistical refutations* (*Sophistici elenchi*), apparently into Syriac, which was then translated by someone else into Arabic.[31]

Finally, there was a "fine work of history"[32] now called the *Syriac common source*, but which I will simply gloss as the *Chronicle* (Hoyland 2011): see below.

Now let us return to 'Umayyad history and Theophilus's role in it. The quick decline of the 'Umayyads began in 743 AD, with the death of the Caliph Hishām. Like the Roman "year of the four emperors" in 69 AD, he was followed in quick succession by three other Caliphs, and finally in 744 by the powerful governor, Marwān II. At first it may have seemed that matters would stabilize, but in the end there were too many internal divisions in the Caliphate for it to continue in its current form. There were several interrelated problems. For example, geographically the government was located in the west (broadly, Syria), which was resented by those in the east (especially in the formerly Sasanian lands); ethnically the Caliphate leadership structure and largesse favored Arabs, which was resented by the Persians; economically it favored Syria, which was resented by the more prosperous Iraqis. All of this was on top of the (perhaps exaggerated) criticism that the 'Umayyads had become too comfortable with infidel culture, and worries that their family relation to Muhammad was not close enough: that is, critics were equating tribal kinship with spiritual purity and leadership. This last view came especially from more puritanical elements in the east.

---

[26] Hoyland 1997, p. 401; Sezgin, p. 49.

[27] Sezgin, p. 49.

[28] Hoyland 1997, p. 401.

[29] Sezgin, p. 49.

[30] See the fuller citation for this attribution by Bar Hebraeus in Pingree 2001, p. 13.

[31] Al-Nadīm, p. 601.

[32] According to Bar Hebraeus (Hoyland 2011, p. 6).

Enter the 'Abbāsids and the central figure of Abū Muslim, a low-born man who spearheaded their rise to power. For decades, Arab immigrants to formerly Sasanian lands had intermarried with local Persians, and a hybrid culture had emerged with its own eastern identity: this was especially so in the province of Khurāsān, which in Persian meant "east," and had been the eastern quarter of the former Sasanian empire. It had retained much of its identity and independence despite being formally conquered, and was also more sympathetic to various ethnic groups, including Turkic peoples. It also housed a clan claiming descent from al-'Abbās, an uncle of Muhammad. In the mid-740s Abū Muslim was sent by the 'Abbāsid family to lay the groundwork of a later takeover. By 748 he had ousted the governor of Merv, and soon set out to destroy the 'Umayyads. Because the 'Umayyads were already in the midst of a multi-factional civil war, the path was made easier for the 'Abbāsids.

Things came to a head in 749-750. Abū Muslim arranged the early proclamation of the first 'Abbāsid Caliph (al-Saffāh, r. 749-54), and then in January 750 the 'Umayyads were defeated at the battle of the river Zāb (between Mosul and Erbil, modern Iraq). Marwān II fled (to be killed later in that year), and the gates of Damascus were opened to the 'Abbāsids. The 'Umayyad dynasty was at an end.

At this point we must introduce the *Chronicle* of Theophilus mentioned above, because Theophilus was not simply a generic subject of the Caliphate during these years: he seems to have been actually present at the Zāb. That is, we are not simply rehearsing historical facts for their own sake, but also because Theophilus gives us a front-row seat both to the events and the very serious role of the military astrologer.

In his 2011 book, Robert Hoyland explains that Theophilus wrote— partly on the basis of previous material—a chronicle of Islamic politics and conquests from about 589 to 754 AD.[33] Especially strong is the portion from 630 AD onwards, and the *Chronicle* is filled not only with details of political events, but it records plagues, eclipses, comets, and other omens of interest to a mundane astrologer (sometimes with specific days given). He apparently did not always give precise dates, but fortunately other chroniclers are able to help put the events in the correct order. This *Chronicle* forms a common

---

[33] To my mind, the fact that he stopped around 754 shows that he either got tired of writing his *Chronicle*, or perhaps his astrological duties and current events were too engaging to really keep up with it.

source for several later chroniclers, namely Theophanes (760-818), Dionysius of Tellmahre (d. 845), Michael the Syrian, the chronicler of 1234, and
Bishop Agapius of Manbij (fl. 945). Agapius himself relies almost exclusively
on it for the years 630-750, and we know this is Theophilus because he explicitly tells us so. In the midst of his account of the battle of Zāb, Agapius
quotes Theophilus as saying, "I myself was a constant witness of these wars. I
would write things down so that nothing of them should escape me."[34] He
adds that while Theophilus had written much more on all of these events,
Agapius himself has presented only some of it.

At that key battle, opposite the ʿUmayyad Caliph Marwān II was ʿAbdal-
lah b. ʿAli, uncle of the new ʿAbbāsid Caliph al-Saffāh. The ʿUmayyads or
"Syrians" crossed eastwards over the Zāb via a pontoon bridge, and dug in.
Although they had superior numbers, the ʿAbbāsids or "Khurāsānis"
Khurāsān got the upper hand, and near sunset many of the ʿUmayyads fled.
Some drowned in the river, others were trampled underfoot while fleeing
across the bridge;[35] Marwān fled as well and cut the bridge behind him, es-
caping to Harrān (the capital since 744). The ʿAbbāsids raced in and seized
tremendous amounts of gold and other booty.[36]

All of this may sound very exciting and glorious, but other events and
their aftermaths were more cruel and gruesome. Upon his gaining the Caliphate in 744, Marwān II had entered Damascus and made an example of the
body of his predecessor Yazīd III and some other enemies. He had Yazīd's
body disinterred and crucified, and then had many others' arms and legs cut
off, in addition to crucifying yet others.[37] This brutal violence, and the
knowledge that Theophilus witnessed these kinds of events, should remind
us that being a military astrologer was no laughing matter. One did not do
this for the romance of travel. Caliphs did not want to hear about the evolu-
tion of their consciousness. And if the astrologer was wrong about a chart,
many of his employer's men (of his employer himself) might be slaughtered,
mutilated, or crucified.

Now, Agapius does not explicitly claim that Theophilus was at the Zāb,
but the quote above seems sufficiently like someone looking back on events

---

[34] Hoyland 2011, p. 278.
[35] Agapius's quotation of Theophilus (see above) occurs approximately here.
[36] Hoyland 2011, pp. 275-78.
[37] Hoyland 2011, pp. 252-53.

he had personally witnessed, and anyway we can be sure that the events of that day were probably typical of the kinds of battles Theophilus saw. But now we should ask a question: what was the 55-year-old Theophilus doing there? For if he was a practicing astrologer under the 'Umayyads (that is, part of the elite class), why did he change allegiance to the 'Abbāsids, and how could he then be trusted? For at that time he was not a rookie astrologer eager to work for anyone who would hire him, but surely he was an established figure with allegiances and a history. Was he available for the highest price? If he had changed allegiance, whether for money or due to a change of heart, I should think we would have heard about that. On the other hand, there is another possibility: that despite his childhood in Edessa and the west, he had long worked in Khurāsān, and probably for those who later became the 'Abbāsid elite. A long-term relationship with Khurāsān could easily explain how he could have been trusted at such a momentous time, during such a quick succession of events. To my mind this also helps to soften and explain Ibn Khaldun's apparently distancing description of him as a "Byzantine astrologer of the 'Umayyad period." For on the one hand, it is true that unlike the younger and ethnically more eastern astrologers who worked in the Baghdad court (such as Māshā'allāh, al-Tabarī, Nawbakht the Persian, and Kankah the Indian), Theophilus was a western, Greco-Roman astrologer who had stemmed from the previous era. But on the other hand, he was not wholly identified with the vanquished 'Umayyads. For (under my interpretation) while he had always been part of the 'Umayyad elite, it was the *Khurāsāni* part of that elite. In other words, due to his age and experience he was chronologically an 'Umayyad, and simply moved into the halls of power with the 'Abbāsids when they properly became "the 'Abbāsids." Nevertheless, for many years he was probably not recognized as being a central figure in the Baghdad court, for reasons I will explain. So again, we are reminded of the essential ambiguity of Theophilus: 'Umayyad and 'Abbāsid, Baghdadi and Khurāsāni, Greco-Roman and Perso-Arabic, Hellenistic and medieval.

Al-Saffāh was succeeded by his son al-Mansūr (r. 754-775), who famously moved the capital of the empire to Baghdad and hired astrologers to elect the moment of its founding on July 31, 762 AD JC. As I mentioned, this group of astrologers included Māshā'allāh, 'Umar al-Tabarī, and Nawbakht the Persian—but Theophilus is never mentioned among them. The reason seems to be that Theophilus was busy doing other things: we do know from

Labors (Ch. 1, **8**) that he was part of a campaign to Margiana (in Khurāsān) in the winter of 758-759, which he says was both very cold and difficult.

As mentioned before, 'Abbāsid power was heavily dependent upon support from Khurāsān in the east; the problem was that this area had always been semi-independent. That was all well and good when trying to destabilize the 'Umayyads, but now that the 'Abbāsids were in charge they could not allow rebellion within their power base. In 758-59 the governor of Khurāsān, named 'Abd al-Jabbār al-Azdī, whose family was from Merv (in Margiana), rebelled. So al-Mansūr sent his son, the future al-Mahdī and employer of Theophilus, to Margiana in order to put down the rebellion. The move was successful, and in the end the people rose up against al-Jabbār and handed him over to al-Mahdī. Al-Mansūr then gave the governorship to al-Mahdī, who spent many more years in the east before returning to Baghdad.[38]

These events tell us several interesting things and suggest one other intriguing possibility. First, al-Mahdī was acquainted with Theophilus by 758-759, perhaps as the family astrologer. Indeed al-Mahdī was born only in about 745 AD, so a roughly 65-year-old Theophilus would have been closely advising a 15-year-old al-Mahdī, and did so for many years. Al-Mahdī was also obviously impressed enough to retain Theophilus in 775 when he acceded to the throne (if not retain him for the entire 13 years up until them). So all of this probably explains why Theophilus was not part of the team in al-Mansūr's court, and was therefore never mentioned with them: he was in the east much of the time, helping al-Mahdī put down the rebellions that ensued in the 760s. And if he had been with al-Mahdī the whole time, then they had a roughly 27-year working relationship. That is impressive.

Second, these facts show that important astrologers worked in many places and capacities, and were not simply padding the carpeted halls of capital city palaces. Both al-Mansūr and al-Mahdī had their *own* astrologers, likely with very different types of experience. For instance, while Māshā'allāh wrote an astrological piece on how long a king will rule,[39] that does not mean he was a military astrologer with actual battlefield experience of the type that Theophilus had. Indeed it makes one wonder what Theophilus might have thought of his "colleagues" in Baghdad: did he view them as dilettantes who

---

[38] Hoyland 2011, p. 300; Kennedy p. 135; Pingree p. 2001, p. 15.
[39] Contained in Sahl's *On Times*, Ch. 11 (my edition from the Arabic forthcoming, 2017).

lacked his vast experience? Did he feel threatened by this younger genera-tion? And did he have any strong professional reason to share his precious books—carefully adapted from Dorotheus and others—with astrologers he may not have known well and could have been his rivals? Below I will sug-gest he did not.

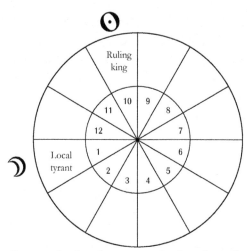

Figure 1: Significators for local tyrant and ruling king (*Labors* Ch. 12)

But a more intriguing point that connects his astrology with history, is this. In *Labors* Ch. 12, Theophilus adapts *Carmen* V.37 on runaways, to the situation of rebellion. At first the parallel may not be clear, but Theophilus reasons as follows. The Ascendant (the initiator of action) and the Moon indicate a runaway, while the Midheaven and the Sun indicate his master or the one seeking him. Just so, the Midheaven and the Sun indicate politically a ruling king, while the Ascendant and Moon signify a local tyrant or warlord who has decided to independent and "escape" the king's authority: he is a "runaway." So, using Dorotheus's rules for such an inception or event chart, Theophilus is able to answer questions about what will happen to the local tyrant who has initiated a rebellion: will he have local support, will he be "brought back," and so on. But this scenario is, precisely, the situation of al-Jabbār mentioned above, whose rebellion al-Mahdī suppressed in 758-59 (not to mention others in the 760s). It is extremely tempting to suppose that by 758-59, Theophilus had decided that this was the model to use for al-Jabbār, so that he would have interpreted charts for al-Mahdī in just this fashion. If so, then *Labors* Ch. 12 is not simply an intellectual exercise, but evidence of an astrologer adapting Dorotheus to very real battlefield and political conditions. I hope we will eventually identify charts which can reliably be attributed to Theophilus, to show his application of these theories to known events.

After 758-59, we have no reliable information about Theophilus's life until his last months. A story related by Bar Hebraeus, edited in the *CCAG* V.1 (p. 230), reports the following about an interaction between Theophilus and a known concubine of al-Mahdī, probably in the summer of 785 AD:

> It is related that when al-Mahdī, deciding to set out for Masabdanus,[40] ordered his concubine Hasanah[41] to go with him, when he sent her she said to Theophilus son of Thomas (a Christian astrologer from Edessa, [and] chief of the astrologers of al-Mahdī): "You were the author of this journey for the Emperor of the faithful, and you imposed the journey on us, which had not come into [his][42] mind; may God hasten your death, so that by it we may be freed of you."
>
> But when her letters reached [Theophilus], he said to the girl who delivered them, "When you return you should tell her: 'This advice is not from me. But what you have prayed for me, [namely] that I die quickly, this was decreed by God, and my death does draw near. You shouldn't think that your prayers were heard, but rather you should prepare much dust for yourself, and when I have died, you should put it on your head.'" She did not cease to seek the interpretation of his statement after he died, until, twenty days afterwards, al-Mahdī died.

In light of the personal influence Theophilus must have had on al-Mahdī, we can imagine that others besides the concubines might have resented decisions being made by the court astrologer.

From here we turn to the events after the death of Theophilus, and his legacy. Near the end of his life a student or associate of Theophilus, named

---

[40] Unknown at this time, but Kennedy (2004, p. 139) says that al-Mahdī died in a hunting accident in the Zagros mountains, a broad range east of Baghdad. MacBean lists a Massabatica, near "mount Zagrus."

[41] "The good," "the beautiful."

[42] I assume that since the concubine had no business intending any state journey, she means that the journey was not a good idea *for al-Mahdī*, but that he went simply because Theophilus had suggested it.

Stephanus,[43] moved permanently to Constantinople with numerous books (including apparently those of Theophilus), where he set about to "restore the study of astronomy and astrology" neglected by the Romans since the time of Heraclius.[44] One problem, he noted, was that the Byzantine Romans were no longer using Ptolemy's calendrics, so it was hard for them to practice Ptolemy's astronomy; in response, he created tables and an ephemeris for 796 AD, based on the Byzantine calendar.[45] This was apparently the way in which works preserved by Theophilus, and the other practices of the Perso-Arab astrologers, passed over to Constantinople and revived astrology there. But these works never made it to the Latin West, except for a few short passages in authors like al-Rijāl (see Appendix A).

In thinking about Theophilus's legacy, it seems to me there are two related questions to ask. The first is: how separate from Islamic culture and their own colleagues did Stephanus and Theophilus feel? The second is: why did Theophilus not seem to influence his colleagues very much? For one would think that people like Stephanus and Theophilus had good positions in the Caliphate, after a long-standing relationship with people like al-Mahdī; and Pingree argued for decades that Theophilus gave a copy of Rhetorius to Māshā'allāh, which should have made quite a splash. Indeed, if he had a better Greek copy of Dorotheus, one would think that that would have immediately been translated into Arabic and superseded 'Umar's version. The list could go on. But as I will argue, there is no evidence that Theophilus gave Rhetorius to Māshā'allāh, and very little of Theophilus's other works appears later in Arabic: for the most part they are only small sections from *Labors* and the otherwise unknown works on questions and nativities (Appendix A).[46] Moreover, we have seen that later biographers like Ibn Khaldun and al-Nadīm barely mention him or his astrological works at all; in later Arabic manuscripts his name is even spelled incorrectly as Nūfil (نوفيل) ra-

---

[43] He has variously been called Stephanus of Alexandria and Stephanus the Philosopher (Pingree 2001, p. 240); but Principe (pp. 24-25, 29) identifies a Stephanus of Alexandria involved in alchemy in the 600s, so we should not be too quick to identify him in any particular way.

[44] Pingree 2004, p. 239.

[45] Pingree 2004, p. 540.

[46] The student of Abū Ma'shar, Shadhān (*Albumasar in Sadan* Section 25, **1**), reports that Abū Ma'shar claimed to have found a book by "Theophilus, son of Thomas" in a library; but he does not say what was in it, and its mysteriousness and inaccessibility further underscores that Theophilus's works were not widely available.

ther than the better Thūfil (ثُوفيل), as though later writers were not even sure who he was.

I propose that the answer is partly professional, partly cultural. The professional side can be understood in terms of normal professional protectiveness, as well as his long years away from Baghdad and the close attachment to al-Mahdī. Remember: for the military astrologer, casting charts is a life-and-death business, so books like those of Theophilus would have comprised important trade secrets. Despite dedicating books to Deucalion (whom we know little or nothing about) and having a few bits of his books published in Arabic later, Theophilus had a prima facie reason to keep his library to himself, especially since for many years he probably had little-to-no contact with the Baghdad astrologers. We know from the introductory chapter of *Cosmic* that he did not learn the "eastern" approach to Aries ingresses until after the founding of Baghdad, so for some time he must have been isolated indeed, until he had to cooperate with others in Baghdad during the Caliphate of al-Mahdī. As for his colleagues, we should remember that he was brought in as the chief astrologer by al-Mahdī at a time when other astrologers (like Māshā'allāh) had already been attending the previous 'Abbāsid Caliphs for between thirteen and twenty-five years. It is easy to imagine professional resentments, especially if Theophilus had to be taught the Persian mundane astrology that the others would already have been practicing. So the lack of evidence for a transmission of Rhetorius or the rest of his library, or most of his own books, leads me to believe that both his lack of sharing and later writers' relative silence was intentional. On the other hand, later astrologers were certainly engaged in transforming inceptional texts into horary questions just like Theophilus was, so perhaps he did communicate something of his style and approach to them, if not much of the content.

The cultural issue is more speculative, but there are a few bits of evidence to consider. The first is that Stephanus left the Islamic world entirely for the Christian Byzantine culture of Constantinople, endeavoring to restore astrology there, even to the extent of—possibly—writing a Christian commentary to an edition of the *Handy Tables* or to the ephemeris for 796 mentioned above.[47] The second comes from the odd statements in *Cosmic*

---

[47] Pingree 2003 (p. 82) seems to say that he wrote the ephemeris but did not "use" the *Handy Tables*; Pingree 2004 (p. 540) says he did write a *commentary* on the *Handy Tables*.

Ch. 1, **7-8**, in which Theophilus describes the "ruling city of the Saracens" as being called Baghdad "in the dialect of the Syrians." Now, the words *Sarakēnē* and *Sarakēnos* were already centuries old, the former being used by Ptolemy himself in his *Geography* to designate certain peoples and areas of western Arabia, the northeast of Egypt, and the Sinai;[48] but they were imprecise terms and only much later came to mean Muslims generally. So why did Theophilus, who knew very well who the Arabs, Persians, Khurāsānīs, and ʿAbbāsids (indeed, Muslims) were and what they wanted, refer to all of them as "Saracens" and speak of the dialect of the "Syrians" (where he had grown up) in the third person like this? The text does not actually say that *Cosmic* is dedicated to someone like Deucalion, but this is a reasonable assumption, and would make this distancing language even more stark: for instead of addressing a book generically to "the world," he would be speaking to a contemporary who already knew him and what he was doing, and wouldn't need to be told about "the dialect of the Syrians." (Could this also mean that Deucalion lived somewhere far away from the world of Baghdad and the Caliphal wars?) So this suggests a sense of alienation and lack of cultural allegiance to the region he worked in. The third bit of evidence is that al-Mahdī himself had directed renewed attacks against the Byzantines, invading Asia Minor in 782 AD. The fourth is the reference by Ibn Khaldun about Theophilus being a "Byzantine astrologer of the ʿUmayyad period."

From these suggestive facts I propose that while Theophilus had worked for the ʿAbbāsids for many years, culturally and religiously he was still a Greek Christian loyal to Byzantine civilization. Especially while off in Khurāsān, he may not have fully appreciated the kinds of regional consolidation and civilizational clashes that were taking place: unlike us, he did not have the benefit of centuries of hindsight. As I mentioned, Ibn Khaldun reports him as saying that the Muslim or Arab dynasties would last a long time, but even then he might have thought of the Persians (in the form of the Khurāsān elite) as just a regional power, and the Arabs as just one more conquering group in the area. Over time he may have been increasingly conscious of his cultural and religious isolation in a world that had changed much since the days when the Khurāsānīs basically carried on rather independently, in what was in some respects still Sasanian culture. The way of the world was becoming clear: the trend was towards Persian administration, Arabic translations, and more Islamized philosophy and sciences,

---

[48] See for example his *Geography*, Book IV, Ch. XVI, p. 129.

especially as embodied in the so-called "house of wisdom," the intellectual movement which was already underway in the reign of al-Mansūr.

In light of these professional and cultural ideas, it might make sense that neither Stephanus nor Theophilus had a great and direct professional impact on their colleagues. Theophilus was elderly, a relative outsider, and a Greek writer. The younger Stephanus might have seen that the time was right to leave the East for good, and take Theophilus's inheritance with him.

Section 2: The works in this book

Labors Concerning Military Inceptions

As the title indicates, *Labors* is a work on military astrology, dedicated to Deucalion. For people who are used to treatments of war in books of questions (such as in Bonatti or Sahl), this may not seem particularly new. However, Theophilus *is* new, for two reasons. First, in his introduction (**7-8**) he says that before his time there were not many astrological treatments of war—unless it was simply to ask whether there would be war. But commanders in the field need to know much more than this, because war is a multi-faceted and complicated business. So, he explains (**8**) that he was forced to adapt both natal and inceptional texts to military purposes, and even mentions the harsh winter weather in 758-59 AD during the campaign with al-Mahdī against al-Jabbār (see above).[49] So apart from any other military astrology the Indians had, Theophilus was very conscious of developing something new, which his other colleagues and professional competitors would not have had. It would also not be far off to say that this is "horary" astrology or questions proper, because while many chapters still have an inceptional character, plenty of others fit right in with the genre of questions.

The second reason why Theophilus is new, is that he is largely new to us. We might think that such a well-known figure would have been used again and again by later Arabic writers, but he was not. Only a few chapters from *Labors* can be detected in Sahl's *On Questions* and *On Times*, and pretty much all later military astrology handed down to Latin writers comes from

---

[49] This is another reason to doubt that Theophilus used Indian sources for his military astrology, else he would have mentioned them.

Sahl. So, most of the book appears as a novel composition, in a little-explored branch of astrology, which was neglected almost as soon as it was written! Given that Theophilus actually used his material and tested it in the field, it makes it all the more valuable and rare.

Most of the chapters in *Labors* are based on Dorotheus, both his natal and inceptional books.[50] For example, Chs. 5-8 on aspect combinations are based on *Carmen* II.14-17, but adapted to military purposes. These chapters are pretty straightforward because they are based on natural significations and combine basic qualities: here, Saturn seems to represent the actions of the king's general, so when in trine to the Sun it brings a good reputation; in trine with Mercury, wisdom and clever words; and so on. But in many other cases, Theophilus has creatively adapted unexpected chapters from Dorotheus to very different and complicated scenarios. For instance, *Labors* Ch. 20 on besieging a city is taken from *Carmen* V.26, the inception for launching a ship into the water.

Also interesting are Theophilus's explicit statements about planetary significations (**2-4**). So for instance, we all know that Mars is a planet of war (**2**); but Saturn can also indicate war, particularly the capturing of cities and destruction of kings (**3**). For cities, Theophilus is probably thinking of building, stone, and the immovability of settlements and real estate, all of which are Saturnian; for kings, he is no doubt thinking of Saturn as the king in the way other Persian astrologers do (or as the king's general). For Saturn is the highest, most remote, and slowest planet, and instead of moving towards other planets, all others move towards him: just so, the king is remote, ideally steady and resolute, and others must come to him. In both this passage and *Cosmic* Ch. 1, **10-11** he lists other significations, but the reader should especially consult *Labors* Chs. 3-7 to see how Theophilus applies planets in combination and uses Dorotheus to shape his astrological thinking.

Readers of Pingree's articles on Theophilus will also know that he sometimes speaks of *Labors* being in two "editions," with Chs. 1-24 being the first edition, and the last 17 chapters being the second edition. I know of no evidence for this claim, but I think it is related to his views on Rhetorius, and will return to it below. (Note however that the title of *Apotelesmatics* does say that *it* is a second edition.)

---

[50] According to Pingree, Chs. 35-37 are from Book VI of Rhetorius (Greek edition still unpublished in 2017).

Collection on Cosmic Inceptions

The *Collection on Cosmic Inceptions* is devoted to mundane astrology. It is based partly on Dorotheus (*Carmen* IV and some version of III.1), partly on other material attributed to Nechepsō (and possibly Petosiris), with a few special mundane Lots. There may have been more to this work, because as mentioned above Ibn Khaldun stated that Theophilus had made some mundane predictions about Islam on the basis of Saturn-Jupiter conjunctions. It is also possible that he wrote about such things in another work, and we have already seen that there is evidence for other, unrecorded works by Theophilus.

Like the introduction of *Labors*, we can get a rough sense of when Theophilus wrote *Cosmic* (or at least, its introduction): in Ch. 1, **7-8**, he says that he learned his method of mundane ingresses in "the ruling city of the Saracens," which he says that "the Syrians" call Baghdad. Now, there had long been a small town on the site of Baghdad, and it was not far from the old Persian city of Ctesiphon, but Baghdad was not formally established until 762. So, we can assume that all or most of *Cosmic* was written after 762 AD, and that he himself was not doing mundane astrology of this type before then. This is interesting information, because it suggests that in his own practice he had primarily been adapting inceptional astrology for al-Mahdī, and had to be taught historical astrology by others while in his 60s.

In Chapter 1, Theophilus points out that there has been much disagreement on how to calculate and understand mundane ingresses. He lists four approaches:

- "The Egyptians" (**1-3**). The Egyptians reckoned the beginning of the year as the heliacal rising of Sirius, at which time they looked at the Moon and configurations of other stars. But as Theophilus points out, this was only the beginning of the year because of the local flooding of the Nile, which is irrelevant to other lands. So, he rejects this.
- "The Greeks" (**4**). These unnamed people drew on "the laws of nature" and looked at the first New Moon when the Sun approached the beginning of Aries. It is not clear to me whether they looked at both charts or not, and whether or not the New Moon itself was more important.

- Ptolemy (**5**). The method of Ptolemy was to look at the New and Full Moons immediately prior to all four seasonal ingresses.[51]
- The "eastern" astrologers, who admired the wisdom of the Persians, and translated Greek authors (**6-7**). These astrologers use only the Aries ingress, regardless of the associated lunar phase, calculated for the ruling city of the region.

Of these, Theophilus uses the fourth, "eastern" method (**7**), which he says also follows the method of Critodemus, Valens, Dorotheus, and Timocharis (**6**).[52] As another testament to the fact that Theophilus's methods did not largely affect his Arabic-language successors, most medieval Arabic treatments seem to follow either the "Greek" method or the Ptolemaic method, pairing annual or quarterly ingresses with New and Full Moons.[53] Nowadays most astrologers follow the "eastern" method of the Aries ingress without any Moon, but that is probably due to older methods being lost (or simply by analogy with a natal solar revolution), rather than any roundabout influence by Theophilus.

Theophilus also describes the use of four special mundane Lots which are worth investigating:

- The Royal Lot, from the Sun to the Moon, projected from the Midheaven (Ch. 3).[54]
- Lot of the month: from the Sun to Cancer, projected from Leo (Ch. 6, **1-2, 18, 34,** and **46**).[55]
- Lot of the king: from the Moon to Leo, projected from Cancer (Ch. 6, **19, 46,** and **49**).[56]
- A third lot, concerning the populace: from the Sun to Moon, projected from the Ascendant (Ch. 6, **58-62**).[57]

---

[51] *Tet.* II.10 (Robbins, pp.197-99).

[52] But in *Cosmic* Ch. 5, **1-2** he still seems to look at the preceding New or Full Moon. For his mundane lord or ruler of the year, and more information about interpreting ingress charts, see also *Labors* Ch. 38, where he does quarterly ingresses without the lunations.

[53] See my *Astrology of the World* Vols. 1-2.

[54] I suspect that this is only the diurnal calculation, and in a nocturnal chart it should be from the Moon to the Sun. In this way, it is a Lot of Fortune for a ruler (Midheaven) rather than for a normal native or the people (Ascendant).

[55] Note that the two versions of this chapter give two different calculations.

[56] Note that the two versions of this chapter give two different calculations.

One puzzling feature of Theophilus's treatment of monthly lords comes from *Cosmic* Ch. 5, **3-7**, which he adapted from the passage on monthly profection lords in *Carmen* IV.1, **46-50**. Part of the confusion comes from what I see as the lack of clarity in Dorotheus himself: this again suggests that Theophilus might have had a Greek prose summary of Dorotheus, but one which (like *Carmen*) was a bit uncertain. The operative sentence in *Cosmic* is this:

3 On the month, otherwise: from the transiting Sun to the Moon at the fixing of the year, and the same [amount] from the annual Hour-marker, and wherever the number leaves off, there we consider to be the beginning of the month.

The interpretation of this sentence depends mainly on whether we place a comma after "Sun." Without a comma, Theophilus seems to mean that we count from the Sun to the Moon, both of them within the annual ingress chart, and then project that from the Ascendant of the ingress. The sign we reach is the first month, and its lord is the lord of that month. Presumably then, each *successive* sign and lord will rule the *following* months. This is my preferred reading. So, in this 2017 ingress for London, from the Sun to the Moon is 267° 29'. We project that from the Ascendant, and reach 4° 39' Aries. Therefore, the first month of this tropical year (March 20 – April 19) falls on Aries, and the lord of the first month is Mars. Presumably then, the next month will be Taurus, ruled by Venus, then Gemini and Mercury, and so on. If we do this, then the calculation is essentially a Lot of Fortune at the ingress—and indeed, the Lot of Fortune here does fall precisely on that place. This leads us to ask whether we should reverse the calculation by night, as with a normal Lot of Fortune. One argument against reversal is that this is a solar ingress, so we must begin with the Sun. But I suspect that this is simply a normal Lot of Fortune, so it should be reversed at night.

---

[57] Again, this seems like a normal Lot of Fortune in parallel with the Royal Lot; it seems to be calculated on a monthly basis.

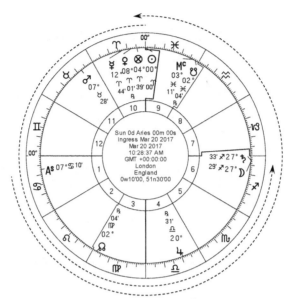

Figure 2: Monthly signs and lords (*Cosmic* Ch. 5, 3-4)

On the other hand, suppose we read this sentence with a comma, as "from the transiting Sun, to the Moon at the fixing of the year." That would mean counting from the transiting Sun *at each monthly ingress*, to the same position of the Moon which she had *at the Aries ingress*. But I don't think that's what Theophilus means. For as the Sun's position moves forward, his distance to the Aries ingress Moon decreases: this would result in each monthly sign going *backwards*, which I have never seen in traditional astrology. For instance, let the Sun be at 0° Taurus next month. Now the distance from him to the ingress Moon is only 237° 39'; projected from the ingress Ascendant would now get us only to Pisces and its lord Jupiter, meaning that the assignment of months to the signs would go backwards. To my mind, this is a big argument against such an interpretation.

Valens (*Anth.* V.4) also attributes to Nechepsō a method similar to *Cosmic* Ch. 5: from the transiting Sun to the Moon in the natal solar revolution ("the turning," *ektropē*). Again, a lot depends on how we might place a comma or read the phrase: from the transiting *Sun to the Moon, both* in the solar revolution, would yield my preferred solution above, so that we essentially find a Lot of Fortune in the revolution and then count successive signs for successive months. But Valens also says that this is for nocturnal charts (I believe he means for nocturnal *revolutions*, not nativities): for diurnal ones, measure from the transiting Moon to the natal Sun, and project from the Ascendant (presumably, of the solar revolution).

Finally, for a similarly problematic situation, see the "Lot of the month" by Nechepsō in *Cosmic* Ch. 6, which may also assign the months backwards, unless the method is only designed to find the first sign and month, moving forward sign-by-sign after that.

Apotelesmatics

Apotelesmatics, which lacks a name in the manuscripts but was called this by Pingree based on its opening sentences,[58] is a pastiche of many different things, and can be broken down in the following way:

- Ch. 1: Theological and cosmological.
- Chs. 2-17: Mundane, sources uncertain (but possibly some in-spired by Ptolemy).
- Chs. 18-31: Inceptions of many types, and especially natal material converted into inceptions. Of these:
  o Chs. 18-24 are based on Rhetorius.
  o Ch. 25 seems to share a common source with Firmicus Mater-nus IV.9-IV.14.
  o Chs. 30-31 are based on Ptolemy.[59]

Chapter 1 is a charming and impassioned theological and cosmological essay designed as an appeal to Deucalion. Theophilus begins by distinguish-ing mathematics from apotelesmatics—that is, between the calculation of a chart and judging what a chart *means* (**1-2**). He makes an appeal to Deucali-on, whom he says has a greater interest in mathematics and really needs to spend more time on apotelesmatics (**2-7**), not letting critics of astrology inhibit his confidence and desire (**5-6**). Turning to a grand religious view of the cosmos, Theophilus engages in a bit of hexameral or heptameral writing, a medieval type of writing in which one relates the days of creation to various

---

[58] Pingree 2001, p. 17.
[59] Pingree (2001, p. 18) claimed that Ch. 30 (in his counting, Ch. 29) was drawn from Heph. III.3, but in fact it is based on Ptolemy, not Hephaistion.

metaphysical and physical topics. In this case, he associates each of the planets with one of the days of Creation (**8-21**), quoting *Genesis* in several places. To this he references a "Book of All Wisdom," which he says was written by Solomon and is probably *Proverbs*, because he quotes *Proverbs* 24:3 there (**23**); then he refers to the *Book of Isaiah* (**23**) and the Gospels (**26-30**), pointing out that the three Wise Men were obviously astrologers, which shows that astrology is true and approved of by God. After some other references to the New Testament (**32-34**) he then creatively adapts *I Corinthians* 2-3 and returns to the topic of the soul (**35-38**). In this Biblical passage, Paul describes three paths in life, of which the first is the purely spiritual. Theophilus re-describes these paths so that astrology fits in the second path—not purely spiritual because it involves technical disciplines, but more than merely material and body-based.

Of the remaining chapters, I would like to point to Chapter 18, on the fixed, *paranatellonta* stars. These are fixed stars which are on the horizon or meridian at various times, such as in a nativity. The list appears in many forms throughout astrological literature (albeit with some changes and variations):

1. Anonymous of 379.
2. A Persian version attributed to Hermes, which later found its way into:
3. Zarādusht's *Book of Nativities* (Arabic).[60]
4. Rhetorius Ch. 58.
5. The Arabic original of the *Book of Aristotle*.[61]
6. Theophilus, *Apotelesmatics* Ch. 18.
7. Sahl's *Book of Nativities*.[62]

Sahl (7) most likely got his from (5), which got it from (2) or (3). Zarādusht (3) probably got his from (2). Theophilus (6) would have gotten his from Rhetorius (4), who probably got it from (1).

---

[60] I am preparing a translation of this book, with other works attributed to Zarādusht.

[61] See my translation of the Latin version, in *Persian Nativities* I.

[62] Translated and published by me in 2017, in a volume of Sahl's works.

There are a few differences between Theophilus and Rhetorius:

- Theophilus omits Algol in the Jupiter-Saturn group (**11-13**).
- Theophilus makes Pollux be Mars-Saturn (**14-15**), whereas for Rhetorius it is Mars alone.
- Theophilus seems to add Vindemiatrix to the Saturn-Venus group (**26**).

But more importantly, in Theophilus almost all of the longitudes in this text are precisely 2° 40' more than what appears in Rhetorius. So, we should be able to apply precession to figure out either when Rhetorius wrote his book, or for what year the values he did find, were written. But this will not be as easy as it seems.

The standard rate of precession defined by Ptolemy was 1° every 100 years (too slow). In the 9th Century at least—after Theophilus's death— Arab astronomers were said to have made new measurements that yielded 1° every 66 years (too fast, but better).[63] So if the values in Theophilus are 2° 40' more than in Rhetorius, Ptolemy's rate gives us 266 years, and the Persian/Arab rate 176 years.

Source	Rate	Result
Ptolemy	1° / 100y	266 years
Persian/Arab	1° / 66y	176 years

Now, Pingree claimed[64] that the stars for *Apotelesmatics* were calculated for about 770 AD, and the reason for this was probably because the editors of *CCAG* V.1 (p. 212) had compared the Theophilus values to *Ptolemy's* original values, and given a date of 768 AD. To me it seems more appropriate to compare the values to Rhetorius rather than Ptolemy, since the material actually comes from Rhetorius; but let us assume 770 AD anyway. If Theophilus himself added the 2° 40', this would date Rhetorius's book to about 509 AD (Ptolemy) or 599 AD (Persian/Arab).

Now, Pingree had argued as early as his translation of *Carmen* that because of some planetary values listed in Rhetorius Ch. 110 (which could be

---

[63] Evans, pp. 275-76.
[64] Pingree 2001, p. 16.

dated, with some massaging, to 601 AD), Rhetorius flourished sometime in the 7th Century.[65] And this would harmonize with the Persian/Arab rate of precession (about 599 AD). But contrary to Pingree, Holden argued in his edition of Rhetorius (p. 158) that this chapter does not represent a chart example at all, but merely illustrates applications and separations discussed in the previous one (Ch. 109). Holden's argument was straightforward: the positions in Ch. 110 list no Ascendant, and say nothing about a human being—unlike the natal charts described and interpreted later on in Chs. 113 and 118. Since the chapter follows a discussion of applications and separations, and without an Ascendant cannot be—and is not—used to delineate a chart, it does not represent a datable nativity at all. I think Holden's argument is quite strong, and we cannot use Ch. 110 to date Rhetorius.

Well, what can the precession dates tell us? The Persian/Arab rate would give us Pingree's usual preferred date in the early 600s, which he had deduced from the planetary positions in Rhetorius Ch. 110. But leaving the question of those positions aside, this could only be true if two other things are *both* true: (1) that Theophilus only had a copy of Rhetorius very late, around 770, and (2) the Persian/Arab rate had actually been calculated by the reign of al-Mahdī. But (2) seems to be false, as 770 is decades before the astronomers made the calculations. And (1) seems unlikely to me: do we have any reason to believe that Theophilus did not discover Rhetorius until he was 75 years old? Let us remember that there are also Rhetorian chapters and references in *Labors* (in both later chapters and possibly in Ch. 17) and *Apotelesmatics*, as well as OVI (Ch. 1.5, 7), which Pingree believed had no Rhetorius in it at all.[66]

Clearly then, we have a problem. Rhetorius could not have lived around 601 AD and *also* be the source of a Persian/Arab rate of precession in 770, which had not even been measured yet. The only other option is the Ptolemaic rate, which—if we still use 770 AD—would yield a date of approximately 509 AD. Indeed, I think it more likely that Theophilus got Rhetorius years earlier, which would put Rhetorius's life even closer to the

---

[65] Pingree 1976 (p. *xii*). He reaffirmed this in 2003 (p. 79), giving a date of 620 AD—but this was *after* conceding two years earlier (2001, p. 7) that the early 500s was correct, on the basis of the fixed stars in Theophilus.

[66] Pingree 2001, p. 16.

datable nativities in his Chs. 113 and 118, which were those of Pamprepius (440-484 AD), and a royal child who died early (463 AD).[67]

We still might ask, "but aren't the stars calculated for the year 768/770?" Perhaps not. Cumont and Boll believed it was 768, by comparing Theophilus with Ptolemy. But Theophilus got his star list from Rhetorius, not Ptolemy. So how did Theophilus know the year when Rhetorius wrote his book (and presumably calculated his stars)? He could only have added his 266 years of precession based on that. One possibility is this: the native discussed in Rhetorius Ch. 113 was said to have died at age 44, namely in 484 AD. So it was reasonable to assume 484 AD as the earliest date Rhetorius could have completed his book. If we add 266 years to 484 AD, we get 750 AD, precisely when we know Theophilus was actively working as a military astrologer, in his mid-50s.

From all of this I conclude that Rhetorius was late 5th or early 6th Century, and that Theophilus most likely had a copy of his book long before 770 AD.

On Various Inceptions

Of the four works here, *On Various Inceptions* is the most confusing and disorganized. The first thing to note is that all of the eleventh and twelfth houses are missing, as is much of the ninth and tenth. But even so, the arrangement of chapters is in some cases puzzling. For example, Theophilus has put his chapters on runaways and theft in the second house, when Dorotheus himself clearly understands them more as seventh house and lunar topics. Some chapters also seem to be out of order, and in the appropriate places I have rearranged them and noted where they originally appeared.

In other cases the chapters almost seem like notes by Theophilus to himself. One instance is Ch. 1.6, **14-16**, on prices: it is based on Dorotheus, but so compacted and brisk one cannot really draw out a practical interpretation. Likewise, Ch. 1.7 is on travel and generically resembles Dorotheus, but is again so compacted and full of unusual terms, it's hard to understand.

---

[67] It is also worth pointing out that many of Rhetorius's stars are about 1° (or a little bit more) greater in longitude than Anonymous of 379: this again points to a date in the late 400s.

As for sourcing, it is often uncertain.[68] I have just mentioned Dorotheus, but we can also point to Ptolemy in Chs. 1.21, 1.22, maybe 1.10, and 5.3. Much of Ch. 1.7 is based on Demetrius, as can be seen in Schmidt 1995 (*Sages*). What makes this work even more strange is that Ch. 9.8, **1-2** has one definite Arabic transliteration, and a mistaken adjective which could easily have been a misread of a certain Arabic adjective. It also constantly uses "and" to introduce sentences and clauses, which is very typical of Arabic. This suggests that either the Greek manuscript came from an Arabic intermediary (which was itself a translation of Theophilus's Greek, as seen in Appendix A), or perhaps Theophilus himself even translated something from Arabic.

But there are two notable points. The first is that in Ch. 1.13 Theophilus preserves quite detailed material on thought-interpretation, which I have discussed in many places before but especially my translation of Hermann of Carinthia's *Search of the Heart*.[69] We can see here that Theophilus is blurring the lines between inceptions, thought-interpretation, and questions.

The second is the "feminine Saturn." Normally, Saturn indicates male humans, as do the Sun, Jupiter, Mars, and Mercury (especially as a morning star). But in *OVI* Ch. 5.5, **5** we read the following, in the context of a question about the sex of an unborn child:

"**5** For the stars that foster feminine births are Saturn, Venus, and the Moon; masculine, Jupiter, the Sun, and Mars."

This is quite surprising, and would seem to be a manuscript error. But both al-Qasrānī (Berlin 5877 or Landberg 70, f. 85b) and al-Rijāl's *Book of the Skilled* I.46 contain this same material in Arabic, attributed to Theophilus, and report the same thing. In passage #3 of Appendix A below, from *Skilled* we read:

4 And the planets indicating males are the Sun, Jupiter, and Mars;[70] and [those indicating] females are Venus, Saturn,[71] and the Moon. **5**

---

[68] Pingree (2001, p. 16) claimed that *OVI* shows signs of influence from Hephaistion, but again without evidence and I have not seen it.

[69] See also *Apotelesmatics* Ch. 30, which is based on the *Tetrabiblos*.

[70] Reading with **N** and *OVI* for **B**'s "Saturn."

[71] Reading with **N** and *OVI* for **B**'s "Mars."

And If Mercury was eastern, he indicates males, while if he was western, he indicates females.

6 And in the matter of Saturn and Mars, I say that the majority of the ancients differed on this statement about them, so they made Saturn be male and Mars female, and in that they saw evidence for each one.

I must remind the reader that manuscript **B** switches Saturn and Mars in sentence **4**, contrary to Theophilus and al-Qasrānī. But that would not make sense of sentence **6**, which is only coherent if **4** had really made Saturn female and Mars male. So here we have a confirmation, from multiple languages and manuscripts, that Theophilus made Saturn female. Nor is this the only place we can find the attribution:

- In *Carmen* I.10, **18**, the Arabic Dorotheus makes Saturn feminine as well, in a totally different context. In this case, the manuscripts contain a marginal note that says "in the root copy I have found Saturn to be female and Mars male, and it is an error." So the copyist of *Carmen* saw this in *his* master copy of Dorotheus, and thought it was strange enough to comment on it.
- A more ambiguous case is *Carmen* I.23, **21**, where Dorotheus uses a chart example and says that because Saturn is in a certain sign, and the sign is female, a sister will die. Now, we might take this to mean that while Saturn is male, the female nature of the sign converts him into indicating a sister. But later in the sentence, the Sun is in the same sign and indicates a brother—suggesting that Saturn can indicate females all by himself.
- Sahl's *Nativities* Ch. 6.1, **9** likewise implies the femininity of Saturn in the context of illness: "And if you found the Ascendant made unfortunate, then it is bad, and especially from a planet which is not of its essence (and that is that the share of male [planets] is by day, and the share of female ones by night—except that Mars is by night, and the share of Saturn is by day)." In other words, Saturn is especially assigned to the day here, because it is implied that he would normally be assigned the night and femininity.

- The *Yavanajātaka* Ch. 1.115 treats Saturn as neuter (at least under some conditions):[72] "Jupiter, Mars, and the Sun are masculine, Venus and the Moon feminine; Saturn and Mercury are neuter, their sex depending on their situations."

If we leave aside the *Yavanajātaka* as perhaps being too culturally distant and of uncertain influence, we can see four instances, across three authors and in independent topics, where Saturn is either explicitly or implicitly feminine. And as the scribe in *Carmen* and al-Rijāl show, this both ran counter to other views, and (in the case of al-Rijāl) was a specific topic of debate.

Are there reasons to prefer Saturn as male or female? Each way does have its own astrological rationale. If we go by sect, then Saturn should be male and Mars female (al-Rijāl's implied, preferred solution). But if we go by the natural qualities of heating and cooling, then it makes sense for cold Saturn to be associated with femininity, and hot Mars with masculinity—for unlike Ptolemy, medieval Persian and Arab astrologers tended to make both Venus and the Moon *cold* and wet. Therefore, all three cold planets would be female (excluding Mercury, who varies), and all three hot planets male. And indeed, it is notable that Theophilus, Sahl, and the Pahlavi Dorotheus were all part of the Persian milieu. It is also worth pointing out that, unlike the Ptolemaic system so common in the later West, both of the gender systems here are balanced: three female, three male, and one common to both (Mercury). This kind of balance is very typical of Hellenistic astrology, and it has always struck me as odd that Ptolemaic astrology would be so lop-sided by having four male, two female, and one common.

When discussing this with my friend and colleague Charles Obert, I pointed out that in Western Qabalah, Saturn is associated with the Sephirah Binah, considered a feminine sphere and a "Great Mother" image; he then pointed out that a feminine Saturn could be a Crone archetype, forming a triad with the feminine Venus and Moon. I would like to briefly expand on that here in the following table, for your consideration:

---

[72] See Vol. 2, pp. 9 and 246.

Female		Male	
Saturn	Crone	Sun	King, father
Moon	Mother	Jupiter	Priest
Venus	Maiden	Mars	Warrior

Figure 3: Possible archetypal assignments, with feminine Saturn

The order of works and Pingree's chronology

In a certain sense there is not a lot to say about the order in which The-ophilus wrote these four books, because only two dates are certain, and one more ambiguous. The first certain date is 758-59 AD (implied by the intro-duction to *Labors*), when he went with al-Mahdī on campaign to Khurāsān. The second date is from the introduction to *Cosmic*, when he mentions Baghdad, which was founded in 762. All we can conclude from that is that the bulk of these two works were completed, and their introductions written, after those dates.

The more ambiguous date pertains to the fixed stars in *Apotelesmatics* Ch. 18, which I discussed above. We don't know exactly why or how Theophilus calculated his particular 2° 40' and added it to the longitudes in Rhetorius, and I argued above that based on internal evidence in Rhetorius, he could have calculated the longitudes for as early as 750 AD.

This is the extent of our current knowledge of the books' chronology. None of the books refers to any of the others, so apart from little details there is no other internal information we can use.[73] So it is certainly possible that he wrote *Cosmic* shortly after 762, *Labors* shortly after 758-59, and *Apotelesmatics* after 770 (or 750), with *OVI* being the wild card. But it is equally possible that he wrote the first edition of *Apotelesmatics* before 750 and just kept updating a second edition with star values over the decades, while only putting the final touches on *Cosmic* and *Labors* at the end of his life. Since *OVI* sometimes reads like a bunch of unconnected and com-pressed notes, it could simply have been a sheaf of papers in a box, preserved

---

[73] For example, in the Introduction to *Cosmic* Theophilus says he uses the Aries ingress, apparently without the preceding lunation; but in Ch. 5 he *does* seem to recommend the lunation (and in *Labors* Ch. 38, again not). So maybe Ch. 5 represents an earlier view he did not revise, or perhaps he just included it later anyway. Either way, it does not change the dating of *Cosmic* to being after 762. I should add that *OVI* Ch. 10.1 is equivalent to *Labors* Ch. 25, but with no indication which came first.

since his early days as a jobbing astrologer, which Stephanus bundled up and took with him. We have no way of knowing.

But again, since Pingree built up so much around Theophilus, and began to date Theophilus's books based on his theories, we ought to examine them here lest others be confused when reading other articles and accounts. Following is Pingree's final chronology (2001):

- *Labors* Chs. 1-24 (the "first edition"): early 760s, because of his recent military work, and because it has no Rhetorius in it.[74]
- *Cosmic*: after 762, due to the mention of Baghdad.
- *OVI*: about 765, because *Apotelesmatics* allegedly refers to it, and while *Apotelesmatics* has Rhetorius, *OVI* allegedly does not. Therefore, *OVI* is earlier than *Apotelesmatics*.
- *Apotelesmatics*: about 770, because of the fixed stars.
- *Labors* Chs. 25-41 (the "second edition"): sometime late.

Just about everything is wrong with this chronology. First of all, despite Pingree mentioning the "first" and "second" editions of *Labors*, I have seen no internal or external evidence that there are two editions; chapters do not even repeat, as one would expect in a second, separate edition. The entire basis of the claim seems to be that not every manuscript has all parts of *Labors*, and since Rhetorius appears only in later chapters, the last half of *Labors* was written later. This claim makes no sense: see below.

Nor is true that *Apotelesmatics* refers to *OVI*, thereby post-dating it (even apart from the presence of Rhetorius). Pingree's argument is that *Apotelesmatics* Ch. 1, **2** refers to *OVI* because it speaks of "universal" or "cosmic" apotelesmatics as well as "inceptions by inquiry."[75] It is true that *OVI* has the word "inceptions" in its title, but so do *Cosmic* and *Labors*, and *Labors* is virtually nothing but inceptions: what does that prove? In fact, the reader can see that Theophilus is explaining to Deucalion that Deucalion has been neglecting some higher and spiritual aspects of knowledge, and Theophilus is going to tell him some very important things he has learned from such apotelesmatics and inceptions. He is not referring to another work, but rather trying to speak seriously to Deucalion. In fact, it seems to me that the "universal" apotelesmatics could easily refer to the cosmological discussion

---

[74] But see *Labors* Ch. 17, **6**.
[75] Pingree 2001, p. 16.

that ensues, as well as the following chapters on mundane astrology, while the "inceptions by inquiry" are illustrated by the latter chapters of *Apotelesmatics*. Apart from the close similarity of *Apotelematics* Ch. 27 and *OVI* Ch. 8.7, these books do not overlap: there is no reason to look elsewhere to explain this reference.

So in the end, Pingree's entire theory of dating comes down to two principles: (1) the dating of the Rhetorian fixed stars to about 770 AD, and (2) that if a book (or portion of a book) does not have Rhetorius in it, then Theophilus did not have Rhetorius at that time. Once again, we see that Pingree is willing to overlook everything in order to usher Rhetorius onto center stage.

As for (1), I have already discussed the dating of the stars several times, both how he could have dated them originally around 750 but also kept updating them over the years. So nothing is gained by focusing on these stars. As for (2), it is not only unbelievable, but the opposite could equally be true. For example, Theophilus quotes the Bible many times in the introduction to *Apotelesmatics*, but not in *Labors*: therefore it follows that he had never seen a Bible at the time he wrote *Labors*. *Labors* also does not seem to have any Ptolemaic material:[76] therefore he did not have the *Tetrabiblos* until later in life. Obviously this kind of argument is not credible.

But the opposite could also be true: what if Theophilus only used Rhetorius sparingly because after experimenting with it early, he decided it wasn't very useful? (The same could be said about Ptolemy, to explain his scarcity.) After all, according to Pingree, *Labors* only uses a few chapters from Rhetorius Book VI, which were drawn from Julianus of Laodikaia on war: maybe he didn't think much else was serviceable? Compared with *Carmen's* systematic combinations of planets by aspect and on the angles, transits, detailed delineations, not to mention *an entire book on inceptions*, maybe Theophilus figured he'd better stick with Dorotheus instead? If we look at the Rhetorian chapters in *Apotelesmatics* (Chs. 18-24), they seem rather strange anyway for a second, expanded attempt by an elderly father to impart his greatest wisdom to a son: chapters on madmen and robbers, whether someone has died, natal passages on twelfth-parts, and some general advice on inceptions. This does not sound like someone who is receiving Rhetorius for the first time and mining its depths, but perhaps one

---

[76] This is despite Ch. 12, **14**, which may be based on Heph. III.

returning to Rhetorius after a long hiatus, to see what else he can do with it. We ought to conclude that our texts offer little to suggest any definite chronology beyond the dates of 758-59, and 762.

At this point I think we can leave the chronology of Theophilus behind; perhaps in the future more information will be discovered.

Section 3: Pingree's hypothesis about Theophilus, Rhetorius, and Māshā'allāh

Above we saw that Pingree attempted to date the various books of Theophilus through his use of Rhetorius. Here I will address another theme of Pingree's, namely that Theophilus played a pivotal role in transmitting Rhetorius to future generations. I will argue that he did not, and that the evidence actually shows the contrary. Specifically, Pingree's source texts and Appendix A of this book indicate the following:

- Rhetorius as a named author was virtually unknown to the later Arabic writers, as well as the Latins.
- Rhetorius (so far as he did get transmitted) came chiefly via al-Andarzaghar.
- Numerous Arabic passages attributed to Theophilus, do not show the influence of Rhetorius.

In the 2001 summary of his view,[77] Pingree argued that Rhetorius was passed on to later generations via two paths: one was through Māshā'allāh, to whom he gave a copy of Rhetorius; the other is through his student Stephanus, who brought the Greek Rhetorius to Constantinople around Theophilus's death.[78] I see no reason to doubt the part about Stephanus—in which case it was Stephanus who brought Rhetorius to the Byzantine Romans, not Theophilus. Here I am concerned with the Theophilus-Rhetorius-Māshā'allāh connection.

The two key elements of Pingree's argument are as follows. The first is that we can date Theophilus's works through his use of Rhetorius; and *because* we can roughly date his reception of Rhetorius, we can use it to say

---

[77] Pingree 2001, p. 3.
[78] Pingree 2001, p. 12. .

when he gave it to Māshā'allāh. The second is that Māshā'allāh wrote the Arabic version of the *Book of Aristotle*,[79] and *because* it contains source material from Rhetorius, he *must* have gotten it from Theophilus.

Right away we can remove the first part of the argument. Even if it were valid to date Theophilus's works though his use of Rhetorius, it would have no bearing on the Māshā'allāh connection. He could have gotten Theophilus early and given it to Māshā'allāh late, or he could have gotten it late and given it early. The dating has nothing to do with the crux of the issue.[80] For Pingree to be correct, Māshā'allāh must have written the original *Book of Aristotle*, and had no other way of getting Rhetorius. So, only this second part of the argument matters. Let us review Pingree's reasons for believing in Māshā'allāh's authorship of the *Book of Aristotle*, and then I will show that it was most likely written by the earlier Persian astrologer al-Andarzaghar, the real transmitter of Rhetorius.

In the Introduction to the 1997 edition of the Latin *Book of Aristotle*,[81] Pingree points to his 1989 article[82] for his argument in favor of Māshā'allāh's authorship. First, a certain Greek manuscript lists a number of books which form a library or bibliography of Māshā'allāh (Gr. *Masala*),[83] and this list is very similar to the one at the beginning of the Latin *Book of Aristotle*—although there is no book attached to the Greek list, and the *Book of Aristotle* does not name Māshā'allāh at all. Now, at the end of this Greek list (but again, not in the Latin *Book of Aristotle*), the author of the list claims that he has made an effort to compile and publish the present book as a synopsis of these works, in four parts—and indeed, the *Book of Aristotle* is in four parts. So, the implication is that Māshā'allāh wrote a book in four parts on the basis

---

[79] At the time I translated the Latin *Book of Aristotle* and published it in my *Persian Nativities I*, I simply assumed that Pingree was probably right. As I will suggest below, the whole thing could have been translated into Arabic by Māshā'allāh, so that he had something to do with it; but I no longer believe he was the actual author.

[80] One related question is this: in what language was Rhetorius allegedly given to Māshā'allāh? Surely Greek. But I do not know of any clear evidence that Māshā'allāh knew Greek, nor have I heard of any Pahlavi version of Rhetorius. Significantly, Sezgin does not even mention any *Arabic* translation of Rhetorius!

[81] Burnett and Pingree 1997, p. 3. Although Burnett and Pingree probably wrote the Introduction together, the theory is Pingree's, so I will refer only to him here.

[82] Pingree 1989, pp. 227-89.

[83] Vaticanus Gr. 1056 (ff. 242r-242v), edited and printed as Appendix I of the edition of the 1997 *Book of Aristotle*.

of these authors, and the *Book of Aristotle* is that book. Second, in one of its two manuscript versions, the Latin *Book of Aristotle* is immediately preceded by a book on nativities by Māshā'allāh, in 14 chapters—but which is unrelated to the Greek list.[84] Here, the implication is that Hugo was already translating multiple works by Māshā'allāh together, so it is reasonable to suppose that the *Book of Aristotle* was by Māshā'allāh because of its proximity to the other work—although this other work does *not* appear next to the *Book of Aristotle* in the other manuscript.

To sum up, we have (1) an independent list of books in Greek that mentions Māshā'allāh and a compilation in four parts, which is very similar to a list in a Latin book of four parts that does not mention Māshā'allāh, and (2) one manuscript of this Latin book which does not mention Māshā'allāh, in which it is preceded by a book that is attributed to him. This is suggestive, but not very strong. As for (2), scribes would have included in their manuscripts whatever their employers told them to, so this connection between two works of Māshā'allāh is rather tenuous. Evidence (1) is a bit stronger, but there alternative scenarios. For instance, perhaps Māshā'allāh did not write the *Book of Aristotle*, but translated it into Arabic from an earlier author: in that case, these statements about writing a four-part book are from the earlier author (namely, al-Andarzaghar), and the Greek translator of the list confused Māshā'allāh's own role as a translator, for his authorship.

Nevertheless, there are six more important reasons to doubt Pingree's theory:

Problem 1: The "Māshā'allāh" book list never mentions Rhetorius. One of the more surprising facts is that the book list does not mention Rhetorius, which is remarkable given that the *Book of Aristotle* clearly makes use of him. We would certainly expect that such a major work, if handed over intact to Māshā'allāh, would have been prominently mentioned. Instead, the bibliography mentions dozens of works which do not exist at all, or certainly not in the way they are listed. For example, it lists a thirteen-book edition of Dorotheus, with 89 chapters on historical astrology. Of course, Dorotheus never wrote such a book.

Problem 2: Absence of Rhetorius in the Arabic Theophilus. In Appendix A I present 14 sets of Arabic passages which explicitly credit Theophilus. This

---

[84] Oxford, Bodleian Savile 15, ff. 177v-184v. Apparently the version in Savile 15 is less complete than Oxford Bodleian Digby 149 and London, BL, Cotton App. VI, 97v-108v (according to David Juste, personal communication).

means that at least some portions of *Labors, On Various Inceptions,* and his otherwise unknown natal work, were available in Arabic. But none of the passages can be traced to Rhetorius, nor are they attributed to him. So although Theophilus does sometimes use Rhetorius, it is not clear that any of those passages made it into Arabic, much less a volume of Rhetorius itself. So a general transmission via Theophilus's own Rhetorius chapters does not seem likely.

Problem 3: Book IV of the Book of Aristotle is by al-Andarzaghar. As Burnett and al-Hamdi showed in their 1991/1992 translation of a work by al-Dāmaghānī, pretty much every sentence in Book IV of the *Book of Aristotle* can be attributed to al-Andarzaghar. This by itself should have raised red flags about the authorship of the *Book of Aristotle* as a whole, since al-Andarzaghar is not mentioned in the "Māshā'allāh" bibliography, either! (Nor would al-Andarzaghar be mentioned, if the book list was his own.)

Problem 4: Sahl's Nativities and Māshā'allāh. Long passages in Sahl's *Book on Nativities* are clearly lifted directly from the Arabic *Book of Aristotle,* and follow it closely, sentence by sentence. But unlike the *Book of Aristotle,* Sahl often states exactly who his sources are, and his numerous passages citing Māshā'allāh are *never* any of these *Book of Aristotle* passages. It would be surprising if Sahl had a major natal work by Māshā'allāh such as the *Book of Aristotle,* and decided never to credit him, while constantly quoting him elsewhere.

Problem 5: Sahl's Nativities, al-Andarzaghar, and Rhetorius. For me the definitive argument against Pingree is that Sahl attributes thirteen passages to al-Andarzaghar, which *do* appear in the *Book of Aristotle* (sometimes consecutive paragraphs), and five of these *are* directly from Rhetorius. They are as follows:

Sahl attributions	Book of Aristotle	Rhetorius Book V
Ch. 1.25, **8-14.**	III.1.2, **1-7.**	Ch. 55 (Holden p. 41).[85]
Ch. 1.30, **36-50.**	III.1.3, **1-17.**	
Ch. 2.16, **1-5.**	III.2.3, **1-5.**	
Ch. 3.2, **12.**	III.3.3, **18-19.**	
Ch. 3.2, **13-16.**	III.3.3, **20-23.**	Ch. 108 (Holden p. 155).[86]
Ch. 3.2, **17-24.**	III.3.4, **1-7.**	
Ch. 3.2, **25-26.**	III.3.4, **8-10.**	Ch. 108 (Holden p. 155).
Ch. 3.2, **27-30.**	III.3.4, **11-12.**	
Ch. 3.2, **31.**	III.3.4, **13.**	
Ch. 3.2, **1.**	III.3.6.	
Ch. 4.2, **1-3.**	III.4.1, **1-6** *passim.*[87]	Ch. 97 (Holden pp. 145-46).
Ch. 8.7, **5-6.**	III.8.1, **21.**[88]	Ch. 77 (Holden p. 128).
Ch. 11 Intro, **5.**	III.12.1, **1-2.**	

Figure 4: Al-Andarzaghar in relation to Sahl, *BA*, and Rhetorius

Now, Sahl does quote al-Andarzaghar in other places which do not correspond to the *Book of Aristotle*, and he also has *Book of Aristotle* material based on Rhetorius which he does not connect to al-Andarzaghar. But from the above it is clear that al-Andarzaghar had some kind of access to Rhetorius. It is also worth pointing out that despite all of his cited sources and the presence of Rhetorian material, Sahl never mentions Rhetorius himself. This suggests that he had no idea who Rhetorius was.

Problem 6: The Bizīdaj. In the biographical section on Theophilus above, I mentioned that due to the reach of the 'Umayyad empire, it is reasonable to think that others besides Theophilus could have had copies of Rhetorius. Indeed, Sahl's *Nativities* shows just this. In one passage attributed to "the

---

[85] Like the Sahl passage, Rhetorius specifies that the malefics are in the Ascendant, which neither *Carmen* I.3 nor Heph. III, Appendix A do. Rhetorius also includes the Moon being besieged, which *Carmen* does not, and Hephaistion does but attributes to Manethō. Again, *Carmen* does not speak of the Moon being in the straight signs, but both Hephaistion and Rhetorius do.

[86] Cf. also Rhetorius Ch. 106.

[87] This paragraph is blended with material about the planetary joys.

[88] This is Ch. III.8.2 in Pingree and Burnett's Latin edition.

Roman *Bizīdaj*,"[89] Sahl presents material from Rhetorius Ch. 103. And another passage on the fixed stars also attributed to the *Bizīdaj*[90] is based on the first few stars of Rhetorius Ch. 62. Holden's footnote (p. 117) says that the degrees have been advanced at a rate of precession to yield 481 AD, and that Cumont thinks Rhetorius might have taken this material from Julian of Laodikaia. But no matter where Rhetorius got it, it shows that the *Bizīdaj*, which *was* a Persian work, also had Rhetorian elements: in other words, Rhetorius was known to the compiler of the *Bizīdaj* long before Theophilus, just as he was known in some form to al-Andarzaghar.

So if (3, 5) fully one book and more of the *Book of Aristotle* was written by al-Andarzaghar, with (5) multiple references in Sahl connecting al-Andarzaghar to Rhetorius (but with apparently no knowledge of Rhetorius himself), and (1, 3) no mention of either Rhetorius or al-Andarzaghar in the "Māshā'allāh" book list, and (4) Sahl never connecting Māshā'allāh with the passages from the *Book of Aristotle* he obviously had, and with (6) other evidence that the Persian *Bizīdaj* also drew on Rhetorius, but (2) no other known Theophilus material in Arabic reflecting Rhetorius, it follows that the theory of transmission by Theophilus to Māshā'allāh must be wrong. Māshā'allāh may have edited or possibly even translated the Arabic *Book of Aristotle* from Persian, but he did not write it or even compile it in any major, identifiable sense; nor was Theophilus his only possible source of Rhetorius. The most sensible conclusion is that al-Andarzaghar is the key figure in this story, that he had a copy or summary of Rhetorius long before Māshā'allāh, and that Māshā'allāh may not even have known who Rhetorius was.

From these considerations, I conclude and suggest the following. Theophilus did have a copy of Rhetorius, but he probably did not share it with anyone in his circle. Instead, for personal or professional reasons he kept it for himself and only bequeathed it to Stephanus, who took it to Constantinople.[91] In this way, after 785 Rhetorius essentially disappeared from the

---

[89] Sahl, *Nativities* Ch. 3.13, **5-13**.

[90] Sahl, *Nativities* Ch. 6.2, **69-71**.

[91] Indeed, we might as the following: why *would* he share the book with Māshā'allāh, or anyone else? After all, by the 760s he would have been around 70 years old, and would already have had his own valuable student. With Rhetorius, he had a valuable book that helped secure his professional position. The fact that Stephanus immediately high-tailed it to Constantinople is suggestive of his *not* wanting to spend more time among the professional astrologers of Baghdad.

Arabic-language scene, apart from passages in works like the *Book of Aristotle*, which was copied by various authors but with no idea of its real source. Instead, people like Sahl knew the *Book of Aristotle* as a work of al-Andarzaghar, who (along with the *Bizīdaj*) was the real source of their Rhetorian material.

Section 4: Theophilus's Dorothean source

As my numerous footnotes show, Theophilus relies heavily on some version of Dorotheus, especially for *Labors* and *Cosmic*. But what was this Dorothean source? So far, we know of three possibilities. The first is the verse *Pentateuch* itself, which lasted at least into the early 5th Century because Hephaistion quotes from it. The second is the Pahlavi translation from the 3rd Century, which lasted (with some changes) into the 8th Century, when 'Umar al-Tabarī put it into Arabic.[92] The third is some kind of Greek prose paraphrase of parts of Dorotheus, and we have evidence of this in the Greek *Fragments* and *Excerpts*.[93]

My own view is that Theophilus had something like the third possibility: a Greek prose version of Dorotheus, but one which was more complete than what 'Umar translated from the Pahlavi. Let us look at some evidence for this.

First, I don't think it likely that he had access to the *Pentateuch* itself. One piece of evidence I think is clear is *OVI* Ch. 1.6, **14-16**, on buying and selling. We are fortunate to have both 'Umar al-Tabarī's version (*Carmen* V.44) and the actual verses from the *Pentateuch* (Heph. III.16, **13-17**). In the *Pentateuch*, Dorotheus does *not* use the Moon's declination or her presence in the crooked or straight signs. But *Carmen* does use them—or rather, it blends declination with latitude in a confused way. Theophilus follows the Persian approach of *Carmen*, or at least he has his own ambiguity and confusion: see my footnote to this passage. But likewise, in Appendix A #7 below al-Rijāl quotes Theophilus on the same topic, where he speaks of the Moon being in a "declining" sign, which again sounds like declinations rather than

---

[92] I published my own translation of this in 2017.

[93] The *Fragments* included reports, summaries, and paraphrases in Greek which Pingree included in his 1976 translation of *Carmen*. The *Excerpts* were further, short sentences and paragraphs he later discovered, which are translated by Eduardo Gramaglia in Appendix C of my 2017 translation of *Carmen*.

latitude. So Theophilus probably did not have the *Pentateuch* itself but either a separate Greek prose summary, or perhaps even a Greek prose summary which was *itself* the basis of the Pahlavi version.

Second, there is plenty to suggest that his own version of Dorotheus was more complete than 'Umar's *Carmen*, and probably something closer to the original *Pentateuch*. I will list six passages here.

1. In *Cosmic* Ch. 2, **2**, Theophilus uses a passage parallel to the odd one about the easternness and westernness of planets in *Carmen* III.1. But significantly, instead of the unusual use of 9 days for a planet to make a solar phase (*Carmen*), Theophilus uses the more common 7 days, which Hephaistion also uses in Heph. III.44, **2** and III.45, **19** (both of which derive from the original *Pentateuch*).

2. *Labors* Ch. 22a, **5** contains a (partly missing) sentence which is reflected in the *Pentateuch* (in Heph. III.40, **21**), about the Moon being under the rays and connecting with Venus. But *Carmen* lacks this sentence, which should have occurred around its V.28, **22-23**.

3. *Cosmic* Ch. 4, **47** is a sentence applied to mundane astrology, which is clearly drawn from Dorotheus's natal material on illness: see *Carmen* Ch. IV.2, **8**. However, whereas *Carmen* just has a generic interpretation that gestures at the gender of the sign, Theophilus specifically raises the distinction between an eastern Venus and a western Venus, with different interpretations; he also speaks of the sixth "place" rather than its "house." This is a sharper and more detailed interpretation that suggests a better Greek version.

4. Sahl's *Nativities* Ch. 2.11, **12-14** (in Appendix A below, #9), is an Arabic passage attributed to Theophilus, on assets. The parallel is to *Carmen* I.28, **25-26**, but Sahl's Theophilus is clearer and more fleshed out. This is so even though *Carmen* mentions the Lot, of assets, while Theophilus is discussing the second place.

5. *Labors* Ch. 2, **3**, suggests through the phrase "looks on" that Theophilus had a copy of Dorotheus closer to the original *Pentateuch* than *Carmen*, because the *Pentateuch* source shown in Heph. III.38, **11** says to "keep watch" on a fixed sign rising. But somehow the sentence be-

came confused or garbled, because in this part Dorotheus is referring to marking the Hour.

6. *Labors* Ch. 37, **3** contains a very late Greek term in a sentence where Theophilus specifically cites "the verses of Dorotheus."

From these passages I think it is safe to conclude that Theophilus's Dorotheus was more complete than *Carmen*, closer to the intent to the original Greek, but not the *Pentateuch* itself, because in at least one place (prices, above), it may have been affected by the Pahlavi edition or even been the cause of the confusion in it.

Section 5: Special Vocabulary

Most of the vocabulary that might seem special to Theophilus is actually standard Greek, and can be found in Hephaistion. The most common are:

- **Having a word, having a relationship** (Gr. *logon echōn*). This seems to mean that a planet has rulership over some place, and so has authority in the matter: it "has a word" on the matter.
- **Pivot, post-ascension, decline** or **pre-ascension**. In order, these are equivalent to an "angle" or "stake" (Ar.), a "succeedent" house or place (because it ascends after the pivot), and a falling or cadent place (because it declines from a pivot, or ascends prior to it).

One unusual case is:

- **Pious** places or signs. I believe that these refer to the eight angular/pivotal and succeedent or post-ascending places, although whether these are by quadrant divisions or signs, I am not sure. *OVI* Ch. 1.25, **5** uses phrases like "higher repute" and "depressed," which makes it sound like exaltation and fall, and Ch. 1.29, **1** contrasts the pious signs with depression or fall. But *OVI* Ch. 5.4, **4** speaks of "eight" pious signs, which matches the pivots and post-ascensions, as well as the notion that these places have to do with coming to a peak, versus declining and going down. The reader should especially consult Chs. 1.25 and 1.29 for vivid terms applied to these signs.

Section 6: Manuscripts

The four works of Theophilus were compiled primarily based on the following manuscripts (all incomplete):

- **A**: Parisinus suppl. Graecus 1241 (*CCAG* VIII.1)
- **B**: Parisinus graecus 2506 (*CCAG* VIII.1)
- **Ber**: Berolinensis graecus 183 (*CCAG* VII)
- **E**: Angelicus graecus 29 (*CCAG* V.1)
- **L**: Laurentianus 28, 34 (*CCAG* I)
- **P**: Parisinus graecus 2417 (*CCAG* VIII.1)
- **R**: Parisinus graecus 2425 (*CCAG* VIII.4)
- **S**: Escurial I.R.14 (*CCAG* XI.1)
- **V**: Vaticanus graecus 1056 (*CCAG* V.3)
- **W**: Vindobonensis phil. Gr. 115 (*CCAG* VI)
- **Y**: Vaticanus graecus 212 (*CCAG* V.1)

Each manuscript was described in its associated *CCAG* volume, and sometimes excerpts were edited in it. But over time, the *CCAG* editors began to cross-reference chapters of Theophilus so as to add more manuscript sources, such as Laurentianus 28, 13. As a result, when possible we were able to use at least two manuscript sources for each chapter, or else an edited version in the *CCAG* from multiple manuscripts. In his 2001 article, Pingree summarized the primary manuscript groups as follows:

First group: **L**, **W**. These descend from the same manuscript, but the scribe of each "omitted his own choice of undesirable chapters."[94]

Second group: **A**, **Y**. These are both coped from the same source.

Third group: **P**.

To these Pingree added a few comments about **B**, **E**, and **R**, which the reader may consult.

---

[94] Pingree 2001, p. 17.

Section 7: Editorial principles

Following is how we use brackets in the text:

[ ] Square brackets are inserted based on *our* view of how they clarify the text for the *reader*, and make a clearer English sentence. We also put subsection titles in these brackets, when we believe it makes the text work better, even though they are not strictly necessary to insert.

< > Pointed brackets represent material which we deem *necessary* to insert. For example: <*lacuna*>, <*missing*>, or a sentence which is incomplete but we can be sure how it is completed.

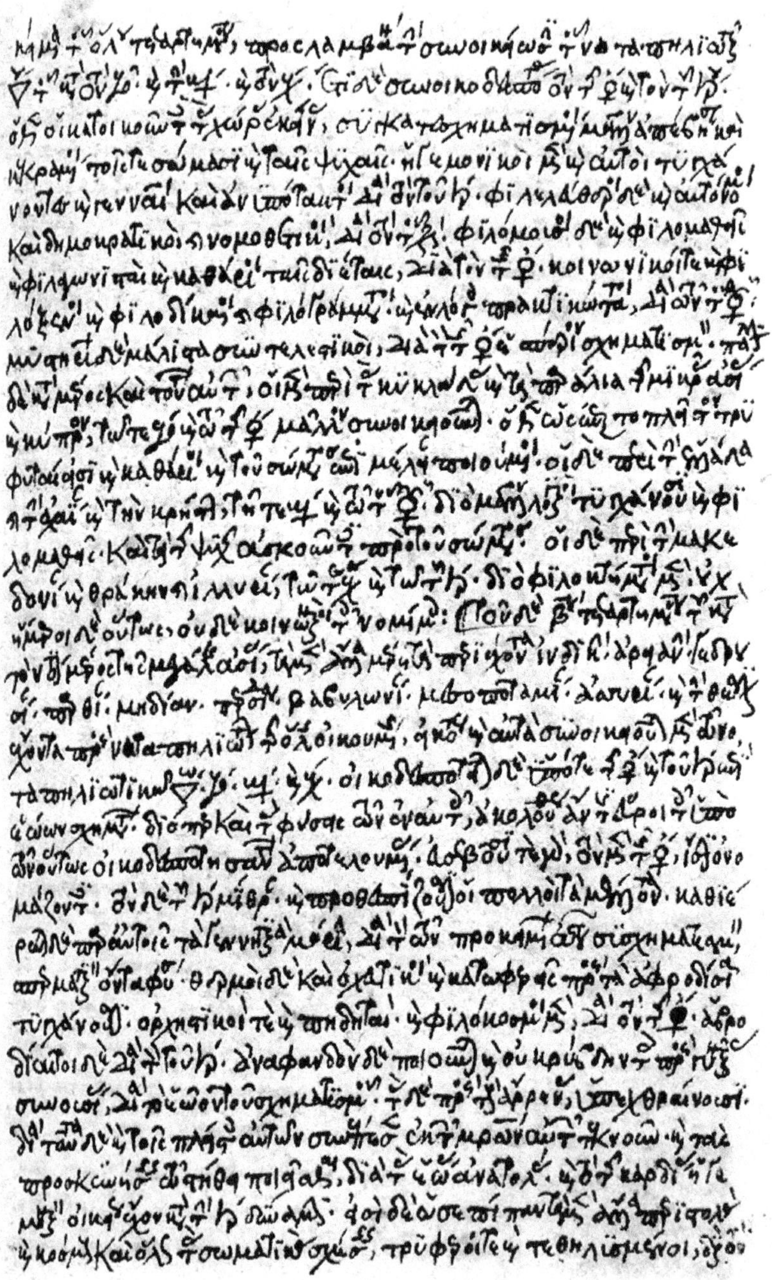

Page from MS Angelicus Gr. 29

LABORS CONCERNING MILITARY INCEPTIONS

Chapter 1: Introduction[1]

1 The *Labors* of Theophilus the philosopher on inceptions of war, military campaigns, and tyranny, by which he became experienced and which he collected from the ancients, addressed to his son Deucalion.

೮ഠ   ഔ   ൚

2 The natural and peculiar quality of the stars, oh most orderly[2] Deucalion, does not have one single, but a many-colored as well as a distinct force,[3] most suited to every completion of events,[4] even when for the most part each of them is recognized by one most generic quality, in consequence of the arrangement assigned to it, and its characteristic significance—such as Mars in war matters, Mercury in speech, Saturn in agricultural pursuits, and Venus in erotic affairs. **3** And yet, as it turns out, not only does Mars activate war, but also Saturn, which accomplishes the destruction of kings and the capture of cities, just as one can find in the universal completions of events; but then in addition Mars produces burnings, pestilential <illnesses> and a scarcity of fruits. **4** In the same way, Mercury [brings also] robberies, anarchies, irregularities in life, he is called "Messenger,"[5] and he will arbitrate for peace. **5** Likewise, in the natal completion of events we find the stars operating differently or giving different meanings in relation to their configurations and their exchanging of places: that is, when those that do evil act as those that do good,[6] and when the benefics are weak; though indeed, as regards the completion of events, one should consult the disposition of the stars and the determination of their degrees.

---

[1] Edited in *CCAG* V.1, pp. 233-34.

[2] *Kosmiōtate*, from the adj. *kosmios* ("orderly, well-behaved, moderate").

[3] *Energeia.*

[4] **BD:** *Apotelesma*, from here through 7.

[5] *Diaktoros.* **EG:** A common Homeric epithet for Hermes, such as in *Iliad* 2.103 or *Odyssey* 5.43.

[6] **BD:** That is, when malefics act in benefic ways. **EG:** This translation is meant to preserve the play of words between *kalopoios* ("one that does good," or a benefic) and *kakopoios* ("one that does evil," or a malefic).

6 Having observed this, the men wise in celestial influences made use of the commixed quality[7] of the stars, not only in the most particular and individual [cases], but also in the most universal and generic, as if those dealing with war [matters] made use of all the stars and the luminaries for one delineation of the outcomes and assistance.[8]

7 So I, having pondered this, and having learned that a method of approach[9] to [the subject of] war is seldom found among the ancients, except only [the inquiry] *whether* in the cosmic completions of events there will be war and captivity in the land (clearly leaving aside the most specific [issues], that is to say, especially the military campaigns against the enemy, those launched by the enemy, or the siege of cities and the tyrannies), I also write on the things that are set in motion or sharpened at specific times, by two armies facing each other, taking up a position, or pitched over against each other, on which matters the accurate records in the books of the ancients are found to be helpless.

8 Having given heed to precisely these things, I deemed it necessary to shift and divert some inceptions of war from the [current] natal and inceptional systems[10] which contained at the same time the plausible[11] and the true, precisely because, having put many to trial, I was compelled (as you know) by those who held power at that time, to get busy with these things at the time when we made the military campaign with them eastward to the land of Margiana,[12] where we withstood mutual misfortunes of war, with much icy-cold and immoderate winter, as well as the greatest fear, and opposition beyond measure.

9 Now, arranging these inceptions sequentially, and by some natural succession, I did not neglect any of those rolls[13] bound fast and requested in the lines of battle, but I organized that particular book, the most complete,

---

[7] *Schesis* (or, "nature").

[8] *Sympraxia*, lit. "joined work." **BD:** I do not understand the role of "assistance" in this sentence, but what Theophilus seems to mean is that his predecessors did not fully appreciate the different significations that planets can have in war, and tended to treat this topic as though it were a natal chart, with only the standard significations.

[9] *Ephodos*.

[10] **BD:** That is, natal and electional astrology; this is a clear indication that Theophilus is conscious of breaking new ground, not simply in terms of subject matter (war), but in terms of how to approach a chart.

[11] *To pithanon*.

[12] **BD:** See my Introduction for information about this campaign.

[13] **BD:** I.e., scrolls or books on rolled paper.

which contained inceptions of war, also those concerning inquiries on tyrannies, besieged cities, and the like.

10 However, it is necessary that you undertake this very business with high attention and care, and, with a plain view,[14] consider the commixture of signs and stars: I mean, of the wandering and the fixed, as well as those of the luminaries, the Lots involved, and their lords, and you will not stumble, with God helping in the work.[15]

Chapter 2: An inception of war[16]

1 If[17] someone will start a war (says Theophilus), or a campaign, or a question arises on this, search this way: **2** The one who initiates [it], from the Hour-marker; the one made war upon and against [whom he has] taken the field, from the setting. **3** And if indeed a fixed sign marks the Hour,[18] the war will be lasting, or else the campaign; if bicorporeal, the one drawn up in battle comes into regret, and changes to another issue by himself; if the sign marking the Hour is tropical, his undertaking will be unaccomplished.

4 Gain[19] knowledge of the affair of war from the Midheaven, and from the stars that are on and bearing witness to it. **5** If both benefics and malefics simultaneously have a relationship[20] with the Midheaven, victory and defeat will be uncertain for both sides. **6** If benefics are related to the Hour-marker and the Midheaven, victory (whenever it happens) will be inclined towards the pursuing one, and defeat towards the fleeing one. **7** But if the benefics have a relationship towards the setting and the Midheaven, victory will incline towards the fleeing one. **8** Again, if indeed one of both sides (namely,

---

[14] **EG**: That is, with a plain approach that is unadorned by special theories.

[15] **BD**: This is a typical phrase in Arabic works, which would be بعون الله.

[16] Edited in *CCAG* XI.1, pp. 230-33.

[17] For this paragraph, cf. *Carmen* V.34, **1-4**; Heph. III.37, **1-2**.

[18] Reading with the sense of *Carmen* and Hephaistion for "looks on." Theophilus may have taken this from the original Dorotheus, because Heph. III.38, **11** says to "keep watch" on a fixed sign rising.

[19] For this paragraph, see generally *Carmen* V.34, **8-13**; Heph. III.37, **3-7**.

[20] *Logon echōn*. **EG**: Or more literally, "has a word." **BD**: This is a common phrase in Theophilus, and we will not always point it out.

the Hour-marker or the setting) has a relationship to the Midheaven[21] along with good testimony, victory will incline towards him.

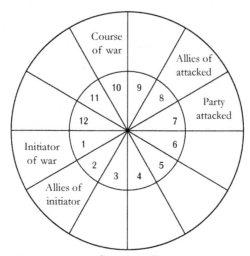

Figure 5: House significations for an inception of war

9 The[22] pursuer will indeed have assistance from the post-ascension of the Hour-marker, and the fleeing one from the eighth place. **10** The rulers of the second place, when well-posited, and when benefics are in the place or looking upon it, [mean] the pursuer will have the friendliest and well-disposed comrades. **11** In a similar way also, the rulers of the eighth place having the same disposition [means] the fleeing one will have good assistance. **12** In the same way also when the rulers of both places are in the opposite position,[23] they indicate the contrary. **13** And if the master of the Midheaven looks upon the second place, if it chances to be in familiarity with it, the pursuer will have victory; but if it is in the eighth place, or in familiarity with it, or setting, the fleeing one will have victory.

---

[21] **BD/EG:** That is, if the *lord of* either the Hour-marker or seventh has a relationship.

[22] For this paragraph, cf. *Carmen* V.34, **21-23**; Heph. III.38, **22-24**.

[23] *Kata tēn enantian thesin.* **BD:** In context, this probably means that instead of benefics there are malefics, and instead of being well arranged they are poorly arranged. But this also echoes *Carmen* and Heph. III, which deals with the sign "opposite" the Ascendant (i.e., the seventh) and the relation of the lord of the Midheaven to it.

14 If[24] the Moon separates from one of the rulers of the Hour-marker, or connects with any of these, victory will incline towards the pursuer.[25] **15** If [she] separates from one of the lords of the Hour-marker, and connects with any of the masters of the setting [pivot], the fleeing one will have victory. **16** In the same way, consider this about the masters of the setting [pivot].

17 Moreover,[26] the Moon increasing in light indicates the one who makes war, and the Sun the one made war upon. **18** If [the Moon] is waning, or decreasing in light, she then indicates the one made war upon. **19** And of course if the Sun has a good position, and is testified to by benefics, the party meant by him will have victory; but if the Moon is posited in good places, and is supervised[27] by a benefic, the one indicated by the Moon will have victory.

20 Also[28] examine the Lot of Fortune at that time, and should it approach[29] the Hour-marker (that is, if it or its lord chances to be in the arising part),[30] the one making war will have victory. **21** If Fortune or its lord approaches the setting or is found in the western parts, the one made war upon will have victory. **22** Now, if the master of the Lot of Fortune is found under the earth, there will be a deliverance from the war, and there will be agreement between both sides. **23** But if the Lot of Fortune is found on the Midheaven, it indicates that there will be a quick deliverance from the war <due to the judges>.[31]

24 The Sun or the Moon occupying the Midheaven indicates that the victory of the king or of his armies will be conspicuous and much talked about. **25** The luminaries chancing to be in the setting, or benefics being on it, announce victory for the one made war upon. **26** The benefics being under

---

[24] For this paragraph, cf. *Carmen* V.34, **24-25** and Heph. III.38, **25-27**, although neither of these are as detailed as Theophilus.

[25] **BD:** This seems to be backwards. One would think that if she separates from the lord of the *seventh* and connects with the lord of the *Ascendant*, victory will go to the pursuer (the Ascendant). And this would be in parallel with **15**. However, **16** specifically addresses the seventh or setting in the same way, leaving **14** unclear.

[26] For this paragraph, cf. *Carmen* V.34, **26-29**, and Heph. III.38, **1-3** and **28-30**.

[27] *Epitreō.* **BD:** This sounds like it should mean "overcoming," but Heph. III.38, **26** is equally generic.

[28] For this paragraph, cf. *Carmen* V.34, **30-33**; Heph. III.38, **31-32**.

[29] *Prosneuō*; also, "incline."

[30] **BD:** Or perhaps more generally in the rising (i.e., eastern) half of the chart.

[31] **BD:** Adding with *Carmen* V.34, **33** and Heph. III.38, **32**.

earth indicate defeat for the one made war upon, through treachery and wrong-doing; but if benefics are on the pivot under the earth, then the one making war will be justly defeated.

27 And[32] this way speaks Theophilus: In addition, we say that it is necessary to also examine the benefics and malefics. **28** And if a benefic is found on the Hour-marker, it shows victory for the one making war; but if a benefic is found on the setting, it indicates defeat.

29 Again, thus speaks Theophilus: When Taurus[33] rises in feminine signs in nocturnal inceptions or inquiries, it shows victories for the one making war; but if a malefic, it indicates defeat.

30 When in the inquiry the lord of the Hour-marker is found retrograde, it shows weakness and the turning around of the one making war. **31** When the lord of the setting is [so] found, it shows the same things for the one marched against.

32 It is also necessary that the wise one make a comparative examination of the configurations, and declare that victory will incline towards the one who is found with the greatest number of good testimonies.

33 Moreover one should also know that, should the benefics be found on the underground pivot, a great slaughter is indicated.

34 When there is a favorable beholding[34] between the lord of the Hour-marker and the lord of the setting, then peace is indicated; and the first of the two to the beholding,[35] shows the one who seeks after peace.

---

[32] For this paragraph, see broadly *Carmen* V.34, **19-20**.

[33] **BD/EG:** This should probably read "benefic."

[34] *Theōria.*

[35] *Peri tēn theōrian.* **BD:** This probably means the lighter planet which is making the application, as Sahl has it (*Questions* Ch. 7.2, **8**).

Chapter 3: On the four pivots, configurations, post-ascensions, places, and degrees of each one[36]

1 Saturn[37] marking the Hour to Jupiter[38] kills the general, and reduces[39] the army, and causes it to be oppressed by the enemies. **2** But Saturn marking the Hour to Mars[40] with the Moon, while Jupiter is not observing, indicates that the leaders are unjust and rapacious. **3** Saturn in his own place, being of the same sect as the Hour-marker,[41] indicates a good and fortunate campaign, for it will also afford victory and spoils; though if he chances to be in the places of the Moon and Mercury this harms the army, bringing toils and vexations, with much fear and sluggishness.[42] **4** Saturn marking the Hour while Venus is setting, indicates destruction for those in the campaign.

5 Saturn[43] culminating produces the same things as when he is marking the Hour, especially when he is of the sect; and when he chances to be in another's sign, it brings a sure maltreatment, though when maltreated in a bicorporeal [sign, he] will again rise from [his] fall. **6** Saturn culminating while Mars himself is setting,[44] indicates evident slaughter for those who have marched to war, provided there is not a benefic on the Hour-marker.

7 Saturn[45] on the setting is troublesome for both those marched against and their shield-fellows, also bringing dangers from rivers, or chilling and disturbances from waters; except that the enemies will be thrown again into agitation. **8** Saturn setting with Venus makes the soldiers more faint-hearted, effeminate, and unsuccessful.[46] **9** Saturn[47] setting with Mercury handles bad-

---

[36] Edited in *CCAG* XI.1, pp. 233-42.

[37] For this paragraph, cf. *Carmen* II.27, **1** and **5-7**.

[38] In *Carmen*, this means that Jupiter is in the west.

[39] *Tapenoi*. **EG**: Aside from being reduced in number, this can also mean "abase."

[40] Again, in *Carmen* this means that Mars is in the west.

[41] Or rather, it being a diurnal chart (*Carmen*).

[42] Or, "carelessness" ('*rathumia*).

[43] For this paragraph, cf. *Carmen* II.27, **9-10**.

[44] *Carmen* has Mars with Saturn, but perhaps Theophilus had a more complete list.

[45] For this sentence, cf. *Carmen* II.27, **11**; but *Carmen* has Saturn on the IC here.

[46] *Apraktos*. Or, "impotent, unavailing."

[47] For this sentence, cf. *Carmen* II.27, **12**; again, *Carmen* has Saturn on the IC.

ly the auxiliary [troops] of those at war, and their possessions, also lessening the good fortune.[48]

ဩ   ဩ   ℜ

10 Jupiter[49] marking the Hour indicates good luck and agreement for those who make war; it also renders the leaders most manly and of good courage. **11** Jupiter marking the Hour in a masculine sign renders the leaders manlier and more efficient. **12** Jupiter marking the Hour in a bicorporeal [sign] shows the army to be managed by two generals. **13** Jupiter marking the Hour while Saturn sets, kills the general and harms the king; it also indicates that the enemies drive the soldiers into violent agitation. **14** With Jupiter in this condition, if Mars also post-ascends or decimates him,[50] the good luck lessens, except that it allows [him] to prevail over the enemies.

15 Jupiter[51] culminating increases victory, and renders the generals well-disposed towards the army. **16** Jupiter culminating, and watched closely by a Mars testified to from a familiar[52] and good place, increases the victories and profits.

17 Jupiter[53] setting and having a relationship with the Hour-marker makes the end of the campaign better than the beginning; if a destroyer is also present, it strengthens those made war upon, and brings slaughter to those making war. **18** Jupiter culminating[54] and watched closely by Mars from a congenial place, makes the campaign fortunate and held in honor. **19** Jupiter setting together with a malefic, brings dangers and treachery for the army. **20** Jupiter setting in a tropical sign indicates putting the ruling king to flight. **21** With Jupiter setting and watched closely by Venus while Mercury and Mars are testifying, there will be a plot in the army. **22** If Jupiter is setting and looking upon the Moon, the one making war will not attain booty nor any of the suitable things. **23** Jupiter setting, Venus marking the Hour

---

[48] At this point Theophilus must have had a paragraph on Saturn coming to the signs of other planets based on *Carmen* II.32, just as with the other planets below.

[49] For this paragraph, cf. *Carmen* II.28, **1-4.**

[50] In *Carmen*, this seems to mean that Mars is in the tenth or the eleventh (i.e., what post-ascends the *Midheaven*).

[51] For this paragraph, cf. *Carmen* II.28, **6-7.**

[52] In *Carmen*, this means that Mars is in one of his own dignities.

[53] For this paragraph, cf. *Carmen* II.28, **10-13.**

[54] **BD:** This should be "setting," with *Carmen*.

and looked upon by the Moon, indicates that there will be a guarding and salvation of the army.

24 Jupiter[55] underground, Mars culminating: the wealth will come from things sacred[56] to the army; besides [that] it also makes friends enemies, and it will bring victory for the one making war only after some time.

25 Jupiter[57] in the inception coming to the place[58] of Saturn affords the alleviation of a pre-existing grief. **26** Jupiter coming to the place of Mars is good, and brings favor and action to the army; it also brings enemies into subjection, and increases fortunate things.

ဆ   ဆ   ର

27 Mars[59] marking the Hour in a male sign, in a diurnal inception, affords a hostile end to the war, and a short attack; seen by Saturn, it brings imminent danger for the one making war, but [if] testified to by Jupiter, a bright victory with toil. **28** Mars marking the Hour while the Sun and the Moon are setting, or when one of them is setting while the other is underground, and Jupiter in aversion to them, causes the violent death of the general, and [makes] the soldiers be exposed to the sword and wounds. **29** Mars marking the Hour in a nocturnal and military inception, especially in a feminine sign, is good and a great fortune for the one marching to war; though even more so when the sign in which he is placed chances to be of the sect. **30** It is much better when Jupiter himself looks, for it renders the army ready[60] and confident,[61] even though with distress and work. **31** When Mars is post-ascending the Hour-marker, if no benefic testifies to him, the one making war will be plundered and looted; but if a benefic should look upon it, he will be partially looted, and will partially save what is his.

32 Mars[62] culminating and in sect,[63] or post-ascending the Midheaven, makes large expeditions and delayed meetings with the enemy; but if the

---

[55] Cf. *Carmen* II.28, **14**, but *Carmen* does not mention Mars here.

[56] *Aporrētos.* **EG:** Also, "forbidden, secret." **BD:** The notion of secrecy seems more appropriate to Jupiter being under the earth.

[57] For this paragraph, cf. *Carmen* II.32, **1-2**.

[58] This should be "house," not the actual body of Saturn (per *Carmen*).

[59] For this paragraph, cf. *Carmen* II.29, **1-4**.

[60] *Empraktos.* **EG:**Also, "active."

[61] *Tharsaleos.* **EG:** Or, "courageous."

[62] For this paragraph, cf. *Carmen* II.29, **5-7**.

sign in which he stands is tropical or bicorporeal, the army will retreat back to their own land, after scattering most of their wealth. **33** Jupiter testifying means a bright victory, and especially when Mars in sect testifies.

34 Mars[64] underground disintegrates the arrangements of the army, though if a benefic testifies, it brings fresh profits and rewards, as well as gains from spoils.

35 Mars setting,[65] <if> [he] overtakes the others,[66] it indicates burning wherever someone makes war. **36** Mars setting in his own places while Jupiter looks upon him, reconciles the enemies. **37** Mars setting and the Sun or the Moon looking upon him, sets the army apart and causes separation, rendering the campaign irregular. **38** Mars setting, and seeing a Moon increasing in light, brings on great dangers for the army, in terms of betrayal and imprisonment; and much more so if Jupiter is not observing.

39 Mars[67] coming towards Saturn (that is, where Saturn is in the inception),[68] makes those marching to war resolute, zealous, and effective against the enemies. **40** Mars in the inception coming to the place of Jupiter, Venus, or even Mercury, brings suffering and great distress to the army. **41** Mars coming to the places of Jupiter brings loss and damage for those drawn up in battle-order; and [Mars moving to the place] where the Sun of the inception is, and coming to be under the rays, [means] an illness will befall the army, but it will also cause danger and destruction for the general. **42** Mars coming towards Venus indicates murmuring and quarreling within the army. **43** Mars coming towards Mercury sows treachery and suspicion within the army, and also lessens the ability.[69] **44** When[70] Mars is coming to the place of the Moon (as well as that of the Sun), while the benefics are not testifying, an illness falls on [the army]; and if the sign is also bestial, it brings death to the horses and mules, except that it causes the army to prevail over the enemies.

---

[63] *Carmen* has this in diurnal nativities, i.e. contrary to his sect.

[64] Cf. *Carmen* II.29, **8**.

[65] For this paragraph, cf. *Carmen* II.29, **9-13**.

[66] *Katalabei*. **BD**: This could be a synonym for "decimates" or "overcomes"; it is not reflected in *Carmen*.

[67] For sentences **39-43**, cf. *Carmen* II.34, **1-4**.

[68] This may be Theophilus's view, but *Carmen* treats this as being a sign *ruled by* these planets, not a connection with their bodies.

[69] *Praxis*. **EG**: This is in the sense of "practical ability"; but it might simply mean "action."

[70] For this sentence, cf. *Carmen* II.37, **3-4**.

හ   හ   ෂ

45 The Sun[71] marking the Hour in inceptions of war, and testified to by benefics, indicates a bright victory for the one making war, and especially when he is in his own place, or exaltation, or in a masculine sign; if in addition benefics decimate him, the victory will appear to be even brighter.

46 The Sun culminating produces the same things, just as when marking the Hour, except that it does not give a truce or arrangements.

47 The Sun[72] setting brings grief to the one making war, and inspires joy to the one set opposite. **48** The Sun setting and being in places alien to his own, and testified to, opposed, or squared by malefics, brings on captivity and quick destruction for the enemy; but if the Moon at that time travels along with[73] the Sun, the above-said things will become more certain.

49 When[74] the Sun is in the pivot under the earth and harmed by malefics, he acts in accordance with what has been said, unless he is in his own house or exaltation.

50 The Sun[75] chancing to be in Saturnian places according to the above-said disposition, indicates that the soldiers are vigorous and effective. **51** The Sun being in the places of Mars in the same disposition, indicates unpleasantness and the conflict of the army.[76] **52** When both luminaries come to be in the places of Jupiter, they indicate that the soldiers are prudent and the generals good. **53** The Sun being in the places of Venus means that the generals are competent and thoughtful. **54** The Sun being in Mercurial places renders the generals efficacious and lucky. **55** The above-stated things will be more powerful when the lord of the sign and of the bounds looks upon the luminaries, or bears witness to them.

---

[71] For this paragraph and the next, cf. *Carmen* II.26, **1-2**.

[72] For this paragraph, cf. *Carmen* II.26, **3** and **5**.

[73] *Synodeuō*. **BD**: That is, assembles or meets with him in the same sign.

[74] Cf. *Carmen* II.26, **6**.

[75] For this paragraph, cf. *Carmen* II.37, **9-10**, **12**, **14**, and maybe **2**.

[76] **BD/EG**: We believe this means that there will be dissatisfaction *within* the army about their situation.

ଓ   ଓ   ଓ

56 Venus[77] marking the Hour or post-ascending the Hour-marker in a war inception, and Mars configured with her, she being eastern,[78] makes the leaders effective and lucky, and also causes the obedience of the army; but the good things will be more certain when the Moon also looks upon Venus; Mercury, together with Mars, being configured with her and Saturn, makes the generals rapacious, unjust, and very scandalous. **57** Venus marking the Hour in a bicorporeal sign, with Mars also in a bicorporeal [sign], shows the division of the army, and [also] that it has two generals. **58** Venus marking the Hour or culminating with Mercury, and she being eastern, makes the army ready to obey the one in authority, and the generals be wise, and especially when the sign is feminine or tropical. **59** Venus marking the Hour or culminating when the Moon, with Mars, looks upon it, makes the army obedient to the leaders. **60** Venus marking the Hour with Mercury, while Mars is setting, unsettles the army and excites [it] against the generals; but correction will come with Jupiter's transit into the place which looks upon[79] the Hour-marker in the root. **61** Venus marking the Hour, Saturn setting: the general is destroyed by his own army. **62** Venus marking the Hour, the Moon being under the earth, means the good luck of the army, bright victory, and a quick and good return. **63** Venus marking the Hour in a feminine sign indicates nobleness of mind and the righteous dealings of the general. **64** Venus marking the Hour and being eastern, or post-ascending the Midheaven, makes the campaign easy to accomplish, and the attacks hard [for the enemy] to meet, and especially when Saturn is not looking upon her.

65 Venus[80] culminating in a feminine sign accomplishes sluggish wars and slow-moving attacks, and especially when Mars is not configured with her. **66** Also, if Jupiter and Mars do not distribute[81] to her, there will not be war at all. **67** Venus in a masculine sign, or post-ascending the Midheaven, the Moon being in a masculine sign and testified to by Mars and Mercury,

---

[77] For this paragraph, cf. *Carmen* II.30, **1-14**. However, I do not see a source for sentence **62**; perhaps this was in the version of Dorotheus used by Theophilus.

[78] *Anatolikē.* **BD:** This probably means she is coming out of the rays, but maybe simply that she is rising before the Sun.

[79] *Epiblepei.* **EG:** This is possibly a synonym for "decimates."

[80] For this paragraph, cf. *Carmen* II.30, **15-16**.

[81] *Epidōsin.* **BD:** In *Carmen*, this means that they (or rather, Saturn) looks at or aspects her.

makes the army most masculine in spirit, and most reckless, and accomplishes victory through contrivances[82] and negotiation.[83]

68 Venus setting, Mars not looking upon her: the campaign turns to peace and truce.

69 Venus culminating and seen by a Saturn in his own place, makes the leaders of the army strong and most competent, and especially when [Saturn] is in tropical signs.

70 Venus[84] culminating, or in the underground [pivot], and testified to by Saturn and Mars from alien places, if Jupiter is not assisting, makes the leaders of the army wanton and shameful, and unsettles the army against them; but if in addition the Moon is harmed as well, then it means the defeat of the army.

71 Venus setting when Mars is culminating grants a famed victory against the enemies. **72** Venus setting, seen by Jupiter, strengthens the enemies. **73** Venus setting,[85] Saturn or Mars culminating and in tropical signs: the evil will not happen just once, but many times.

74 Venus[86] in the underground [pivot] fosters grief for those in campaign, and especially when she is in masculine signs.

75 Venus[87] coming towards Saturn is favorable for every pursuit, and will turn the scales:[88] for the enemies will turn their steps [around]. **76** Venus coming towards the places of Jupiter indicates that the army is in good hopes. **77** Venus coming towards the Sun unsettles the army and causes disputes. **78** Venus coming towards Mercury increases good fortune, and fosters victory for the one making war. **79** Venus coming towards the Moon is favorable, productive of cheerfulness, and effective.

ℬ ℬ ℭ

---

[82] *Mēchanēmatōn.* **EG:** This can include mechanical devices.

[83] *Traktaismōn.* **EG:** Only the verb *traktaizō* is found in the lexicon, which is equivalent to the Latin *tractare,* "to treat, handle, negotiate."

[84] This bears a resemblance to *Carmen* II.30, **17** and **19-20**. But in *Carmen,* Venus is setting.

[85] Cf. *Carmen* II.30, **20-21**, although *Carmen* has Venus in the IC, not the west.

[86] Cf. *Carmen* II.30, **20**.

[87] For this paragraph, cf. *Carmen* II.35, **1-2** and **4**; also *Carmen* II.37, **11**. However, I cannot see a source for sentence **77**.

[88] *Epirrepō,* lit. "to lean towards, incline."

80 Mercury[89] marking the Hour and [being] eastern, indicates the happiness[90] and sharp action of the army. **81** Mercury marking the Hour with a benefic: the pursuer is bribed with money, and keeps back from the undertaking. **82** Mercury marking the Hour or culminating, in a bicorporeal sign, and being eastern,[91] prepares a great deal of captivity for the soldiers. **83** Mercury [being] with Venus, marking the Hour or culminating, provides a popular reputation for the army; but if Jupiter bears witness, the campaign will appear more illustrious. **84** If Mercury were under the rays in the same placement, this renders the generals malignant and insidious.

85 Mercury[92] culminating or post-ascending, in the Midheaven or in the Hour-marker,[93] brings popular repute and success for the soldiers, and makes the campaign transient: during that time it leads the enemies to a truce, and it decides on peace.

86 Mercury[94] setting destroys a great mass of the army, and especially when he is in a tropical or bicorporeal sign, and Mars looks upon him. **87** Mercury underground produces the same things. **88** Mercury rejoices with both benefic and malefic stars,[95] because the former make it effective, the latter villainous.

89 Mercury marking the Hour with Saturn brings on damage for the one arranged for battle. **90** Mercury being looked upon by malefics in the same inceptions, also renders the leaders and the soldiers unjust.

Ꞷꝏ   ꝏ   ꝏ

---

[89] For this paragraph, cf. *Carmen* II.31, **1, 3, 6-8**. However, I do not see a source for sentence **81**.

[90] *Eudaimonia*, lit. "good spirit."

[91] *Anatolikos*. **BD:** Again, this could also mean rising out of (or simply being out of) the rays, or at any rate rising before the Sun. See **84**, which has Mercury explicitly under the rays.

[92] Cf. *Carmen* II.31, **2**.

[93] **BD:** In *Carmen*, this means being in the Midheaven, eleventh, or second: that is, post-Ascending the Midheaven or the Ascendant.

[94] Cf. *Carmen* II.31, **9-10**.

[95] **BD:** This seems to be a garbling of *Carmen*. Instead, *Carmen* has Mercury "rejoicing in his own glow," and simply points out that being with benefics indicates good Mercurial qualities, and malefics bad ones.

91 The[96] Moon marking the Hour, and increasing in light, helps the one arranged for battle. **92** The Moon marking the Hour or culminating in a diurnal inception, exposes trivial things[97] and impedes good fortune, and especially when a malefic distributes to[98] her, or post-ascends her: for it brings disappointment after the victory. **93** When the Moon, [being] in her own house or exaltation in such position, is testified to by a benefic, victory will become illustrious and have much help.[99] **94** The Moon marking the Hour or culminating in a nocturnal inception, as well as post-ascending the said pivots, provides with an illustrious and much-helped victory, diminishing the stock of supplies. **95** If a benefic also beholds her, the victory will be very much illustrious and talked about, and the stock of supplies will be plentiful.

96 The Moon[100] in the setting means quick victory for the enemies, banishment for those arranged for battle, and quick plundering, as well as uncontrolled turning around.[101]

97 The Moon[102] being in the pivot underground, and harmed by malefics, produces destruction through the ambush, obstruction, and treachery of the one having a relationship to the places of both parties; but if also benefics were [present] or looked upon her, then it brings help from ambush and treachery for the said party.

98 The Moon[103] being in the places of Mars, according to the above-mentioned position, indicates that the soldiers are bold, active and manly. **99** It is also appropriate to consider the testimonies of the stars, for if the benefics looked upon the luminaries in the above-stated places, they would indicate a just selection of the generals; but if a malefic should look upon the luminaries, it means that the generals are unjust and treacherous.

---

[96] For this paragraph, see broadly *Carmen* II.25, **1-5**.

[97] **BD/EG:** This seems to mean that the army is engaged in petty concerns and things, as opposed to great actions.

[98] **BD:** *Epidōsin.* As before, in *Carmen* this seems to mean simply that it looks at her.

[99] *Periboēthos.*

[100] Cf. *Carmen* II.25, **6**.

[101] **BD:** This seems to mean, "a rout."

[102] Cf. *Carmen* II.25, **7-8**.

[103] For this paragraph, cf. *Carmen* II.37, **7-8**.

100 The Moon[104] being in the places of Venus indicates good fortune and effectiveness through the good thinking of the generals. **101** The Moon coming towards her own place in which she was at the inception of the campaign, fosters disturbance[105] for the army. **101** If she also chances to be in a tropical sign, the army changes from one activity to another; but if in the root [of the inception] Venus or Jupiter chances to be there, it brings joy and much rejoicing for the army. **102** The Moon coming to the place of the Sun is good for standing together and the obedience of the army. **103** The Moon coming to the places of Mars while the benefics testify, means an illustrious victory; but if a malefic looks upon her, it shows imminent danger for the army. **104** The Moon transiting Venus, while no malefic testifies, shows the success of the army. **105** The Moon coming towards Venus, while Mars comes close to her, indicates that there will be an agreement and truce with the enemies.

106 The Moon coming towards Saturn while Saturn is in his own triangle, and she increasing in light, indicates assistance for the army. **107** The Moon[106] coming towards Mercury, if Mercury turns out to be favorable and testified to by benefics, shows favorable things for the army; [but] he being corrupted and testified to by malefics, evil things.

108 The Moon coming to the Hour-marker of the root buoys up the army and fosters empty hopes. **109** The Moon coming towards the Midheaven of the inception brings glory and good progress[107] for the army. **110** The Moon coming towards the setting of the inception is good for plots against the enemies. **111** The Moon coming to the underground [pivot] of the inception is in the same way good for plots and secret dealings, hiding-places, and the manipulation of enemies.

---

[104] For this sentence only, cf. *Carmen* II.37, **11**.

[105] *Meteōrismos*. **EG**: Or, "delay."

[106] For this sentence, cf. *Carmen* II.37, **13**.

[107] *Proagōgē*. **EG**: Also, "eminence."

Chapter 4: On connection and separation[108]

[Connections of the Moon][109]

1 The Moon connecting with Saturn and she being in a decline, shows the weakness and cowardice of the army and its leader, as well as wintering, and much danger; but if Jupiter testifies to the Midheaven or the second place, it loosens the evil, and especially if Jupiter <is> in tropical signs.

2 The Moon connecting with a pivotal Jupiter following a straight course,[110] brings good repute for the leader, though when she connects with an unfavorably-placed Jupiter, this brings a reduction of repute and honor for the leader. **3** The Moon connecting with Jupiter and she being pivotal, indicates that the army is well-reputed and lucky.

4 The Moon connecting with Mars and she being in a decline, shows the irregularities of the campaign, dangerous attacks, and bad fortune; however, they indeed terrify the enemies. **5** The Moon connecting with Mars, and she being pivotal, Jupiter looking upon her, indicates that the leader is active and effective, and that he will be crowned with an illustrious victory. **6** The Moon <connecting> with a favorably-placed Mars, and diminishing her light, renders the generals practical, hot-headed, and lucky, and the soldiers brave; but if the Moon, increasing her light, is going to connect with a badly-placed Mars, she becomes mean and averse for both those who rule and those ruled; and especially when Mars chances to be subtractive.

7 The Moon connecting with the Sun in a masculine sign brings glory and magnificence for the leader, except that it causes grief and the scattering of wealth at the beginning; but as time goes by it brings good fortune and very joyful reasonableness.[111]

---

[108] Edited in *CCAG* XI.1, pp. 242-46.

[109] **BD:** This subsection may be a reworking of the interpretation of transiting Moon in *Carmen* IV.4, **13-22** (see also Schmidt 1995, p. 5), but if so then Theophilus either has a much fuller text to work with, or has filled out many details himself based on his own military interpretations.

[110] **EG:** I take *euthupos rounti* to be *euthu-pourounti*, otherwise it does not make any sense. There is no mention of this in the critical apparatus, and one should probably expect a slash instead of the final *sigma* in *euthupos*.

[111] *Epieikeia*. **EG:** Also, "goodness, virtuousness."

8 The Moon connecting with Venus, while Mars is configured and in busy[112] places, shows that the generals are conquerors and extremely virtuous.

9 The Moon connecting with Mercury, she being pivotal or post-ascending the pivots, while Mars is favorably posited and testified to, leads to an illustrious victory, and leads the subdued ones to the paying of tributes.

[Combinations of separations and connections][113]

10 The Moon separating from Saturn and connecting with Jupiter in inceptions of war, produces acquisition and preservation from toil and from any trouble, also with the exchange of many lands, and a good campaign and return home; taken from Jupiter towards Saturn, she produces for the campaign the opposite things to those already said.

11 [The Moon] being taken from Saturn to Mars on the occasion of the campaign, produces a release from evils, and renders the soldiers bold and brave; taken from Mars to Saturn, it causes the opposite things.

12 The Moon being taken from Saturn to Venus <at> the time of the campaign is easy for everything, and fosters the enslaving of female persons, and intercourse with them. **13** [The Moon] being taken from Venus to Saturn <at> the said time, or at the outbreak of war, produces victory against the enemies, and especially when Saturn is an evening [star]; when a morning [star], Saturn brings the army grief after the victory.[114]

14 The Moon being taken from Saturn to Mercury <at> the time of the battle, sows malice and strife among the leaders, and brings sluggishness to the army; if Mercury is a morning [star], it produces release without danger; if an evening one or under the rays, it prepares the treachery of the army. **15** Taken from Mercury to Saturn, she causes hindrances to victory, and hurls sicknesses into the army.

---

[112] **BD**: That is, the advantageous (*chrēmatizontōn*) places.

[113] This entire subsection (**10-32**) *may* be a creative reworking of the transit delineations in *Carmen* IV.4, **27-51** (and see Schmidt 1995, pp. 1-5). In *Carmen*, these are (for example), transiting Saturn to the natal Jupiter, without any involvement of the Moon; but in Theophilus, he makes the Moon separate from Saturn and connect with Jupiter (**10**). But Theophilus also gives the contrary combinations (Saturn-Jupiter, Jupiter-Saturn), which *Carmen* generally doesn't do. For more of these types, see *Apotelesmatics* Ch. 25.

[114] **BD:** To me it does not make sense that Saturn means something better when an evening star; but maybe this has to do with Venus being a nocturnal planets.

16 Taken from Mars to Jupiter in inceptions such as these, the Moon is completely favorable, and especially when Jupiter chances to be a morning [star]; if an evening one, it brings relief from distressing things. **17** The Moon being taken from Jupiter to Mars brings decrease and a lack of things necessary to the army; if she is also increasing in light, [it is] much worse.

18 The Moon coming from Jupiter to Venus is good for all things related to the army, though it also shows that there is lewdness and dissoluteness within the army. **19** Taken from Venus to Jupiter in battles, [the Moon] is favorable and productive of victory; she also grants glory and magnificence to the leaders, especially when she makes the connection upon the pivots.

20 Taken from Jupiter to Mercury, she brings victory through treachery; taken from Mercury to Jupiter, she gives good fortune and favorable interactions.

21 Taken from Mars to Venus, when both are evening [stars], she produces acquisition and slavery; but if both are morning [stars], they also grant an illustrious victory. **22** Taken from Venus to Mars, both being evening [stars], they make the leaders very scandalous; if morning [stars], they make the soldiers manlier and of good courage, except that they arouse rebellion against the leaders and cause controversy.

23 The Moon being taken from Mars to Mercury in inceptions of this kind, both being morning [stars], makes the soldiers obedient and submissive; when evening [stars], they are made unstable, careless, and uncertain. **24** Taken from Mercury[115] to Mars, both being morning [stars], the Moon shows the soldiers to be rapacious and unjust.

25 The Moon being taken from Mercury to Venus renders the soldiers cheerful and extravagant, especially when both are evening [stars]; if morning [stars], they also give good fortune.

26 The Moon connecting with benefics by co-travelling in inceptions belonging to generals, is favorable for success and good luck; coming together with malefics, [it is] unfavorable and inconvenient.

27 The Moon separating from the Sun and taken to Venus, with Venus herself not being severely damaged by the malefics, brings honor, glory, and praise to the leaders. **28** If Venus is harmed by destroyers or is not in a good place, she makes the soldiers ill-sounding, controversial, and braggarts.

---

[115] Reading for "Saturn."

29 The Moon separating from Venus, when Venus is unfavorably placed, makes the soldiers ineffective and unfortunate.

30 The Moon separating from Mercury, while Mercury is well-placed, makes the soldiers be fortunate and effective.

31 The[116] luminaries coming to benefic places are fortunate and glorious; but if both luminaries are maltreated by Mars or Saturn, they make the leaders deranged and malignant.

32 The[117] malefics coming to pivots are unsteady, and are filled up with ill repute in everything, and especially when the benefics are in aversion.

Chapter 5: On triangles[118]

1 Saturn[119] trine Jupiter in such inceptions renders the leaders most competent, strongest, and best-disposed towards their kings, with also a dominion over the enemies. **2** If also Mercury is configured with these, it shows them to be shrewd and inventive as well. **3** If also Mars (he being well-placed) is configured with them, it brings victory through bloodshed, except that it brings murder and blame in their actions.

4 Mars trine Saturn in such inceptions makes the actions more effective.

5 Saturn trine the Sun in inceptions of war, brings promotion and good repute; if they also are in the visible hemisphere, [it is] much better.

6 Saturn trine Venus in such dispositions produces stability and the solemn bearing of the army.

7 Saturn trine Mercury reveals the leaders to be sagacious and experienced, contriving victory through words and thinking; or also[120] through bloodshed.

8 Saturn trine the Moon provides illustrious and great victories, and especially when the light [of the Moon] is[121] increasing; when decreasing, it diminishes the above-said things.

---

[116] Cf. *Carmen* IV.4, **50**, and its fuller version in Schmidt 1995, pp. 4-5.

[117] Cf. *Carmen* IV.4, **51**, and Schmidt 1995, pp. 4-5.

[118] Edited in *CCAG* XI.1, pp. 246-47. **BD:** Where necessary to make the English sound better, I will use "trine," else the text would read as the awkward "Saturn triangle Jupiter."

[119] For all of these aspects of Saturn, cf. *Carmen* II.14, **1-9**.

[120] **EG:** Reading from **S** as reported in the critical apparatus, otherwise it does not make sense.

[121] Reading with *Carmen* II.14, **7**, for "lights are."

ဢ   ဢ   ᘉ

9 Jupiter[122] trine Mars makes the leaders effective and successful.

10 Jupiter trine the Sun means the splendor and good fortune of those in command, as well as glory and honor for the kings.

11 Jupiter trine Venus renders the leaders graceful, merry, and causes them to be regarded with affection.

12 Jupiter trine Mercury shows the commanders to be thoughtful and effective.

13 Jupiter trine the Moon renders the general well-reputed, well-known[123] and able, but also renders the army obedient to their leaders, especially when the Moon is waxing.

ဢ   ဢ   ᘉ

14 Mars[124] trine the Sun shows the leader to be efficacious and high-spirited.

15 Mars trine Jupiter, Jupiter being pivotal and the Moon well-placed, brings victory to both the leaders and the army, and especially when he chances to be in a masculine sign.

16 Mars trine Venus makes the leaders powerful, of strong body, and high-minded.

17 Mars trine Mercury renders the soldiers vigorous and lucky at war, as well as quick.

18 Mars trine the waning Moon indicates a quick action of the army, as well as good fortune; if Jupiter is looking on, it adds splendor.

ဢ   ဢ   ᘉ

19 The Sun[125] and the Moon trine each other, and testified to by benefics, is favorable and glorious.

---

[122] For these aspects of Saturn, cf. *Carmen* II.14, **10-13** and **15**.

[123] *Polygnōstos.* **EG**: But perhaps, "knowing many things."

[124] For these aspects of Mars, cf. *Carmen* II.14, **16-20**.

[125] For this aspect, cf. *Carmen* II.14, **22**.

Chapter 6: On squares[126]

1 Saturn[127] decimating Jupiter on the inception of war diminishes the victory, and sows contrariety of purpose and controversy within the army; it also causes hindrance in actions, and awakens rebellions. **2** Jupiter decimating Saturn in the same inception makes the aforesaid things less, and makes the army have good will towards those in power.

3 Saturn decimating Mars in the inception of war is difficult, for it brings greediness and grief to the army, and much distress. **4** Mars decimating Saturn kills the leader first, and also causes the manipulation of the army, with much ill-will and dispute.

5 The Sun decimating Saturn during the campaigns scatters public property, and turns the allies towards the enemies; it lessens the good fortune as well. **6** Saturn decimating the Sun awakes rebellions and tyranny against the king; this chancing to be so, it also causes his death.

7 Saturn decimating Venus shows the abandonment[128] of the army, as well as sorrow and sluggishness, with evil fortune; it also causes the leaders to be deceived in their expectations. **8** Venus decimating Saturn makes the campaign glorious.[129]

9 Saturn decimating Mercury introduces opposition, cold, and sluggishness in the army. **10** Mercury decimating Saturn does not improve the above-said things, but spoils them.

11 The Moon decimating Saturn indicates the rapaciousness and sluggishness of the army. **12** Saturn decimating the Moon causes plagues for the cattle belonging to the army; if also in a feminine sign, it is even worse.

13 Jupiter[130] decimating Mars renders the leader glorious and remarkable, and strengthens the army against the enemies. **14** Mars decimating Jupiter renders the soldiers bold, imperious, and most reckless, except that they fail at something.

---

126 Edited in *CCAG* XI.1, pp. 247-50.

127 For these aspects of Saturn, cf. *Carmen* II.15, **2-14**.

128 *Ekptōsis*.

129 *Endoxon*. **EG**: This is meant in the sense of "held in high esteem" or "much talked about."

130 For these aspects of Jupiter, cf. *Carmen* II.15, **15-24**.

15 The Sun decimating Jupiter indicates a most brilliant and high-spirited leader, except that it lessens the property upon warding off the enemies. **16** Jupiter decimating the Sun indicates good things for both the leaders and the soldiers.

17 Jupiter decimating Venus makes a truce and treaties in the campaign. **18** Venus decimating Jupiter makes the soldiers stupid and of good courage.

19 Jupiter decimating Mercury provides victory by means of subtle contrivance and inventiveness. **20** Mercury decimating Jupiter renders the leaders undistinguished and unfair, also stealing and plundering the booty and weapons of the army.

21 Jupiter decimating the Moon is beneficent for both the leaders and the soldiers, for it brings glory and victory. **22** The Moon decimating Jupiter is favorable and praiseworthy[131] for everything, and it also helps the leaders.

ଅ   ଅ   ଓ

23 The Sun[132] decimating Mars is not favorable, neither for the leaders nor the soldiers, for it causes the army to be stripped of its arms, and also sows oppositions. **24** Mars decimating the Sun hurls sickness upon the army.

25 Mars decimating Venus is wholly evil and troublesome, and causes oppositions; if it is in tropical signs, it renders the soldiers careless and frivolous. **26** Venus decimating Mars causes the above-said things.

27 Mars decimating Mercury becomes the cause of many evils, for it harms and creates conflicts, hindering the matters of war as well. **28** Mercury decimating Mars renders the soldiers rapacious and robbers.

29 Mars decimating the Moon causes the soldiers to be stripped of their weapons and throw away their shields; the evil becomes even worse when Mars is in Saturnian places, and the Moon in Mercurial or Martial places. **30** The Moon decimating Mars hints at the unsociability and lack of capacity of the leaders, as well as the evil fortune of the army, and the cessation of hostilities.[133]

---

[131] *Doxastikē*, reading as late (including modern) Greek; the classical meaning ("pertaining to conjecture") seems to make no sense.

[132] For these aspects of Mars, cf. *Carmen* II.15, **25-32**.

[133] *Ekecheiria*. **EG**: Reading with late or modern Greek, for the ancient "rest from work," "holiday."

ʚᴑ   ʚᴑ   ᴄ᧞

31 The[134] luminaries decimating each other, pivotal, and testified to by benefics, indicates a successful and glorious campaign; but when testified to by malefics, it means danger for the army. **32** If the luminaries in their decimation are declining, with good testimony, it shows the mediocre state of the affairs.

ʚᴑ   ʚᴑ   ᴄ᧞

33 Mercury[135] and Venus decimating each other provides victory by means of waters.

34 The Moon[136] decimating Venus indicates good fortune for the army; Venus decimating the Moon brings one victory after another,[137] and the survival of those taken captive.

35 Mercury[138] decimating the Moon produces victory by means of inventiveness and thought; if Mercury in the same chart[139] is in turn decimated by a destroyer, it prepares victory through wrongdoing.

Chapter 7: On diameters[140]

1 Saturn[141] diametrical to Jupiter brings grief to the army; but if Saturn marks the Hour and Jupiter sets, it provides a delayed victory.

2 Saturn diametrical to Mars introduces controversies, tumults, and rebellions in the army; it also awakens tyranny against the leaders. **3** If they were also pivotal, and diametrical to each other, this reveals ruin for the army; in the post-ascensions, they cut off the hopes of the army; but being in the declines, they harm less, although they also bring hardships and failure.

---

[134] For this sentence only, cf. *Carmen* II.15, **33**.

[135] Cf. *Carmen* II.15, **35**.

[136] Cf. *Carmen* II.15, **36-37**.

[137] *Allepallēlos*. **EG**: Reading with late or modern Greek, as it is not attested to in ancient Greek.

[138] Reading with *Carmen* II.15, **38** for "Venus."

[139] *Thesis*.

[140] Edited in *CCAG* XI.1, pp. 250-52.

[141] For all of these aspects of Saturn, cf. *Carmen* II.16, **1-3**, **7-12**, **14**, **16-18**.

4 Saturn diametrical to the Sun, when Jupiter is not testifying to them, means the death of the leader and much struggle for the army, and especially in feminine signs.

5 Saturn diametrical to Venus indicates an unjust leader and rapacious soldiers.

6 Saturn diametrical to Mercury indicates <*omitted*>.[142]

7 <Saturn diametrical to the Moon indicates>[143] the plundering of the soldiers, as well as much grief; but if they also are in four-footed signs, they bring the destruction of the horses and mules of the army; if the signs are of human shape, the distress will be from enemies; if the signs are watery, the disgrace for them will come from rivers and storms.

ଏଠ   ഗ   ଓଃ

7 Jupiter[144] diametrical to Mars causes the soldiers to become deserters and throw away their weapons in the lines of battle.

8 Jupiter diametrical to the Sun is not favorable, for it makes the soldiers be despoiled by the enemies.

9 Jupiter diametrical to Venus is not favorable, for it makes the soldiers be raisers of rebellion and controversy.

10 Jupiter diametrical to Mercury makes victory by means of contrivance and treachery, and it does not give a profitable end.

11 Jupiter diametrical to a rising Moon is favorable, for it renders the soldiers brave; but if setting and diminishing in light, it also awakens tyranny against the leaders. **12** If the Moon is under the rays as well, it indicates opposition and the failure of the army.

ଏଠ   ഗ   ଓଃ

13 Mars[145] diametrical to the Sun indicates a horrible death for the leader, and makes the army ineffective.

14 Mars diametrical to Venus indicates the anarchy of the army.

---

[142] See *Carmen* II.16, **12-13**.

[143] Adding based on *Carmen* II.16, **14**.

[144] For all of these aspects of Saturn, cf. *Mathesis* VI.16 (only *Carmen* II.16, **24** survives).

[145] For all of these aspects of Mars, cf. *Carmen* II.16, **26-27, 29-30**.

15 Mars diametrical to Mercury produces victory through treacheries, especially when in the bounds of Saturn or in the houses of Mercury.

16 Mars diametrical to the Moon is evil, for it indicates danger for the army.

ಙ಼   ಙ಼   ಅ

17 Venus[146] diametrical to the Moon is not favorable for attacks on the enemy nor ambush.

18 Mercury[147] diametrical to the Moon sows cowardice within the army.

Chapter 8: On hexagons[148]

1 The[149] stars casting a hexagon to each other cause the same things as when casting a triangle, though a little less for good or for evil.

Chapter 9: On war, according to Theophilus[150]

1 When[151] someone departs to war and wishes to march against the enemies, search this way. **2** Let Mars be for you the battle; the one marching to war, the star from which Mars has flowed away; the enemy, the star with which Mars connects.

3 If indeed Mars[152] is borne from Saturn, or from a western Mercury, the one going to war will be harmed and undergo a reversal of fortune.[153]

4 But if Mars connects with Saturn himself or a western Mercury, the enemy will be harmed, and will be offered to the gods.[154] **5** If Mars himself is

---

[146] Cf. *Carmen* II.16, **32**.

[147] Cf. *Carmen* II.16, **33**.

[148] Edited in *CCAG* XI.1, p. 252.

[149] Cf. *Carmen* II.17, **1**.

[150] Edited in *CCAG* XI.1, pp. 252-53.

[151] For this paragraph, see also Ch. 35, **1** below, material ascribed to Julianus of Laodikaia.

[152] Following **S**, for "Jupiter."

[153] *Tropē*, lit. "a change." **EG:** But this can also mean "turning about," suggesting that the one going to war will be put to flight.

[154] *Trapēsetai*, lit. "he will be set on the table."

injured by being under the rays or enclosed[155] between the Sun and the Moon, the war will not be convenient nor helpful, either for the one making war or for the one made war against.

6 If Mars is borne from a benefic to another benefic, it profits not only the one making war, but also the one made war against: both sides turn to a truce and peace—although if the twelfth-part of Mars falls into a bound of Jupiter,[156] while Jupiter has a relationship with[157] the Hour-marker, the Mid-heaven, and the second sign from the Hour-marker, then the one making war will have victory. **7** But if on the contrary Jupiter has a relationship to the setting, the eighth sign, and the underground, the one made war against will have victory. **8** If the twelfth-part of Mars falls into the bound of Saturn, Saturn having a relationship to the setting, the eighth place, and to the underground pivot, the one made war against will prevail. **9** If the twelfth-part of Mars falls into the bound of Saturn, Saturn having a relationship to the above-mentioned places with which Mars has a relationship, it sows fear and cowardice in each of the two parties. **10** If the twelfth-part of Mars[158] falls into the bound of Venus, Venus having a relationship to one of the said parties, that side with which she has a relationship will propose peace to the other one, which will be begged. **11** But if the twelfth-part of Mars falls into the bound of Mercury, Mercury having a relationship to one of the above-mentioned parties,[159] it will introduce inventions[160] and manipulation[161] to that party.

---

[155] **BD:** According to Antiochus and others (Schmidt 2009, pp. 195ff), this is the degree-based version of "besieging." If this is what Theophilus means, then the Sun and Moon must be within 7° on either side of Mars, with no other planet making an exact aspect to those spaces between them.

[156] **BD:** Meaning unclear. This could mean that the twelfth-part in which Mars currently is, is also in a bound of Jupiter—but why not simply say Mars is in a bound of Saturn?

[157] *Logon echōn*, lit. "having a word on," here and below.

[158] **BD:** Reading for "Saturn."

[159] Again, *meros*. **EG:** P reads differently, namely that the relationship is to "one of the above-mentioned pivots."

[160] *Mēchanē*. **EG:** This mainly refers to war machinery, especially those which lift weights (cranes, etc.).

[161] *Traktaismos*. **EG:** This word is not found in lexicons of ancient or modern Greek, but the verb (*traktaizō*, "to bleach") is also the equivalent of the Latin *tracto* and the Greek *kakourgeō*, "to work evil, maltreat, corrupt, falsify." **BD:** The Latin derivative *tracto* can also mean to "manipulate," so we have decided to use that word here.

Chapter 10: If someone wishes to become a tyrant[162] and free himself from subjection to those in power[163]

1 If[164] someone searches concerning tyranny, let the Moon be without maltreatment and looked upon by the benefics: for this way the rulership and independence[165] will be lasting. **2** If the Moon flows away from a benefic and connects with a malefic, the first subjection to a ruler will be better.

3 Otherwise:[166] let the Hour-marker be the tyrant, the setting the ruled; the reason for the tyranny[167] is examined from the middle;[168] of what sort the tyranny[169] will turn out to be, from the underground.

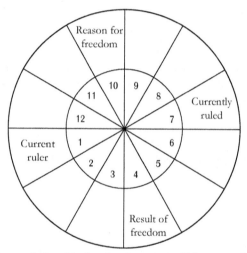

Figure 6: Angles for freeing oneself from a ruler

---

[162] *Tyranneuō*. **EG:** This is meant in the Greek sense of being a "ruler of the people," without moral connotations.

[163] Edited in *CCAG* XI.1 (pp. 253-54). **BD:** The context of this inception might not be clear at first. Most of this material is found in *Carmen* V.14 (but see Heph. III.21), which is about a master (Ascendant) freeing a slave (seventh), so the initiator of the action is indeed the Ascendant. But here, the client and initiator is the one who is *currently* being ruled and wants to be free – namely, Dorotheus's slave, the seventh.

[164] For this paragraph, cf. *Carmen* V.14, **1-3**; Heph. III.21, **5**.

[165] *Autonomia*, lit. "self-rule."

[166] For this sentence, cf. *Carmen* V.14, **5**; Heph. III.21, **1**.

[167] **BD:** In context, this probably means "the rulership he desires."

[168] *Mesos*. **EG:** That is, the Midheaven.

[169] **BD:** Again, this must mean the future rulership and freedom he desires.

4 Also[170] examine both hemispheres, that above the earth, and that under the earth, as well as the stars which are in each. **5** For those which are underground show what is about to be, especially that star that is about to rise from the hemisphere above the earth into that above the earth. **6** If benefics were in the hemisphere underground, what is yet to be will be favorable for the tyrant; if malefics, evil.

7 The Moon[171] in the setting pivot, a malefic being together with her: declare that the ruled will quickly be ruined.

Chapter 11: If someone (of those making war or those against whom war is made), sends a herald to the other in order to seek favor or a truce[172]

1 Having[173] sent someone as ambassador, let the Moon be on the Hour-marker or in the triangles of it, or the squares, adding in number and light; also let the ruler of the Hour-marker be with the Moon, travelling direct, or let it connect with the Moon, for in this way he who asks and is sent as an ambassador will not fail. **2** However, it is even better if the Moon moves into her own house or looks upon it.

3 In[174] a similar way, let also Mercury chance to be with Jupiter; but should he also be with Saturn in the same inception, it would be better if [the herald] did not nod assent, whatever the request to him is. **4** Mercury chancing to be with Venus brings about good fortune. **5** If Jupiter as well happens to hold a straight course, not being harmed by Saturn, it is a cause of good fortune; but if Jupiter goes retrograde, being also harmed by Saturn, the ambassador will not succeed.

---

[170] This paragraph may be an expansion of *Carmen* V.14, but can definitely be found in Heph. III.21, **6-7**.

[171] For this sentence, cf. *Carmen* V.14, **6**; Heph. III.21, **8**.

[172] Edited in *CCAG* XI.1, pp. 254-55.

[173] For this paragraph, cf. *Carmen* V.15, **1-2**; Heph. III.25.

[174] For this paragraph, cf. *Carmen* V.15, **2-5**; Heph. III.25.

Chapter 12: On tyranny[175]

1 Let[176] the tyrant be the Hour-marker and the Moon; though let the ruling king be the Sun and the Midheaven.

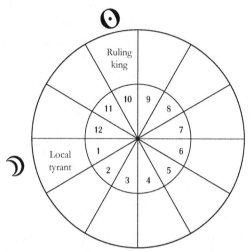

Figure 7: Significators for local tyrant and ruling king

2 The sign[177] marking the Hour being fixed, and the Moon being in such signs: the tyrant will hold power for a long time.[178] **3** If the sign marking the Hour is tropical and the Moon is in a tropical sign, the ruler will not last in his tyranny for a long time. **4** If the sign marking the Hour is bicorporeal, and the Moon is in such, it indicates that the mass of people will join in against the ruler, but then change their mind regarding what they have done.

---

[175] Edited in *CCAG* XI.1, pp. 255-59. **EG**: This word (*tyrannōn*) comes from the verb *tyranneō*, "to be a ruler, absolute monarch." **BD**: The original context of this chapter in Dorotheus (*Carmen* V.37) was the capture of a runaway (the Ascendant, Moon) by his or her owner or master (Midheaven, Sun); the runaway is the Ascendant because he or she has initiated the situation by running away. But in this military version, Theophilus seems to be considering a local tyrant or warlord (Ascendant, Moon) who is trying to escape the authority of a more powerful king or Sultan (Midheaven, Sun). The question then is whether the ruling king will be able to bring the local tyrant back under his control. For a discussion of this in relation to Theophilus's life, see the Introduction.

[176] For this sentence, cf. *Carmen* V.37, **1**; Heph. III.47, **1**.

[177] For this paragraph, cf. *Carmen* V.37, **2-3**; Heph. III.47, **2**.

[178] **BD**: In context, I believe this means that the local warlord will be able to rule for a long time.

5 The Moon[179] marking the Hour in crooked signs indicates an uncertain purpose and affair, not profitable for him. **6** A straight sign marking the Hour, and containing the Moon, is profitable for the tyrant, and prepares for him a convenient rulership.

7 The Moon[180] being within the first fifteen degrees of the bicorporeal signs declares that the tyrant has ruled for the first time; if in the last [degrees], he has ruled before this time.

8 The Moon[181] marking the Hour on the east declares that the tyrant is, or has gone, there; if culminating, to the south; setting, to the west; under the earth, towards the north; being in between two pivots, in the middle of the winds, it indicates a turning of his course.

9 The Moon[182] connecting with Mars, or testified to by him by square or diameter, indicates bondage and flight for the tyrant, or that he has been taken by force and oppressed because of the ruled. **10** The Moon connecting with stationary Saturn indicates that the tyrant has been plotted against by comrades. **11** The Moon connecting with Saturn, Saturn not being stationary, indicates the destruction of some of those belonging to him, though it also shows that he comes to the king with great distress.

12 The Moon[183] being testified to by benefics, or connecting with them, an insurrection will fall upon the tyrant.[184]

13 The Moon with Saturn, being within 15° above the earth, means a fast betrayal of the tyrant.

14 The Moon[185] being unconnected from[186] the Hour-marker and with the Sun gives indications for the madness of the tyrant. **15** The Moon travelling together with the Sun[187] shows the same things.

---

[179] For this paragraph, cf. *Carmen* V.37, **4-5**; Heph. III.47, **3**.

[180] Cf. *Carmen* V.37, **6-7**; Heph. III.47, **4**.

[181] Cf. *Carmen* V.37, **8-9**; Heph. III.47, **5-6**.

[182] For this paragraph, cf. *Carmen* V.37, **10-14**; Heph. III.47, **16-20**.

[183] Cf. *Carmen* V.37, **15-16**; Heph. III.47, **10**.

[184] **BD:** I believe Theophilus meant to say, "the king." For in *Carmen*, the influences of the benefics on the Moon mean that the runaway (here, the local tyrant) will escape. So it probably means he will get his way, and there will be an insurrection against the king.

[185] For this sentence, cf. Heph. III.3, **3**, based on Ptolemy's account of monstrous births (*Tet.* III.8, Robbins).

[186] **BD:** This probably means "in aversion to."

[187] *Synodeuousa.*

16 If you find the ruler of the Hour-marker going retrograde, it makes the tyrant change his mind, and himself go against the ruled. **17** The lord of the Hour-marker being in its own house, and not retrograde, he lasts in his tyranny. **18** And if it is found in the hemisphere under the earth, it makes the tyranny lasting; but in the setting pivot, quickly dissolved.

19 The[188] Sun setting or culminating with any of the malefics, and looking upon the Moon from a square or diameter: the ruled will perish before the tyranny is dissolved.[189] **20** The Sun seeing the Moon above the earth: the tyranny will quickly be dissolved, and the tyrant will be betrayed by one of his comrades.

21 The Moon marking the Hour with Saturn: the tyrant will give himself up.

22 When[190] benefics are marking the Hour or looking upon the Hour-marker, they will release the tyrant entirely from fear and war. **23** Venus looking upon the Hour-marker and the Moon indicates that the tyrant will go by himself and endure no evil from those in power, but he will be thought worthy of great royal honors.

24 The[191] Moon increasing in light does not release the tyrant so easily, though it also indicates that he is daring. **25** The Moon diminishing in light indicates that the tyranny is brief, and dissolved within a short span of time.

26 The Sun[192] setting and Saturn being in the eighth place shows that the king is destroyed by him. **27** The malefics being on the Midheaven or with the Sun: say that the those under the sway of the tyrant will be subdued and defeated by the tyrant.[193]

28 The Moon[194] being on the setting pivot, and Mars following[195] her, brings a violent death upon the tyrant and gives burnings by fire. **29** The Moon setting, Mars and Mercury following, brings a terrible death upon the tyrant.

---

[188] For this sentences, cf. *Carmen* V.37, **18**.

[189] **BD:** That is, the more powerful king will not be able to help him. Theophilus should have said that the *king* will die before removing the tyrant, so as to parallel *Carmen* better.

[190] For this paragraph, cf. *Carmen* V.37, **15-16**; Heph. III.47, **10-11**.

[191] For this paragraph, cf. *Carmen* V.37, **17**; Heph. III.47, **12**.

[192] For this paragraph, cf. *Carmen* V.37, **18-19**; Heph. III.47, **13-14**.

[193] **BD:** I.e., because the king (the Midheaven, Sun) is too weak to help.

[194] For this paragraph, cf. *Carmen* V.37, **20-21**; Heph. III.47, **15-16**.

[195] *Epikatapheromenos.*

30 The Moon setting while Mars is in the [place] under the earth, shows the same things.

31 The Moon[196] without light, observed by Mars, sets the tyrant on fire or kills by iron.

32 Saturn[197] looking upon the Moon when she is waning in Libra: say that the evil for the tyrant is certain and insufferable.

33 Mercury[198] looking upon the Moon with the malefics: declare that the tyrant will come to commit suicide.

34 The Moon[199] brought to Mars while she is descending towards southern or northern regions, Jupiter[200] himself not looking upon her, indicates fear and danger for the tyrant.

35 The malefics[201] being in the underground, or on the setting pivot, while none of the benefics is there, nor testifying, show the death of the tyrant.

36 The Moon[202] culminating, if the malefics cast a diameter or square: say that the tyrant will hang himself or be crucified. **37** The Moon culminating or being under the earth, or setting, surrounded by the Sun and sojourning[203] Saturn:[204] the tyrant is burnt alive.

ᔥ   ᔥ   ᘇ

38 [To enquire][205] about when the tyranny will be completed, search from the recurrences[206] of the diametrical figures of the Moon and the

---

[196] Cf. *Carmen* V.37, **22**; Heph. III.47, **17**.

[197] This may be loosely based on *Carmen* V.37, **28** (see also Heph. III.47, **20**). But in those texts, Saturn is looking from a watery sign, and Libra has nothing to do with it.

[198] Cf. *Carmen* V.37, **29**; Heph. III.47, **21**.

[199] This seems to be loosely based on *Carmen* V.37, **31-32**; Heph. III.47, **23** (which however both read rather differently).

[200] Reading for "Mars," with V.37, **32** and Heph. III.47, **23-24**.

[201] Cf. *Carmen* V.37, **33**, but more accurate is Heph. III.47, **25**.

[202] Cf. *Carmen* V.37, **34-36**; Heph. III.47, **26-27**.

[203] *Epidēmios*.

[204] **BD:** This should be Mars, in accordance with *Carmen* and Hephaistion.

[205] **BD:** This paragraph is similar to *Carmen* V.23, **1-3**, concerning when a traveler will turn back and return home.

[206] *Apokatastikos.* **EG:** Lit., "to bring back to a point," usually used to refer to planet returning to their natal places.

Sun.[207] **39** And also, when the Sun in the inception is in a tetragonal figure to the Hour-marker or the Moon, [search from] the tetragons; if diametrical, from the diameters; if in a triangular figure, in the triangles of the Hour-marker and the conjunction of the Moon; and the two-and-ten degrees[208] of the Hour-marker having fallen on the Hour-marker, it indicates that the tyranny will have an easy release.[209]

Chapter 13: In what kind of land the war will take place[210]

1 If in the inceptions of war you found Mars in the first decan of Aries, in a rough and dirty land; in the second decan of Aries, on a land high and rich in vines; in the third decan, on a plain and pastoral [land].

2 [In] Taurus in the first decan, on a fallow land just broken up; in the second, in a place high and full of trees; in the third, on flat lands with mill-stones.

3 Gemini in the first decan, on mountains and in thickets; in the second, on rough land and [land] with dwellings; in the third, in ravines and deep gullies.

4 In Cancer in the first decan, in humid and thickly-wooded places; in the second, on barren and unsown lands; in the third, on high and thickly-wooded places.

5 Leo in the first decan, on steep places and mountains; in the second, on hilly and grassy lands; in the third, in rugged [land] and deserts.

6 Virgo, in the first decan, on a land sown with grain; in the second, in a fallow land just broken up, and olive groves; in the third, on mountains, and also in rough and rocky places.

7 Libra in the first decan, in a moist meadow or on a plain; in the second, in mountains and high places; in the third, in cultivated places and dwellings.

---

[207] **BD**: Meaning unclear. It might mean that we are to look at successive Full Moon charts. But in comparison with the next paragraph, perhaps this is some kind of transit.

[208] **BD/EG**: This seems to mean its twelfth-part, even though the text does not use the standard word *dōdekatēmorion*.

[209] **EG**: Another possible reading based on the other MSS, would be: "And the Sun in the inception being in a square figure to the Hour-marker, or squaring the Moon, or opposing her diameter; or else in triangle, in the triangles of the Hour-marker and of the conjunction of the Moon...it indicates that the tyranny will have an easy release."

[210] Edited in *CCAG* XI.1, pp. 259-60.

8 Scorpio in the first decan, in rough places; in the second, in vineyards; in the third, in briny and salty places.

9 Sagittarius in the first decan, in rough and dry places; in the second, in lands rich in vines; in the third, on mountains, elevations, mounds, or places full of seaweed.[211]

10 Capricorn in the first decan, in places humid and abounding in pasture; in the second, in mountains and thickets, as well as in forested, rushing streams; in the third, in vineyards and irrigated places.

11 Aquarius in the first decan, on the seashore or on a river; in the second, in seas and marshes; in the third, in moist meadows and nearby places.[212]

12 Pisces in the first decan, in humid places; in the second, in places for irrigation and abounding in pasture; in the third, in vineyards and thickly-wooded places.

Chapter 14: When there is war[213]

1 On[214] the subject of when there will be war, Theophilus says that if the luminaries make a triangle with each other and look upon the Hour-marker, the war will be made to cease easily; but if a tetragon, [the war] will not be over easily, but the one making war will move from battle to battle, and from place to place. **2** If the luminaries are diametrical to each other, the war breaks out slowly and will come to an end only after a long time.

3 The[215] Moon being distant from one star by more than 8°, neither in an adherence[216] nor connecting with it, indicates that the war will break out even more slowly.

---

[211] *Bruōdesi.* **BD:** This word can also connote moist, mossy places.

[212] **EG:** I take this to mean places near the meadows.

[213] Edited in *CCAG* XI.1, pp. 260-61. **BD:** This material is adapted from *Carmen* V.36, the material on recovering stolen items: where *Carmen* says that the item will be recovered quickly or slowly, Theophilus says war will break out quickly or slowly.

[214] For this paragraph, cf. *Carmen* V.36, **1-3**.

[215] **BD:** I do not find this in *Carmen*, but since every other sentence can be traced to it, it may represent a missing sentence.

[216] *Kollōmēne*, but a better reading from **S** (a source of the *CCAG* passage) is *koloumēne*. **BD/EG:** That is, a bodily conjunction (usually within 3°).

4 The[217] Moon traveling in company with[218] any of the stars in her own house indicates the swiftest war, especially when the Sun bears witness to them.

5 If[219] the Moon's twelfth-part moves onto the Hour-marker or the Mid-heaven, or the Sun itself, or its ruler, or even onto any other star which is on the east,[220] it indicates that the war will break out quickly.

6 When[221] the Moon is in the sixth or seventh from the Hour-marker, there is not war, provided the Sun does not testify.

7 The[222] Moon being on the ecliptical place makes the attacks hard to carry out.

8 The[223] Moon being on the Lot of war or looking upon it, indicates that the war has not come to pass easily. **9** If none of the luminaries looks upon the Lot of war, it means that there is not war.

10 The Moon[224] marking the Hour indicates that war will come to pass easily.

11 The Sun[225] marking the Hour in Libra, Aquarius, or Gemini, means that there is not war.

Chapter 15: Otherwise, when there is war[226]

1 See[227] how many signs chance to be between the Hour-marker and the Moon, and again how many between the Sun and the Hour-marker, and put

---

[217] Cf. *Carmen* V.36, **4-5**.

[218] *Sunodeousa*. **BD:** For Antiochus and Serapio, this means being in the same sign as another planet, between 3°-15° from it (Schmidt 2009, p. 165).

[219] Cf. *Carmen* V.36, **6**.

[220] Sahl (*On Times* Ch. 8, in Appendix A) has "a planet just arisen," which plausibly suggests a planet which has just gone eastern, rising before the Sun in the morning.

[221] Cf. *Carmen* V.36, **7**.

[222] Cf. *Carmen* V.36, **9**. **BD:** In *Carmen* this is the "burned path" or *via combusta*, roughly from the last half of Libra through the first half of Scorpio.

[223] For this paragraph, cf. *Carmen* V.36, **12-13**. **BD:** In *Carmen*, this is the Lot of Fortune, not a Lot of war: so Theophilus simply changed the identity of the Lot. But which one did he mean? I suggest the Hermetic Lot of Courage, or the Dorothean Lot of expedition.

[224] Cf. *Carmen* V.36, **14**.

[225] Cf. *Carmen* V.36, **17-18**.

[226] Edited in *CCAG* XI.1, p. 261. This appeared in the MSS as the last paragraph of the previous chapter.

both numbers together: after such an amount of days or months there will be war.

Chapter 16: Whether the army is large or small[228]

1 Taking[229] from the degree of the Moon till that of Mercury, consider how many signs and degrees it adds up to. **2** And if the summed-up [numbers] are even, as you heard [the amount of troops], double them; if odd, say that they are just as you heard them. **3** According to the quantity of signs, say that the mass [of soldiers] is either smaller or larger.

Chapter 17: On treachery[230] and betrayal[231]

1 When[232] Saturn and the Moon are testifying to the Hour-marker, say that there will be treachery or betrayal for the army. **2** With Jupiter testifying to the Moon and the Hour-marker, say that there will be neither treachery nor betrayal. **3** When Mars testifies to the Moon in the inception of war, say that there will be ruin[233] and sedition.[234] **4** When Venus testifies to the Moon and the Hour-marker, say that there will not be treachery. **5** When Mercury looks upon[235] the Hour-marker and the Moon, declare treachery and knavery.

6 When[236] the Moon is unconnected from Mars in the inceptions of war, she makes the soldiers wretched, cowardly, deprived of strength, and disobedient to the commanders.

---

[227] **BD:** Source uncertain, but since the previous and following chapters are all from Dorotheus, I suspect this probably represents a missing sentence from the *Pentateuch*.

[228] Edited in *CCAG* XI.1, p. 204.

[229] Cf. *Carmen* V.36, **72**.

[230] *Dolos*. Or, "cunning."

[231] Edited in *CCAG* XI.1, p. 205.

[232] For this paragraph, cf. *Carmen* V.36, **122-26**.

[233] *Anatropē*. Also "overthrowing," "overthrowing," or the "capsizing" of a ship.

[234] *Stasis*. Or, "faction."

[235] *Epiblepō*.

[236] For this sentence, cf. perhaps Rhetorius Ch. 52 (Holden p. 31).

7 When Mars spear-bears for the Sun, he renders the commanders manlier and more fearsome, and the soldiers more daring[237] and effective.[238]

8 When Mars marks the Hour, he makes those marching to war[239] hotheaded,[240] reckless, and bold.

Chapter 18: On war[241]

1 When[242] someone inquires from you about the two encampments, whether they have moved from the place where they were, search as follows. **2** If the lord of the Hour-marker and that of the Moon are declining, either all or most of them, say that those marched against have moved from one place to another. **3** If the lords of the Moon are together declining [from] those opposite the Hour-marker,[243] say that the ones marched against [have moved] from one place to another.

Chapter 19: When they set out moving[244]

1 Look at the lords of the Hour-marker, and of what is opposite the Hour-marker, whether they are on the pivots, or on the post-ascensions, and which position they have with regard to the whole.[245] **2** For if they are morning [stars], either <all> or most of them, say that they make the movement quickly. **3** For how long, look at their change from one place to another after

---

[237] *Parabolōteros.*

[238] *Epiteuktikōteros,* lit. "able to attain or achieve."

[239] **BD/EG:** Greek reads "those marched against," who are signified by the seventh. But this does not make astrological sense, so we have read this as those marching to war, viz. the Ascendant.

[240] *Thermos,* "hot."

[241] Edited in *CCAG* XI.1, pp. 205-06.

[242] **BD:** I have not found an earlier source for this material, but this material shows up in Arabic texts on questions, when a querent wants to know if the man he is going to visit is still there or not.

[243] *Anthōroskopountas (anth-'ōroskopeo).* **BD:** But as it stands the sentence does not make sense to me. It seems as though the sentence should read something like "declining *from the Midheaven or are* opposite the Hour-marker."

[244] Edited in *CCAG* XI.1, pp. 205-06. It also appears in *CCAG* XI.1 (p. 265), as its own chapter.

[245] *Kosmikos,* "of the world/universe." **EG:** Theophilus is clearly referring to solar phases.

the configuration[246] of the luminaries: how long they take to do this, and say they will make the movement in such a quantity of days. **4** If they are evening [stars], or making a stand-still,[247] say that the movement will be slow, according to their change[248] and figural description.[249]

Chapter 20: On besieged cities[250]

1 As[251] regards besieged cities, one should consider in which sign the Moon chances to be at the hour of the siege. **2** And if she happens to be in Aries, while the benefics testify to her, say that the retreat of the besiegers will be quick, and the release of the besieged very harmless. **3** In Taurus, the siege will last a long time. **4** In Gemini, with the testimony of the benefics, it means an unprofitable retreat of the besiegers. **5** In Cancer, it means the retreat of the enemies after three days. **6** In Leo, a long-lasting siege and war. **7** In Virgo, with the malefics testifying, it means that there will be treachery for the besieged ones [by the besiegers]. **8** In Libra, the fast retreat of the besiegers. **9** In Scorpio, long-lasting war and captivity. **10** In Sagittarius the besieged ones will come out, secured by a treaty. **11** In Capricorn, it indicates famine and death for the city; when Mars is configured, it gives much shedding of blood besides. **12** In Aquarius, it means that the siege will be long-lasting; also [a cause of] suffering, hardship, and pain. **13** In Pisces, it indicates that the siege will be without end, and that there will be war.

---

[246] *Suschēmatisis*, lit. "similar situation" or similar "configuration."

[247] **BD**: That is, stationing.

[248] *Metakinēsis*, lit. "movement from one place to another." **BD**: Examples of these kinds of changes can be found in Sahl's *On Times*.

[249] *Schēmatographia*.

[250] Edited in *CCAG* XI.1, p. 206.

[251] For this chapter, cf. *Carmen* V.26, **1-12** (on the topic of pushing a ship into the water).

Chapter 21: In reference to besieging a city[252]

1 Let[253] the Moon be waning, descending southward, contemplated by[254] benefics, either by any figure or by being with her. **2** In a like manner, let Mars cast a <tri>angle to her, and let him be in female signs, and also let the same stars look upon the Hour-marker. **3** Also, let the straight signs mark the Hour (and not the crooked ones): for this way, the besieged city will be taken without much toil.

4 Otherwise:[255] examine the Moon descending southward, and being contemplated by Mars (and not by Saturn), but rather[256] connecting with Mars—for should it be Saturn, [let it be] by day.[257] **5** Mars signifies a sharp matter,[258] while Saturn the slowest [matters].

Chapter 22[a]: On besieged cities[259]

1 Look[260] at the Hour-marker and the second place from the Hour-marker, and their lords: what kind of position they have, and the stars bearing witness. **2** For when the benefics are testifying to those places or their lords, or else when they are well-placed, they declare a quick seizing of the city.

⁗   ⁗   ⁗

---

[252] Edited in *CCAG* XI.1, p. 207.

[253] For this first sentence, cf. *Carmen* V.7, **1** and V.8, **1**.

[254] *Theōreō.*

[255] For this paragraph, cf. *Carmen* V.6.

[256] **EG**: That is to say, *preferably* connecting with Mars by body rather than by aspect.

[257] **BD**: The key here is that the Moon is waning. First of all, she is waning so as to signify the destruction of something; second, because in a waning phase she is said to be cooler, it is better for her to be with hot Mars than with the very cold Saturn. But if it must be Saturn, then it should be when he belongs to the sect of the chart, viz. by day. Finally, Mars is better for destruction than Saturn is.

[258] *Oxupragia.* **EG**: In contrast to what Saturn indicates here, this surely means a "quick" matter.

[259] Edited in *CCAG* XI.1, pp. 207-08.

[260] For this paragraph, see broadly *Carmen* V.23, **7-8**; but also V.28, **19**.

3 The Moon[261] diminishing in light produces a fast release of the siege; increasing, it prolongs the war. **4** The Moon releasing her bond[262] means a city hard to conquer. **5** The Moon under the rays, connecting with Venus, <or with Mercury when he is>[263] setting[264] and an evening [star], announces a quick salvation of the city.

6 The Moon[265] staying in the signs from the Midheaven to the setting ones, and connecting to Venus along with Mercury, means the release of the siege. **7** When the Moon is in a triangle [coming] from Jupiter and Saturn, say that some siege is solved by a treaty,[266] though not quickly.

8 The[267] Moon going to[268] those signs from the Midheaven to setting (precisely those called "leading down") while Mars looks upon her, means that there is a fast seizing of the city. **9** The signs from the Midheaven to setting, and to the underground [pivot], are "leading down"; those from Midheaven to the Hour-marker, and to the underground, are "leading up."[269] **10** When the Moon is in the signs leading down, a diameter or square [to her] being made from Mars, say that the seizure of the city is quick. **11** The Moon in the signs leading down, with Jupiter looking upon her, means the retreat of the besiegers. **12** Saturn being with the Moon in the signs leading down, with Jupiter decimating him, means the same things. **13** Mars squar-

---

[261] For the rest of this chapter, cf. *Carmen* V.28, **19-32**, and Theophilus's own natal rearrangement in Appendix A (from al-Rijāl). In *Carmen*, this is an election or event chart about whether or not a man will be released from bondage. For this paragraph, cf. *Carmen* V.28, **20-23**; Heph. III.40, **19-21**. This passage is evidence that Theophilus had access to a Greek version of Dorotheus or at least a better Pahlavi edition, because *Carmen* does not mention the Moon connecting with Venus while under the rays.

[262] In *Carmen* V.28, **21**, this refers to her opposition to the Sun.

[263] **BD:** Adding with the original Greek Dorotheus quoted in Hephaistion.

[264] *Dutikē.* **BD:** This probably means sinking under the rays of the Sun.

[265] For this paragraph, cf. *Carmen* V.28, **23-24**; Heph. III.40, **23-24**.

[266] *Spondilōn.* **EG:** This is not in the lexicon, but its familiarity with *spondē* ("libation," "drink-offering") can clearly be seen. Also, *spondai* (pl.) means a solemn treaty or truce, mainly because solemn drink-offerings were made upon concluding them. **BD:** The Latin *spondeo* is the same, and its uses also include the pledge of money to settle an agreement: so we might also consider that the agreement could include ransoms, tribute, etc.

[267] For this paragraph, cf. *Carmen* V.28, **26-31**, and Heph. III.40, **26-31**.

[268] **BD:** That is, being moved to that quadrant by primary motion.

[269] **BD:** These regions are identical to the western and eastern halves of the chart respectively, and can be said to go "down" and "up" by primary or diurnal motion.

ing the Moon while Saturn is setting,[270] [means that] the siege will last for a long time. **14** Mars making a triangle with the Moon while Saturn squares, produces the same things, except <that those> inside the city will be set free from the siege by managing to escape.

15 It[271] is also appropriate that we examine the underground pivot: by day it takes upon itself the result [of the matter]. **16** And if benefics are looking upon it, declare the retreat of the besiegers; if malefics, the seizure [of the city].

Chapter 22[b]: On ambush, treachery, and trickery[272]

1 If[273] anyone wishes to manage [to set] an ambush, or [work] some treachery or trickery upon the enemies, let the Moon be in Aquarius, Taurus, Leo, Pisces, or Sagittarius, waning or under the rays, and subtractive in numbers; and with Jupiter, Venus, and Mercury testifying to her, or being with her, or let her be connecting with them, or else with them testifying to the Hour-marker: in this way can treachery and contrivance be created for the caught one.

2 Otherwise: let Mercury be with the Moon (says Theophilus), eastern, unharmed, and holding a straight course. **3** In the same way, make the lord of the Hour-marker be making a morning phase or let him be in his own

---

[270] **BD**: *Carmen* V.28, **30** has Saturn in a trine here; but Heph. III.40, **30** has an opposition (which could be plausible because he would then be setting opposite her).

[271] For this paragraph, cf. *Carmen* V.28, **32**.

[272] Edited in *CCAG* XI.1, pp. 208-09. **BD**: This chapter could be considered a second half of the previous one, as it does not have a separate number in the table of contents but fits between Chs. 22 and 23. Moreover, it is adapted the same chapter in *Carmen* as Ch. 22 is.

[273] **BD**: This paragraph is an unusual adaptation from *Carmen* V.28, **3**, **6**, **10**, **12**, and **14-15** (see Heph. III.40), because Theophilus wants to do two contrasting things with the Moon. First, the original topic was determining how long someone will be kept in chains, based on the sign of the Moon at the time he is put into bondage: so the Moon is the one captured. Now, the signs mentioned here are indeed the signs which Dorotheus says will never result in freedom, so we can imagine that the Moon indicates the intention of the captor and the situation of the captured or betrayed person. But in the second half of the paragraph, according to Dorotheus the Moon's relation to Venus, Jupiter, and Mercury shows a later *release*—whereas Theophilus wants these to show good fortune for the captor, namely that his tricks will work and there will *not* be release.

chariot, being in aversion to the malefics, the Hour-marker and the Moon inclining[274] and hurling rays[275] towards the lords of the sign.

4 Otherwise: let the Moon be on the Hour-marker or in its triangles, her ruler being with it, the Hour-marker holding a straight course,[276] or let the Moon connect with the lord of the Hour-marker, coming to her own exaltation or her own house; or let Mercury be with Jupiter. **5** For this indeed contributes to both night battles and the sudden launching [of attacks].

Chapter 23: On military campaigns[277]

1 When[278] someone inquires from you about a military campaign, whether to make war or not, investigate as follows. **2** Let the Lot of expedition be for you [the arc] from Saturn till the Moon, and the same from the Hour-marker. **3** If the Lot falls in Scorpio or Aries, in Capricorn or Aquarius, launch the campaign.[279]

4 Mars rising through the Hour-marker, looking upon[280] the luminaries, means [that one should launch] the expedition.[281]

5 The Lot of expedition or Mars falling in Aries or Taurus, in Leo or Sagittarius, means that the campaign will be on horses.

6 The Lot of expedition or Mars being in Cancer or Sagittarius, in Scorpio or Aquarius, makes the [...] release [...][282] of the campaign be through the sea or large rivers.

7 The Lot of expedition and Mars (or [their] rulers), being testified to by benefics, indicates good campaigns; by malefics, bad ones. **8** The campaigns

---

[274] *Prosneuō.* **BD**: It is not exactly clear to me what it means for her to "incline" toward a planet.

[275] *Aktinoboleō.*

[276] **BD/EG**: This seems to mean the straight signs, or signs of long ascension.

[277] Edited in *CCAG* XI.1, p. 209.

[278] For **1-4**, see Heph. II.19 (Schmidt p. 68), a natal chapter which includes related lines from the *Pentateuch.*

[279] Natally, Dorotheus says that this means the native will be involved in military campaigns.

[280] *Ephorōn.*

[281] Dorotheus does not specify that Mars must be in the Ascendant, but says it is better if there is daylight.

[282] Corrupt text.

become remarkable when Jupiter and Mars are configured with each other, and especially if they are pivotal.

Chapter 24: The inception of war[283]

1 When someone departs to war, let the houses of Mars mark the Hour, and have Jupiter and Mars culminating or changing each other's places, being configured with each other and with the Lot of Fortune. **2** If they and the signs in which they are placed have good dealings,[284] the matter of the expedition and war chances to be good, remarkable, and productive of victory. **3** Proceed thusly, and [when] engaging in attacks of the campaigns and army, you will not stumble then.

Chapter 25: By [Theophilus], on the proposal of a ruler [for election][285]

1 If[286] you were asked about a proposal for the election of someone from beside[287] the king or satrap, [for a position of power], either over a territory or in the army, take the king or satrap himself from the Hour-marker; and the one proposed for election, that is, the one who is led to power, from the setting; the office itself, and the land, or city, from the Midheaven; the result of undertaking rulership, from the underground sign; the election of the proposed one, from the setting sign itself.

---

[283] Edited in CCAG XI.1, p. 204.

[284] **BD:** This must at least mean that they are in the good or busy or advantageous places (*kalōs de chrēmatizontōn*), but perhaps also with other good configurations.

[285] Edited in CCAG IV, pp. 93-94. **EG:** This chapter seems to concern a proposal, *by* the king or satrap, *of* someone else, in order to have that proposed person elected to a position of power.

[286] **BD:** Sentences **1-6** seem to be based broadly on *Carmen* V.9, **1-7**, on contracting and leasing.

[287] That is, someone around or accompanying the king.

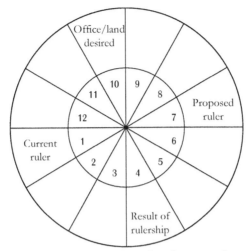

Figure 8: House significations for election of new ruler

2 But if the seventh sign turns out to be crooked, corrupted by one of the malefics, or its lord being either under the rays, retrograde, or in a bad disposition, say that the man is deceitful, malignant, and unsuitable. **3** If the seventh sign is straight and is testified to by a benefic, and its lord is out of the rays, going well forward, and has a good disposition, say that the man is straightforward, incorruptible, and efficacious.

4 If a benefic is on the Midheaven, or testifying to its own ruler,[288] say that the man will be a powerful, active, and useful ruler in his authority; if a malefic is on the Midheaven, or testifies to it, its ruler being in a bad disposition, say that his office will be of a strange nature, and strong, or else that he will not finish it.

5 If a malefic is on the setting sign or culminating, it indicates that the one voted for will decline his office.

6 A malefic looking upon the underground, or [being] on it, puts an end to the authority.

℧   ℧   ℺

7 If[289] you are asked about two or three [people], observe the triangle lords of the setting sign (the first, the second and the third): what kind of

---

[288] **BD:** Or perhaps simply to "its" ruler, namely the ruler of the Midheaven.

[289] This use of the triplicity lords sounds typical of Dorotheus, but is not from *Carmen*.

phase or disposition they have, and by which stars they are testified to, clearly assigning the first [person] to the first triangle lord, the second to the second, and the third to the third, and thus formulating a judgment of the signs and the stars.

8 See[290] also the Moon: for if she connects with a benefic, it shows that the result of the office will be favorable; if a malefic, evil.

Chapter 26: On abandoned cities[291]

1 If[292] you are asked about an abandoned city, or place, whether it is rebuilt or not, whether it is settled or not, and by whom it is built: from the Hour-marker one must take the city, its disposition, and its place; from the setting pivot, the builder; from the Midheaven, the [activity of] building itself, whether it is built up or not built up; and from under the earth, the result of the affairs, and the conclusion of its being set aright.[293]

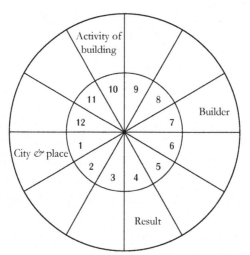

Figure 9: Abandoned cities

---

[290] **BD:** This may represent *Carmen* V.9, **8**, the last sentence of the chapter on leasing.

[291] Edited in *CCAG* XI.1, pp. 210-11.

[292] For this paragraph, cf. *Carmen* V.9, **1**.

[293] *Diorthōsis.* **EG:** That is, when the work is completely finished, with all of its corrections and amendments.

2 When[294] a malefic is on the Hour-marker, or casting a diameter to it, or in square, a deserted place is indicated. **3** The Descending Node marking the Hour means the same thing. **4** The triangle rulers of the Hour-marker being under the rays or having a bad disposition, means an uninhabitable place. **5** The Moon [being] empty in course and [occupying the place] of Bad Fortune,[295] and overcome by the malefics, indicates a deserted place.

6 A malefic[296] being on the Midheaven does not show the building of the city. **7** The triangle rulers of the Midheaven having a bad disposition, or being injured by the malefics, show the same thing. **8** A benefic being on the Midheaven, and the triangle rulers having a good disposition, indicate building. **9** If they make a rising phase, they show that the building will be quick. **10** The luminaries having a good disposition, and configured to the benefics and the Midheaven, show building.

11 If[297] the benefics are on or examining the setting pivot, it means that the builder will build with peace and freedom from fear; if malefics, the opposite: that is to say, with war, distress, and fear. **12** The setting sign[298] having a relation to the Hour-marker means a founder not foreign; not having a relation, a foreign and strange one.

13 The underground[299] being harmed means that the result of the building will be bad; [seen] by benefics, it indicates that the result of the building will be magnificent, beautiful, and well-arranged.

ℬ   ℬ   ℭ

14 It is also necessary for us to study the Lot of Fortune and [the Lot] of building:[300] and if these Lots and their lords have a good position, we say that the building is fortunate and useful; if these and the Lots lie badly [positioned], and are testified to by malefics, we say that the building undergoes harm, or that there is no building at all. **16** In fact, by carrying out the examination and combination of these, we define what is likely to happen. **17** The

---

[294] For this sentence only, cf. *Carmen* V.9, **2-3**.

[295] **EG:** That is, the sixth.

[296] For this sentence only, cf. *Carmen* V.9, **6**.

[297] For this sentence only, cf. *Carmen* V.9, **4-5**.

[298] **BD:** This probably means the *lord of* the setting sign, or perhaps a planet in it.

[299] For this sentence, cf. *Carmen* V.9, **7**.

[300] **BD:** See the formula for this in **17**.

Lot, of building is taken from the ruler of the underground to the ruler of the Midheaven, and the same [projected] from the Hour-marker.

18 We take the time of building (that is, when to build), from the most authoritative places of the inception, and from the stars that are in both places: that is to say, from the change of their figures, or from their transits to their phases, their [bodily] adherences and connections [by aspect].

Chapter 27: If you are asked whether a city is besieged or not, and—if it is—whether it is taken prisoner or spared[301]

1 Let[302] the Hour-marker be the city, says Theophilus: should a malefic be on the Hour-marker, say that the city has been besieged; on the pre-ascension of the Hour-marker, say that it will be set free from the siege; in the post-ascension of the Hour-marker, it means that it has never been besieged, but it is about to be.

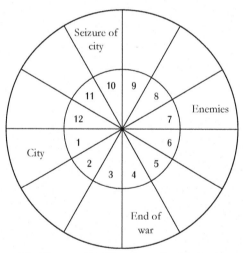

Figure 10: House significations for besieging a city

---

[301] Edited in *CCAG* XI.1, pp. 212-13. **BD:** This chapter as a whole is probably adapted from *Carmen* V.34, **1-14**, on court cases.

[302] For this paragraph, see Heph. III.47, **71b**, on the topic of whether a runaway has fled before.

2 A benefic being on the Midheaven means that the city is not seized, but it is saved. **3** When a malefic is on the Midheaven, it indicates the seizing of the city.

4 If a benefic post-ascends the Midheaven while a malefic culminates, say that the city has been freed through a treaty or truce; but if a malefic post-ascends while a benefic culminates, say that they were taken alive, but [they were put] to slavery. **5** In the same way, if a malefic is declining from the Midheaven, while another malefic has become pivotal, say that the city has already been captured, and the citizens spared alive.[303] **6** [It is] in the same way with regard to the setting of the said stars.

7 Also the Moon's separations, connections [by aspect], attachments [by body], and enclosure give meanings, as well as her third, seventh, and fortieth day. **8** But also, the Lot of Fortune thus understood has the same meaning.

9 The setting pivot having a benefic renders the enemies most civilized; having a malefic, most savage and uncivilized.

10 The underground having a benefic, and testified to by a benefic, means that the end of the war has a useful result; if malefic, the opposite.

Chapter 28: An inception of war[304]

1 From[305] the Hour-marker one must take the one launching the war, or the one who enquires from us about the one making war and the one marched against. **2** From the setting pivot, the enemy and the one made war upon. **3** Further, from the Midheaven one must investigate the war itself, whether it will come to be or not, and if there is war, [whether] it lingers or lasts, or whether both sides will move on towards agreement or peace. **4** Besides [that], from the underground [one should know] the cause and result of the war, that is, towards which side victory will incline.

---

[303] **EG:** It may seem strange that the malefics would spare them, but this was not necessarily a good thing in the mind of the ancients: it likely means they were put into slavery.
[304] Edited in *CCAG* XI.1, pp. 214-16.
[305] Sentences **1-16** seem to be adapted from *Carmen* V.34, **1-14**, on court cases.

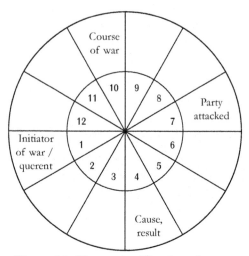

Figure 11: House significations for war

5 And if Saturn marks the Hour, the one marching to war is unjust, villainous, competent,[306] slow, heavy, and unable to climb. **6** Jupiter marking the Hour means that the one going to war is just, able to attain, or a king. **7** Mars indicates someone daring, reckless, and undisciplined. **8** The Sun and the Moon: a king, distinguished, and a large army. **9** Venus: a cultivated, most pleasant[307] general, concerned with the army. **10** Mercury, an intelligent and sagacious general.

11 Saturn culminating means a prolonged war. **12** Mars culminating indicates that the war has swift actions.[308] **13** Jupiter culminating shows that those [in war] will turn towards peace and agreement. **14** In a similar manner, Venus indicates the same. **15** Mercury culminating means that the war will be through treachery and cunning.[309]

16 If the stars chance to be on the setting pivot, they indicate such things as those meant by their being on the Hour-marker.

---

[306] *Hikanos.* **BD:** It seems to me this should be *in*competent, given the rest of the adjectives here.
[307] *Hedutaton,* lit. "most sweet."
[308] *Oxypragia.* **BD:** Or perhaps, actions that are "intense" or "sharp."
[309] *Kleuēs.* **EG:** Or perhaps, "theft."

17 If[310] Saturn happens to be underground, it means that the war has arisen from some ancient matters and shameful motives; and the defeat will be for the one who has marched to war if he has Saturn on the Hour-marker; if on the setting pivot, for the adversary. **18** When Mars obtains the underground pivot, it indicates that the war has arisen from recent attacks, and an attempt on unlawful matters; it also means defeat for the one to whom the pivot is attributed. **19** Jupiter and Venus occupying the underground indicates that the war was produced by famous and venerable people, and victory will be for those whose pivots they occupy. **20** Mercury [gives indications] according to how he receives their testimony.

21 Furthermore, the Sun being maltreated in the part where Saturn holds dominion,[311] indicates defeat; [similarly with] the Moon maltreated in the part where Mars rules. **22** If the maltreatment of the Moon is on the Midheaven, it indicates damage for both parties. **23** The Lot of Fortune or its lord being maltreated indicates defeat for the part in which it falls.

24 The Moon empty in course shows the ceasing[312] of the war [by truce].

25 The Moon under the earth in a feminine sign, or the Sun under the earth in a masculine sign, means victory for the royal army.

Chapter 29: If someone wishes to besiege a city, and at the same time find peace[313]

1 One[314] must take care that the Sun and the Moon, as well as the lord of the Lot of Fortune, are without maltreatment, and that they are not in the second place nor in the eighth from the Hour-marker.

2 In a similar manner, the lord of the Hour-marker must also be without maltreatment.

---

[310] This paragraph seems to be adapted from *Carmen* V.34, **35-40**; but there, the reason for the court case is given by the signs in which the lord of the Ascendant and seventh are: if in Capricorn or Aquarius, then because of Saturnian people, etc.

[311] *Meros*. **EG**: This might refer to each side (or "party") in the battle. **BD**: *Meros* also refers to degrees of the zodiac. But what astrological scenario does Theophilus envision here?

[312] *Echecheiria*. **EG**: This is found in Morell's *Lexicon Graeco-prosodiacum* under *spondē* ("truce"); synonyms include "reconciliation," "friendship," and so on.

[313] Edited in *CCAG* XI.1, pp. 216-17.

[314] This chapter seems to be a select summary of advice taken from Dorotheus, most clearly seen in Heph. III.1, **1, 3-4**.

3 The same Lot of Fortune must be in the friendly place,[315] or in the Good Fortune,[316] or the Midheaven, or in the ninth.

4 Also harmonize the Moon with the Hour-marker, and let Mercury be eastern,[317] and witnessed by benefics.

5 Beholding such figures, either all or most of them, take the city peacefully and without a fight.

Chapter 30: A military inception, from which the whole beginning (and reversal) of the war is known[318]

1 From the Hour-marker, says Theophilus, is known the beginning of the war, its cause, and all of the ongoing attack, that is, of those making war, and their enemies: and this [is] from the disposition of its triangle lords, and also from the attendant stars, and from those testifying, as well as from their strength.

2 From the <post>-ascension of the Hour-marker, whether there will be war or not; and whether what comes to pass will turn out to be favorable or evil.

3 From the third, how many weapons of war there are, or of what kind are those necessary for victory: for it is useless having things unfit for war.

4 From the underground, the place in which the war will take place: for instance, whether it is a plain, or mountain, by the sea or a lake, or else by a great river, in ravines, in places with trees, or deserts.[319]

5 From the fifth place, the zeal or carelessness of the soldiers, and their courage or cowardliness.

6 From the sixth place, the cattle of the army: that is, horses, mules, and camels.

7 From the seventh, the machines: both those created by art, and those without art.

8 From the eighth place, their victims of wounds, captives, runaways, and the lack of order in the army.

---

[315] **BD:** The ninth.
[316] **BD:** The fifth.
[317] *Anatolikos.* **BD:** Again, this could mean in the Ascendant, or outside of the Sun's rays, or rising before the Sun (and out of his rays).
[318] Edited in *CCAG* XI.1, pp. 213-14.
[319] **BD:** See also Ch. 13 above.

9 From the ninth, spies, and all the knowledge of the enemies.

10 From the tenth, the place of the leader and the commanders with him.

11 From the eleventh, the lines of battle, the constitution of the ranks, and the attack on the enemies.

12 From the twelfth, the maltreated nation, or the land, or the city made war upon, against which it is marched.

13 It is necessary to calculate the arrangement of these twelve places with utmost attention and accuracy, as well as their lords, their disposition, the stars in them, along with the configuration of the luminaries, having also sought after the Lots: that of Fortune, that of war,[320] and [that of] victory,[321] as well as the preceding New Moon, simply just as we have calculated them; this way we will not fail.

Chapter 31: From Zoroaster, by Praxidicus,[322] on expected war or some evil: when it will take place[323]

1 Examine Mars, and if you find him attending one of the pivots, say that[324] war is coming; but if Mars is on the post-ascensions of the pivots, the war will take place in <*missing*> days within the month; if Mars is in the declines, this war and the expected evil[325] have already taken place.

2 If you are asked about a war yet to occur, count the degrees between Mercury and Mars, how many there are, beginning the release from Mars.[326] **3** When indeed Mars comes to it, then there will be war.[327] **4** The benefics, in

---

[320] **BD:** Perhaps the Hermetic Lot of Courage?

[321] **BD:** Perhaps the Hermetic Lot of Victory?

[322] **BD:** Pingree suspects (2001, p. 14) that this Praxidicus ("avenger") was a Sundbādh, a general in the ʿAbbāsid period under the famous leader Abū Muslim; this Sundbādh was a patron of translations of Zarādusht from Pahlavi into Arabic, in about 750 AD. He was an "avenger" because he unsuccessfully tried to avenge Abū Muslim's assassination by Caliph al-Manṣūr in 755.

[323] Edited in *CCAG* V.3, p. 87.

[324] Not found in **E**.

[325] **EG:** "And the expected evil" not found in **E**.

[326] **E** reads: "... and give as many from the degrees of Mars. See which month is the last, and these things will happen when Mars ...".

[327] **EG:** **P** adds: "the attack at this time" (*amphibolia*, "the state of being attacked on both sides").

the inception of war, going to the left square, indicate a release from war.

Chapter 32: On undertaking an office or service, how many years and months he continues[328]

1 Examine, the Moon and Mars, how many signs and degrees there are between them: for each sign shows one year and[329] one month (and if Saturn is closer to the Moon, see how many degrees there are between the Moon and Saturn): after these degrees, he will fall weak. **2** But if the North Node chances to be closer to the Moon, see how many degrees there are between them: in such a quantity of months he will become weak, or there will be war.

3 And if you wish to know when good things will occur, see how many degrees there are between the Moon and Jupiter, beginning from the degrees <of Jupiter>.[330] **4** And according to the number found,[331] good things will befall him. **5** But if it happens that Saturn or Mars is joined to the Moon, he will be quickly succeeded [by someone else] and will quickly be withdrawn from it.

Chapter 33: On a man who wishes to come to the king and see whether the mighty one fulfills the promises that were made, or not[332]

1 See when he comes to [the king], and mark which of the seven stars is on the Midheaven. **2** For if it is a benefic, good things will happen to him, and whatever he promises, trust that it will come true. **3** But if it is a malefic, it is not good for him, and whatever he promises, say that it is false.

4 And if a benefic chances to be on the Hour-marker, good things are about to happen to you because of him. **5** But if a malefic, they are not good for you, but what he promises that he would undertake for you, he does not do, but deceives you.

---

[328] From **E**, f. 108v.

[329] This should be understood as "or."

[330] **EG**: This is a conjecture, as the text does not say who to begin with.

[331] **EG**: This seems to mean that the number of degrees is converted into units of time.

[332] From **E**, f. 108v.

Chapter 34: On kings and powers[333]

On powers, and if you want to know whether one conquers or is defeated[334]

1 Look[335] at the Sun and the Midheaven, and in what kind of degree it is, either that of a benefic, or of a malefic. **2** Count from the Midheaven's degree up to that of the malefic, for each degree is a day, month, or year. **3** Moreover, look at the Midheaven: which [star] is looking upon it from a ÷[336] (that is, by casting a diameter to it). **4** If indeed it is a benefic, the king will prevail: he will seize his enemy. **5** If a malefic, terrible things and very difficult conditions will come upon the king on that day. **6** And if you wish to know whence these things happen to him, [then] if one inquires by day and it comes to pass that Mars looks upon the culminating pivot from a diameter,[337] the affliction that falls upon him is awakened by a man; if by night, having fallen ill, he will quickly die. **7** But if Saturn looks upon it from the fourth place T[338] he will be weak with a difficult illness, and he will perish in his own house without heirs.

8 If Saturn and the Sun are on the Hour-marker, that king will rule in that place for the year.

Chapter 35: On war, from Julianus of Laodikaia[339]

[Mars as the indicator of warfare]

1 When, there is war, Mars will be the war; the belligerents, [the stars] from which [Mars] is taken or flows away (be it bodily or by rays); the one

---

[333] From **E**, 108v.

[334] **EG**: This is the title actually given in **E**.

[335] **BD**: The paragraph breaks in this chapter are somewhat speculative, as the material seems to be a grab-bag of unrelated techniques.

[336] **EG**: In the margin is a remark about this symbol: "triangle or square or diameter."

[337] **EG**: Between the lines is written: "or square."

[338] **EG**: In the margin is a remark about this symbol: "from a square or diameter."

[339] Edited in *CCAG* V.1, p. 183. **BD**: According to Pingree (2001, p. 18), Chs. 35-37 are based on apparently untranslated material from Rhetorius, which ultimately goes back to Julianus of Laodikaia.

made war upon,[340] [the stars] which he connects with. **2** If indeed he were taken from benefics, the outcome is fair; if from malefics, unfair. **3** If he is flowing away from or connecting with [stars] of the sect, it shows that the warriors are of the same family or race; but if it is connecting with or flowing away from stars of the opposite sect, they are not of the same stock.

4 And when depressed,[341] it makes war not great; [but] exalted, great.

5 But if he is in tropical [signs] or pivotal, [the war will be] notable; if in fixed ones or not pivotal, not notable.

6 Otherwise, when stationary, either he himself or those connecting [with him], [it will be] long-lasting; not stationary, of short duration.

7 Culminating, say that [the war] is fought about rulership; marking the Hour, about life; setting, about [the means of] living; underground, about land and graves. **8** In the ninth, about neglected gods or laws; in the third, about families[342] and female gods; in the sixth, about some mutilated remains,[343] and about injustice; in the twelfth, about [political] subjects; in [the place] of the Good Daimōn, because of friendship and offspring; in the fifth, because of a woman or city; in the second, because of riches; in the eighth, because of ancient and death-related matters.

9 Mars being under the rays, carries the war forward with cunning; eastern,[344] conspicuously; in the tropics, by public consent; in bicorporeal [signs], with many.

[Mercury as the indicator of spies]

10 Mercury approaching those which Mars connects with ([Mars] being well-placed and with good testimony), will reveal the affairs of the belligerents to the enemy; but in separation, and being configured, it causes the opposite.

11 With Mercury under the rays, the traitor will escape notice; eastern,[345] he will not.

---

[340] *Polemoymenos.*

[341] **BD:** That is, in his fall.

[342] *Genos.* **EG:** This refers broadly to one's clan, family, descendants, offspring, etc.

[343] *Akrōtēriasmos.* **EG:** Also, "amputation."

[344] **BD:** That is, being out of the rays (or even being out of the rays, rising before the Sun).

[345] **BD:** See the footnote above.

12 Mercury being in another's sign, eastern and uncorrupted, clearly causes the escape of the traitor; but if he had with himself the ruler of the sign, [the traitor] will have accomplices.

13 When overcome by benefics, even if he is caught, nothing will happen to him; if by malefics, he will be punished. **14** When the overcoming star is witnessed by Jupiter, by a prominent person; by the Sun, by the multitude and publicly; by Mars, by a general or soldier.

Chapter 36: Another inquiry on war[346]

1 Otherwise: the belligerents will be taken from the Hour-marker; those against whom they march, from the setting; the cause, from the Midheaven; the result, from the underground. **2** The stars surrounding the places show the taking of the citadels and the alliances; when attaining exaltation or adding in numbers, they indicate aid for them; but when they suffer dejection or are subtractive in numbers, the destruction of city-walls—or else lands, when Saturn (surrounding [these places]) is maltreated; but machines, when Mercury [is maltreated]; sacred places and temples, when Venus is; foundations, when the Moon is; allies, when Jupiter is; the government,[347] when the Sun is.

3 On[348] the other hand, if the rulers of the Hour-marker and the setting are well-configured with one another, or are in a common sign, the enemies will reconcile with each other; when squared by benefics, for expediency; if by malefics, for the sake of insult. **4** If the rulers of the post-ascensions were subject to the same conditions, the allies will also reconcile to them.

---

[346] Edited in *CCAG* V.1, p. 184. **BD:** According to Pingree (2001, p. 18), Chs. 35-37 are based on apparently untranslated material from Rhetorius, which ultimately goes back to Julianus of Laodikaia.

[347] *Dēmos*. **EG:** This could also refer to the common people, or the public life. **BD:** But since Jupiter indicates powerful people it is probably someone prominent.

[348] For this paragraph, cf. *Carmen* V.34, **3** and **21**.

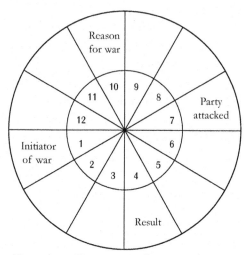

Figure 12: House significations for war

5 If a lunar eclipse occurs, there will be much slaughter; but if a solar one, utter destruction, according to the magnitude of the eclipse. **6** The [evil effect of the] eclipse will be for those with whom it has familiarity; but if it holds familiarity with both [parties], having become evil for both [sides]... <*lacuna*> ...<7>...inconvenient for the aggressors, but when already embarked upon the war, [then it becomes inconvenient] for those made war upon. **8** We declare the same about an earthquake, war-trumpet,[349] meteor, or comet.

9 The anomalous stars[350] foretell that those to which they are attached will also become anomalous.

10 When the rulers of the Hour-marker are going retrograde, or passing over the lord of the setting, or those of the setting over the [ruler] of the Hour-marker, they indicate their migration to one another. **11** However, they being in congenial places (like Jupiter in Pisces, Mars in Aries), if any star appeared to go direct or retrograde into the two mentioned signs, there will be some mediators, either betraying or being favorable, just as the testimony declares. **12** If it turns out to be benefic, or closely observed by a good one, the mediators will be sincere and guileless; but if, being a malefic, it was also looked at by another malefic, deceitful and fickle. **13** But if, having passed over that place, it is made benefic, then [the mediator] will be reliable

---

[349] **EG**: A class of comets, according to Ptolemy (*Tet.* II.9).
[350] **BD**: I am not entirely sure what kinds of stars Theophilus means here.

for that. **14** And if it passes over from congenial places towards alien places, he will be sent from his own stock to foreign lands; if from alien places towards its own, then from foreign countries to his homeland. **15** When it makes the direct or retrograde movement in its own sign, having with itself in its place the stars that indicate the persons of the belligerents, it will give notice of what each party will want. **16** Mercury will hold the character of the messenger, Jupiter the ruler, Mars the soldier, Saturn the elder or an honored person, the Sun the chief officer, Venus gods or images of gods, the Moon the elements or plants[351] (such as when those carrying branches,[352] earth, or water, beseech the more powerful).[353] **17** The same [stars] (that is, the Moon and Venus), will also show women, for many times they, through the same kind of service, act as mediators reconciling one side to another, such as did the women in the Roman war against the Sabines: having come forward to the middle of the armies, they acted as arbitrators for each side.

Chapter 37: On the resolution of war[354]

1 It is not easy to clearly and accurately ascertain the moment of the end of the war, though one only has to survey from the ruler of the underground, and from those coming to the places of Mars (or their squares), in such a way that the benefics bring about a resolution for the war when they move free and uncorrupted (and let them be in fixed signs, so that there will not be war again); the malefics [bring about] an increase [of hostilities], especially when they are out of sect or when they urge towards corruption.

2 What comes to pass on a certain day for each one,[355] will be known from the transits[356] of the Moon, if we observe how she was configured first, or how she is configured at the moment, with the inception of both parties:

---

[351] *Phyton.* Also, offspring, creature.

[352] *Klados.* Like laurel branches used in temples, and presented by suppliants. The verb *pempō*, used here, is not merely "to send," but also "to take part in a procession."

[353] *Kreittōnas.* Clearly, the gods.

[354] Edited in *CCAG* V.1, p. 186. **BD:** According to Pingree (2001, p. 18), Chs. 35-37 are based on apparently untranslated material from Rhetorius, which ultimately goes back to Julianus of Laodikaia.

[355] **BD:** I take this to mean "each party in the conflict."

[356] *Parodos.*

those marching out following the results [of the chart of the attack], and those making war either when the enemies attack them, or when they are told by a messenger that the enemy would do so.[357]

3 Moreover, from the things said in the verses of Dorotheus about how the villain[358] will return,[359] it is possible to investigate whether it is the aggressor or the attacked one who will prevail.

4 If there is a nativity of the one made war upon, it is necessary to make a judgment of what will befall him based upon it. **5** But if someone could also determine the nativity of the leader, the forecast of the future would be accurate and unambiguous, since from the luminaries, or malefics, or... [*corrupt text*] ... <**6**> ... of the squares, they obtain from the months; but should the benefics transit [on them], they predict peace and solution for them.

Chapter 38: On the turning points of the four seasons[360]

1 If you wish to know what is yet to happen in the nativity and also to a particular person, at a given latitude, calculate when the Sun comes to Aries in one minute,[361] on which day and at what time. **2** And after determining this, calculate accurately the stars at that time. **3** Also find out where the Moon and the Descending Node are. **4** And after determining this, calculate the pivot of the Hour-marker as it is at that time in which the Sun has made the equinox in the sign of Aries, as well as the remaining pivots; also find the post-ascensions and the declines. **5** And after determining the twelve places, accurately find the releaser, lying in a releasing place, and also as lord of the distribution of times. **6** After finding the releaser, examine its ruler: this will show what is about to happen.[362]

---

[357] **BD:** Theophilus seems to be distinguishing two inception or question charts: (1) the chart for the attack, whether a question about it or the inception for actually setting out; (2) the chart for the defenders, either when they hear about the attack or the attack is actually made.

[358] *Praksas.* **EG:** This is late Greek.

[359] **BD:** This is probably some of the Dorothean material on whether fugitives will return: see *Carmen* V.37.

[360] Edited from **E**, f. 95r. For more on Theophilus's mundane astrology, see *Cosmic.*

[361] **BD:** That is, into the first minute of Aries.

[362] See **10ff** below. This ruler is the mundane equivalent of the longevity house-master (also known as the *kadkhudah* or *alchocoden*). If so, the bound lord is preferred, if it sees the releaser. See also *Cosmic Inceptions* Ch. 2.

7 Immediately look at the Hour-marker and its ruler, in which place it has fallen into; in the same way also the Sun, in which place he is. **8** One must examine both of them: if indeed you find the Sun in a bad place and the ruler of the Hour-marker in a good place, that year will become good for the populace, but bad for the rulers. **9** But if the Sun is well placed and the ruler of the Hour-marker badly so, say the opposite: that it is good for the rulers and bad for the crowd.

10 Then see the ruler of the releaser, which has been found: what kind of testimony it bears towards the Hour-marker, the Sun, and to the ruler of the Hour-marker. **11** [See] as well whether it looks upon the Sun (he being in a good place), or whether it looks upon the rulers of the Hour-marker, and the Hour-marker itself (falling in a bad place): [for] then the year will be good for the rulers, but more insignificant for the multitudes. **12** Then look at the ruler of the releaser, in what kind of place it has fallen into, which star receives it, and which hurls its rays on it. **13** If it is a benefic star, it is favorable; if a malefic one, say that it is not good. **14** But if the ruler of the releaser is indeed eastern, and found in the upper hemisphere, in a voiced sign, the things signified by it will become evident; but if it is found in the underground, or in the lower hemisphere, it accomplishes its effects in a hidden manner.

15 Saturn[363] found with the Ascending Node on the Hour-marker is significant of good things for the populace and evil things for those in office. **16** If a malefic star is found in the second place from the Hour-marker, say that the maltreatment will come in relation to livelihood; if in the third, in relation to relatives; and thus conclude successively according to the twelve places. **17** But if indeed Jupiter or Mercury falls in any of such places with the Descending Node, they become favorable for those who rule; and together with this, take a look at the nature of the sign in which the star is, which is significant of these effects, and declare according to its evil or good qualities. **18** But if Mars with the Ascending Node is the releaser, it is indicative of war and bloodshed, as well as discord within the same family or people and in the country that is assigned to the sign in which Mars is placed. **19** If Mars is found in a tropical sign, it shows that the ruler will move from one place to another; if another star is found squaring or opposing the

---

[363] **BD:** Based on **18**, Theophilus seems to mean that Saturn is the releaser.

Sun, and especially if it is of the other sect and is a malefic star, it indicates war, plots, and treachery.

[Who prevails]

20 When you wish to know who prevails,[364] consider where the Sun is placed, and the above-mentioned star (that is, that which squares or opposes the Sun), as well as the rulers of both of them, and the disposition of both the Sun and the star. **21** If Mars is found on the Hour-marker or the Midheaven, and the Sun in the seventh or the underground, and the malefics[365] post-ascend the Sun, and the malefic stars are with him, it indicates that the king is miserable and sick, and bad things will befall him; though it is a different matter when the benefics post-ascend the Sun, and the king becomes strong and powerful. **22** And the star that is higher is stronger, since it is found in a pivot, be it on the Hour-marker or the Midheaven. **23** His people are miserable and become ill when malefics post-ascend; but if they are in favorable places, and testified to by benefic stars, they show good things. **24** Being a malefic and witnessed by [malefics], it foretells bad things. **25** Also look at the rulers of both stars, and that which is witnessed by benefics: say that that is [the significator of] the conqueror. **26** But if Mars squares or opposes the Sun, it is bad for the rulers. **27** Now, if by the same figure it looks upon the Hour-marker or its ruler, say that the harm will be upon the populace, according to the sign assigned to each specific latitude—such as if in Aries, Persia; if in Leo, the Turks; if in Scorpio, Syria; in Cancer, Rome; in Aquarius, India. **28** But if Mercury is corrupted by another star, say that the harm will come to what belongs to Hermes: that is, traders, those who write, and likewise. **29** If Venus is likewise maltreated, it causes corruption in men's livelihood; and especially when in a feminine sign, it shows that there will be harm inflicted upon women. **30** If it is an authoritative sign,[366] misfortune will come to ruling women.

31 Also take a look at the eighth place from the Sun, and if Mars is found there it will be significant of much slaughter and fear in that place where

---

[364] **BD:** That is, in the war or plots mentioned in **19**.

[365] **BD:** Reading for "benefics."

[366] *Hegemonikon zōdion.* **BD:** Meaning unclear; perhaps Theophilus is referring to the royal signs (i.e., the fiery ones).

Mars is. **32** Similarly, see the eighth place from the Moon, and thus declare as was said about the Sun.

[Death versus slaughter]

33 When you wish to know whether there will be slaughter or death, look at Mars, which star is with him, and which sees him. **34** For if Jupiter looks upon Mars from a sign of human shape, say slaughter; if from a sign related to cattle or beasts, say death, though not slaughter. **35** Now, should Saturn be looking upon Mars from a square or diameter, say that there will be death but not slaughter; but if Saturn is in a triangle with him, it becomes significant of slaughter. **36** Mars comes to signify death for men when in a masculine sign; if in a feminine one, for women. **37** As regards this, some examine the Moon, as well as any malefic star with her, or the eighth place from her: if Mars is found there, it shows slaughter; if Saturn, death. **38** If Jupiter chances to be with the Ascending Node, witnessed by Mars, it shows slaughter; but if Saturn looks upon him, death. **39** Also consider the nature of the signs and stars, thus declaring according to what has already been pointed out.

[Timing]

40 Now if you want to know when the influences will take place, examine the Moon and the malefic stars: if they are in tropical signs, and in square, diameter, or conjunction, in so many days as there are degrees between them; but if in bicorporeal signs, in so many months; in fixed ones, years.

41 Also look at the Hour-marker and its ruler: find out how many degrees there are between them, giving the same quantity of ascensional degrees as days, months, or years, as described above, that is, one day for each degree, from the rising degree until that of the ruler (and the other way round, from the ruler until the rising degree). **42** However, some count from the ruler up to the ruler of its sign, and as many signs as are found, they say such a quantity of days, months, or years will pass in order for the effects to be accomplished. **43** However, should a bicorporeal sign be found within those lying between the Hour-marker and its ruler, some say that one should double the days, months, or years.[367]

Chapter 39: On the delivery of letters, from Zoroaster

Comment by Dykes. There are two versions of this chapter, which differ enough that it is worth listing them both:

- A (left column): from *CCAG* II (pp. 192-95), edited from Marcianus Gr. 335 (now 645), ff. 121*ff.*
- B (right column): from Bidez and Cumont 1938, pp. 209*ff*, edited from a combination of **E** (ff. 116*ff*), and Ambrosianus Gr. 38 (ff. 118v*ff*).

(A) On the delivery of letters, from Zoroaster

1 If a letter is delivered to you, and you wish to find out the intention of what is written inside, whether there is cunning or not, and whether it is just, unjust, good or evil (and the same when someone, having sent a message, brings it to you), you will know what is hidden there as follows:

(B) On the delivery of letters

1 If a letter concerning certain matters is delivered to you, and you wish to know what has been written, what kind of message it conveys, and whether it was sent with [the intention of] treachery or a plot, or with a noble aim ([and] in like manner when you wish to find out by whom the letter was written, or even what is inside before the seal [is broken]), you will proceed as follows, both if you receive the letter by night or by day, and the same if the messenger approaches and wishes to deliberate with you.

---

[367] **BD:** Theophilus is no doubt getting this hint from Dorotheus, who doubles the number of things which appear in common or double-bodied signs.

[Saturn marking the Hour or culminating]

2 Fix the pivots and the position of the stars as in a nativity, and if Saturn marks the Hour or culminates at the time you received the letter, the message is exceedingly hard to bear.

3 If the Moon comes into contact with him or squares [him], the bringer is double[369] and very strict.

4 But if Saturn, marking the Hour or culminating, stands still, it contains terrible news about some necessary matters.

5 If Mercury is there as well, everything will be further confirmed for the worse, and the letter has been written by an evil man: the deliverer and the writer are your enemies and adversaries; but among all [of them], the most hostile to you is the one to whom the handwriting belongs.

2 If the Shining One[368] marks the Hour or culminates at the time the letter is delivered to you, it indicates that what is inside announces things exceedingly hard to bear, and which will be fulfilled: know each of them beforehand.

3 If the Moon chances to be on her own, either in square or happening to be equilateral[370] <*lacuna*>, the giver will turn out to be double, and the writings will be much more austere.

4 But if the star marking the Hour or culminating chances to be at a standstill, it will bring round to difficult announcements on necessary things.

5 If the Glittering One[371] is present as well, everything will be confirmed for the worse, and the letter itself has been written by some treacherous and evil man; the deliverer and the writer are enemies and adversaries, and especially he to whom the writing belongs is, of all [of them], the most hostile and hateful towards you.

---

[368] Saturn.

[369] **BD**: This probably means that he has a secret mission, or says one things but means another: "two-faced."

[370] *Isopleura.* **BD:** This word plus the lacuna that follows must have meant a conjunction or opposition.

[371] Mercury.

6 If Jupiter is together with Saturn, the written things are mixed, here good, there evil, though the evil will not prevail: the letter comes from a prominent man, a hater of knavery, and just. **7** If Venus is also there with Saturn, the writing participates in both evil and good, and the message is written with female intention, and the character of what has been written is a mixture of both wickedness and righteousness, though mainly inclining towards the good.

6 If[372] Jupiter is there as well, or even Venus, the writings will be mixed, here good, there evil, in such a way that, in relation to what has been written, you will in some places rejoice, and in others be given false hopes, though indeed the evil will not prevail.

7 If Jupiter is there as well, the letter will be from a man prominent in public affairs, a hater of evil, and just. **8** If Venus is also present, the writings will have both good and evil in common; the letter has been written down enclosing a female intention; [the character of the writer] will participate in both evil and usefulness towards you, though as far as common knowledge goes, more admirable than worthless.

[Mars marking the Hour or culminating]

8 If Mars marks the Hour or culminates, or is on the setting of the Sun,[373] the message contains a great plot; and the one carrying the letter is privy to the plot, and the things within [the letter] are hard to bear.

9 But if Mars chances to be standing still on the Hour-marker or on the Midheaven, it contains a great

9 If the Fiery One[374] equally marks the Hour, culminates, or comes to the setting of the Sun, the letter will contain a plot and a great loss, and the deliverer of the message will be privy to the plot, and the things inside will be hard to bear.

10 If he chances to mark the Hour or culminates while at a standstill, it will contain a great struggle

---

[372] **BD:** This sentence is a variation on the more complete one that follows.
[373] **BD:** This probably means that he is an evening star, coming out of the rays at the setting of the Sun.
[374] Mars.

struggle[375] and some destruction of high authorities; it has been written by an evil, choleric, hot-headed, and impious man.

10 If Jupiter is also present, the written stuff is of a mixed nature; if Venus, the things in it are also mixed, but they have been written by a woman or a eunuch.

11 If the Moon is together with Mercury, consider the same things as those with Saturn.

12 If Mars is together with it,[376] and if the star is alone, in a row,[377] [the letter] contains knavery, stealing, cheating, futility, and deceit: the writer is a partner, or manager of affairs, or is someone having a mercantile business.

13 But if it stands still, the things under consideration are even worse, more deceitful and contentious.

and destruction of some prominent people; it was written by an evil man, hot-headed, choleric, and impious.

11 If Jupiter is there as well, the things inside will be mixed, just as with Saturn; if Venus, they will be common in the same way, though the letter has been written by a woman or a eunuch.

12 If the Moon is there as well, she will bring to completion in a similar manner, just as has been shown with Saturn.

13 If Mercury joins [Mars] in marking the Hour or culminating, if the star happens to be alone, the letter will contain laziness, stealing, and a stratagem for plundering;[378] there will also be some futility,[379] though nothing true: the writer of the letter will be a partner, manager of affairs, or from those who work with mercantile affairs.

14 If it[380] chances to be at a standstill, the things written inside will be worse.

15 However, should Saturn be together with Mars, the contents of the letter will be difficult, and the

---

[375] *Agōn.* **EG:** This could also refer specifically to a legal action.

[376] **BD:** This seems to be Mercury, as in the right column.

[377] *Monostoicheō.* This seems to mean that it is moving direct, as it is contrasted with being stationary in the next sentence.

[378] *Dolos diaphorikos.*

[379] *Periergia.* Also, "needless questioning," and "meddling with another's affairs."

[380] **BD:** It is unclear whether this is Mercury or Mars.

message will contain nothing sound, but treachery, imposture, and struggle.

14 If the Moon is also present, it will bring about even worse things, like those spoken of about Saturn, and the bearer of the letter is privy to evil, and has tampered[381] along his way with the seal and the letter.

16 And the Moon, when present, will bring about the worst things, in agreement with what has been explained about Saturn: the carrier of the letter will be privy to the plot, and the message is not to be trusted; he has given advice on what is written inside, and he has given advice to have its seal counterfeited, either on the way, or on the ship <*lacuna*>[382] the deceit; the news told is from an enemy, and hazardous to life.

17 The letter contains <*lacuna*>.

[Mercury marking the Hour or culminating]

15 If Mercury marks the Hour or culminates, the letter contains great good as regards livelihood and preservation, for things both present, and those that have come to pass, and everything is true.

16 If Jupiter is also there, he who wrote the message is a just man, excelling in glory; if Venus, a young man who has lately embarked upon some business, cheerful, playful, and good; the one carrying the letter is

18 <If Mercury marks the Hour or culminates, it brings> great good as regards livelihood and preservation, as well as present and past things, and increasing good things, and everything is true.

19 If Jupiter comes to assist, the writer of the letter <is> a man prominent in life and fame, just and happy; if the Light-bringer,[383] the writer will be a young man[384] recently embarked upon some business,

---

[381] Reading with Schmidt 1995 p. 27 (*Sages*), for "plotted, schemed."

[382] According to Bidez-Cumont, some words seem to be missing, so they indicate a lacuna.

[383] Venus.

[384] **EG**: *Phosphoros* stands for *Aphrodite*, that is, Venus. The author of the letter is a *neaniskos* or "young man," because *Phosphoros* himself (as a noun, masculine in this text) is represented by a child bearing a torch. Cumont himself (p. 219) wonders why the Byzantine Phosphoros is assimilated to Venus.

just and well-intentioned.

cheerful, merry, playful, excellent, and the deliverer of the letter will be just, and with a good disposition of soul.

[Jupiter marking the Hour or culminating]

17 If Jupiter marks the Hour or culminates, it contains great good, true and well-meaning things, relating to affairs past, present and future: it has been dispatched by a great and truthful ruler, [and] the one who wrote the letter is held in esteem, and a friend of yours.

20 If Jupiter in the same way marks the Hour or culminates, the letter will have great and true good things, in such a way that one would rejoice in the news told; it will include [words] in relation to beneficial affairs past and present, which will be fulfilled. **21** It has been dispatched by a man prominent in all affairs, happy and truth-loving; the writing will likewise be from someone well-known and raised to leadership, being truthful towards you at that time.

18 If he marks the Hour together with the Moon, the good that has been pointed out will increase.

22 If he marks the Hour together with the Moon, it will increase the written things a lot, as if being transcendently good and beneficial.

19 But if Jupiter stands still, the good is double.

23 Still, should Jupiter be at a standstill, the good will be double.

20 If Mercury is also present, the good already indicated will increase, and it contains [information] about some gain and superabundance: it has been written with the judgment of two men, one of whom is just and noble, and the other just but deceitful, [but] the one who carries the letter has a good disposition of mind towards you.

24 If Mercury is present as well, he increases the good, and the letter will contain an excessive amount of words on surplus profit; the letter will be written with the judgment of two men, one of whom is just and excellent, the other treacherous and unjust, [while] the deliverer of the letter is coming towards you with good feelings and a familiar spirit in

21 If Saturn is together with him, or Mars, consider the things within the letter as mixed, some of them good, some others, evil.

intention.

25 But if any of the destroyers joins in marking the Hour, consider what is inside of a mixed nature, some good, some evil.

[Venus marking the Hour or culminating]

22 If Venus marks the Hour or culminates, the letter contains cheerful and reasonable things.

26 If Venus marks the Hour or culminates, the letter contains cheerful things, and what is written inside is so cheerful that you rejoice in mind, enjoy yourself, and exult in the recognition of the news received.

23 But if she marks the Hour in a male sign, it has been written by a good <man; if in a feminine sign, a>[385] woman who is disposed in a good way towards you.

27 If a masculine sign marks the Hour, the letter was written by a good and just man, and well-intentioned towards you; if in a feminine sign, by a good woman well-disposed towards you.

24 If Venus stands still, the good news will be double.[386]

25 If the Moon or Mercury is also there, it will confirm the good; even more so with Mercury. **26** But with Mercury, it will contain ambiguous[387] words, and elegance of language: it has been written by a cheerful young man, though he is also crafty, dissembling, sociable, stealing, a perjurer, and a liar, also cleanly and unsuspectedly robbing from what is yours.

28 If in a fixed sign, consider the good news to be double.

29 And if Mercury is present as well with the Moon, the good will be much reinforced, and exceedingly so if Mercury comes to help: the letter will contain excellent words and praises; it was written by a visible and cheerful young man, very sagacious and thin and, with Mars, a partner in affairs, an embezzler, perjurer, and a liar, also cleanly and unsuspectedly robbing from what is yours.

---

[385] **BD:** Adding in accordance with the right column.
[386] **BD:** Again, like **3** this probably indicates deception.
[387] *Diaphorikos.*

27 If Mercury is not present, it was written by a public woman; the carrier of the letter is just by nature and well-intentioned towards you.

28 If Saturn or Mars come together with Venus, what is written is of a mixed nature, [both] fine and fearful, [and] the good things are commanding and lavishly [stated]; it has been written with a certain haste by a prominent man, [and the written things are] lavish and miss the mark.[389]

29 But if [it] sets,[390] the letter contains some accusation, and the manuscript will be of someone exceedingly arrogant; but the deliverer of the letter will also be that way.

30 If Mercury is not present, it was written by a common woman; the deliverer of the letter is a governor, just by nature <and well-intentioned>[388] towards you.

31 If indeed any of the destroyers joins in marking the Hour, you will consider the things written to be mixed, some of them good, some others difficult: the letter will contain within [it] commanding and lavish words; it was written and sent by a prominent man, and it will contain lavish words and [those] missing the mark, [written] with superiority <and> zeal.

32 If it[391] is taken down towards the setting, the letter will contain someone's allotment [of land]; the writing will be from someone overly arrogant, [and] the carrier of the letter will be such as well.

[The Moon marking the Hour or culminating]

30 If the Moon marks the Hour by herself, while none of the planets is brought above the earth[392] or culminates, the letter contains some expectation and a public announcement concerning things that have

33 If the Moon equally marks the Hour by herself, while none of the planets is taken up above the earth or culminates, the letter will contain an expectation and a public announcement on things done and

---

[388] **BD:** Adding with the left column.

[389] **BD:** Or as Schmidt puts it, "not to the point."

[390] **EG/BD:** Lacuna. The critical apparatus suggests that this is Venus setting (along with the malefics), which matches the implied meaning in the right column.

[391] **BD:** I take this to refer to Venus along the malefics, setting in the west.

[392] **BD:** That is to say, is brought into the Ascendant.

been done and completed; the letter is the word of a bystander,[393] or of some individual, a partner, an inferior, or someone of the same stock. **31** If the Moon leads to a conjunction, the letter contains a summons; the deliverer is meddlesome and busy with many things.[394]

fulfilled; the letter will be from someone versed in science, or from a private individual [who has no professional knowledge], or from a partner, some person of lower rank, or even from someone of the same stock. **34** If she is led to a conjunction, the letter strengthens the summons, and the deliverer of the message will be very meddlesome, and very busy about many things.

[The signs, if the Hour-marker and Midheaven are empty]

32 But if neither the Moon nor any one of the five stars marks the Hour or culminates, [the letter] contains what is signified by each sign, when the seven stars are absent.

33 Aries marking the Hour or culminating makes the written stuff authoritative.

34 Taurus marking the Hour or culminating, given to trouble and inclined to anger.

35 Gemini, the things [indicated] will be mild, austere and numerous, and they will be brought to fulfillment.

36 Cancer gives indications on present things.

37 Leo, from prominent and very harsh people.

35 If neither the Sun nor the Moon, nor any one of the five stars marks the Hour or culminates, they (in addition to the Sun and the Moon) being absent, and the letter is delivered, it will contain what is indicated by each of the twelve signs.

36 When Aries marks the Hour or culminates, if delivered, the contents are authoritative.

37 Taurus marking the Hour or culminating, the contents incite trouble and incline to anger.

38 If Gemini marks the Hour or culminates, it will contain mild, very austere and numerous commands, which will be brought to fulfillment.

39 Cancer marking the Hour or culminating, the news received are

---

[393] *Epistatou.* **BD:** This can also mean an overseer (as Schmidt has it), but the normal sense of the word (and in context here) is of someone who provides support, who stands in the rear, etc.

[394] **BD:** Or perhaps, is a busybody, getting involved with many things.

38 Virgo shows things connected with the Mysteries, which will also be fulfilled.

39 Libra, from prominent people, though mainly those things pertaining to livelihood.

40 Scorpio shows an announcement and expectation of some good person, which will be fulfilled.

41 Sagittarius, authoritative and austere things, which will be fulfilled.

42 Capricorn shows cheerful things from some companion, but they are not true.

43 Aquarius provides profitable things, which in the end will be upset.

33 Pisces gives indications for a summons and a plot.

about things that have been instituted.

40 Leo marking the Hour or culminating: from an authority, and hard to understand.

41 If Virgo, it will include matters related to the Mysteries, and they will be fulfilled.

42 If Libra, the written content is from an authority, and rather aggressive.

43 If Scorpio, it will have an announcement and the expectation of some good thing.

44 If Sagittarius, the matters inside will be authoritative and very austere, and they will be fulfilled.

45 If Capricorn, the written content will be cheerful, and it has been written by some companion, but it is not true.

46 If Aquarius, it will contain some kind of advantage, and it will be carried forward to the end.

47 If Pisces, it will contain a summons and a plot.

Chapter 40: Again, on letters

Comment by Dykes. No sources are given in the *CCAG* or by Pingree.

Chapter 41: When it is convenient to send letters[395]

1 When[396] you send letters, seek concerning Mercury that he should be with the Moon, and none of the malefics be together with them, nor configured. **2** Moreover, Mercury should be rising,[397] and neither under the rays nor retrograde. **3** If you send the letter under such conditions, your intention will not fail.

---

[395] From Laurentianus 28.14, 235v.

[396] Cf. *Carmen* V.16, **1**; Heph. III.27, **1**.

[397] *Anatolikos.* **BD:** In this context, Theophilus means being outside of the rays, though whether rising before the Sun or after him is unclear.

THE COLLECTION OF THEOPHILUS ON COSMIC INCEPTIONS[1]

[Chapter 1: Four approaches to ingress charts][2]

1 First: The eldest and wisest of the Egyptian star-watchers determined that the beginning of the year was from the [heliacal] rising of the Dog;[3] and indeed, from a close examination of the position[4] of the Moon, and the position by degrees of the other stars, as well as of the figures described by them, they said that the celestial influences[5] of the year are produced. **2** [And] these things did not take place because of some magical oracular pronouncement that had a persuasive sign, but due to the fact that the rising of the Nile throughout the land of the Egyptians occurred at that time, overflowing Egypt, and for this reason they proclaimed that that was the beginning of the year. **3** However, this is not suitable for the rest of our inhabited lands.

4 Those of later times, as they thoroughly understood the knowledge of the laws of nature, and partook of this plain speculation, I mean, those astrologers from among the Greeks, foretold the [first] New Moon of the year when the Sun approaches the beginning of Aries, observing the sign marking the Hour and the positions of the wandering [stars], together with those of the fixed stars, as well as how the pivots come out in the nativity,[6] and thus they forecast the celestial influences of the year.

5 But I say that the wisest Ptolemy employed a more detailed method for such a prognosis, [based upon] all the four turning points of the annual cycle,[7] the New and Full Moons prior to those turning points (as well as their

---

[1] *Kosmikē katarchē.* That is, "cosmic" or "mundane" inceptions.
[2] Edited in *CCAG* I, pp. 129-31.
[3] Sirius.
[4] *Epochē.*
[5] *Apotelesma,* or the result of the position of the stars on human destiny.
[6] **BD:** That is, the *cosmic* nativity: see also **7** and **9**.
[7] **BD:** That is, the seasonal ingresses into Aries, Cancer, Libra, and Capricorn. See *Tet.* II.10.

rulers, together with the fixing of the pivots of the nativity),[8] and the power of the co-rising fixed stars.

6 Throughout all the eastern lands, the admirers of the wisdom of the Persians, who translated the Greek books into their own language, made use of only the astronomical tables for the annual cycle (namely, that of the position of the Sun at the beginning of Aries), just like Critodemus, Valens, Dorotheus, and Timocharis, as well as their colleagues [did]. **7** Whence, oh utmost lover of learning, I also, though more ambitiously, deemed necessary to make use of this tradition, which the eastern people eagerly embraced, and this is the yearly nativity: I mean, when the Sun comes to the first minute of the first degree of Aries, in the ruling city, wherever it might be; but those in the ruling city of the Saracens, where I received my method of calculation, which is more eastern than Babylonia, as I examined[9] the hours of Alexandria, 203° 15',[10] [...][11] which is 10-300-30.[12] **8** This is called Eirēnopolis,[13] [but] in the dialect of the Syrians, *Baghdad*;[14] its latitude, considered from the equinoctial semicircle, in the decline of the northern region, is of 33° degrees.[15]

9 When I found that the sages of the East used such a turning point of the annual cycle in relation to Babylon, and that from such a study they foretold things about wars, droughts, rainfalls, kings, and any distress or misfortune happening in every land, I certainly judged it excellent and wisely thought to fix the birth – I mean, the *cosmic* birth – of the whole inhabited land from the ruling city, as if from the starting point[16] of the universal amphitheater. **10** And besides the position of the Hour-marker, we shall have to treat everything as in the nativity: through the testimony of the benefics and of malefics, as well as the placement of the lights—except what concerns the

---

[8] **BD:** The use of pre-ingress lunations in mundane astrology is probably partly in imitation of the use of pre-natal lunations in nativities.

[9] *Endokimasai.* **EG:** This does not make sense, so the *CCAG* editor conjectured *edokimasa*, "I tested."

[10] **BD:** Pingree 2001 (p. 16) reads this as: "2/3 1/6 1/15 of an hour."

[11] Corrupted text.

[12] **BD/EG:** ιτλ, indicating Greek alphanumeric characters: ι is 10, τ is 300, λ is 30. Pingree 2001 (p. 16) reads this as 13° 30'.

[13] "The City of Peace," مدينة السّلام.

[14] *Bagdada.*

[15] **BD:** Modern Baghdad is indeed slightly above 33° N.

[16] *Balbis.* **EG:** This was a rope drawn across a race-course at the starting and finishing of the race, or the posts to which this rope was attached; hence, any starting point (and goal).

king, which we should take from the Royal Lot, the positions of its trigon lords, and from the degree of the Midheaven, the trigon rulers of the Midheaven, their placements, and, with them, that of Jupiter. **11** And accordingly, what concerns war [is taken] from the position of Mars, [and] the major accidents from that of Saturn, making use of the combined attendance of the signs and of the stars, according to their natures, as well as of the authority of the rulers of the year, together with the preceding first syzygy of the year (that is, of the New or Full Moon).

12 In general, the most generic turning point of the year is that found in the sign of Aries. **13** But there is still another more detailed [method], considered most special, which the wise Ptolemy employed: the one from the rest of the turning points (that of the summer, autumn and winter) as well as their preceding syzygies.[17] **14** And an even more detailed monthly change [is taken] from the transit of the Sun through each sign, and the horoscopic and pivotal position in that [sign], as well as that of the syzygy of the lights that take place in it, and that of the star ruling it. **15** You should indeed work on the turning point of the yearly cycle, [and] then you will thus successively discover how we arranged the celestial influences.[18]

[Chapter 2]: The study of the celestial influences of the ruler of the year, such as they are collected from the ancients[19]

1 How one should understand the ruler of the turning of the year.[20]

2 When[21] the day of the turning-point has come (that is, when the Sun has come into Aries), it is appropriate to understand the co-mixtures of Saturn, Jupiter, and Mars, which of them is making an eastern phase, or reaching its first or second station, or achronycal phase[22] or occultation: for indeed if any of the three previously-mentioned stars should make one of the

---

[17] See *Tet.* II.10.

[18] **EG: B** adds, "just as was received from the ancients."

[19] From **L**, 60v-61v.

[20] **BD:** That is, the mundane revolution of the year, or Aries ingress. For more on this, see *Labors* Ch. 38.

[21] **BD:** For this paragraph, cf. *Carmen* III.1, **1-3**. This is material on longevity, but adapted for mundane purposes.

[22] **BD:** This is when a planet rises when the Sun sets, and vice-versa.

above-mentioned figures, [within] seven days preceding or seven days following the turning-point, this one will have dominion.

3 But if within seven days Mercury will be stronger as an evening or
morning riser, take the position (to the second) of the Sun himself in Aries,
in whatever the ruling city may be, <as well as> the preceding conjunction or
Full Moon, or the quarters of the Moon occurring with the position of the
Sun at the beginning of Aries. **4** For indeed among all these already-
mentioned stars, the one having full word will have the rulership of the year;
but if these fail in the rulership, when none thenceforth of the above-said
figures has word, then <take> the most pivotal of them, and especially when
one is in its own place, and happens to be of its own sect. **5** These[23] conditions having been fulfilled, it is also appropriate to carefully examine the sign
marking the Hour, for that will be the releaser, when those around it are has-
tening towards a phase. **6** This will have dominion when its ruler, as I say, of
this place, chances to be out of the Sun's rays.

7 One[24] should even examine the lord of the turning-point of the year like
this: when the Sun is in Cancer,[25] on the Hour-marker or Midheaven, or in
the place of the Good Daimōn, he holds rulership. **8** If his ruler, or the ruler
of his bound, is not under the rays of the Sun or similarly on the setting pivot
or in the eighth place (the Sun having fallen into this place) when the day of
the turning-point has come, it pertains to the Moon to rule. **9** If she is on the
Hour-marker, Midheaven, or in the place of the Good Daimōn, and in a feminine sign (though not in a masculine sign); <or>, the Moon being on the
setting pivot, or <in the eighth>,[26] in masculine and feminine signs she rules
(because the Moon rejoices in the eighth place, precisely when she first appears [after] having come from the conjunction [with the Sun], and these on
the equinoctial turning point <or> on the nocturnal turning point above the
earth; being under the earth, the Moon only rules when she is on a pivot, in

---

[23] For **5-6**, cf. *Carmen* III.1, **13-14**.

[24] **BD:** What follows is Theophilus's version of finding the longevity releaser (often known
as the *hyleg* from Arabic, or *apheta* from Greek), normally used in natal charts but here
adapted for mundane purposes. See also *Labors* Ch. 38. For this paragraph, see broadly
Carmen III.1, **16-21**.

[25] **BD:** This is either a mistake for "Aries," or else it reflects an alternate Egyptian tradition
in which the summer solstice (in the northern hemisphere) is the beginning of the year.
This tradition is reported by Ptolemy in *Tet.* II.10, and mentioned by Theophilus above in
Ch. 2, **13**.

[26] **EG:** The manuscript is blurred here.

her own bound, and out of the rays.[27] **10** But if it is under the rays of the Sun, or else if the Moon herself is diminishing in her light, one should instead examine the Sun when he is in the underground pivot or in the post-ascension of the Hour-marker.

11 But[28] if the luminaries do not chance to be in the above-said places, it will be necessary to find which of them[29] is on the rising degree. **12** And if their ruler[30] is under the rays of the Sun that will be a difficult year, as well as troublesome, especially if none of the benefics is on the Hour-marker.

13 And[31] if the Moon rules the years, and is in Cancer, it is necessary to find the lord of her bound, and see whether it casts a trigon, square or diameter [to her]. **14** But if the Sun rules the year,[32] one should examine these things as with the Moon. **15** If the Moon is in the place of another, it is necessary to examine her ruler, as well as that of her bounds. **16** For instance, if in the first degrees of Libra (which is the house of Venus and the bound of Saturn), we need to examine the quality of its[33] figures in relation to each other, and if they make at least one of the above-mentioned phases, not only themselves, but also their rulers (as I say, Venus and Saturn): because not all the co-mixtures of all the stars happen to be effective, but <some are> weak and unreal[34] as well.

17 The certain and unmixed: on the other hand, the [candidates are] certain, when in the bounds of a star, and either making a phase before seven days, or gaining the mastery of the luminary of the turning-point, have a trine or square cast [upon them], or <are> witnessed through another figure. **18** They are not certain, though, when the star which is master of the turning-point chances to be in the bounds of one, while the other bears witness in the house of another, and its ruler does not look upon it.

---

[27] **BD:** This probably means that *her* bound lord is not under the rays, in parallel with the Sun above.

[28] For this paragraph, cf. *Carmen* III.1, **23-25**.

[29] **BD:** This probably means "whichever of the *other planets*." But in *Carmen* we are simply supposed to look at the degree of the Ascendant.

[30] **BD:** Again, in *Carmen* this is the lord of the Ascendant, so "its" ruler.

[31] For this paragraph, cf. *Carmen* III.1, **26-27**.

[32] **BD:** That is, if he is in Leo and is the releaser (*Carmen* III.1, **26**).

[33] **BD:** Theophilus seems to be speaking of the candidate releaser (here, the Moon), but the use of plurals later on and the separate mentioning of Saturn and Venus again makes it unclear what exactly he means.

[34] *Oneiros*, or "of dreams."

19 The[35] Lot of Fortune will have dominion over these places, their rulers, and ruled, when it is in one of those places, or witnessed by its own lord.

20 Now,[36] when the Lot of Fortune is not capable of having dominion, the Full Moon will hold sway, or its ruler, when it is in one of such places.

21 However, when all of them are declining from the pivots, then the Hour-marker will be the master.

22 Once the ruler is found, also examine the rays hurled to the ruler of the year by hexagon and diameter, observing as well which of them is either pivotal or declining, and not only that, but also the hurling of rays to the luminaries and to the Hour-marker, thus making a judgment and understanding, when examining closely concerning the things concerning kings.

23 And in this way proceed next to find out about the rest of the things.

[Chapter 3:] On the Lot of the king, from the Sun up to the Moon, and the same from the Midheaven[37]

1 The[38] triplicity rulers of the Royal Lot, and the Lot itself, being in a good place, indicate the strength and health of the king; moreover, when they are in the bounds of benefics, they are still more powerful. **2** But if a malefic conjoins the Royal Lot, its ruler, or looks upon them, grief and sickness will fall upon the king.

3 Both the Lot and its triplicity rulers having a bad position, the king will suffer the sedition of disparaging and much inferior men.

4 However, should the Lot be in a good place, while its trigon rulers in a bad one, the king will have good expectations, though he will waste his wealth because of the enemies. **5** Now, if the Lot falls in bounds of malefics, it means the ill-luck and cowardice of the king.

6 If the Lot falls in disreputable[39] signs, and its triplicity rulers in distinguished signs, the king will rise from the grief and cowardice, and will be more courageous.

---

[35] Cf. *Carmen* III.2, **12**.

[36] Cf. *Carmen* III.2, **13**.

[37] Edited from **L**, f. 61v-62v. This is probably the diurnal calculation, so that it would be Moon-to-Sun by night. In this way, it is a kind of Lot of Fortune for rulership.

[38] For sentences **1-8**, see *Carmen* I.13, **2-10**.

[39] *Adoxos.*

7 The first triplicity ruler of the Lot being well-placed, and the second badly, say that the beginning of the year will be good for the king, and the end bad. **8** When the second one is well-placed and the first badly, say the opposite.

9 A malefic[40] seeing the Royal Lot, when it[41] is declining, grief will fall upon the king.

10 The ruler[42] of the Royal Lot, if it makes an eastern phase, indicates prosperity and victory for the king.

༒   ༒   ༓

11 Examine[43] closely the diameter of the Royal Lot, and whether the ruler of the diameter is on the Lot, clearly opposing its own place: another king will come forth to the kingdom and rule.

12 Mars[44] and Saturn casting a square or opposing the Royal Lot, while no benefic is bearing witness, indicate the death of the king. **13** Jupiter being cast a square or diameter by the malefics, while Venus and Mercury, and the luminaries, are not looking upon it,[45] indicate the death of the king as well. **14** The lights not bearing witness either to each other or to the Royal Lot, mean the destruction of the king.

15 If[46] a malefic goes stationary, opposing or squaring the Royal Lot, apart from the testimony of the benefics, declare the death of the king.

16 Mars[47] being decimated by the Sun, or post-ascending the Sun, while the benefics are not looking upon him, destroys the king.

17 The Sun[48] pivotal or post-ascending the pivots, being with the malefics, or squared or opposed by them, indicates the destruction of the king; in the same way, it means the same when he is in a bad place.

18 Saturn[49] transiting[50] the Royal Lot indicates the ruin of the king.

---

[40] Cf. *Carmen* I.13, **11**.

[41] This must mean the Lot.

[42] Cf. *Carmen* I.29, **21**, the Lot of assets.

[43] Cf. *Carmen* I.14, **6**, and the discussion of similar passages there.

[44] For this paragraph, cf. broadly *Carmen* I.16, **6-15**.

[45] **BD:** It is unclear whether this is Jupiter or the Lot; probably the Lot.

[46] Cf. *Carmen* I.23, **39-41**, but this could be based on different version of *Carmen* I.17, **1**, since the following passages are based on I.17.

[47] Cf. *Carmen* I.17, **2-3**. But *Carmen* has Mars decimating the Sun, which makes more sense.

[48] Cf. *Carmen* I.17, **4**.

19 A malefic[51] stationary in the place of the Royal Lot signals the death of the king; but if a benefic hurls its rays, it does not mean death, but he suffers vexation and sickness.

20 Mars[52] pivotal in a diurnal turning-point,[53] and Saturn in a nocturnal one, are most evil, for they cause the dispersion of the royal wealth.

21 The Sun,[54] when he chances to be in the Bad Daimōn or in the Bad Fortune,[55] and when he is witnessed by a malefic, indicates grief for the king, and causes the loss of possessions. **22** And Jupiter in a bad place also means grief for the king, and irregularity in the royal affairs.

23 The[56] Royal Lot falling in a bad place, with a malefic on it, or squared or opposed by such a malefic, indicates a bad death for the king.

24 The[57] rulers of the Royal Lot and of the Sun being unconnected from the Hour-marker, the Sun himself not looking upon the Hour-marker, signals a bad death for the king.

25 Jupiter[58] decimated by Saturn causes meanness of spirit between the king and his subjects. **26** Saturn opposing Jupiter makes the subjects of the king his enemies.

ಠಿ   ಠಿ   ಜ

27 And in the same way as we have examined the Lot, we shall busy ourselves as well with the triplicity rulers of the Midheaven.

---

[49] Cf. *Carmen* I.17, **13**.

[50] *Epembainō*.

[51] Cf. *Carmen* I.17, **13**.

[52] Cf. *Carmen* I.18, **5**.

[53] Per *Carmen*, this is a diurnal ingress (and a nocturnal ingress, for Saturn).

[54] For this paragraph, cf. *Carmen* I.18, **6-7**.

[55] **EG**: That is, the twelfth and sixth houses, respectively.

[56] Cf. *Carmen* I.18, **8-9**.

[57] Cf. *Carmen* I.18, **10**.

[58] Cf. *Carmen* I.18, **11**.

[Chapter 4:] On the ruler of the year[59]

1 The[60] ruler of the year: whether it chances to be benefic or malefic.

2 This was received [from tradition] about the change of the year: when eastern and moving forward, say that the year is good; but if it makes an occultation, or moves backward, declare the year rotten.[61]

3 The good will be certain when the ruler of the year itself bears witness to the Hour-marker and the lights.

4 Examine as well the stars and signs in relation to sect, and look for the triplicity ruler,[62] so that this star is in sect.

[The ruler of the year in a bad condition][63]

5 The ruler of the year, if it chances to be under the rays and in its own places, it indicates a truce for the king, his army, as well as the idleness and sluggishness of the necessary affairs. **6** The ruler of the year being in an alien place, under the rays, is difficult, for it causes sicknesses among men, according to the nature of the sign; in a similar way, the year also brings loss to traders and business agents.

7 When Mars has ruled the year, being under the rays and in an alien place, it awakens plots against kings, secretly prepares the engines of war, and hurls feverish illnesses upon men, causing damage and loss. **8** And when he comes out of the rays, it also brings bloodshed and battles with much seizure and piratical attacks. **9** But if he is in the watery signs, droughts, and bad and terrible famine.

10 Saturn ruling the year, and being in alien places under the rays, brings upon men great and unhealthy disturbances from humors and humid condi-

---

[59] From **L**, f. 62v*ff*; see also Laurentianus 28.13, f. 146r*ff*. Omitted here is the following opening sentence only found in Laurentianus 28.13: "We shall investigate on these things, concerning kingship, as well as on the other events occurring in the year, the following way." **BD:** The following material is drawn from Dorotheus, but pertains to the (natal) lord of the year *by profection*. Theophilus seems to be adapting it to his special ruler of the year, which is based on the techniques of the natal longevity releaser and house-master (Ch. 2 above, and *Labors* Ch. 38).

[60] For **1-4**, cf. *Carmen* IV.1, **3** and **5-7**.

[61] *Sapros.*

[62] **BD:** This is probably the triplicity lord of the sect light.

[63] For **5-14**, cf. *Carmen* IV.1, **7-13**.

tions; it also makes the winter frosty, snowy, and ice-cold, and in all cycles of life it causes slowness, sluggishness, and the delay of the good things.

11 Jupiter ruling the year, and being in an alien place under the rays, causes the scattering of the royal treasury, and causes the king to be concerned about temples, sacred places, and having foreknowledge about[64] his subordinate commanders and army, except that it only shows moderate speed and the suitable size of fruits.

12 When Venus rules the year, being in an alien place under the rays, it instills disorder and censure between rulers and ruled, though the winter will be appropriate in its production of fruits, but without much abundance.

13 Mercury ruling the year, being in an alien place under the rays, the merchants will suffer loss and damage; it is also harmful for kings and their secretaries. **14** It feeds false hopes among men and renders the year useless, except that slaves and beggars enjoy advantages; the winter will be drier, and the changes in the weather[65] will be threefold.[66]

[The ruler of the year in a good condition][67]

15 Mars ruling the year, being eastern, and particularly when in his own place as well, is completely favorable, since it makes those that engage in war practical, quick, and effective; it instills intelligence and agreement within the army. **16** There will be a scarcity of money for thieves, and quick action among men. **17** The winter will be mild, and men and cattle will enjoy timely fruits.

18 Saturn ruling the year, especially when eastern, and in his own places, indicates a good year for the king, and means strength and power, and a time without sickness; it increases the rains and snowstorms, aids in the production of fruits, and is productive as regards all cultivation of trees. **19** It also provides for construction in every place.

20 Jupiter ruling the year, when he is a morning riser, and especially if in his familiar places, is most favorable, for it causes the royal subjects to have

---

[64] **EG**: Meaning unclear. Perhaps this means anticipating their movements so as to guard against plots, or else Theophilus is simply combining the two Jupiterian significations of "foreknowledge" and "officials."

[65] *Episēmasiai.* **EG**: This could also mean, "bodily symptoms," and the excess of an illness.

[66] *Tritai.* Meaning unclear.

[67] For **15-21**, cf. *Carmen* IV.1, **16-20**.

good will toward the king, this king will be successful,[68] and will provide benefits for his subordinates; the year will be well-arranged, and most healthy, overflowing with all profitable prosperity and abounding in fruitfulness.

21 When Venus rules the year, when both Venus and Mercury are eastern, and particularly when in their own places, the year is beautiful, and indicates a well-arranged year, especially for the officials and secretaries of the rulers; there will be much profit and good weather for the merchants; the winter will be with much rain, mild, and abounding in every fruit.

[Other planets in relation to the Hour-marker][69]

22 When Saturn does not have word on the year, and he opposes, squares, or is on the Hour-marker, it fosters instability, madness, and ill-repute in life, and causes dangers among each other; it sows hate and enmity among men, as well as enmity, antagonisms, and subversion against kings.

23 Mars not having a word in relation to the year, and being on the Hour-marker (or opposing or squaring it) means a difficult year, for it makes the people rise up, and incites wars with dangerous fires.[70] **24** If Jupiter looks upon Saturn or Mercury, it softens the evil.

25 If Jupiter does not have a word on the year, but marks the Hour or sees the Hour-marker from whichever figure, it does not diminish the good of the year; but if in addition a malefic beholds,[71] it brings the good of the year to an end, and causes the generals below the king to be either destroyed by the people, or banished.

26 Venus not having a word in relation to the year, and being on the Hour-marker or in a figure with it from whichever place, indicates a good year. **27** But[72] if Mars squares or opposes [her], it indicates disorder and irregularities.

---

[68] *Euemereō.* More literally, "he will spend his days cheerfully."

[69] For **22-32**, cf. *Carmen* IV.1, **22-34**. **BD:** In *Carmen* this is about the profected natal Ascendant coming *to* a natal planet, and that same planet *by transit* at the revolution, being configured to that sign. But Theophilus is adapting this to the Ascendant of the ingress.

[70] *Puretos*, which can also mean "fever."

[71] *Epidoi.* **BD:** It is unclear whether this malefic is beholding Jupiter or the Ascendant.

[72] **BD:** This probably represents a missing sentence in *Carmen*, or the end of its Ch. IV.1, **30**.

28 Mercury not having a word in relation to the year, being on the Hour-marker or in a figure with it, means that the year will not be difficult. **29** But if Saturn is with [him], or squares or opposes him, it indicates that there will be deadly slaughter in that year, as well as the destruction of men, and much damage.

30 The Moon marking the Hour at the change of the year, and being configured with benefics, indicates a good and manageable[73] year. **31** But if Saturn opposes or squares [her], it means an unhealthy and dangerous year. **32** If Mercury is also with Saturn, the evil will be worse, for it sows madness, opposition, and disorder, and there will be much corruption among men.

[The lord of the year in the pivots][74]

33 If the ruler of the year is on the Hour-marker, witnessed by the malefics, the year will be most utterly evil,[75] for there will be sorrows and a decrease of the good.

34 If the ruler of the year is in the underground or setting pivot, while Saturn is with it, or squares or opposes it, it indicates a difficult year, for it brings sicknesses, the destruction of necessary things, as well as loss.[76] **35** If also Mars is configured in the same manner as the ruler of the year, the year will be even worse, for it indicates that wars will burst out,[77] and that there will be afflictions, madness, and feverish illnesses; in the same way, burnings in [certain] places.

36 The star ruling the year being on the Midheaven, when it also chances to be looked from above[78] by a square from a malefic star, much opposition will be suffered in that year, in such a way that every evil will be succeeded by another evil, and the evil will be spread throughout, while the good will only remain in hope.

---

[73] *Euphoros.*

[74] For **33-39**, cf. *Carmen* IV.1, **35-45**. **BD:** In *Carmen*, this is about the profection of the Ascendant coming to the natal angles; but Theophilus is adapting this to the ruling planet being *in* one of the angles of the ingress.

[75] *Pankakiston to etos.*

[76] *Elatōsis,* or "diminishing."

[77] *Sugkrousmos polemōn,* lit. "a collision of wars." **EG:** A rare word, but a text by Nechepsō in *CCAG* VII, p.148 also employs it in relation to war.

[78] **BD:** That is, decimated.

37 Saturn opposing the Hour-marker of the year implies a bad year, in a similar way as Mars. **38** When the malefics do not look upon [it], examine the conjunctions[79] that take place on the Hour-marker of the year, as well as on its diameter, [and] also in its two squares: for if such conjunctions are witnessed by malefics from a square or diameter, they bring sorrows to the kings and rulers. **39** But if they were witnessed by benefics, they would bring good things to the kings and rulers, besides everything that we have already explained.

[The sixth sign of the ingress chart][80]

40 Before we proceed to judge about cosmic events, we should also examine the sixth sign from the annual Hour-marker, of what kind it is—that is, whether it is in watery, or beastly signs, or those of human form. **41** The sixth sign from the annual Hour-marker, and also its ruler, when maltreated,[81] bring destruction, slaughter, and corruption to the world according to the peculiarities of each country and the rulership that they hold in relation to those lands, and the particular nature of the stars in their placement.[82]

42 You investigate of what kind the corruption is, the following way. **43** When the sixth place is watery, and its ruler is found in watery signs, maltreated (namely, squared or opposed by Saturn), distilling, chilling, and much moisture and ill-treatment will take place, since illnesses and deaths will result from them for those beings whom the above-cited signs are concerned with.

44 This place and its rulers being maltreated by Mars (namely, by being squared or opposed), causes burning symptoms and bodily conditions with fevers; drought and a lack of rains occur; also the attack of robbers and movements of armies, as well as captivity—this [is] when Mars is eastern. **45** If Mars is under the rays, it causes dissension among slaves and people of the crowd, as well as madness and revolutionary movements.

---

[79] *Sunodos.* **EG**: That is, the New Moon. **BD**: In *Carmen* IV.1, **43-44**, this refers to monthly profections.

[80] For **40-51**, cf. *Carmen* IV.2, **2-10**, on illness in nativities.

[81] *Kakoumenos.*

[82] **BD**: Note that in *Carmen*, this refers to each signs rulership over some part of the body; Theophilus is adapting this to rulership over geographic areas.

46 Jupiter being the ruler of the sixth sign, witnessed by malefics, indicates that there will be damage in grapevines and in some other fruits from trees.

47 Venus being the ruler of the sixth, and harmed by the malefics, should she happen to be eastern, it instills sicknesses among young women; if she is setting,[83] in married women;[84] [it also causes] destruction to beings related to the signs that do not hear the star of Venus.[85]

48 Mercury being the ruler of the sixth place, and harmed by malefics, indicates droughts and lack of rain, and brings about illness of the ears, moistening, and sharp and burning fevers.

49 The lights ruling the sixth place, and maltreated, bring about troubles in the eyes. **50** The Sun, maltreated and in rulership, brings destruction to those beings related to the signs that do not hear the Sun. **51** The Moon ruling the sixth place, and maltreated, introduces illnesses of the liver among men, as well as ruin and destruction to the beings signified by the signs that do not hear her.

[The Lot of corruption][86]

52 Aside from all this we also have the Lot of corruption, which we must calculate for a diurnal turning-point[87] from Saturn to Mars, and the same amount from the Hour-marker; in nocturnal turning-points, the other way around. **53** If the ruler of this Lot is maltreated, it shows evil things; but if it is seen by benefics, it indicates a year without sicknesses and subject to no malignant influence.[88]

54 If, on the other hand, this Lot falls in between the Hour-marker and the Midheaven, it means that the influences will be given in more eastern parts; though if in between the Midheaven and the setting pivot, in southern

---

[83] **BD:** This probably means sinking under the rays.

[84] **EG:** Lit., "women who are under men" (*hupandros*).

[85] **EG:** Reconstructed from Laurentianus 28.13. In 28:34, it reads: "destruction to the beings (*zōōn*, meaning both animals and human beings) that do not hear Venus." **BD:** This must refer to signs which do not hear the sign in which Venus is. But in *Carmen* this just means being in a *male* sign, and *Carmen* has nothing correlating to the similar phrase in **50-51** below.

[86] For **52-54**, cf. *Carmen* IV.2, **11** and **15**. **BD:** In *Carmen* this is the Lot of chronic illness.

[87] **BD:** That is, "ingress."

[88] *Akakōtos.*

lands; if between the setting and the underground, toward western parts; between the underground and the Hour-marker, in northern lands.

[The Moon][89]

55 The[90] Moon in the turning point of the year, when she is full, and flowing away from malefics, indicates sicknesses, especially if she separates from a pivotal star while the other malefic looks from above. **56** If the Moon flows away from a pivotal Saturn at the turning-point of the year, the Moon being waning, it brings chilling and humors upon men, and causes long diseases and emaciation with coughs. **57** The Moon separating from Mars at the turning-point of the year, Mars being pivotal and the Moon waning, prepares piratical onslaughts, and causes premature childbirth in women. **58** The Moon separating from benefics at the turning-point of the year, and coming to a connection with one of the malefics (which is in the 13th degree),[91] shows a healthy beginning of the year and an unhealthy end.

59 But if she makes contact[92] with Saturn, it instills some disease from moisture. **60** If with Mars, it brings burning fevers and difficult conditions.

61 Saturn[93] and Mars in the place of the Evil Spirit,[94] and opposing or squaring the Moon: they hurl sicknesses upon men, and especially if Jupiter is not looking upon them.

62 In[95] turn, if the stars that cause corruption and diseases happen to be in the quadrant from the Midheaven to the Hour-marker, they cause evil at the beginning of the year; if in the quadrant from the Midheaven to the setting, in the middle of the year; between the setting and underground pivots, between the middle and the end; if between the underground and the Hour-marker, at the end of the year.

---

[89] This subsection was drawn from *Carmen* IV.2.

[90] For this paragraph, cf. *Carmen* IV.2, **62-64** and **66**.

[91] **BD**: This interval is generally taken to be the "orb" of the Moon when she applies to other planets (see Schmidt 2009, pp. 150-53). However, *Carmen* IV.2, **66** has 30°, which would be the equivalent of the Hellenistic void of course Moon (Schmidt 2009, p. 192). Both of these make sense.

[92] *Sunaptō.*

[93] Cf. *Carmen* IV.2, **67**.

[94] **BD**: This seems to mean, "if *Saturn is with* Mars is in the place of the Evil Spirit" (i.e., the twelfth).

[95] Cf. *Carmen* IV.2, **78-81**.

63 Consider[96] the following regarding benefics, and on the other hand, the stars that bring evil: when they are evening [stars], they bring corruption slowly; when morning [stars], quickly.

[Chapter 5:] On the month[97]

1 It is necessary that we examine, when the Sun enters each sign, and comes within 60' into the beginning of the sign, where the Hour-marker and the other pivots fall, in the same way as in a nativity. **2** Also calculate the Moon and the rest of the stars after the preceding syzygy, and search for the stars holding dominion, comparing their figures with those at the beginning of the year, and making the combination of influences of the stars, thus drawing from these the monthly study of celestial influences.[98]

3 On[99] the month, otherwise: from the transiting[100] Sun to the Moon at the fixing of the year, and the same [amount] from the annual Hour-marker, and wherever the number leaves off, there we consider to be the beginning of the month. **4** And if we find the ruler of the month to be eastern, both in the [annual] nativity and according to [later] transit, we say that it is an indicator of good things taking place in that month. **5** Now, if it is setting[101] in the nativity, and eastern according to transit, [it is in the] middle. **6** If [it is] under the rays in both the nativity and according to transit, we say that the month is unsuccessful. **7** And if eastern in the nativity and setting according to transit, we declare the month bad.

8 If[102] the Moon becomes the ruler of the month, one should examine whether she is adding,[103] or mounts to the heights:[104] for the Moon is excel-

---

[96] Cf. *Carmen* IV.2, **81-82**.

[97] From **L**, f. 65r; also Laurentianus 28.13, f. 148.

[98] **BD:** This may mean that we compare successive lunar charts with the original lunar chart of the year (around the Aries ingress), or perhaps that we compare each set of lunar and solar charts, with the original set around the Aries ingress.

[99] For this paragraph, cf. *Carmen* IV.1, **46-50**. **BD:** For a discussion of this passage and chart, see the overview of *On Cosmic Inceptions* in the Introduction.

[100] *Parodikos.*

[101] **BD:** This probably means sinking under the rays.

[102] For this paragraph, cf. *Carmen* IV.1, **51-55**.

[103] *Prosthetikē.* **EG:** That is, moving faster than average, or perhaps moving faster than the previous day.

lent when completely elevated and adding in numbers. **9** When [she is] subtractive in numbers, [it is in the] middle; and if depressed, and subtractive in numbers, as well as diminishing in light, most evil. **10** If the Sun rules the month, and increases the day,[105] we say that the month is good; if it decreases the day, bad.

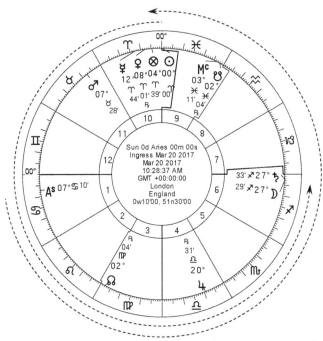

Figure 13: Monthly signs and lords (*Cosmic* Ch. 5, 3-4)

---

[104] *Hupsos hupsoutai.* **EG:** This may mean that the Moon is climbing to the northern latitudes of the ecliptic.

[105] **BD:** This means that the days are getting longer.

[Chapter 6:] On the month, according to Nechepsō[106]

[First Version: Laurentianus 28.13, ff. 148v-149r]

1 It is necessary to count from the transiting Sun until Cancer, adding the same amount from Leo, for the two lights chance to be the kings of the universe. **2** Leo was called a royal sign, because it is the house of the Sun; Cancer, as an amphibious sign,[107] is of the Moon. **3** This is why, by adding the same amount from each of them,[108] we have the beginning of the month.

4 For instance,[109] let [the ingress into] Libra be the month of Thoth. **5** The Sun being at the beginning of Libra, count from the beginning of Libra until Cancer, and there are ten signs. **6** Add the same amount from Leo, and I find Taurus, the house of Venus, since the ruler of the royal diadem [of that sign][110] is Venus.[111] **7** If she chances to be found sinking under the Sun, the month is of sad countenance, and will cause anxiety. **8** But if she is found on the east, it makes it relaxed and unconcerned. **9** The good and the evil will be known in a clear manner <from this>.[112]

---

[106] **EG:** Sentences **1-33** represent a first version of this chapter; the second version is in **34-62**, and contains an extra paragraph that does not appear in the first version. A third version, in Laurentianus 28.14 (f. 77v) is only a summary and does not help settle any disputes between the first two. **BD:** This method might not actually reflect Nechepsō, as Valens V.4 attributes the method above (Ch. 5, **3**) to Nechepsō.

[107] **EG:** lit. "of double life," or "of two worlds." This is said of the Moon, because she can be seen both at day and night.

[108] See **18ff** below, which explains the two Lots of the month more clearly.

[109] **BD:** In this example (see figure below), Nechepsō is using the Egyptian month Thoth, the first month of the Egyptian year, when the Nile flooding reached the delta, and when the Libra ingress occurred. The Sun is at the beginning of Libra. Counting inclusively, Libra through Cancer is ten signs (or, Cancer is the tenth sign from Libra). Now count ten signs (or to the tenth sign) from Leo, and reach Taurus. Therefore Taurus is the sign of the month, and Venus its lord. But note that as the Sun enters Scorpio, the distance is nine signs, and nine signs projected from Leo is Aries (and its lord Mars). In other words, we run into the same issue we did in the alternative interpretation of Theophilus's monthy profections above: the monthly signs are moving *backwards*.

[110] **BD:** Or perhaps this should read something like "*wherefore* the ruler of the royal diadem is Venus," with the sense of **36** below.

[111] **BD:** Nechepsō is counting inclusively.

[112] Adding on the basis of **39** below.

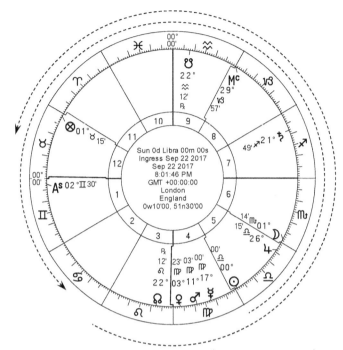

Figure 14: The Lot of the month (*Cosmic* Ch. 6, 4-6)

10 When Mars or Saturn are assigned the month,[113] and they chance to be in a good place, that is to say, setting under the Sun,[114] it breaks down the corruption brought to the month.

11 It will also be necessary to examine the ruler of the sign to which the month was allotted: for when a benefic happens to be in a place of a malefic, the good of the month will be more moderate. **12** In the same way, a malefic chancing to be in the place of a benefic lessens the evil. **13** When a benefic chances to be in the place of a benefic, it makes the good of the month great. **14** If a malefic in the place of a malefic, it makes the evil great as well.

15 We should also examine the two Lots, on which I will speak shortly, as well as their rulers:[115] that is, whether each happens to rising or setting. **16** For when benefics chance to be on the setting, they become powerless in relation to the undertaking of any matter, just as when the malefics to which

---

[113] **EG:** MS **L** has "and the days" here.

[114] **BD:** Theophilus might mean, "being in a good place *and* being under the rays."

[115] **BD:** That is, the Lot of the month, and the Lot of the king: see **18ff** below.

the month was assigned, chance to be setting, they make the rising up of the crowds powerless. **17** In the same way also, the benefics and malefics, when they chance to be eastern, they make the events brought about by them powerful.

[The Lot of the king]

18 Always calculate the Lot of the month from the transiting Sun up to Cancer, adding the same amount from Leo, just as we said at the beginning of the chapter. **19** Then, [for the Lot of the king] from the transiting Moon up to Leo, adding the same amount from Cancer.[116] **20** Thus we obtain the two Lots of the month, on which we have spoken in another place. **21** Once having found both Lots, then we should examine in which phase the ruler of each chances to be, whether it happens to be rising or setting, subtractive or additive, and thus, in relation to the strength of the star to which the month was assigned, as well as to the phase it is making, the completion of events regarding war and people will be revealed: whether they mean good or bad things.

22 After[117] we have clearly talked about the Lot of the, month (we now find the Lot of the month in Taurus, whose ruler is Venus),[118] let us now cast the Lot of the King. **23** Let the Moon be in Scorpio. **24** From Scorpio to Leo there are ten signs. **25** We thus add ten signs from Cancer, and the Lot falls in Aries, the house of Mars: so Mars is the ruler of the Lot of the king. **26** If Mars is found to be eastern, it moves the mob and causes slaughter. **27** When setting, it also stirs the crowds, but will bring no harm. **28** If Venus happens to be in the house of Mars, in that month the opposite will befall the king. **29** Mars chancing to be in Saturnian places, and having been allotted the month, there will be discord with ties of kindred and sailing. **30** When Mars chances to be in the house of Jupiter, it produces a month of hardships

---

[116] **BD**: This is the Lot of the king, as mentioned below.

[117] **BD**: Although the Lot of the month will always fall in the same place, the Lot of the king will differ because of the Moon's own motion. In the figure above, the Moon in the same ingress chart is in Scorpio. Counting inclusively, from Scorpio to Leo is ten signs (or, Leo is in the tenth sign from Scorpio). The tenth sign from Cancer is Aries, so the Lot of the king *in this month of this year*, falls in Aries, with its lord Mars. An alternative would be to treat this more like a normal Lot, so that one counts the actual degrees from the position of the Moon to 0° Leo, and then project that from 0° Cancer.

[118] **BD**: This is the Lot which was described in **4-6** above.

in the life of merchants and workers. **31** When Mars happens to be in the house of Mercury, it produces a troublesome month for those keen about writings and occupied in business. **32** If Mars is found in the sign of the Moon, the month will be completely full of a [morally] weak mob, and sudden deaths. **33** Finally, when Mars happens to be in the sign of the Sun, there will be much violence in that month, and many will be plundered; but the misfortune will not be given ear to.

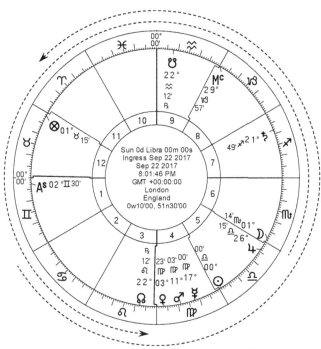

Figure 15: The Lot of the king (*Cosmic* Ch. 6, 19)

*[Second version: **L** f. 65r]*
Petosiris <and> Nechepsō on good and evil months[119]

34 This is not strange for you to know, great king, not only from the examination of the nativity, but also from another method, as follows: in the month of Thoth, the Sun is in Libra; it will then be necessary to count from the transiting Sun up to Cancer, and add the same number from Leo. **35** For both lights chance to be kings of the universe, and the Sun <is the reason why> Leo is called a royal sign, while the Moon <rules> Cancer, "amphibious" and "full of movement,"[120] wherefore it brings the mob together. **36** Count then from the Sun (transiting Libra), through Cancer, and again the same number from Leo, and the number leaves off in Taurus, the house of Venus: so Venus is indeed the lord of the royal diadem. **37** If she happens to be found setting under the Sun's rays, the month is of sad countenance[121] and causing anxiety. **38** Though when she is found on the east, it makes the month relaxed and unconcerned. **39** Thus indeed, oh great king, will be known the clear manner of the good and evil around us.

40 When Mars or Saturn are allotted the month and the days, and they chance to be in a good place, for instance, setting under the Sun,[122] it breaks down the corruption brought to the month.

41 It will also be necessary to examine the ruler of the sign to which the month has been allotted: for when a benefic happens to be in a place of a malefic, the good of the month will be more moderate. **42** In the same way, a malefic chancing to be in the place of a benefic, makes not a bad month. **43** In the same way as when <a benefic>[123] chances to be in the place of a benefic <it makes the month good>, when <a malefic is> in that of a malefic, it makes the evil of the month greater.

44 We should also examine the rulers of the two Lots, that is, whether they happen to be on the east or setting: for when benefics chance to be setting, they become powerless in relation to the undertaking of any matter, just as when the malefics to which the month was allotted chance to be setting, they make the rising up of the crowds powerless. **45** In the same way

---

[119] From L, f. 65r.
[120] *Polykinētos.*
[121] *Katastygnon.*
[122] See the footnote to **10** above.
[123] **BD**: Adding material in brackets on the basis of **13-14** above.

also, the benefics and malefics, when they chance to be eastern, make the events brought about by them powerful.

[The Lot of the king]

46 Always calculate the Lot of the month, from the transiting Sun up to Leo, in a similar way also [the Lot of the king] from the transiting Moon up to Cancer.[124] **47** See the number of the sign in which it leaves off, [and] examine the ruler of that sign, in which phase it chances to be, whether it happens to be rising or setting, subtractive or additive. **48** Thus, based on the phase of the star to which the month was allotted, declare about war, or, considering this, declare about people, that is, whether it causes good or evil things, or rather, of the second Lot.

49 We indeed calculate the second Lot from the transiting Moon until Cancer, since the sign of Cancer is amphibious and full of movement, and with a tendency to bring together in itself, and the lady of the house[125] is more remarkable than the other stars when she is adding in numbers, for it makes the turning about in this sign faster. **50** So the number from the Sun in Libra up to Leo is 11, and the second [one is] from the Moon being in Gemini: the number leaves off in Aries, the house of Mars. **51** When indeed you find Mars sinking into the solar rays, the mob will be agitated, and there will be deaths. **52** But when the star of Mars chances to be in the house of Venus, it will indicate the opposite for the king in that month. **53** Mars chancing to be in Saturnian places, and having been allotted the month,

---

[124] **BD:** Note that this calculation is different from the first version in **18-19**, and clashes with the fact that both texts already agree on Taurus-Venus being the Lot of the month (**6, 36**). Now, at first glance this alternative could be a legitimate alternative, because the relation between a planet and its own sign is very important. However, note that the worked example in **50** is not carried out correctly and seems to mix the two instructions. In **50** the Moon is in Gemini: but if we counted from her to Cancer, then that would only be two signs, and projecting from Leo would put the Lot of the king in Virgo. The passage reads as though we must project 11 signs from Gemini in order to get Aries, but the 11 signs pertained to the relation of the *Sun* in Libra, and Leo. This version seems to put the Moon in Gemini by mistake because that is eleven signs from *Leo*. So the scribe mixed up both the instructions and the positions. This is so even though it does make astrological sense to measure from a luminary to *its own* sign, and project from the other's sign (as in this version).

[125] *Despotis.* That is, the Moon.

there will be discord with ties of kindred and sailing. **54** When Mars chances to be in the house of Jupiter, it produces a month of hardships in the life of merchants and workers. **55** When Mars happens to be in the house of Mercury, it produces a troublesome month for those keen about writings and occupied in business. **56** If Mars is found in the sign of the Moon, the month will be completely full of a [morally] weak mob, and sudden deaths. **57** When Mars chances to come to the sign of the Sun, there will be much violence at that time, many will be seized as plunder, and their misfortune will not be given ear to.

[A monthly Lot about the populace][126]

58 It is necessary to make use of such speculation about the populace each month, beginning the influences from the number of the transiting Sun, till <the Moon>, adding the same number from <the Hour-marker>, since thus the enquiry on the influences of the month on the populace will be easily understood. **59** [For instance], as regards the earth and things shaped by nature,[127] Virgo takes the lead. **60** Thus, let the Moon be in Virgo, marking the Hour, and the Sun in Libra. **61** The number of signs from the Sun till Virgo being 11, [if we add] the same number from Virgo marking the Hour, the number leaves off in Leo (and indeed the ruler of Leo is the Sun): and at the time the Sun comes into the sign, the earth will turn humid. **62** But if the Sun is eclipsed in the month of Thoth,[128] it is prejudicial for the earth in relation to sowing; on the subject of sowing and vegetables, it will be favorable when in Cancer, especially if the rest of the stars assist.

---

[126] **BD:** This Lot seems to be simply a Lot of Fortune (without a reversal by night), carried out in a separate monthly ingress chart (rather than projecting from the Aries ingress every time). This paragraph does *not* appear in the first version of this chapter from Laurentianus 28.13, above.

[127] *Fytos.* **EG:** But mainly trees and plants are understood by this here.

[128] When the Sun is in Libra.

[Chapter 7:] On the universal effects of the Nodes[129]

1 The Moon suffering eclipse in Gemini, Libra or Aquarius, will be deadly for the whole world.

2 If the eclipses occur in the opposite signs (namely Leo, Aries, and Sagittarius), the evil will become worse, for this indicates famine, battles, and falling of cities, on every place of the inhabited world, with the loss of wild beasts, and all kind of creatures and cattle, especially of camels and sheep, especially in the latitudes of the signs that do not hear.

3 In Cancer, Scorpio, and Pisces it will cause a lack of waters in lands close to them, forcing the men in those lands to banishment because of the lack of necessary things. **4** There will also be lack of fish in the sea and the rivers.

5 When in Taurus, Virgo, and Capricorn, there will be much affliction among men, as well as a scarcity of trees, fruits, and seeds, particularly in those nearby latitudes.[130]

[Chapter 8:] Portents[131] of the New and Full Moons[132]

1 Take the New and Full Moons that take place—more specifically, the degree on which both lights are—and examine in which bound such a degree falls. **2** Observe the ruler of the bound, to see what kind of phase it makes. **3** The accomplished effects indicate as follows:

4 Saturn ruling the bound of the lights, being under the rays, or achronycal, brings darker[133] winters; if he is found in Sagittarius or Pisces, it

---

[129] From L, f. 66r and Laurentianus 28.13, f. 149v.

[130] **EG:** That is, on the latitudes/countries that match those of the signs. This seems to indicate, for instance, that if an eclipse occurs in Capricorn (which is 23° 45' below the equatorial line), then the lands along that latitude will be most affected. **BD:** But since the ancients knew little of lands south of the equator, he might mean this in a general way, so that Capricorn (being the sign of greatest southern declination) means "everything in the far south."

[131] *Episemasia.* **EG:** That is, the changes in the weather brought about by the Moons.

[132] **BD:** This passage appears as a scholion in in L (f. 65v), but as a chapter in Laurentianus 28.13 (f. 149r); we have decided to make it a chapter in its own right.

[133] *Melania* ("blackness"). **EG:** That is, many storms with black clouds.

causes much sailing at sea, fears and watching by day;[134] in Cancer, also on rivers; as regards sailing, it causes excessive frost towards the Northern Bear. But if he is eastern, it will cause mildness.

5 Jupiter ruling the bound of the New Moon, when he is setting or an evening [star], will bring rainstorms (though not black, since the clouds will be like fleeces of wool). **6** But if eastern or achronycal, it causes fair weather and increasing of fruits. **7** If he is also in watery signs, it produces an increase of fish, as well as a release from illnesses for men. **8** If he is in Virgo, it especially makes the fruits grow.

9 Mars ruling the bound of the syzygy, if besides that he is also under the rays, is indicative of fair weather, and a cessation of winds. **10** But if arising, it will bring upheaval and movements, and there will be much lightning and thunder.

11 Venus ruling the bound of the conjunction, being eastern, is indicative of fair weather and the birth of animals; setting, it brings winds and frost.

12 With Mercury, eastern, ruling the bound of the New Moon, the air will be clean. **13** If western,[135] moderate. **14** But if he is under the rays, it awakes winds from the west, and brings down hail, even to places free from inundation. **15** Now, if he chances to be in [crooked][136] signs, towards the latitude of Egypt; in tropical signs, in places by the sea; in bicorporeal, in both.

---

[134] *Hemeroscopia*. **BD**: Maybe this means many changes that force people to make daily assessments of the weather.

[135] *Hesperios*. Or, "evening," i.e. as an evening star.

[136] **EG**: There is a difficult abbreviation here; it could also be "Saturnian places."

APOTELESMATICS

Chapter 1: Introduction[1]

By the same Theophilus the philosopher, from the second edition

From Theophilus to his son Deucalion, greetings:[2]

1 Be satisfied, O Deucalion, my son, with such things as I, with much philosophy, have very (even exceedingly) well written down for you before in defense of mathematical science, making use of appropriate testimonies from the divine writings and from the revered philosophers, [both] those from without,[3] and those who instructed in the name of Christianity, and established the faith with work and truth. **2** But because I hold you to be excellent and good-natured, engaged in high philosophy and having by far a greater longing for mathematics, I have deemed it also necessary to now address, for your edification, the things neglected by your developed certainty, together with some other chapters on what has been understood by me from the universal completion of events, and from the inceptions by inquiry, so that through these, and those previously gained by me by training, the true Science is elucidated to you.

3 It is indeed necessary that you follow closely the astrological science with utmost attention and care, without hesitating to refrain from whichever stumbling block keeps you away from it, for it is the delightful and most excellent Queen of all Science, even when it is mocked and ridiculed by the majority, especially by some of the ecclesiastical leaders. **4** For this reason, of those who ridicule it, some wish to state that this [science] does not exist at all, while others [admit] that it exists but it is liable to fail. **5** However, O my son, let this slander neither scare you, nor hinder either your aim or the willingness that is within you, for in the Treatise before this one I opposed the attack of those who extorted by false charges, and abusively threatened, the most sacred and sublime astrology.

6 However, in this Treatise I would not hesitate to indicate the little things which are meaningful, and to present, from the divine writing, with some natural examples, the plausible and the unambiguous, so that you, with

---

[1] Edited in *CCAG* V.1, pp. 234-38.
[2] Lit., "be well," "fare well."
[3] **BD**: That is, pagans.

others, having confidence in these [little things], may be impartial, unshaken in your thought, firm and infallible in your assumption. **7** For in the Treatise preceding this one I gave heed to the seven days of the creation of the universe, and precisely [reminded you] that they had been assigned to the seven stars in a sequential order; but now I thought it would be beauty-loving to make clear, before anything, the doctrine of the seven days, and refer to the natural and particular quality of each and every day, and the mixtures and forces of the seven stars, and therefore in this way confirm the heptad by means of graphic examples.

8 The Hierophant[4] Moses called the first day that one to which the Sun is especially assigned, and very fittingly so: for on that one was manifested God's first work. **9** For indeed the Prophet says:[5] *"In the beginning God created the Heavens and the Earth,"* and with this he shows that, just as the Sun is the luminary of the Above and the Below, so also the first work, which came to be on his day, brought to light the creation of the Heavens and the Earth—precisely because of this, every place below the Heavens is shadowy and idle without the brilliance of the Sun. **10** He went on:[6] *"the Earth was invisible and unformed, and darkness was over the face of the deep,"* and, shortly after confirming that the day was of the Sun, he went on:[7] *"and God said, let there be light,"* and what follows [that], for it was fitting that on the day of the Sun, the light be born, so that, throughout the whole, the first day was manifested (that is to say, the one day of the Sun).

11 Immediately following the Sun, the Moon was distributed the second day:[8] for on this one the waters were brought together to their assembling, and water was separated from water in the midst, and the dry [land] was seen, because the Moon is watery by nature, and is distinguished among the lights in regard to her phases: crescent-shaped, first and third quarters, and gibbous. **12** Moreover, the Moon wanes and waxes due to her figures, and brings about great tides of the waters of the oceans, as well as the lack and overflow of rivers, together with many other alterations, which great experience has taught men.

---

[4] Lit., "sacred revealer."

[5] *Gen.* 1:1.

[6] *Gen.* 1:2.

[7] *Gen.* 1:3.

[8] *Gen.* 1:6-10.

13 The third day[9] was given to Mars, for on this one the Earth yielded everything tree-like and grassy for nourishment and consumption: because Mars, chancing to be fiery and dry by nature, is a waster and corruptor of all matter, and for this reason the third day is assigned to him.[10]

14 The fourth day[11] was assigned to Mercury, as being speech-related and a cause of all wisdom, for on this day the creation of the world is said to have labored on the luminaries and the stars at the same time, for signs and for seasons.[12] **15** For by means of thought and scientific observations we grasp the course of the Sun and the Moon, and the motions of the stars, in length and width, as well as their retrograde and direct motions, with their phases and settings, and all their influence, quality, and force.

16 The fifth day[13] was distributed to Jupiter, and very fittingly so, as being the most productive and a cause of every mildness of the airs. **17** Also because of this, on this day [God] brought forth the waters, and all the cattle [and] beasts, together with all the winged creatures, so that all the Earth, and its surrounding air, would be filled with all kinds of living beings.

18 The sixth day[14] was assigned to the star of Venus, because this star chances to be mild-tempered and most fruitful as well as quite full of all cheerfulness: on this day indeed, the most generic man was molded and became a living soul, and king of all that is upon Earth. **19** And in the same way that the star of Venus has fame and splendor over all the stars, and differs from them in beauty and glory, so also man has virtue over each living being, and appears eminent in speech, mind, glory, and brilliance, and became the husbandsman of Paradise, that is, the one in charge of all things on Earth.

20 The seventh day[15] is, with good reason, attributed to Saturn, for it is said that on this [day] the Creator rested from His own works, and that it is a day of leisure and inaction. **21** For Saturn is idle, unfruitful, due to his natu-

---

[9] *Gen.* 1:11-13.

[10] **BD:** I would also point out that the original Roman God Mars was an agricultural god, responsible for the vigorous growth of vegetation; this is fitting for the day on which vegetation developed.

[11] *Gen.* 1:14-19.

[12] **BD:** That is, astrology and the use of it for calendrics, planning agriculture (and therefore economic planning), etc.

[13] *Gen.* 1:20-23.

[14] *Gen.* 1:24-31.

[15] *Gen.* 2:1-3.

ral coldness: he is neither generative in living beings, nor efficacious in the remaining nature of the creations, but rather more idle and hard.

22 These things, O my son, have I advanced to you, as concisely as possible, on the seven days of the creation of the Universe, as well as how the days are naturally assigned to the seven stars, one after another. **23** [I also said] that the seven stars were built by the Creator, and Solomon calls them to mind in his own *Book of All Virtue*,[16] where he reveals that Wisdom had built a house for herself, and had supported it with seven pillars;[17] in the same way also Isaiah[18] the Prophet speaks of the seven eyes of the Lord looking at the inhabited world. **24** And what is clearer or truer than this, that there are seven stars, precisely those which make the contrary movement in the circle bearing the forms of animals? **25** By means of their configuration and position relative to one another, they transform the changing nature of the things that are under the Moon, having been entrusted this by the Creator: namely, birth, destruction, and renewal of the creatures.

26 In my first Treatise I even cursorily gave heed to the Magicians that came from the East to do reverence to our Lord Jesus Christ; but now I wish to elucidate the prophecy[19] more clearly, to you and to those that judge well, who come across my writing, [which consists of] a certain dialectic argument,[20] so that those who are not persuaded of this will become so, through the argument[21] of truth. **27** From where did the Magicians learn of the King being born at Judea? **28** From a certain oracle, or from the rising of a star (or comet, or some other appearing[22] [star])? **29** If from an oracle, the interpretation[23] of the star was superfluous, for what need was there of astral phase and signification? **30** If the star appeared to the Magicians, it is clear through astrological science that they moved in order to know the birth of the King,

---

[16] *Panaretos.* **BD:** Theophilus is probably thinking of the *Book of Proverbs*, which does mention Solomon's name, and contains the following quote about Wisdom in 24:3. But this name is also give to a book attributed to Hermes, which contains information on certain Lots: see Paul of Alexandria Ch. 23, and Commentary 22 by Olympiodorus (pp. 41*ff* and pp. 111*ff*.).

[17] Cf. *Proverbs* 9.1.

[18] **EG:** But this is actually Zechariah 4:10.

[19] *Chrēma.* Or, "oracle."

[20] *Dialektikē logos.*

[21] *Logos.* Or, "word."

[22] *Epitolēs.* Or, "shining."

[23] *Logos.*

and the star itself became the significator of the moment of birth of the Lord, and if this is evident to those who have sense, then astrology is true.

31 Judge well, you listeners, and any who has broken free from blame, and honor those who practice astrology, suitably recognizing the Creator in His creations. **32** But even so, son, as I learned, there is no single way towards the step[24] of virtue: there is, in the holiest and all-wise Paul a step of the Spirit, one of the soul and another of the flesh.[25] **33** Accordingly he teaches [us] about our Lord Jesus Christ, for He is our Savior, teaching the perfect path in the Gospels to his holy disciples, [which is] to forsake their family, parents, children, and wife, to speak with simplicity for one's whole life, to take up His cross and follow Him,[26] and He spoke at that time of the spiritual and highest wisdom in riddles, beyond which there is no further step.[27] **34** For indeed through the knowledge that not all men are able to set foot on such a step, he also taught other paths, lesser than this one, when afterwards he mentioned the five talents, two talents, and one talent,[28] and the economy of injustice, subtly suggesting by means of this that whoever is not able to grasp the highest path of the virtues, let him take another path, that is, a middling and freely-giving one, so that such may be perfected in the tents of the chosen ones, such as indeed at that time the manager was praised by his own master.[29]

---

[24] *Bathmos*, a step or rung of a stair or ladder, as well as a degree in rank. **EG:** Clearly, the idea is that of a "ladder" of virtue. See *I Corinth.* 15:44.

[25] **BD:** Theophilus seems to be doing some creative interpretation here. First, the notion of steps or rungs on a ladder toward virtue is more appropriate for a Platonic philosopher (such as with the famous "ladder of love" in Plato's *Symposium*). Second, Paul is trying to draw a simple contrast between the physical body and mortality on the one hand, and the spiritual body and immortality on the other—clearly favoring the latter. But Theophilus will suggest that there are two paths leading to God (which include sciences like astronomy and astrology), which was not Paul's point at all.

[26] See Luke 14:26-27.

[27] See Luke 14:28-32 immediately following the previous passage, which does contain puzzling parables.

[28] See Matthew 25:14ff.

[29] **BD:** This passage is much clearer than the parable in Matthew, and unlike Matthew Theophilus seems to have a clear point—unfortunately it is obscured by his trying to blend it with the parable. As I mentioned before, Theophilus is trying to say that there are many paths to God, one of which is astrology.

35 So[30] now know well, my son, that there is a spiritual Wisdom, that of the initiates,[31] who [*corrupt text*] when passing away have not made use of the mathematicians, nor of any other sophistic complication, but with simplicity of character they exercised lofty virtue, with revered virginity. **36** There is also a Wisdom of the soul, which seeks after the cosmic philosophy by word and act, holy wedlock, moderate virtue, and blameless virginity. **37** <This> the children of the physicians and astronomers <exercise>, both Platonic and Aristotelian, [but] outside any censure or madness: for he who is not able to become the Sun, let him be the Moon, and he who is not able to become the Moon, let him become a luminous star, and he that is not competent to provide for gold or silver, cultivates wheat, and becomes a thinker for the economy of life. **38** The third step is that of those pertaining to the body, and those bearing a body and making predictions of cosmic fraud and imposture; that you abstain from that, my son, is something I pray for, and will pray for.

39 Have strength[32] in practicing the truth, and help Justice to your utmost.

Chapter 2: On the winds occurring in the settling of the airs,[33] which indicate rains, thunder, hurricanes, earthquakes, and the rest of such things[34]

1 Saturn ruling the bounds of the conjunction of the lights[35] in Aries, when he is under the rays, causes heavy rains and completely clouded skies,

---

[30] Now Theophilus creatively uses Paul (in I Corinth. 2-3) to describe three paths in life. The first (**33, 35**) is the spiritual (2:15), those who are more or less infused with the Holy Spirit and lead pure lives. The second (**36-37**) is the soul life (2:14), which is followed by philosophers, astrologers, and others who use the human intellect and various sound disciplines to gain knowledge. The third, lowest, and least suitable (**38**) is the life of the body (3:1), which apparently includes all sorts of other kinds of divination.

[31] Or, "perfect ones."

[32] *Errōso*. **EG:** One of the classical closing formulae of the epistolary genre, meant to send good wishes to the reader.

[33] *Katastasis tōn aerōn*. **EG:** But the sense of this could also be, "the establishment of the seasons."

[34] Edited in *CCAG* IV, pp. 83-84. In a footnote to the Greek text (p. 83), this chapter is said to be an abridgment of a longer text found in **L** ff. 95-98, attributed to the "Chaldeans and Egyptians."

and among men sicknesses with flux, and difficulty in breathing. **2** When he is an evening [star] it indicates very cold blasts of winds; when a morning [star] and rising it means mildness and freshness of the air. **3** If stationary, thundering and lightning.

4 In Taurus, being under the rays, it is an indicator of mild temperature. **5** When an evening [star] it causes dryness, as well as want of rain in the weather; as a morning [star] it is mild. **6** Stationary, rainy and with thunder.

7 In Gemini, under the rays, dry and without moisture. **8** As an evening [star], with droughts and lack of rains; as a morning [star], mild and harmless. **9** Stationary, pestilential.

10 In Cancer, under the rays, it causes darkness during daylight, violent winds, and storms. **11** As an evening [star], shipwrecks at sea; as a morning [star], good and mild weather. **12** Stationary, it is pestilential.

13 In Leo, under the rays, it causes flux and disturbances of the waters, as well as dryness in the air. **14** As an evening [star], it is dry; as a morning [star], mild, and a cause of great health. **15** Stationary, it is hot and dry.

16 In Virgo, under the rays, it makes illnesses fall upon men. **17** As an evening [star], badness of the air; as a morning [star] it turns dry. **18** Stationary, it causes sicknesses.

19 In Libra, under the rays, it causes pains in the eyes. **20** As an evening [star], irregularities in the airs; as a morning [star] it is productive of cold and dry winds. **21** Stationary, it produces illnesses with quartan fever.

22 In Scorpio, under the rays, it indicates dry air. **23** As an evening [star], rains with violent noise; as a morning [star], cold and hoar-frost. **24** Stationary, irregularity in the air.

25 In Sagittarius, under the rays, it indicates rains and a good season for fruits, and cloudy skies. **26** As an evening [star], a want of rain and dryness; as a morning [star], cold and frost. **27** Stationary, it hurls illnesses upon men.

27 In Capricorn, under the rays, it causes storms from the black north. **28** As an evening [star], frost; as a morning [star], very cold winds from the north. **29** Stationary, darkness during the day.

30 In Aquarius, under the rays, it causes harsh winters. **31** As an evening [star], fears at sea and in rivers; as a morning [star], frosts and storms. **32** Stationary, it is snowy and glacial.

---

[35] **BD:** That is, conjunction of the Sun and Moon, either in any month or perhaps especially just before the Sun's ingress into one of the signs.

33 In Pisces, under the rays, it is snowy. 34 As an evening [star], damp; as a morning [star], of mild temperature. 35 Stationary, it causes irregularities of the airs.

Chapter 3: On Jupiter[36]

1 Jupiter ruling the bounds of the conjunction of the lights in Aries, being under the rays, causes rains. 2 As an evening [star], clouds like locks of wool; as a morning [star], good production of fruits, fair weather. 3 Stationary, an increase of fruits, the health of cows and sheep.

4 In Taurus, under the rays, it shows suitability of the air. 5 As an evening [star], rains; as a morning [star], good production of fruits. 6 Stationary, it is favorable for the production of fruits, the health of men, and the pasturing of animals.

7 In Gemini, being under the rays, it shows a good temperature. 8 As an evening [star], health for men; as a morning [star], mildness and health. 9 Stationary (and not unprofitable), a release from sicknesses and health.

10 In Cancer, under the rays, it indicates fair weather at sea, and an increase of fish. 11 As an evening [star], it is mild in relation to the air; as a morning [star], it is a cause of mildness of temperature and health. 12 Stationary, it is not unprofitable under any condition.

13 In Leo, under the rays, it causes periodic winds. 14 As an evening [star], it provides good temperature; as a morning [star] and rising, it indicates strength and good health. 15 Stationary, a release from illnesses.

16 In Virgo, being under the rays, it indicates the good production of fruits. 17 As an evening [star], mild temperature; as a morning [star], health. 18 Stationary, the same.

19 In Libra, under the rays, it is mild. 20 As an evening [star], it makes the weather healthy; as a morning [star], it drives illnesses away. 21 Stationary, it turns the air calm.

22 In Scorpio, under the rays, it indicates rains. 23 As an evening [star] it is mild; as a morning [star], calm and increasing the fish in the waters. 24 Stationary, the stillness of the sea and a release from illnesses.

---

[36] Edited in CCAG IV, pp. 84-85.

25 In Sagittarius, under the rays, it indicates temperate rains. **26** As an evening [star], much [rain], more than needed; as a morning [star], fair weather. **27** Stationary, good health for men.

28 In Capricorn, under the rays, it indicates humid air. **29** As an evening [star], it means rains; as a morning [star], fair weather at sea and in rivers. **30** Stationary, thunderstorms.

31 In Aquarius, under the rays, it is temperate. **32** As an evening [star], repeatedly freshly-infused; as a morning [star], healthy. **33** Stationary, damp and hot.

34 In Pisces, under the rays, it indicates an increase of fish. **35** As an evening [star], it is temperate; as a morning [star], it causes fair weather at sea and in rivers. **36** Stationary, it is waterless.

Chapter 4: On Mars[37]

1 Mars ruling the bounds of the conjunction of the lights in Aries, being under the rays, is indicative of good weather. **2** As an evening [star], the contrary; as a morning [star], turbulent. **3** Stationary, with thunder and lightning.

4 In Taurus, under the rays, it indicates stillness in the air. **5** As an evening [star], it is mild;[38] as a morning [star], it moves the winds. **6** Stationary, it turns dry.

7 In Gemini, under the rays, it hurls illnesses upon men. **8** As an evening [star], it is a cause of heat; as a morning [star], it introduces disturbances. **9** Stationary, it is heating and drying.

10 In Cancer, under the rays, it causes burning heat. **11** As an evening [star], it introduces illnesses; as a morning [star], it causes disturbances in the weather. **12** Stationary, it is irregular, scorching, and dry.

13 In Leo, under the rays, it instills illnesses into <the weather>. **14** As an evening [star], burning hot; as a morning [star], it produces disturbances. **15** Stationary, it is unhealthy.

---

[37] Edited in *CCAG* IV, pp. 85-86.
[38] *Eudieinos*. **EG**: Also, "warm," "calm."

16 In Virgo, under the rays, it is harmful for the weather, for it instills ill-nesses. **17** As an evening [star], it is choking; as a morning [star], it introduces disturbances. **18** Stationary, it indicates the dryness of the air.

19 In Libra, under the rays, it turns the air dry and without moisture. **20** As an evening [star], it is rainy; as a morning [star], turbulent and with thunder. **21** Stationary, dry and without moisture.

22 In Scorpio, under the rays, it indicates the stillness of sea. **23** As an evening [star], stillness of the airs; as a morning [star], it moves the winds. **24** Stationary, dry and without moisture; it also causes thunder and light-ning, moves the army, and <it means> the death of a great man.

25 In Sagittarius, under the rays, it is without moisture. **26** As an evening [star], unhealthy and mostly pestilential; as a morning [star], turbulent. **27** Stationary, unfavorable and harmful.

28 In Capricorn, under the rays, it is hot. **29** As an evening [star], mild; as a morning [star], harmful. **30** Stationary, irregular and unfavorable.

31 In Aquarius, under the rays, it means a lack of rains. **32** As an evening [star], the calmness of the airs; as a morning [star], it moves the winds. **33** Stationary, [it is] harmful at sea.

34 In Pisces, under the rays, it announces the scarcity of fish. **35** As an evening [star], it is without moisture; as a morning [star], with lightning and thunder, as well as humid and destructive. **36** <*Stationary missing.*>

Chapter 5: On Venus[39]

1 Venus ruling the bounds of the conjunction of the lights in Aries, being under the rays, indicates calmness at sea. **2** As an evening [star], it causes winds; as a morning [star], it is rainy and with thunder.

3 In Taurus, under the rays, it is thundering. **4** As an evening [star], caus-ing good weather; as a morning [star], mild and beneficial for the weather.

5 In Gemini, under the rays, it is dry. **6** As an evening [star], windy; as a morning [star], causing fair weather and mildness.

7 In Cancer, being under the rays, it shows the calmness of the airs. **8** As an evening [star], it is mild; as a morning [star], it is indicative of good weather.

---

[39] Edited in *CCAG* IV, pp. 86-87.

9 In Leo, being under the rays, it is burning hot. **10** As an evening [star], it introduces illnesses in the cattle; as a morning [star], it is temperate.

11 In Virgo, being under the rays, it is dry. **12** As an evening [star], temperate; as a morning [star], humid.

13 In Libra, being under the rays, it is humid. **14** As an evening [star], temperate; as a morning [star], generative and humid.

15 In Scorpio, under the rays, it is devoid of moisture. **16** As an evening [star], causing good rains; as a morning [star], bringing much rain.

17 In Sagittarius, under the rays, it is rainy. **18** As an evening [star], it is windy and icy; as a morning [star], temperate.

19 In Capricorn, under the rays, it is frosty. **20** As an evening [star], mild; as a morning [star], rainy.

21 In Aquarius, under the rays, it is snowy. **22** As an evening [star], ice-cold and windy; as a morning [star], rainy and misty.

23 In Pisces, under the rays, it is icy and cold. **24** As an evening [star], watery and windy; as a morning [star], mild, generative and sprouting.

Chapter 6: On Mercury[40]

1 Mercury ruling the bounds of the conjunction of the lights in Aries, being under the rays, causes hail. **2** As an evening [star], it is less temperate; as a morning [star], it makes the airs clean.

3 In Taurus, under the rays, it is very rainy and causes flooding. **4** As an evening [star], it is temperate; as a morning [star], it makes the airs clean.

5 In Gemini, under the rays, it awakes winds on earth and at sea. **6** As an evening [star], it is drying; as a morning [star], temperate.

7 In Cancer, under the rays, it disturbs the seas. **8** As an evening [star], it indicates fair weather at sea; as a morning [star], it is temperate and indicative of humidity.

9 In Leo, under the rays, it indicates winds from the west. **10** As an evening [star] it is choking; as a morning [star], with clean airs.

---

[40] Edited in *CCAG* IV, pp. 87-88. **BD:** It is not always easy to figure out exactly how each planet contributes its effects, but we can see here that Mercury as an evening star tends to be drying (and in cold months, cold), while as a morning star he gives refreshing moisture.

11 In Virgo, under the rays, it means that there will be strong and furious storms at sea. **12** As an evening [star], it is drying; as a morning [star], humid with good temperature.

13 In Libra, under the rays, it is indicative of sterile winds. **14** As an evening [star], without rain; as a morning [star], rainy.

15 In Scorpio, under the rays, it is hail-bringing. **16** As an evening [star], without rain; as a morning [star], rainy.

17 In Sagittarius,[41] under the rays, it is very rainy. **18** As an evening [star], without moisture; as a morning [star], mild and healthy.

19 In Capricorn, under the rays, it is snowy. **20** As an evening [star], ice-cold; as a morning [star], rainy.

21 In Aquarius, under the rays, it is snowy. **22** As an evening [star], glacial and Tartarus-like; as a morning [star], humid.

23 In Pisces, under the rays, it brings hail and flood. **24** As an evening [star], it is temperate; as a morning [star], causing good weather at sea.

Chapter 7: The influences[42] of the eclipses of the Sun[43]

1 The Sun suffering eclipse in the first 10° of Aries indicates movements of the army, the continuity of the military expedition, mob-rule, with much noise, controversy, and dryness of the air. **2** In the second 10°, the imprisonment of kings, much distress, the danger of death, and destruction of fruits. **3** In the third 10° it causes grief for men, and indicates also the death of a great woman, and the destruction of cattle.

4 The Sun being eclipsed in the first 10° of Taurus shows the inaction of traders, but the good supply of the seeds of Demeter.[44] **5** In the second 10° it indicates danger for pregnancy in women. **6** In the third 10° it indicates hunger and plague.

7 The Sun being eclipsed in the first 10° of Gemini indicates carelessness in sacred and legal matters, [and] the illness and distress of the king. **8** In the

---

[41] **EG**: Reading for "Taurus."

[42] *Apotelesmata.*

[43] Edited in *CCAG* VIII.1, pp. 267-69. **BD**: The editors of the *CCAG* (p. 267) suggest that this material comes ultimately from an Egyptian source, particularly because of the use of decans.

[44] **EG**: That is, the loss of fruits.

second 10° it indicates theft, rapine, and slaughter of men in battle. **9** In the third 10° it shows the death of the king, as well as anomalies.

10 The Sun being eclipsed in the first 10° of Cancer indicates upheavals and anomalies in the world. **11** In the second 10°, the exhaustion of rivers, a lack of rain, and lots of locusts. **12** In the third 10°, anarchy and ruin for Armenia and Africa.

13 The Sun eclipsed in the first 10° of Leo: the death of the king and the difficult purchase of corn. **14** In the second 10°, great grief for the king, and the destruction of great[45] people. **15** In the third 10°, war, captivity, and the siege of cities.

16 The Sun eclipsed in the first <10°> of Virgo indicates the destruction of great kings, that is, of the Babylonians. **17** In the second 10°, a plague among men: for example, hunger, and much anarchy. **18** In the third 10°, disgrace for writers and scholars, as well as the vexation of the king.

19 The Sun eclipsed in the first 10° of Libra: the corruption of the air, as well as much lingering hunger. **20** In the second 10°, the death of a great king, anarchy and hunger. **21** In the third 10°, quarrels and the clashing of important people, and the scattering of riches.

22 The Sun eclipsed in the first 10° of Scorpio: the bad condition of armies, wars against each other, maltreatments, and the slaughtering of men. **23** In the second 10°, the ruin of the king, and the resistance[46] of the army. **24** In the third 10°, the appearance of a tyrant and contempt for the king.

25 The Sun eclipsed in the first 10° of Sagittarius: much opposition will ensue, and there will be no agreement among them. **26** In the second 10° it indicates the death of camels and mules. **27** In the third 10°, the movement[47] of the king, disturbance, and hunger.

28-30 <*The Sun eclipsed in Capricorn missing.*>

31 The Sun eclipsed in the first 10° of Aquarius indicates grief and poverty. **32** In the second 10°, theft, rapine, earthquakes, and hunger. **33** In the third 10°, the death of sheep and many of the wild animals.

---

[45] *Megistanēs.* **EG:** This is meant in the sense of important people, not necessarily morally great.

[46] *Antitupia.*

[47] *Kinēsis.* **EG:** This is probably a changing of kings. **BD:** But it could also be the king moving around his territories, which was an important political action in antiquity. See Ch. 8, **14** below.

34 The Sun eclipsed in the first 10° of Pisces indicates the exhaustion of rivers and roughness of the seas. **35** In the second 10°, the death of an exalted man, and earthquake in maritime zones. **36** In the third 10°, the anarchy of the armies, much cruelty and the dislike of men.

Chapter 8: On the influence of the eclipses of the Moon[48]

1 The Moon eclipsed in the first 10° of Aries indicates that there will be burning heat, droughts in [certain] places, as well as dryness of the air. **2** In the second 10°, plague, sudden deaths, and the destruction of cattle. **3** In the third 10°, the attempted abortion of women.

4 The Moon eclipsed in the first 10° of Taurus indicates the destruction of wild beasts. **5** In the second 10° it means the death of a queen and the extermination of seeds. **6** In the third 10°, the death of serpents and the other reptiles.

7 The Moon eclipsed in the first 10° of Gemini indicates robbery and the attack of enemies. **8** In the second 10° it shows the sudden movement of the army, and devastation. **9** In the third 10°, the death of a great man and much controversy.

10 The Moon eclipsed in the first 10° of Cancer means that there will be war. **11** In the second 10°, much levying of tribute and payment.[49] **12** In the third 10°, acute illnesses in women, and those bound for death.[50]

13 The Moon eclipsed in the first 10° of Leo indicates the acute illness of the king or the death of an important ruler.[51] **14** In the second 10°, the moving of a king from one place to another. **15** In the third 10°, the movement of the army and military campaign of the Scythians.

16 The Moon eclipsed in the first 10° of Virgo shows the illness of the king, and much resistance among men. **17** In the second 10°, unpleasantness

---

[48] Edited in *CCAG* VIII.1, pp. 269-70. **BD:** The editors of the *CCAG* (p. 267) suggest that this material comes ultimately from an Egyptian source, particularly because of the use of decans.

[49] *Eksargurismos.* **EG:** More specifically, the conversion of payment-in-kind into a monetary payment.

[50] **BD/EG:** The opposition of "sharp (severe)" and "bound for death" illnesses sounds like the distinction between acute and chronic illnesses.

[51] *Probebēkotos.*

and the grief of the king's grammarians. **18** In the third 10°, pestilential plagues are predicted for men.

19 The Moon eclipsed in the first 10° of Libra indicates that there will be much hail. **20** In the second 10°, hoar-frost causing the destruction of vines and the rest of the trees. **21** In the third 10°, the death of a great man.

22 The Moon eclipsed in the first 10° of Scorpio is significant for thunder and hurricanes,[52] sometimes also earthquakes. **23** In the second 10°, the destruction of olive-trees, drought, and burning heat. **24** In the third 10°, madness, murmurs, and controversy.

25 The Moon eclipsed in the first 10° of Sagittarius shows theft and rapine. **26** In the second 10°, the death of mules and horses. **27** In the third 10° it indicates plague and illness among men.

28 The Moon eclipsed in the first 10° of Capricorn is indicative of much opposition and resistance in life, as well as the death or ruin of a great man. **29** In the second 10°, the attacks of armies, piracy, and captivity. **30** In the third 10° it means the death of a king as well as anarchy.

31 The Moon eclipsed in the first 10° of Aquarius shows that the king will need medical assistance. **32** In the second 10°, the scattering of the seeds of Demeter.[53] **33** In the third 10° it indicates release of former evils.

34 The Moon eclipsed in the first 10° of Pisces means the grief of the priests. **35** In the second 10°, the death of a great man. **36** In the third 10°, robbery and rapine, both on land and sea.

Chapter 9: On the influence of the five wandering stars and signs, [beginning with Saturn][54]

On Saturn:

1 Saturn transiting[55] Aries calls forth madness and adversities in life, as well as murmurs about rulers, and indicates the movement of the great king, or the change from one place to another. **2** When his transit takes him to the

---

[52] *Prēstērōn.* **EG**: Also, heavy rains attended by lightning and tornadoes.

[53] **EG**: That is, the loss of fruits.

[54] Edited from **A** f. 34r*ff*, **W** f. 34r*ff*, **Y** f. 138v*ff*.

[55] *Metabasin poioumenos*, where *metabainō* means "to pass or change from one place or state to another."

middle of the sign, he becomes significant of mild weather. **3** When in the northern parts, burning heat and destruction; in the southern parts, cold, with snowstorms and hoar-frost. **4** When he makes a phase[56] in the first decan of Aries,[57] he brings winds and thunder, as well as instability in life, the inaction[58] of evils and the strength of kings; in the second decan, mild weather; in the third decan, burning heat, pestilent sickness, and destruction. **5** In the heart [of the Sun], it means a disease of the king. **6** Making an occultation in the first decan, as regards affairs it shows completeness as well as idleness; in the second one, much irregularity, drought, and war; in the third decan, plague and famine. **7** Stationary in Aries, it means grief and distress; it also shows indifference and ungodliness. **8** Achronycal:[59] the grief of the king, and opposition from his subjects. **9** The increase and decrease in intensity of the influences will more clearly and accurately be known from the testimony of the other stars, and the figures described by the lights, as well as the house relationship of the lands and battles; also the sign itself and its triplicity.

10 Saturn transiting Taurus brings about weakness and illnesses in older men, irregularity in life, unprofitable agriculture, severe famine, and earthquakes in certain places, especially in cities that answer to the rulership of Taurus. **11** If his movement takes him to the middle of the sign, it brings about rains and cold weather. **12** If in the northern parts, it shows mildness in the weather; if in the southern parts, disturbances in the air, pestilence, and confusion. **13** When he makes a phase in the first decan, it shows mist-like airs and earthquakes in certain places, with disturbances and damage caused by the rulers, as well as the uprising of enemies; in the second decan, burning heat and lightning, thunderbolts and ruin by plagues; in the third decan it scatters the royal wealth. **14** <*In the heart missing.*> **15** When he makes an occultation in the first decan, it causes hurtful decisions from the king, as regards both actions and the confiscation of property; in the second decan, oppositions and irregularities, as well as the insurrection of enemies; in the third decan, rapine and robbery, and pestilent diseases; it also indicates early rains and deluges in some places. **16** Stationary, it means the

---

[56] See Ch. 10, **4**: this phase is his morning appearance, eastern of the Sun.

[57] **EG: A** reads "Capricorn," here and in **6**.

[58] **EG**: Reading with **W** (omitted in **Y** and **A**). *Apragia* means there is a lack of energy in the evil.

[59] That is, rising in the east at sunset.

unpleasantness of the king, and the death of an important man; also the diminishing of the public contributions, as well as the opposition of all the army.[60] **17** <*Achronycal missing.*>

18 Saturn transiting Gemini causes the sluggishness and idleness of matters concerning livelihood, the lack of skill of the army, and military campaigns on mountains; also, sudden impacts and reports of portentous rainstorms. **19** If his movement takes him to the middle of the sign, it causes mild weather. **20** If in the northern parts, it brings about earthquakes in certain places, as well as the unleashing of violent winds; if in the southern parts, it causes burning heat and droughts; also a scarcity of fruits. **21** When he makes a phase in the first decan it indicates the inauguration of some laws, rites, and venerable places; in the second decan, the distress of the scribes of the king; in the third decan it means the renewal of ancient documents. **22** In the heart of the Sun,[61] it indicates the business of authenticating by seal the public tributes. **23** Making an occultation in the first decan, it means the disease of the king; in the second decan, the vexation of priests and sacred places; in the third decan, it means the death of the king, or exile. **24** Stationary, it shows the scattering of the royal treasures. **25** <Achronycal>, it indicates the illness and indisposition of the king.

26 Saturn transiting the sign of Cancer brings on diseases among men, especially among those more advanced [in age], and irregularities in livelihood. **27** When his movement takes him to the middle of the sign, it indicates mildness of weather. **28** In the southern and northern parts, drought. **29** When he makes a phase in the first decan, [it indicates the] strength and might of the king; in the second decan it means death of an important ruler; in the third decan it indicates great irregularities in life. **30** In the heart of the Sun it shows the disease of the king and much oppression. **31** When he makes an occultation in the first decan, profits for farmers; in the second decan, it brings about diseases of the eyes and rheum; in the third, it shows the death of women. **32** Stationary, it means the death of an important man. **33** Achronycal, it indicates rainstorms and the overflowing of rivers.

34 Saturn transiting the sign of Leo means plagues and suffocation. **35** If his movement takes him to the middle of the sign, it shows mild weather. **36**

---

[60] **EG**: The MSS omit mention of his achronycal rising.

[61] **EG**: **A** reads, "in trigon."

If in its northern parts, changes in affairs and irregularities; in its southern parts, it is indicative of humidity, heavy rains, and many snowstorms. **37** When he makes a phase in the first decan it is not utterly oppressive, for it becomes significant of prosperity and fertility; in the second decan it brings about diseases and sicknesses among men, especially for kings and rulers; in the third decan it shows unpleasantness in life, want of affection, and opposition. **38** When he is in the heart [of the Sun] it strengthens the king, and it means that he will prevail over those who oppose him. **39** When he makes an occultation in the first decan, [he is]^{62} intelligent as regards livelihood; in the second, disease and the sickness of royal women; in the third decan it shows symptoms of tertian fever. **40** Stationary, it means death and destruction by quadrupeds. **41** Achronycal, it indicates the inundation of rivers.

42 Saturn transiting the sign of Virgo means destruction and plagues for men; it instills oppositions and damages, and it causes loss to prominent men. **43** And when his movement takes him to the middle of the sign, it indicates rainstorms. **44** If in the northern or southern parts, mild weather. **45** Making a phase in the first decan means danger for the king; in the second decan, the death of superior women; in the third, the inspection of scribes, and resistance. **46** Having come into the heart of the Sun, it means profit for priests and consecrated ones. **47** Making an occultation in the first decan, it indicates the illness of the king; in the second, rheum and eye disease; in the third, it means a lack of rains. **48** Going stationary it gives hate and enemies between rulers and the ruled. **49** Achronycal, it means the overflowing of rivers, heavy rains with thunder and lightning.

50 Saturn transiting the sign of Libra is significative of mildness, especially when his movement takes him to the middle of the sign—aside from the fact that it is harmful for women, or leads to dangers originating from a woman; it also causes sickness by moisture. **51** If he passes through the northern parts, it causes movement of violent blasts; if in the southern parts, it means plagues among men. **52** When he makes a phase in the first decan it makes slaves prevail upon rulers; in the second it shows a variation of affairs; in the third it means rapine and captivity. **53** <*In the heart missing.*> **54** Making an occultation in the first decan, it indicates dryness of the air and lack of rains; in the second it brings about the driest cold without rains; <*third decan missing.*> **55** Stationary, it means a lingering illness from inflammation of the

---

^{62} **BD:** I take this to mean the king.

brain, or other attacks, and other similar anomalies. **56** Achronycal, it brings corruption and acute illnesses.

57 Saturn transiting the sign of Scorpio brings serious and dangerous diseases upon men, especially from enemies; it also means freezing and snowy winters. **58** When he passes through the middle of the sign it shows mild weather. **59** In the northern parts, burning heats and choking;[63] in the southern parts, much rain and humidity. **60** When he makes a phase in the first decan of Scorpio it dulls the matters concerning livelihood; in the second decan it causes the scattering of the royal wealth; in the third decan it means earthquakes and the death of the king. **61** When he moves into the heart of the Sun, it indicates sicknesses. **62** Making an occultation in the first decan, it means a neglect of duty by the army; in the second decan, the disease of the king; in the third it indicates the death of a queen. **63** Going stationary it means controversy and many murmurs from the public, with anger, sharpness, hindrances, difficulties, and ineffectiveness in activities; sicknesses follow as well. **64** If achronycal, [it is] utterly difficult, for it stirs up various crises and oppositions against the king.

65 Saturn transiting the sign of Sagittarius is significant of moisture, and it turns harmful for rulers: it causes their destruction. **66** When his movement takes him to the middle of the sign [it means] mildness, though not exempt from fate.[64] **67** In the northern parts it puts winds in motion; in the southern parts it is changeable and not steadfast in any matter. **68** When he makes a phase in the first decan, it gives way to the power to decide on great matters; in the second it means that there will be a levying of tribute for activities; in the third, the building of ships and the establishment of sacred places. **69** Moving to the heart of the Sun, grief and the subjugation of the king. **70** Making an occultation in the first decan, combined misfortunes and distress in life; in the second it shows sluggishness and hindrances to activities; in the third, the rejection and contempt of superior men. **71** Stationary, it means that there will be severe famine. **72** Achronycal, it shows feverish conditions.

73 Saturn transiting the sign of Capricorn is significant of destruction, for it causes a difficult change of affairs and plagues in many places. **74** When his movement takes him to the middle of the sign, it shows the weather to be untempered and irregular. **75** In the southern or northern parts, it is signifi-

---

[63] **EG:** This can also indicate stifling heat.
[64] *Amoiros.*

cant of snowstorms, hoar-frost, freezing cold, and moisture. **76** When he makes a phase in the first decan it is not completely oppressive; in the second decan it indicates the death of the king, as well as plague and ruin; in the third, affliction, grief, and captivity in life. **77** When he comes into the heart of the Sun it causes the departure of those within the king's precincts. **78** Making an occultation in the first decan, it brings about an uprising of enemies and much disturbance; in the second decan it becomes harmful for cattle; in the third it means that there will be storms at sea. **79** Stationary, it indicates upheavals and the loss of possessions, as well as much opposition in life. **80** Achronycal, it causes the death of women.

81 Saturn transiting the sign of Aquarius shows mild weather, but it is harmful for matters undertaken. **82** Passing through the middle of the sign, it becomes the cause of much humidity and heavy rains. **83** In the northern parts it shows destruction of fruits; in the southern parts, disproportionate snowstorms and a mass of clouds. **84** When he makes a phase in the first decan, it brings corruption and much harm upon men; in the second it renders indispensable affairs very slow; in the third, the death of superior women. **85** In the heart of the Sun it causes a lack of farming activity. **86** Making an occultation in the first decan, it will make the evil things more manifest; in the second decan it shows the death of older people. **87** Stationary, it indicates the disease of the king. **88** Achronycal, it brings a sad plight on the king.

89 Saturn transiting the sign of Pisces is temperate at the beginning, but it also produces slander against prominent people and harm to the rulers. **90** When his transit takes him to the middle of the sign it indicates that there will be much moisture and heavy rains. **91** In the northern parts it stirs up blasts of wind; in the southern parts it causes the sudden rush of a massive amount of waters and the overflowing of rivers. **92** When he makes a phase in the first decan it is significant of snowstorms, hoar-frost, and freezing cold; in the second decan it produces a commixture of airs; in the third, an insurrection of enemies and resistance. **93** When he moves to the heart of the Sun, it becomes harmful for authorities. **94** Making an occultation in the first decan, it means rheum and catarrh; in the second decan, the grief of the great king; in the third decan, the movement of enemies and great slaughter. **95** Stationary, it indicates death of an important man. **96** Achronycal, it is significant of a severe want of rains, dry weather, and droughts.

Chapter 10: On Jupiter [in the signs][65]

1 Jupiter transiting the sign of Aries drives away all annoyance and crisis, and produces deliverance from past evils. 2 Passing through the middle of the sign, it is significant of mild weather and good health. 3 In the northern parts it causes much burning heat; in the southern it shows the coldest weather. 4 Making a phase as an eastern star in the first decan of Aries, it unleashes violent thunder and winds; it also causes good fortune and merriment for the army, with good hopes; in the second it means the strengthening and good health of the king, as well as prosperity, healthiness and dejection of enemies; in the third, the progress of well-reputed men, and being well pleasing to the king and to each other. 5 When he comes to be in the heart of the Sun, it indicates prosperous travelling abroad by the king. 6 Making an occultation in the first decan, it protects the highly-valued elders of the senate or council, namely those thought to be worthy of honor, through the esteem and good opinion of the king; in the second decan it puts much joy and distinction into the relatives of the king; in the third it shows the humidity of the weather and an abundance of rain. 7 Stationary, it is harmful and prejudicial. 8 Achronycal, it indicates late-autumn moisture.

9 Jupiter transiting the sign of Taurus accomplishes successfully what concerns religious worship, causing agreement among men as well. 10 Passing through the middle of the sign it means much humidity and cold. 11 In the northern parts, mild weather; in the southern, instability and the irregularity of the weather. 12 Making a phase in the first decan, it indicates periodic winds[66] and good health; in the second, much water in the air within the borders [of the land], and beyond them; in the third it is productive of lightning and thunder. 13 When in the heart of the Sun, joy, healthiness and the prosperity of the king, as well as the fall of his enemies. 14 Making an occultation in the first decan, it shows a sudden outburst of diseases related to water; in the second, the death of the king or a prominent woman; in the third, the death of a superior[67] or important man. 15 Stationary, it prepares plots against the king. 16 Achronycal, it means rains.

---

[65] A continuation of Ch. 9, from **W** f. 34r*ff* and **Y** f. 138v*ff*.

[66] *Ethsiai anemos*. **EG**: Especially those blowing from the north-west during the summer.

[67] *Probebēkotos*. **EG**: Also, a man who has advanced or moved ahead: perhaps a man who has worked his way to a top position?

17 Jupiter transiting the sign of Gemini is significant of healthiness and strength. **18** Moving through the middle of the sign, it shows the winter to be charged with moisture and waters. **19** In[68] the northern parts it becomes cause of winds; in the southern parts, it produces a dry summer and burning heat. **20** Making a phase in the first decan of Gemini means that the king outweighs the enemies; in the second, a good and useful military campaign; in the third, strength, prosperity, and the healthiness of the king. **21** When he gets to be in the heart of the Sun, it means that the king is free from pain or grief. **22** Making an occultation in the first decan indicates sluggishness and a lack of activity; in the second, the cessation of hostilities for the army; in the third, the grief of the king. **23** Going stationary means sedition and the opposition of the army. **24** Going achronycal, rainstorms and a cold winter.

25 Jupiter transiting the sign of Cancer instills false hopes[69] in men and the king. **26** In the middle of the sign it gives much temperateness. **27** In the northern parts it is hot and burning; in the southern parts equally hot. **28** Making a phase in the first decan, it disturbs the king; in the second it fosters the agreement of citizens[70] and goodwill before judges; in the third it means temperate summers and blasts of periodic winds. **29** Coming to the heart of the Sun, it indicates a change of affairs and the laying of foundations. **30** Making an occultation in the first decan, it shows the movement of the king and changing from one place to another; in the second, the loss of royal properties; in the third it disturbs the citizens and instills opposition and rumors. **31** Stationary, it means the death of a prominent man, and the grief of the king. **32** Achronycal, it indicates rainstorms with icy cold.

33 Jupiter transiting the sign of Leo sows some vain imagining in the mind of the king; also anguish, ingratitude, and grief. **34** When he passes through the middle of the sign it means much burning heat. **35** In the northern parts, it shows the movement of winds; in the southern parts, humidity in the air. **36** When he makes a phase in the first decan, it shows the removal and replacement of the king; in the second, the glory and magnificence of the king; in the third, irregularity in life and travel abroad by the king. **37** Coming to the heart of the Sun, it becomes a cause of transition and change.

---

[68] **EG:** Reading with **Y. W** reads: "When in the northern parts, mild weather; in the southern, instability and irregularity in the weather." I find this somewhat suspicious, as Jupiter passing through the northern and southern parts of Taurus has the same meaning.

[69] *Meteōrismos.* **EG:** Or, "mental trouble, wild thinking." See also **49**.

[70] **Y** omits.

38 When he makes an occultation in the first decan it indicates the grief of the king; in the second decan it shows the king needing medical attention; in the third it means the death of a prominent man. **39** Stationary, it shows that the great king is in foreign service, or wandering about. **40** Achronycal, it indicates favorable rainy weather, as well as a mild and auspicious winter.

41 Jupiter transiting the sign of Virgo means mild weather and an early winter. **42** When he has his transit in the middle of the sign it gives signs of peace and agreement among men. **43** Similarly, in the northern parts it causes temperateness; in the southern, rainy weather, both moderate and useful. **44** Making a phase in the first decan, it gives signs of a dry autumn, without moisture; in the second, goodwill and the prosperity of the king; in the third decan, a fitting and honored time for the keeper of archives and scribes, for it indicates profits and prosperity for them. **45** Coming to the heart of the Sun, it means good news and joy for men. **46** Making an occultation in the first decan, unnatural lust[71] and the weakness of the king; in the second, the grief and distress of the public; in the third decan, negligence[72] and the meanness of spirit of the merchants. **47** Going stationary, it means the diminishing of the good. **48** Achronycal, it decreases the rains.

49 Jupiter transiting the sign of Libra instills false hopes and disturbances within the souls of men. **50** Moving through the middle of the sign means mild weather. **51** In the northern parts it brings periodic and helpful breezes; in the southern, it becomes an aider of[73] plague and disease. **52** Making a phase in the first decan, it means increase and the growth of the good; in the second, that there will be heavy rains; in the third, temperateness and healthiness. **53** When he comes to be in the heart of the Sun it shows the marriage of a royal woman. **54** Making an occultation in the first decan, it shows the weather to be without moisture or rains; in the second, cold and very dry weather; in the third it shows that the king will be sick. **55** Stationary, it indicates the marriage of someone royal or of a queen. **56** Achronycal, it brings disease of the eyes and rheum upon men.

57 Jupiter transiting the sign of Scorpio drives away all harm and crisis from men. **58** Coming to the middle of the sign, it indicates a mild and pro-

---

[71] *Malakia.* **EG:** This usually means homosexuality.

[72] *Oligōria.* **EG:** Also, "contempt."

[73] *Aossētēr.* **W:** *Asitia*, "want of food."

ductive winter. **59** In the northern parts, warmth and burning heat; in the southern it means weather without moisture. **60** Making a phase in the first decan, it indicates a change of the army from one place to another; in the second, the strength and healthiness of the king; in the third, a temperate and productive winter. **61** In the heart of the Sun, gratifying good news. **62** Making an occultation in the first decan, it means the truce of the army; in the second, the sickness of the king; in the third, the death of a queen. **63** Stationary, it indicates hindrances because of rainy weather, as well as periodic winds. **64** Achronycal, it brings vexation to rulers.

65 Jupiter transiting the sign of Sagittarius becomes a cause of periodic blasts of wind, and it indicates mild weather as well. **66** When he moves to the middle of the sign, it means that there will be plenty of water throughout the whole winter. **67** In the northern parts it unleashes violent blasts of wind; in the southern, a transition from one good condition to another good condition. **68** Making a phase in the first decan, it shows the quick action of merchants, and the propitious hopes of farmers, with joys; in the second decan, the propitious hopes of farmers, with joys; in the third, the goodwill of the king out of great pain, as well as changing from one place to another. **69** In the heart of the Sun, it means the announcement of good news to the king. **70** Making an occultation in the first decan, it disturbs and troubles the king; in the second it instills grief in the rulers; in the third, the death of a prominent man. **71** Stationary, rainstorms and the king's wrath. **72** Achronycal, a sudden outburst of eye diseases.

73 Jupiter transiting the sign of Capricorn means the ill-will[74] of the king against rulers. **74** When transiting the middle of the sign, a mild winter. **75** In the northern parts, much humidity; in the southern, equally humidity as well as destruction. **76** Making a phase in the first decan, it dissipates the royal wealth; in the second it shows a military campaign during the winter, and beneficial rains alike; in the third, the vigor and good health of the great king. **77** Coming to the heart of the Sun, it profits the king. **78** Making an occultation in the first decan, it shows mob rule; in the second, murmurs and much opposition, also murmuring within the army; in the third it means that the king will be sick. **79** Stationary, it despoils the king, and agitates the mob. **80** Achronycal, it means a suffering of the eyes.

81 Jupiter transiting the sign of Aquarius means mild and moist weather. **82** When moving through the middle of the sign, much humidity. **83** In the

---

[74] **Y**: *krotos* ("rattling noise").

northern parts, proportionate dryness; in the southern, much cloud-like darkness. **84** Making a phase in the first decan, it causes the subversion of old matters in life, as well as a remembering of matters that had been forgotten; in the second decan it helps the appointed royal scribes; in the third, honor and good repute of the royal Council of Elders. **85** When he comes to the heart of the Sun, it exposes hidden matters to the king. **86** Making an occultation in the first decan, it means the disease of the queen; in the second, the death of a prominent man; in the third, it diminishes the rains. **87** When stationary, the serious illness of the king. **88** Becoming achronycal, it means stillness in the weather.

89 Jupiter transiting the sign of Pisces means, as a whole, mild weather. **90** When transiting the middle of the sign, much moisture. **91** In the northern parts it brings periodical breezes; in the southern, the fullness of water and flood-tides. **92** Making a phase in the first decan, it means that the king travels abroad; in the second it grants good repute and honor to the rulers; in the third it strengthens and gives might to the army, and fosters agreement. **93** In the heart of the Sun, it means joy and goodwill for the king. **94** Making an occultation in the first decan, it means hoar-frost and cold; in the second it causes the king to be slightly unstable; in the third, it unsettles those in high command of the legions. **95** Stationary, it is harmful and ineffective in everything. **96** When achronycal, dry and without rains.

Chapter 11: On Mars [in the signs][75]

1 Mars transiting the sign of Aries causes the completion of affairs and quick activity, and is prone to change. **2** When he passes through the middle of the sign it shows dryness in the air. **3** In the northern parts, burning heat and destruction; in the southern parts it gives a winter combined with warmer temperatures. **4** When he makes a phase in the first decan it brings thunderbolts, waterspouts attended with lightning, with thunder; in the second decan, the king gets ill; in the third it means the cessation of hostilities of the army. **5** In the heart of the Sun it brings burning heat. **6** When he makes an occultation in the first decan, it indicates the wasting of the royal treasure; in the second it means the truce of the army; in the third, the at-

---

[75] A continuation of Ch. 9, from **W** f. 34r*ff* and **Y** f. 138v*ff*.

tempted abortion of pregnant women. **7** Stationary, it means torpor and exhaustion, as well as harm and crisis in life. **8** Achronycal, grief, distress, and the disturbance of the mob.

9 Mars transiting the sign of Taurus is not favorable for married women. **10** When coming to the middle of the sign it puts earthquakes in motion, and it also means irregularity of the weather. **11** In the northern parts it is significant of pestilent illnesses; in the southern, instability and the anomaly of the weather. **12** Making a phase in the first decan, it is profitable for naught;[76] in the second it shows destruction and the failure of the seeds of fruits; in the third it means the death of women. **13** When he is in the heart of the Sun it foretells the death of a queen. **14** Making an occultation in the first decan, it brings diseases upon women; in the second, the attempted abortion of pregnant women; in the third, the extermination of grape-vines and olive-trees. **15** Stationary, it indicates the slaughter of cattle. **16** Achronycal, it causes serious droughts and a lack of rains.

17 Mars transiting the sign of Gemini brings pain and harm upon men, particularly traders and scribes; it also shows the deterioration of the air. **18** Having his transit through the middle of the sign, it prevents all temperateness. **19** In the northern parts it means earthquakes; in the southern, burning heat and dryness. **20** Making a phase in the first decan, it means trouble-making in military campaigns; in the second it hurls sicknesses upon men; in the third it shows the unnatural lust of the king. **21** Coming to the heart of the Sun, it means strength and the good health of the king. **22** Making an occultation in the first decan, it means the death of a powerful man; in the second, burnings in some places; in the third, the disease of the queen. **23** Stationary, it brings an outburst of pestilent illnesses. **24** Achronycal, it shows that there will be an intense activity in public businesses.

25 Mars transiting the sign of Cancer brings the opposition of the leaders of the army, and mischief; it also means a cessation of hostilities, and use-lessness and the bad temperament of the air. **26** Passing through the middle of the sign, it is less temperate. **27** In the northern parts, it produces burning heat and droughts; in the southern [it is] similar to the northern parts. **28** Making a phase in the first decan, it means earthquake; in the second it shows the king being under the sway of a powerful man; in the third it means the subjection and good will of the subordinate commanders of the royal army. **29** In the heart of the Sun, it strengthens the royal army. **30** Making an

---

[76] This clause omitted in **W**.

occultation in the first decan, it brings sicknesses upon women; in the second, it causes damage and destruction by burning; in the third, the attempted abortion of pregnant women. **31** Stationary, it shows the death of a distinguished man. **32** Achronycal, it is productive of droughts and drying up, with much nausea.

33 Mars transiting the sign of Leo is less temperate. **34** <*Middle of Leo missing.*> **35** In the northern parts it is productive of burning blasts of wind; in the southern it is less humid. **36** Making a phase in the first decan, it indicates that the king travels abroad; in the second it shows the scattering of the royal wealth; in the third it shows hasty military campaigns, and fosters piracy and robbery. **37** When coming into the heart of the Sun, it makes the king full of cares. **38** Making an occultation in the first decan, it causes contempt, negligence, and the irregularities of the king; in the second it causes burning heat; in the third, some hopelessness in certain affairs, and it also shows that enemies stay within the boundaries. **39** Stationary, it makes envy fall upon the king. **40** Achronycal, it indicates a lack of rains.

41 Mars transiting the sign of Virgo means the deterioration of the air and dryness. **42** When he passes through the middle of the sign it indicates destruction and much aridness. **43** In the northern parts it causes a slight deterioration of the waters; in the southern it does not allow any temperateness. **44** Making a phase in the first decan, it shows quick activities, good order, and tact in the royal affairs; in the second it introduces unforeseen military campaigns; in the third it means the intense activities of business representatives. **45** When it comes to be in the heart of the Sun, good tidings will be brought to the king. **46** Making an occultation in the first decan, it annoys the activities of the scribes; in the second it shows the abortion of a woman;[77] in the third, affliction for farmers. **47** Stationary, it renders the king effeminate. **48** Achronycal, it means the death of the king.

49 Mars transiting Libra shows a neglected opportunity. **50** In the middle of the sign it is not intemperate and unmixed. **51** In the northern parts it stirs winds; in the southern, it is destructive. **52** Making a phase in the first decan, it promotes useful unions and coming together for [the purpose of] livelihood;[78] in the second it grants good repute and honor for the elders of the royal council or senate; in the third, the death of a prominent and royal per-

---

[77] **BD**: This should be understood as "women."

[78] *Sustasis biō.* **EG**: This could also mean coming together (as in friendship) for a lifetime.

son. **53** Coming to be in the heart of the Sun, it causes grief to the king. **54** Making an occultation in the first decan, it shows an autumn dry and with no moisture; in the second it brings diseases upon the elders; in the third it means the cessation of hostilities of the army. **55** Stationary, it brings unforeseen danger from a powerful man. **56** Achronycal, it increases rainfalls with thunder.

57 Mars transiting Scorpio dries up the air. **58** Moving to the middle of the sign, it is less temperate. **59** In the northern parts, arid and dry; in the southern, it turns mild. **60** Making a phase in the first decan, it produces thunder and hurricanes; in the second it causes the vexation of the king; in the third it brings about a change of affairs. **61** In the heart of the Sun, it makes a disease fall upon the king. **62** Making an occultation in the first decan, it means the truce of the army; in the second it causes diseases of the eyes; in the third it is productive of attempted abortion in women and ruin. **63** Stationary, it means a dangerous disease for the king. **64** Achronycal, it causes lack of rains.

65 Mars transiting Sagittarius shows mild weather. **66** Transiting though the middle of the sign, it shows the same things. **67** In the northern parts it is cause of dry winds without any moisture; in the southern, it indicates the change of certain affairs. **68** Making a phase in the first decan, the departure and marching abroad of the army; in the second it becomes a cause of misfortune; in the third, as was said before. **69** In the heart of the Sun, it is unprofitable for the king. **70** Making an occultation in the first decan, it causes oppositions; in the second it means the abortion of pregnant women; in the third, the vexation by the king against the commanders. **71** Stationary, it indicates difficult things for the army, and causes disagreement.[79] **72** Achronycal,[80] it causes much burning heat.

73 Mars[81] transiting Capricorn means dry weather. **74** In the middle of the sign, it indicates mild weather. **75** In the northern and southern parts, it means destruction. **76** Making a phase in the first decan, sickness of the king; in the second, droughts and lack of rains; in the third, strength and thriving conditions for the king. **77** In the heart of the Sun, it causes much dryness. **78** Making an occultation in the first decan, it shows the death of a promi-

---

[79] **Y** now contains the following two sentences: "In the third, it means that there will be rains. Stationary, it means much irregularity and idleness."
[80] **EG**: This sentence only in **W**.
[81] **EG**: Text for Mars in Capricorn only found in **W**.

nent man; in the second it produces grief and the opposition of the army; in the third it means that there will be much humidity. **79** Stationary, it indicates much irregularity and idleness. **80** <*Achronycal missing.*>

81 Mars transiting Aquarius is not less mild. **82** Moving through the middle of the sign causes rains. **83** In the northern parts, it is productive of dryness; in the southern it leads to barren and sterile unions. **84** Making a phase in the first decan, the death of a prominent man; in the second, the intense activity of traders and[82] fair weather for sailors; in the third it unleashes furious winds which cause damage for men. **85** When he gets into the heart of the Sun, it works favorably for the king, and aids him. **86** Making an occultation in the first decan, it is harmful for pregnant women; in the second it causes wreckage to ships; in the third it means the death of a queen. **87** Stationary, it indicates that there will be revolts in certain places. **88** Achronycal, it shows burning heat.

89 Mars transiting Pisces is temperate. **90** In the middle of the sign, moisture, not free from evil. **91** In the northern parts it unleashes winds; in the southern, it indicates rainstorms. **92** Making a phase in the first decan, it is indicative of fair weather; in the second it brings enemies and discord against the people; in the third it means a lack of rain. **93** In the heart of the Sun,[83] it indicates weakness and disease for the king. **94** Making an occultation in the first decan, it causes hoar-frost; in the second, the abortion of pregnant women; in the third, much sluggishness and the cowardice of the army. **95** Stationary, it brings grief pertaining to life conditions, and causes the king to move and change; it also foretells failure of expected things. **96** <*Achronycal missing.*>

Chapter 12: On Venus [in the signs][84]

1 Venus coming to the leading parts of Aries means rain and periodic blasts of wind; towards the middle, it shows the weather to be mild; towards the following parts, dry. **2** In the northern parts, it is warm; towards the

---

[82] **EG:** This clause about sailors is only in **W**.

[83] **EG:** Reading with **W**; the other MSS read, "in the third."

[84] A continuation of Ch. 9, from **W** f. 34r*ff*, **Y** f. 149v*ff*, and **A** f. 23*ff*.

southern, it forecasts hail[85] storms and icy cold. **3** Making an evening phase brings the irregularity of the weather; [making an] evening occultation, unfortunate movements; being at a distance from the Sun, the movements of the army. **4** Making a morning phase means the strength of the army; [making a] morning occultation instills disagreements and causes murmurs; elongated from the Sun means the death of a prominent man. **5** Making a station, it causes thunder and hail.

6 Venus passing through the leading parts of Taurus produces periodic winds, darkness, and a clouded sky; towards the middle, it indicates much rain; towards the following parts, dryness (but if it rains, then it rains heavily, with rays and lightning). **7** In the northern parts it brings about temperate weather; towards the southern parts, the instability of the weather. **8** Making an evening phase is propitious for everything; in an evening occultation it causes the emigration to a foreign land of a prominent man of the sciences; being separated from the Sun means the death of a queen. **9** Making a morning phase, it hints that there will be cheerfulness and prosperity among powerful men; a morning occultation, it introduces grief in the king, and means much trouble; **10** Stationary,[86] it shows instability and anomaly.

11 Venus towards the leading parts of Gemini shows the air to become humid and destructive; towards the middle, it is temperate; in the following parts, anomalous. **12** In the northern parts it unleashes winds; in the southern, it dries up. **13** Making an evening phase is favorable for every activity and progress, especially for traders; making an evening occultation gives rest from work,[87] relaxation, and recreation; being at the farthest separation from the Sun gives censure and blemish to the royal secretaries and scribes. **14** Making a morning phase shows a suitable summer; in a morning occultation it instills mental trouble and grief in men; having her greatest separation from the Sun means the ruin of great scholars and secretaries. **15** Stationary, it renders the weather hot and dry.

16 Venus moving through the leading parts of Cancer shows the air to be cold and works the ruin of flute-players and singers; towards the middle, temperate; in the following parts it produces fresh, pure, and healthy breezes. **17** In the northern, burning heat; in the southern, much warming. **18** Making an evening phase supplies health to men; in an evening occultation

---

[85] **Y**: "sea" (*thalassa*).

[86] **EG**: **W** understands this as being the greatest elongation.

[87] *Ekecheiria*. **EG**: But this can also mean "a cessation of hostilities, armistice, truce."

it causes blame on those in office;[88] having separated herself from the Sun means the death of the king, or of an important man. **19** Making a morning phase shows the safeguarding of riches, and good fortune in life; making a morning occultation introduces grief and distress among rulers; being separated from the Sun indicates the settled and quiet condition of the armies. **20** Stationary it shows death of a queen.

21 Venus transiting the leading parts of Leo makes the air suffocating and very still, plagued with pestilent diseases; towards the middle, fair weather; in the following parts, the deterioration of the air. **22** Toward the northern parts it stirs up fiery air, though in the southern it is temperate. **23** Making an evening phase is indicative of much sullenness and irregularities among men; making an evening occultation indicates the death of a queen; making the greatest separation from the Sun instills grief in the king. **24** Making a morning phase prepares censure for the king within the household, but it also benefits farmers and colonists; making a morning occultation means sluggishness; being separated at the greatest from the Sun means the banishment or death of the king. **25** When stationary, it prepares much grief, meanness of spirit.

26 Venus passing through the leading parts of Virgo heats and dries up; towards the middle parts, it is temperate and healthy; in the following parts, it renders the air cold.[89] **27** In[90] both the northern and southern parts, it is mild and healthy. **28** Making an evening phase shows mildness in late autumn; making an occultation indicates an unhealthy late autumn; making a separation from the Sun produces sicknesses. **29** Making a morning phase brings good tidings from afar; making an occultation means that there will be diseases of the eyes; separated from the Sun foretells the death of a prominent man. **30** Stationary, it brings sicknesses upon women.

31 Venus transiting the leading parts of Libra produces temperateness; towards the middle, it causes strength with temperateness; towards the following parts, cold and rainstorms. **32** In the northern parts, dry breezes; in the southern, it brings pestilent illnesses. **33** Making an evening phase causes men to pursue their private interests; making an occultation instills irritation

---

[88] *In telei.* **EG**: That is, in power, or with authority; but it could also mean, "in the end" or "in age."

[89] **EG**: This last clause only in **W**.

[90] **EG**: This sentence only in **W**.

and provocation; when making the longest separation from the Sun, the death of a queen. **34** Making a morning phase introduces fellow-feeling and sympathy among men; making an occultation causes women to be sick; making her longest separation instills rumors and disagreement among men. **35** Stationary, it blunts fresh gains from men, and shows the death of a queen.

36 Venus transiting the leading parts of Scorpio means icy cold and frost; towards the middle, mild weather; towards the following parts it unleashes winds. **37** In the northern parts it causes dryness; in the southern, darkness. **38** Making an evening phase means anomalies; an evening occultation, dangerous misfortune; separating from the Sun shows the death of a commander or chief of the army. **39** When she makes a morning phase indicates the movement of the army; having an occultation makes the reasoning power and arguments of the rulers uncertain; having her greatest separation from the Sun shows the shedding of blood. **40** Stationary, it awakens opposition.

41 Venus moving through the leading parts of Sagittarius indicates much humidity in the air; towards the middle parts, mildness; in the following parts, dryness. **42** Towards the northern parts, it forecasts violent blasts of wind; in the southern, much moisture and changing of the air. **43** Making an evening phase causes opposition; having her occultation means the death of an important man; making her greatest separation from the Sun hurls sicknesses upon the king. **44** Making a morning phase means the scattering of the royal wealth, by those who appeared to help; <*morning occultation missing*>; having her longest elongation from the Sun shows the death of the king. **45** Stationary, it means the destruction of rulers.

46 Venus passing through the leading parts of Capricorn shows destruction; towards the middle parts, it indicates mildness; in the following parts, much rain. **47** Towards the northern parts it stirs up favorable winds, and grants help;[91] in the southern, cloudy. **48** Making an evening phase means sadness and melancholy; having an occultation brings disease to the royal women; having her greatest separation causes the death of aged rulers. **49** Making a morning phase shows laziness and a lack of cleanliness; making an occultation means a disease of elders; having her greatest separation from

---

[91] **EG:** This last clause not in **W**. **Y** now adds a redundant reading about the northern parts indicating dryness.

the Sun introduces servile persons. **50** Stationary,[92] it shows confusion and anarchy.

51 Venus transiting the leading parts of Aquarius gives mild weather; towards the middle parts, it is moist and mist-like; towards the following parts it is a dispenser of favorable and beneficial winds. **52** Towards the northern parts it is dry; in the southern, cloudy. **53** Making an evening phase profits farmers; having her occultation means still weather and calmness at sea; making her greatest separation from the Sun causes shipwreck at sea. **54** Making a morning phase brings health and strength to men; having her occultation causes winter storms; making her greatest separation from the Sun causes flood-tides of lakes and rivers. **55** Stationary, it causes an outbreak of diseases from waters among men.

56 Venus transiting the leading parts of Pisces is mild; towards the middle, humid; in the following parts, warm. **57** Towards the northern parts it is windy; towards the southern, moist. **58** Making an evening phase causes the king irritation and censure; making an occultation means illness; having her greatest separation from the Sun indicates the death of a powerful man. **59** Making a morning phase harms the rulers; occultation shows that there will be despair regarding expected things; having her greatest separation shows the destruction of the army. **60** Stationary, it means rumors, disagreement, and fear.

Chapter 13: On Mercury [in the signs][93]

1 Mercury coming to the leading parts of Aries is a cause of dry winds; towards the middle it is less mild; in the following parts, burning hot. **2** In the northern parts it becomes destructive; in the southern, temperate. **3** Making an evening phase causes grief to the army; in occultation it is pestilent; having his greatest separation from the Sun indicates war, and at the same time it makes the king submissive to the subordinate commanders. **4** Making a morning phase procures glory and brightness to the people and army; making an occultation, it is changeable; having his greatest separation

---

[92] **EG:** Reading with **W**. For **48-50**, **A** and **Y** read the same as **53-55**.
[93] A continuation of Ch. 9, from **W** f. 34r*ff*, **Y** f. 149v*ff*, and **A** f. 23*ff*.

from the Sun indicates the death of a prominent man. **5** Stationary, it becomes harmful, for it brings plagues and disease.

6 Mercury coming to the leading parts of Taurus mobilizes winds; towards the middle it is temperate; in the following parts, burning hot. **7** Towards the northern parts it is less mild; towards the southern, uncivilized and disorderly. **8** Making an evening phase becomes favorable and healthy; making an occultation causes harm and sickness to cattle; having his greatest separation instills illnesses in the king. **9** Making a morning phase, it is most active and yielding, and it means all types of good things, especially for farmers; making an occultation means the disease of women; having his greatest separation from the Sun indicates the death of cows. **10** Stationary, it brings anomalies to the weather.

11 Mercury transiting the leading parts of Gemini is temperate; in the middle, less temperate; towards the following parts, anomalous and disorderly. **12** Towards the northern parts it is a cause of winds and heat; in the southern, with a tendency to dry up. **13** Making an evening phase brings diseases upon men, as well as feverish conditions; making an occultation is less harmful; having his greatest separation indicates the death of scholars and secretaries. **14** Making a morning phase means the strength and health of men; making an occultation shows burning heat; having his greatest separation hurls pestilent sicknesses upon men. **15** Stationary, it is not unfortunate.[94]

16 Mercury passing through the leading parts of Cancer is indicative of freezing winds; towards the middle parts, it is less temperate; in the following parts it is full of winds. **17** In the northern and southern parts, it becomes a cause of much heat and warming. **18** Making an evening phase, it indicates the strength of women; making an occultation, it grieves the people; having his separation, it becomes a cause of much turmoil and discord. **19** Making a morning phase, it means useful hopes and thriving conditions for the people; making an occultation, it indicates much burning heat; having his greatest separation, it means that bad news will come from afar. **20** Stationary, it foretells the death of a prominent man.

21 Mercury coming to the leading parts of Leo indicates intense heat; towards the middle parts it is not mild; in the following parts, anomalous. **22** Towards the northern parts it stirs hot winds, in the southern, temperate. **23** Making an evening phase produces solicitudes and cares that bring slander

---

[94] *Anaisios* (**W**). In **A** and **Y**, *anaitios* ("guiltless").

to the king; making an occultation renders the air suffocating;[95] having his greatest separation forecasts the death of a great ruler. **24** Making a morning phase introduces disputations between the king and his subordinate commanders; <*morning occultation missing*>; making his greatest separation from the Sun means the death of the king. **25** Stationary, it introduces anomalies in the king.

26 Mercury passing through the leading parts of Virgo indicates burning heat and a hot temperature; towards the middle it is temperate; in the following parts, it gives humidity. **27** Towards the northern parts it causes droughts; towards the southern, mild. **28** Making an evening phase fosters success in traders; making an occultation gives sickness to the king; having his greatest separation foretells the fall of a great man. **29** Making a morning phase shows thriving conditions for men; in morning occultation it foretells the ruin of a great woman; having his greatest separation from the Sun hurls diseases upon men. **30** Stationary, it awakes murmuring and opposition in the cities.

31 Mercury[96] transiting the leading parts of Libra is mild; in the middle parts, parched; in the following parts, dry. **32** Towards the northern parts it moves barren winds; towards the southern parts it is destructive. **33** Making an evening phase means stillness; making an occultation shows diseases; having his greatest separation causes great turmoil in the people. **34** Making a morning phase is indicative of health; making an occultation changes the air; having his greatest separation from the Sun works the good repute of the masses. **35** Stationary, it means help for the people.

36 Mercury transiting the leading parts of Scorpio means cold; towards the middle parts, mild; in the following parts, it excites winds. **37** In the northern parts it is driest; in the southern, temperate. **38** When he makes an evening phase it is significant of useful expectations; making an evening oc-

---

[95] **Y** ends here.

[96] For this paragraph, **W** reads: "**31** Mercury passing through the leading parts of Libra is mild, also meaning warm temperatures and burning heat; towards the middle, it is temperate; in the rear parts, it is moist. **32** Towards the northern parts, dry; the southern, it becomes temperate. **33** Making an evening phase, it brings sickness to the king; <*occultation missing*>; having his greatest separation, it forecasts the fall of an important man. **34** Making a morning phase, it shows thriving conditions for men; making an occultation, it means the ruin of women; having his greatest separation, it hurls sicknesses upon men. **35** Stationary, it means help for the people."

cultation instills faintheartedness, lack of spirit, and solicitudes into the king and rulers; having his greatest separation from the Sun brings bad gossip to the army. **39** Making a morning phase shows the cheerfulness of the king; making an occultation indicates activities of search and inquiry; having his greatest separation from the Sun means most violent wars. **40** Stationary, it indicates irregularities within the army.

41 Mercury having its transit in the leading parts of Sagittarius is mild; towards the middle, less mild; in the following parts, extremely dry. **42** Towards the northern parts it excites biting winds; towards the southern, temperate, changing the air. **43** Making an evening phase increases moisture; making an occultation shows the stillness of the rulers, as well as inactivity; making his greatest separation from the Sun kills a great commander. **44** Holding an eastern phase helps the rulers; making a morning occultation harms the authorities and magistrates, awaking death among them; having his greatest separation kills the king. **45** And stationary, it hurls sicknesses upon men.

46 Mercury having its transit in the leading parts of Capricorn is dry; towards the middle, less mild; in the following parts, rainy and windy. **47** Towards both the northern and southern parts, it is temperate. **48** Making an evening phase means precipitated movements, and of contrary purpose; making an occultation shows the death of a prominent woman; *<elongation missing>*. **49** Holding an eastern phase indicates the health and strength of men in their prime; making a morning occultation means rest, leisure, and a cessation of hostilities; having his greatest separation is significant of pestilent diseases. **50** Stationary, it is favorable and helpful, especially for traders and merchants.

51 Mercury transiting the leading parts of Aquarius is scarcely mild, though towards the middle it is mild; in the following parts it becomes windy. **52** In the northern parts, dry; in the southern, it is indicative of fixed masses of clouds. **53** Making an evening phase causes subversion and the refutation of certain arguments: in an evening occultation, stillness and desolation in activities; having his greatest separation means the death of an aged ruler. **54** Making a morning phase is not unprofitable; *<morning occultation missing>*; having his separation indicates the fall of a great man. **55** Stationary, it brings illnesses upon men.

56 Mercury passing through the leading parts of Pisces is hardly temperate, though in the middle it is temperate; in the following parts, dryish. **57** In the northern parts it is windy; in the southern, watery. **58** Making an evening phase causes opposition among rulers; in occultation it indicates heavy rains; in his greatest separation from the Sun it works shipwrecks at sea and in rivers. **59** Making a morning phase indicates prosperity, good fortune, and the thriving conditions of the rulers; making a morning occultation excites thunder; having his separation, it becomes unfavorable for rulers. **60** Stationary, it is also inconvenient for them in this way.[97]

Chapter 14: What each sign and star indicates, and what they rule[98]

1 Aries rules meadows and plains, as well as pasture-land and flock-animals.

2 Taurus: all arable land and places gained by labor; also, herds of cattle.

3 Gemini: men, mountains, lands left barren, and all the high places.

4 Cancer: watery as well as salty places, woods, also places by the sea, or by the Strymon river, and olives.

5 Leo: deserts, troublesome places; also, tamed and wild beasts.

6 Virgo: men, lands sown with corn and similar things, as well as all winged creatures.

7 Libra: men, plains, places without tillage and of red [soil].

8 Scorpio: those vineyards found in rocky places, and [places of] death.

9 Sagittarius: vineyards found on plains, dry gardens, cedar trees, cypress trees, and those bearing fruits.

10 Capricorn: places with gardens, watered lands, and with goatherds.

11 Aquarius: men, rivers, seas, and everything in them.

12 Pisces: pools of water, and places related to the sea and fish.

---

[97] **EG: A** reads "it is *not* inconvenient," but I have followed **W** for two reasons. First, **W** has proved to be more trustworthy than the other two. Second, because the *kai* ("and, also") indicates something in accord with what has been said before, as does *houtōs* ("thus, in this way").

[98] In Ludwich, pp. 119-20.

Chapter 15: What types of thing belong to each star[99]

1 [The type] of Saturn: onions, garlic, mustard, sesame, pepper, and the like; also wool from goats.

2 Jupiter's: wheat, barley, rice, spelt, and what is gathered in autumn.

3 Mars's: all that is pungent, the sour-tempered plants, and what falls off.

4 The Sun's: wine, fermented liquor and similar things, as well as every sweetmeat.[100]

5 Venus's: every bean,[101] sweet fruits, spring flowers, aromatic herbs, and perfumes.

6 Mercury's: salvia, [Egyptian] bean, vegetable juice, and sweet-smelling green plants.

7 The Moon's: silk-worm, flax, cannabis, *mitaxis*,[102] olive, papyrus, and sedge.

Chapter 16: Also, from metals[103]

1 Saturn's [metals]: lead, litharge,[104] millstones, lignite,[105] claudian,[106] and the like.

2 Jupiter's: tin, beryl, every white stone, red sulphide, brimstone, and the like.

3 Mars's: iron, magnet, pebbles, pumice-stones, red stones, and the like.

4 The Sun's: gold, charcoal, aquamarine, diamond, sapphire, and the like.

5 Venus's: copper, pearl, onyx, amethyst, naphtha, resin, bitumen, watery bitumen, honey, sugar, rock-salt incense.

6 Mercury's: emerald, jasper, topaz, *hesychion*,[107] quicksilver, alloys of gold and silver, frankincense, and mastic.

7 The Moon's: silver, glass, powdered antimony, *xinē*,[108] *chia*,[109] *chandra*,[110] white earth, and the like.

---

[99] In Ludwich, pp. 120-21.

[100] *Tragēma*. **EG**: This generally refers to dried fruits taken as dessert.

[101] *Hospreon*. **BD**: This general word can refer to many types of vegetables.

[102] Unknown at this time.

[103] In Ludwich, p. 121.

[104] **BD**: This can either be a form of lead oxide, or of other metals mixed with lead.

[105] A kind of coal.

[106] *Klaudianos*. Unknown at this time.

[107] Unknown at this time.

Chapter 17: What each star is allotted, of animals[111]

1 Saturn is allotted serpents and snakes, as well as vipers, scorpions, foxes, hares, asses, flies, cats, and the winged creatures of the night.

2 Jupiter: men, lions, and pure[112] birds.

3 Mars: dogs, lynxes, leopards, and the wild and flesh-eating beasts, as well as hogs, apes, and wasps.

4 The Sun: sheep, wild goats, wild sheep, horses, roosters, and eagles.

5 Venus: deer, asses, antelopes, partridges, fish, and locusts.

6 Mercury: reptiles, winged creatures by the water, and the tamer beasts, hawks, falcons, and dogs.

7 The Moon: bulls, camels, elephants, and tame beasts.

Chapter 18: The influences of the *paranatellonta* stars in every inception and question[113]

[*Venus-Mercury stars*]

1 The Ear of Corn[114] is Libra 2° 46', southern, of the first magnitude, and the Lyre[115] in Sagittarius 23° 40', northern, the first magnitude, and the bright one of the Bird,[116] Aquarius 15° 30', southern, the first magnitude. **2** These three are a mixture of Venus and Mercury. **3** When indeed they share the same degrees with the pivots, or the lights, or the Lot of Fortune, in every inception they indicate the brightest of beginnings, easiness of affairs, and popularity. **4** Moreover, if Jupiter were configured or was with any of them, it

---

[108] Unknown at this time.

[109] Unknown at this time.

[110] Unknown at this time. **EG:** *Chandra* is the word for "Moon" in Sanskrit.

[111] In Ludwich, pp. 121-22.

[112] **EG:** This may have to do with the use of special or purified birds in ancient augury and divination.

[113] Edited in *CCAG* V.1 (pp. 214-17), from **E**; also **A**, f. 30ff. **EG:** Reading the title with **A**. **BD:** For a discussion of these stars and their relevance to Rhetorius, see the Introduction.

[114] Spica, α Virgo.

[115] Vega, α Lyra.

[116] Deneb Adige, α Cygnus.

would show that the matter is most distinguished and authoritative; but if Mars, quicker and more active.

5 In a similar way also the Northern Crown[117] turns out to be of the same mixture, for when it is co-pivotal and rises with the lights it indicates famous and successful clerics and chief priests. **6** The one of the southern Fish,[118] being of the same mixture, indicates a very slow beginning, though indeed with a useful end.

[Mars-Jupiter stars]

7 Next, the heart of the Lion,[119] 8° 50' Leo, northern, of the first magnitude; the Bearward,[120] 8° 20'[121] Libra, northern, of the first magnitude; Antares[122] at 19° Scorpio, of the second magnitude; the bright one of the Dog,[123] 24° Gemini, of the first magnitude, southern; and the bright one of the Eagle,[124] 10° 20' Capricorn, northern, the first magnitude. **8** These five are a mixture of Mars and Jupiter. **9** When indeed they are with the pivots in the inceptions, and they rise with the lights, and the Lot of Fortune, they indicate kings and famous soldiers, as well as frightening and unrestrained men. **10** These beginnings are suitable for military campaigns, generalship, and the election of kings, generals and such.

[Saturn-Jupiter stars]

11 Again, the one on the left foot of Orion,[125] 26° <10'> Taurus, southern, the first magnitude, and the middle one of the three stars of the belt of Orion,[126] <3> degrees <40'> Gemini, southern, the second magnitude, and the right shoulder of the Charioteer,[127] 9° 10' Gemini, northern, the second

---

[117] Alphecca, α Corona Borealis.
[118] Fomalhaut, α Piscis Australis.
[119] Regulus, α Leo.
[120] Arcturus, α Bootes.
[121] **BD:** Reading for 3° 20'.
[122] Antares, α Scorpio.
[123] Sirius, α Canis Major.
[124] Altair, α Aquila.
[125] Rigel, β Orion.
[126] Alnilam, ε Orion.
[127] Menkalinan, β Auriga.

magnitude, and the one on the knee of Sagittarius,[128] 23° 20' Sagittarius, northern of Sagittarius, the second magnitude; as well as the bright one of the Goat,[129] 1° 20' Gemini, northern, the first magnitude. **12** These five are of a mixture of Saturn and Jupiter. **13** For indeed when they are pivotal and co-rise with the lights and with the Lot of Fortune they mean that the inceptions promote acquisition and are helpful; such inceptions contribute to the building of ships, cities, and things of that kind.

[Mars-Saturn stars]

14 Next, the [star] on the head of the following Twin,[130] 3° Cancer, northern, the second magnitude, is of the mixture of Mars and Saturn. **15** This one, when rising with one of the pivots, or with the lights, or the Lot of Fortune, indicates some reckless and unruly, irascible, stubborn, greedy, and insolent soldiers, as well as those who have experienced a not-good end.[131]

[Jupiter-Mercury stars]

16 Next, the one on the claws of the Scorpion,[132] 26°[133] Libra, northern, the second magnitude, and the one on the head of the leading Twin,[134] at 29° 40' Gemini, the second magnitude. **17** These two are of a mixture of Jupiter and Mercury. **18** When they are with the pivots, and rising with the lights, they indicate righteous dealings, with goodwill, piety, and wisdom.[135] **19** Such inceptions promote the proposal for election of those who abolish public taxes.

---

[128] Rukbat, α Sagittarius.

[129] Capella, α Auriga.

[130] Pollux, β Gemini.

[131] **EG**: This could also be translated as "those proclaimed by an oracle as not having a good end."

[132] Zuben Eschemali, β Libra.

[133] **BD**: This should be 28° 30'.

[134] Castor, α Gemini.

[135] *Polygnōsia*, lit. "much knowledge."

[Mars-Mercury stars]

20 Next, the one on the front shoulder of Orion,[136] 0° 20'[137] Gemini, southern, the second magnitude, and the front star of the Dog,[138] 5° 44'[139] Cancer, the second magnitude, the one on the right shoulder of Orion,[140] 8° 20' Gemini, the first magnitude; and the one[141] common to the Horse[142] and Andromeda, 24° <10'> Pisces, northern, the second magnitude; also, the shoulder of the Horse,[143] 8° 30' Pisces, northern, of the second magnitude. **21** These five are of a mixture of Mars and Mercury. **22** When they are with the pivots, and rising with the lights, in inceptions they indicate hostile, re-sourceful, and crafty generals, as well as cruel, false, murderers and men-slaying, and those who have suffered a not-good end.

[Venus-Jupiter stars]

23 Again, the one on the right foot of the Centaur,[144] 14° 40' Scorpio, the first magnitude, northern, and the one[145] on the extremity of the River,[146] 5° 40'[147] Aries, the first magnitude, of the mixture of Venus and Jupiter. **24** These, when on the pivots, or rising with the lights, indicate subordinate, honest, pious men, giving good counsel,[148] and with good feelings. **25** This type of inception promotes the prominence[149] of good men.

---

[136] Betelgeuse, α Orion.

[137] **BD**: Reading for 70° 20'.

[138] Procyon, α Canis Major.

[139] **BD**: This should be 5° 30'.

[140] Bellatrix, γ Orion.

[141] Alpheratz, α Andromeda.

[142] Pegasus.

[143] Scheat, β Pegasus.

[144] Toliman or Rigel Centaurus, α Centaurus.

[145] Acamar, θ Eridanus. This is the last and southernmost star in the older form of the con-stellation, and used to be called Achernar (Kunitzsch and Smart 2006, p. 36). But around the Renaissance, the constellation was extended and Achernar became the name for a dif-ferent star, α Eridanus.

[146] Eridanus.

[147] **BD**: This should be 6° 30'.

[148] *Kalosumboulos.*

[149] *Probolē.*

[Saturn-Venus stars]

26 Again, the tail of the Lion,[150] the one north of Virgo,[151] the first magnitude, and the one on the rump of the Lion,[152] 19° 48'[153] Leo, northern, the second magnitude; also, the neck of Hydra,[154] 6° 20' Leo, southern, the second magnitude. **27** These are of the mixture of Saturn and Venus, and indicate the good fortune of the inception, and acquisition, not without some dishonesty and hypocrisy.

[Venus-Mars stars]

28 Last, the bright one of the Hyades,[155] 19° Taurus, of the mixture of Venus and Mars. **29** When it rises or is pivotal in the inception, it indicates a great man, much talked-of, lucky and rich, who subdues cities and countries, especially when Antares is casting a diameter to it.[156] **30** This kind of inception [leads] to the prominence of eastern rulers and generals.

---

[150] Denebola, β Leo.

[151] Probably Vindemiatrix, ε Virgo; but Ptolemy assigns this to Saturn-Mercury.

[152] Zosma, δ Leo.

[153] **BD**: This should be 20° 30'.

[154] Alphard, α Hydra.

[155] Aldebaran, α Taurus.

[156] **BD**: Antares and Aldebaran are roughly opposite each other, so each will rise when the other sets.

	Name	Theophilus nature
1.	Spica, α Virgo	♀ - ☿
2.	Vega, α Lyra	♀ - ☿
3.	Deneb Adige, α Cygnus	♀ - ☿
4.	Alphecca, α Corona Borealis	♀ - ☿
5.	Fomalhaut, α Piscis Australis	♀ - ☿
6.	Regulus, α Leo	♂ - ♃
7.	Arcturus, α Bootes	♂ - ♃
8.	Antares, α Scorpio	♂ - ♃
9.	Sirius, α Canis Major	♂ - ♃
10.	Altair, α Aquila	♂ - ♃
11.	Rigel, β Orion	♄ - ♃
12.	Alnilam, ε Orion	♄ - ♃
13.	Menkalinan, β Auriga	♄ - ♃
14.	Rukbat, α Sagittarius	♄ - ♃
15.	Capella, α Auriga	♄ - ♃
16.	Pollux, β Gemini	♂ - ♄
17.	Zuben Eschemali, β Libra	♃ - ☿
18.	Castor, α Gemini	♃ - ☿
19.	Betelgeuse, α Orion	♂ - ☿
20.	Procyon, α Canis Major	♂ - ☿
21.	Bellatrix, γ Orion	♂ - ☿
22.	Alpheratz, α Andromeda	♂ - ☿
23.	Scheat, β Pegasus	♂ - ☿
24.	Rigel Centaurus, α Centaurus	♀ - ♃
25.	Acamar, θ Eridanus	♀ - ♃
26.	Denebola, β Leo	♄ - ♀
27.	Vindemiatrix, ε Virgo	♄ - ♀
28.	Zosma, δ Leo	♄ - ♀
29.	Alphard, α Hydra	♄ - ♀
30.	Aldebaran, α Taurus	♀ - ♂

Figure 16: Natures of fixed stars: Theophilus

Chapter 19: Different inceptions[157]

1a The[158] Hour-marker in Leo, 3° or 5°; and from Aquarius, 15° or 27°, or 30°; and Virgo, 2°, these being favorable for inceptions, and having every success and favorable reports.

1b Say:[159] *monomoirias*[160] 3° or 5°, and from Aquarius *monomoirias* 15° or 27°; or else Aries 7°, having the Moon: good for inceptions and for every success and report.

[Rhetorius Ch. 52][161]

2 *Another way.* The Moon being unconnected from the Sun in the inception, means the irregularity of the inception and idleness. **3** The Moon unconnected with Saturn is partially good, though the influences will not be fulfilled without toil and distress. **4** The Moon chancing to be unconnected from Jupiter would show failure to attain and the abasement of the inception. **5** The Moon unconnected from Mars shows a middling condition, weakness, and aversion. **6** The Moon unconnected from Venus makes wedlock sad and ineffective. **7** The Moon unconnected from Mercury makes every inception become highly unsuccessful, especially for those who ask for favors or send letters. **8** Examine these figures in the inceptions, based on the ruler of the same belt.[162]

---

[157] Edited from **W**, f. 58v*ff*; **E**, f. 210*ff*; **A**, f. 31*ff*.

[158] From **W**, f. 58v.

[159] From **A**, f. 31.

[160] *Monomoiria.* **BD**: That is, the distribution of the planets to each degree of the zodiac: see for example Paulus Ch. 5. For every sign, its lord rules the first degree, and then each successive degree is ruled by the rest of the planets in Chaldean order. Thus the first degree of Aries is ruled by Mars, the second by the Sun, the third by Venus, and so on.

[161] For this subsection, cf. Rhetorius Ch. 52 (Holden pp. 31-32).

[162] *Homozõnia.* **EG**: That is, houses ruled by the same planet (Aries and Scorpio are of the same belt with respect to Mars, Taurus and Libra with respect to Venus, etc.). **BD**: If Theophilus is connecting this with the previous statements, then he probably means that the Moon's aversion to a planet will affect the houses it rules.

[Rhetorius Ch. 54][163]

9 *Another way.* In every inception, one should not forget to see whether the triplicity rulers of the preceding syzygy are in profitable places, and configured with the lights and with the benefic stars. **10** [It is] the same with the triplicity rulers of the light of the sect, and of the Hour-marker, so that they are not found in their own depressions or, after seven days, they do not come under the solar rays, since this figure indicates error and the contradiction of the inception.

11 Indeed, see also those planets which are with the Hour-marker and the Midheaven of the inception, as well as those which are together with the lights, and with the remaining pivots.[164] **12** Also see whether they chance to be in the bright degrees of the stars. **13** In addition, examine as well the phases of the Moon, and her figures on the third, seventh, and fortieth days: for the third day indicates the undertaking of the inception, the seventh the highest point of the inception, and the fortieth the completion of the inception. **14** Besides [that, examine] all of the first positions[165] as well as the configurations of the stars.

15 And look for the triplicity rulers of the underground pivot, whether they have position or testimony, since the first [triplicity lord] indicates the quality of the result of the inception, the second, the completion itself of the events.

16 Also take a look at the preceding syzygy: which star the Moon connects with, for this star is the beginning of the whole inception.

17 Besides, one must see that the bound rulers of the lights do not stand without dominance. **18** In the same way also the Lot of Fortune and its ruler, that they do not remain unproductive. **19** One should also examine closely the eleventh place from the Lot of Fortune, as well as its ruler, and that of the <Lot of>[166] exaltation of the inception and its ruler.

20 Regarding after how long the influences will take place, this will be known from all the stars, that is, from their adherences,[167] from their figures,

---

[163] For this subsection, cf. Rhetorius Ch. 54 (Holden pp. 32-39). This chapter in Rhetorius concerns a general set of approaches for *natal* charts.

[164] In **A**, *kairois* ("times").

[165] *Prōtē theseia.* **EG**: Meaning unclear: perhaps their positions at the preceding New/Full Moon?

[166] Adding with Rhetorius.

[167] *Kollēsis.* **BD**: That is, a bodily conjunction within 3°.

their cyclic periods, the ascension of the most authoritative signs, and the handing-over of the stars. **21** Still, one should know the first things of the inception from the Lot of Fortune and the end from its lord.

22 It is also necessary to look for the star of the inception having more authority,[168] lest in any way it is found corrupted or without authority, and rendering the whole inception useless.

23 In the same way also the rulers of the sixth and twelfth places marking the Hour harm the beginning of the inception; [in the] setting, [they harm] the end.

24 In a similar manner also, the Ascending Node[169] with the benefics is helpful. **25** The Descending Node with the malefics, though, shows the opposite, for it is harmful.[170]

[Planets in the Hour-marker, from Rhetorius Ch. 57][171]

25 *Another way.* A malefic marking the Hour means that the inception is without result, or ill-sounding.[172] **26** The Sun marking the Hour indicates the success of the inception, as long as he is apart from the malefics.

27 Saturn marking the Hour: say that such man is aged and old; Venus marking the Hour, graceful and pleasant; Mercury marking the Hour, thoughtful and prudent; Mars marking the Hour, courageous and reckless; Jupiter marking the Hour, bright, or some chief magistrate conducting certain affairs.

28 The Lot of Fortune or its ruler marking the Hour: the man enquired about is fortunate and long-lived. **29** The ruler of the Hour-Marker and the Lot of Fortune having chanced to fall under the rays, as well as the house rulers of the Lights, indicates that such [a man] is unfortunate and short-

---

[168] *Pleion echonta logous,* lit. "having more words."

[169] **A** reads "Aries."

[170] **EG:** In **A** (f. 32v) there follows a list of planets ruling the bound of the New Moon, while they rise in each sign. This is not found in the other MSS. The text belonging to this chapter resumes on f. 36.

[171] Cf. Rhetorius Ch. 57 (Holden pp. 48-56).

[172] *Kakemphatos.* **EG:** Perhaps this could be understood as "having an evil word on" the inception?

lived. **30** The ruler of the Good Daimōn[173] marking the Hour, say that such [a man] is full of resources and wealthy.

31 Mercury as a morning riser on the Hour-marker, together with the Sun or Moon, in feminine signs or feminine degrees, indicate that the object enquired about is the cutting-off of necessary things.[174]

32 If the ruler of the ninth place marks the Hour, apart from the hurling of the rays of malefics, say that such [a configuration] brings prosperous living abroad.

33 If the twelfth-part of any of the lights marks the Hour, it indicates good fortune.

34 If the ruler of the seventh place marks the Hour, say that such a man will experience opposition from his own wife, or from an enemy.

35 Saturn pivotal, together with the Sun, Venus, and Mercury, indicates some castrated person or eunuch.

36 The Sun with Venus in Leo marking the Hour means someone lascivious and an adulterer; in a similar way also, Saturn with Mercury marking the Hour in the houses of Venus or Saturn.

37 If the South Node marks the Hour with Venus, the enquiry is about a great man. **38** But if Saturn or Mars together mark the Hour or look upon [it], say that such is knavish and blood-sucking.[175]

39 If the North Node marks the Hour with Saturn or with Mars, apart from the testimony of the benefic stars, say that such a man is powerful and extremely rich.

40 Mars marking the Hour in a place of the sect, or in his own, indicates soldiers and the commanders of the army, fearful and active; when not of the sect and marking the Hour, he indicates someone too reckless, a wanderer, and inspiring fear.

41 The Moon marking the Hour indicates a very important man.

---

[173] **BD:** That is, the eleventh.

[174] **BD:** This phrase about cutting-off sounds very Arabic to me, the phrase would be: قطع الحوائج.

[175] *Haimoboros.*

[Planets in the second and third places, from Rhetorius Ch. 57]

42 The[176] ruler of the preceding syzygy, chancing to be in the second place, causes the loss of riches.

43 If[177] the Moon is found in the third place, it indicates prosperous living abroad.

[The fourth place and underground pivot, from Rhetorius Ch. 57][178]

44 Venus being in the fourth place means a bad marriage for the enquirer.

45 Mars being in the fourth place means wounds and illness.

46 The Moon chancing to be in the underground pivot, harmed by malefics, indicates captivity and imprisonment; sometimes even the loss of the wife and child. **47** However, when the Moon is witnessed by benefics in this place, it means profit from some hidden work. **48** What belongs under the influence of Mars, if it chances to be in it as well; the Moon seen by malefics, indicates a bad death.[179]

49 Saturn being in the underground pivot in the inception, in house or exaltation, while Jupiter is seeing, indicates that the one enquired about finds a treasure.

50 Jupiter being in the underground pivot shows profits from secret businesses, or else from the discovery of treasures; [it also shows that] the end will be good. **51** And if he chances to be eastern in his farthest [elongation], also a noble death.

52 Venus being in this place, and witnessed by the malefic stars, means the death of women; and if besides that she is in a tropical sign, he will not only pay funeral rites to one, but to many. **53** If she is found stationary, it not only indicates an adulterer, but also an effeminate person.

---

[176] For this sentence, cf. Rhetorius Ch. 57 (Holden p. 61).

[177] For this sentence, cf. Rhetorius Ch. 57 (Holden p. 67).

[178] For this subsection, cf. Rhetorius Ch. 57 (Holden pp. 67-71).

[179] **EG:** This is a tricky and confusing sentence, but all of the manuscripts read this way. **BD:** Nor does Rhetorius (Holden p. 67), which discusses this, clearly give the answer. It says that the Moon in the fourth, in a house of Mars and seen by malefics, shows banishment and the loss of inheritance.

54 Mercury being in this place together with Venus indicates false accusations and slander for the enquirer; if a malefic also bears witness, it indicates that there will be poisoning.[180]

55 The ruler of the underground pivot opposing its own house, or being in the twelfth or eighth: say that he will die in foreign lands.

56 The Sun with Saturn in the inception, when in the underground pivot, indicates that such a person is childless.

57 Saturn chancing to be together with Mars and Venus in the underground pivot, in Cancer or Capricorn, means that he will marry a prostitute, and due to this he will fall into many debts.

58 The Descending Node in the underground pivot indicates the good fortune of the inception; but if the Ascending Node were found in the underground, the malefics being with it or bearing witness, the inception will not be profitable.[181]

59 Mars in the underground means that the one presenting the enquiry on whether foundations with iron should be laid, or not, is sick.

[Planets in the fifth place, from Rhetorius Ch. 57][182]

60 The ruler of the Hour-Marker or of the Lot of Fortune in the fifth place shows a commander or tyrant.

61 Saturn being in the fifth place means some landowner or someone undertaking any building.

62 The Moon being in the fifth place indicates good luck and progress.

63 If the house ruler of the twelfth place chances to be in the fifth, and that of the fifth in the twelfth, it indicates that his children will be freedmen.[183]

64 If the ruler of the fifth or the ruler of the Lot of children were found in the sixth place, say that such a person is childless.

65 If the ruler of the wedding-arranger[184] or that of the Lot of marriage, happens to be in the fifth place, it means a good marriage.

---

[180] Or, "witchcraft" (*pharmakeia*).

[181] **BD/EG**: Reading with the sense of Rhetorius, for "would not be *un*profitable."

[182] For this subsection, cf. Rhetorius Ch. 57 (Holden pp. 72-75).

[183] **BD**: In Rhetorius, the native will have foster children. This is probably because the twelfth is the eighth (death) from the fifth; therefore he will raise children because of someone's death.

[184] *Gamostolos*. **EG**: A name for the seventh place.

66 If Saturn or Mars were found in the fifth place, or else the former look upon the latter, it means childlessness. **67** When benefics attend the fifth place, it indicates the blessing of children.

68 If the North Node[185] chances to be in the fifth place, and the benefics[186] are witnessing, it indicates the blessing of children.

69 The Moon in this place, witnessed by benefics, indicates the blessing of children.

70 Saturn in the fifth place means in every inception a very slow prognostication.

71 Jupiter and Venus being in the fifth place indicates quick action and popularity.

72 Mars being in the fifth place, also having a relationship to the inception, is an indicator of honor and glory.

73 Malefics being in the fifth place mean the loss of wealth. **74** Saturn being in the fifth place is deceitful and painful, and means a man ineffective and in need; Mars being there, [means someone] subject to hostile attacks and piratical onslaughts.

75 If Jupiter is in this place, it indicates that the one enquired about will be in public works.

76 The Moon being in this place shows harm through a woman.[187]

77 The[188] ruler of the underground pivot or the lord of the eighth place, being in this place, means that death will come in foreign lands; the ruler of the ninth place shows the same thing when being in the sixth place.

[Planets in the sixth place, from Rhetorius Ch. 57][189]

78 The ruler of the Hour-marker being in the sixth place means that the enquirer will suffer ill from a woman.[190] **79** The ruler of the seventh place

---

[185] **W** and **E** have the South Node, which does not make astrological sense. A reads "Aries" as in **24** above, when the correct term is the Ascending or North Node, as we have it here.

[186] **A** reads "malefics," which does not make astrologica sense; **E** has an abbreviation which could also be read as "malefics" if one letter is read slightly differently.

[187] **BD**: This sentence does not reflect Rhetorius, nor does it make much astrological sense; perhaps the Moon in the sixth?

[188] This sentence is not reflected in Rhetorius.

[189] For this subsection, cf. Rhetorius Ch. 57 (Holden p. 77). Only a couple of sentences are clearly reflected in Rhetorius.

being in the sixth has a similar meaning, that is, some sordid thing coming from women, or having intercourse with children.

80 The Lot of marriage [or] its ruler falling in the sixth, say that he will marry a slave or a freed woman.

81 The ruler of the third falling in the sixth, and witnessed by malefics, shows some sickness or some calamity.

82 If the Ascending Node chances to be in the sixth, it indicates a lack of accomplishment at the beginning of the inception, though the result will be good.

[Planets in the seventh place, from Rhetorius Ch. 57][191]

83 Jupiter in the seventh place means that the result of the inception is good, though the beginning will be hard to manage and harmful; if in a tropical sign, it means a bad marriage.

84 Venus being in the seventh place shows a promiscuous marriage, except when in Taurus or Libra.

85 Saturn being in the seventh place shows misfortune.

86 Mercury setting as well means poisoning.[192]

87 Mars being in the seventh place shows a bad marriage and prostitution; the Moon being conjoined as well indicates some man who loves strangers.

88 The Sun setting shows a bad marriage and childlessness.[193]

89 The lord of the seventh in the twelfth place, or that of the twelfth in the seventh, means an unfortunate marriage or a marriage to slaves.

90 The ruler of the seventh witnessed by the ruler of the eighth means widowhood or divorce.

91 If the ruler of the seventh has become weak, and the ruler of the twelfth is under the rays, it indicates marriage to aged people or to slaves.

---

[190] **BD**: I do not see this happening from the lord of the Hour-marker; perhaps Theophilus means the Moon (see **76**).

[191] For this subsection, cf. Rhetorius Ch. 57 (Holden pp. 80-83).

[192] Or, "witchcraft" (*pharmakeia*). **A** now contains the following sentence (not found in **E**), which is then crossed out as though it was an error: "Mars being in the seventh place shows a bad marriage; when Mercury is setting as well, it also indicates witchcraft and poisoning."

[193] **EG**: **E** seems to add "bad progeny and" before "childlessness," though a lacuna is found at the beginning of the word.

92 If <the ruler of the seventh> is found in the ninth, say that he will marry a foreign or religious woman.

93 If the ruler of the seventh (it being under the rays), chances to be in the underground pivot, and seen by malefics, say that such a man will keep company with slaves and prostitutes.

94 If the Ascending Node chances to be in the seventh place, and you are asked by a woman, say that such a woman is with another man given to feasting. **95** If Jupiter or Mercury chances to be together with it, say that she is of noble birth.

[Planets in the eighth place, from Rhetorius Ch. 57][194]

96 The Lot of Fortune found in the eighth place, and its lord on the Hour-marker: say that the inception is ineffective. **97** If both rulers are malefics, the inception will be worse. **98** If in addition [they are] under the rays, then it indicates the utmost idleness in meaning.

99 Mercury being in the eighth place, or when the ruler of the twelfth place is there, means the contrariety of the inception.

100 The Moon in the eighth is good and helpful.[195]

101 The [ruler] of the underground pivot being in the eighth shows that death will come in foreign lands.

102 Venus being in the eighth shows that such a man is living a shameful and poor life. **103** The ruler of the eighth [sign being] in the <tenth or>[196] eleventh place or in the fifth, bearing witness <*omitted*>,[197] means that such a man will be of service from his position of power, his properties, or such things.

103 If the ruler of the third is found in the eighth place, it indicates that such a man is fond of murder and treachery.

104 The ruler of the seventh place in the eighth means widowhood.

105 The ruler of the fifth place in the eighth means childlessness.

---

[194] For this subsection, cf. Rhetorius Ch. 57 (Holden pp. 84-87).

[195] **BD**: Per Rhetorius, this is in a nocturnal chart, increasing in calculation and light.

[196] **BD**: Adding with Rhetorius.

[197] **BD**: In Rhetorius there is no reference to witnessing; instead, this interpretation is "especially" if it is in its own house or exaltation, and out of the rays, and adding in numbers.

106 The ruler of the sixth (and that of the twelfth) in the eighth place, means the death of enemies and slaves. **107** Mars in such a place shows being harmed by them. **108** Saturn in the eighth place means annoyance.

109 Saturn ruling the eighth place, or looking upon it, indicates an attack of robbers and enemies, as well as burning with fire.

110 The Descending Node in the eighth place shows someone short-lived. **111** If Mars also bears witness, it will give capital punishment.

112 If[198] the Ascending Node chances to be in the eighth place, such man is falsely accused of bloodshed.[199]

[Planets in the ninth place, from Rhetorius Ch. 57][200]

113 The Sun or the Moon bearing witness to the ninth place, shows living abroad.

114 If Saturn or Mars chance to be in the ninth place, eastern or stationary, or configured with the Lot of Fortune, the inception indicates powerful people or tyrants, thieves, or temple-robbers.

115 The ruler of the seventh place, if found in the ninth (when you are asked about marriage): say that such a man will marry a foreign woman; and again, if asked about this subject, when Venus is found in the ninth, say that such an agreement will be unprofitable. **116** Mars in the ninth place: say that such a man is ill-sounding.[201]

117 The Ascending[202] Node in this place means ill luck, and captivity, and settling down in foreign lands.

118 The Descending Node chancing to be in the ninth means a disreputable living abroad.

---

[198] **BD**: This sentence does not accurately reflect Rhetorius.

[199] *Sukophanteō.*

[200] For this subsection, cf. Rhetorius Ch. 57 (Holden pp. 88-89).

[201] See the footnote to **25** above. But in Rhetorius, this means blasphemy.

[202] **EG**: **A** reads "descending" for both, but **E** crosses that out here and corrects it with the symbol for the ascending Node.

[Planets in the Midheaven, from Rhetorius Ch. 57][203]

119 Saturn on the Midheaven, in his own places or exaltation, is helpful in every inception, except that it corrupts marriage. **120** Mars being in aspect makes the inception fallacious, and it also corrupts marriage.

121 Jupiter culminating indicates a glorious inception, with a good marriage and being blessed with children.

122 Venus culminating, being out of the rays and not seen by malefics, causes the one making a beginning to be engaged in necessary public business, and to be associated in a wealthy marriage, and to receive profit from a woman.

123 Mercury culminating means a resourceful man, with an excellent nature, thoughtful and blessed with children.

124 The Sun culminating in the sphere, without the hurling of rays from malefic stars, indicates the brightest inception, royal, a ruling and magnificent man.

125 If the twelfth-parts of the lights are on the Midheaven, say that the inception is the happiest and highly advantageous.

126 If the Lot of Fortune or its lord happens to be in this place, not witnessed by the malefic stars, declare the inception to be of good fortune and most fitting. **127** If the ruler of the seventh bears witness,[204] it fosters a good marriage; the ruler of the eighth witnessing, there will be profits from inheritances; the ruler of the ninth witnessing, indicates good fortune and welfare abroad.

128 The Ascending Node[205] culminating means an exalted inception, but if the malefic stars bear witness together, declare the action of the inception invalid.

129 The Descending Node[206] with benefics, or witnessed by them: say that it indicates irregularity and danger.[207] **130** If a malefic star is with it or

---

[203] For this subsection, cf. Rhetorius Ch. 57 (Holden pp. 91-93).

[204] **BD:** But in Rhetorius, the lords of the seventh, eighth, and ninth are each *in* the Midheaven, not witnessing it.

[205] **EG: A** (f. 38v) reads, "Aries." Reading "Ascending" with Rhetorius.

[206] Reading with Rhetorius for "ascending."

[207] **EG:** Reading with **W.** In **A** there is a lacuna on this word, adding "and *without* danger," which seems reasonable due to the benefics.

bears witness, it means that the beginning of the inception is difficult to handle, and the end easy and profitable.

131 Declare about the influences of the inceptions and actions according to the culminating[208] signs and their natures, as well as their variation.[209]

[Planets in the eleventh place, from Rhetorius Ch. 57][210]

132 Every ruler and Lot that chances to be in the eleventh place indicates all good things, insofar as it is not configured with any malefic, or chances to be under the rays, its depression or diameter,[211] or subtracting in numbers,[212] therefore corrupting the good influence of this place.

133 Similarly, when the malefics chance to fall there, and have a relationship to the inception, being under the rays, in their depression or diameter, it will indicate the taking away of the good meanings, and the increase of corruption.

134 If the ruler of the eleventh (or of the eleventh place from the Sun) is marking the Hour <and the lord of the twelfth is in the setting>,[213] the beginning of the inception is favorable, and the end rotten; if they exchange figures, their strength will be clearly seen.

135 If the Ascending Node[214] happens to be in the eleventh, it means that the expectation of the inception is high and stronger.

136 If the Ascending Node chances to be in the eleventh place, with a malefic or witnessed by it, the beginning of the inception is weak, and the result advantageous and helpful.

137 The lights in the eleventh place accomplish the influences of the inception in a most glorious and graceful manner.

[Planets in the twelfth place, from Rhetorius Ch. 57][215]

138 If the ruler of the Lot of Fortune, or the Lot itself, is found in the twelfth place, witnessed by malefics, declare ill fortune for the inception.

---

[208] **A:** "witnessing."

[209] *Enallagē*; also, "interchange, change."

[210] For this subsection, cf. Rhetorius Ch. 57 (Holden pp. 96-100).

[211] **BD:** That is, its detriment.

[212] **BD:** In Rhetorius this means being retrograde.

[213] **BD:** Adding with Rhetorius.

[214] **BD:** Reading for "Aries," with Rhetorius (Holden p. 97, first line).

[215] For this subsection, cf. Rhetorius Ch. 57 (Holden pp. 43-47).

139 If the ruler of the third is found in the twelfth, it indicates that close people become enemies.

140 If the ruler of the underground pivot is found in the twelfth place, declare harm coming from funeral affairs, as well as death in foreign lands.

141 If the lord of the ninth comes to be in the twelfth place, there will be banishment and exile.

142 If the ruler of the twelfth marks the Hour, say that the beginning of the inception is troublesome.

143 If the ruler of the twelfth place is found with the Sun, say that such a man is some pitiable and low-born servant.

144 If the ruler of the matter of the inception is found in the twelfth place, declare the inception without authority. **145** But if it is with the Moon, a handmaid of a pitiable woman.

146 If the ruler of the twelfth is found with Saturn,[216] say that such a man loves the chase.

147 If the ruler of the ninth turns out to be in the twelfth with Saturn, say that such a man suffers shipwreck, or is in moist places. **148** If it is found with Mars, it shows piratical and military attacks.

149 If the Ascending Node[217] is found in the twelfth place, and the Sun, Moon, Mars, or Mercury is with it, it indicates that distress will occur, and there will be slaying by enemies. **150** If Jupiter or Venus were found with it, it means that the evil will be more moderate.

151 If the Descending Node[218] chances to be in the twelfth place, Saturn or Mars being with it, or testified to by it, say that such a man will find a treasure, or some wealth belonging to another.

152 Saturn chancing to be in the twelfth place means a loss of riches. **153** If Jupiter is also found [there], say that such a man will have trials and struggles, as well as [it indicating] pitiable men. **154** Mars happening to be in the twelfth place means someone servile and who has experienced all misfortunes. **155** Venus chancing to be in the twelfth shows damage coming from a woman, but should a malefic be looking upon her, say that such a man also has a sexual inclination, and is involved in some spiritual misfortune, or else

---

[216] **BD**: In Rhetorius, this is Saturn *as* the lord of the twelfth, in the Ascendant.

[217] **EG**: Again, **A** (f. 39v) reads "Aries," which **E** corrects as "Descending." But we follow Rhetorius here.

[218] Reading with Rhetorius for "ascending."

that he resorts to slaves and other [women] who whip him, or [he falls] into other indignities. **156** Mercury chancing to fall in the twelfth place turns out to be beneficent; but if he is opposed by Mars, it instills controversy due to matters relating to servile affairs.

Chapter 20: On the twelfth-parts[219]

1 If the twelfth-part of the Moon comes to be in trigon with her, it indicates famous people; if in diameter, the opposite, and disreputable. **2** If the twelfth-part of the Moon is in diameter to her, and falls in a four-footed sign, while Mars looks upon her, it makes those who are eaten by wild beasts. **3** If in [signs] of human shape, it makes those who are taken by thieves. **4** If the nativity were nocturnal, it gives active[220] and high-born people. **5** If [configured] with Saturn, the mother will be submissive and a foreigner, and the native himself will be placed in a subordinate position. **6** However, great nativities also fail in livelihood,[221] especially by night. **7** If it falls [on a configuration] with Mercury, learned and educated people; if with Jupiter, pious, godlike; if with Venus, well-disposed,[222] cheerful, and merry; if with the Sun, of good understanding, godlike, and those who search for and speak about divine and universal matters. **8** If [configured] with the Midheaven, with malefics [on it], he will experience prison, and a change for the worse will be seen. **9** If in square with [the Moon], it will be profitable for him; if [configured] with the [place] where Jupiter and Venus are, it is good.

10 If the twelfth-part of Saturn falls into his own trigon, it is disreputable; if it comes to be harmonious with the Moon and the Sun, they will be nativities for royal characters. **11** Similarly, as regards all the remaining stars, if the twelfth-parts fall thus, they mean the same thing. **12** If the twelfth-part of Saturn and Mars fall within the place of the Moon or of the Sun, it is not good. **13** If their twelfth-parts fall in their own trigons, it makes the good even greater, but see whether [they are] of malefics or of benefics. **14** If it falls in the rising sign, they will be distressed because of children, or they will

---

[219] Based on Rhetorius Ch. 60, edited in *CCAG* VIII.4, pp. 184-185.

[220] *Empraktos*.

[221] According to **A** and **V**: "great nativities also give abject people."

[222] *Prosphilēs*: also, beloved, kindly affected.

become sick. **15** If with the setting, there will be dangers from crises,[223] falls, and diseases of the eyes; if with the Midheaven, they will have hindrances to the reputation; if with the underground, there will be disturbances from hidden places.

16 The twelfth-part of Mars causes similar things. **17** But if the twelfth-part of Saturn falls within the place of Jupiter, there will be dissension with the ruling power; if with Mars, he will go through many crises;[224] if with Mercury, he will be distressed because of children and brothers; if with Venus, he will be distressed because of women; <but> if with the Sun, it damages the father's wealth or injures the father himself. **18** If the twelfth-part of Mars falls in the place of Venus, he will be an adulterer; if with Mercury, he will have differences with those privately attached to him,[225] or from his brothers; if with the Sun, he or his father will be at risk from fire and because of wounds.

19 If the twelfth-part of Mercury falls in [the place of] Jupiter, he will be entrusted with money, and will prosper from writings and speeches, and will befriend some prominent man; if with the Moon, he will not be educated, but he will always be among writings and words; if with Mars, or with Mercury or with Venus, he will suffer many blames from women, and will have dealings[226] with elderly or slave women.

Chapter 21: On madmen and epileptics[227]

1 If the Moon and Saturn mark the Hour, and Mercury, in a pivot, sets without the aspect of benefics, they make madmen and deranged persons.

2 If Mars is setting while Saturn and Mercury mark the Hour, apart from Jupiter and Venus, they make madmen and deranged persons.

3 If the Sun and the Moon mark the Hour and Saturn is setting, apart from Jupiter and Venus, they make those who are enraged, as well as madmen.

---

[223] *Krisis.* **EG**: This word can also denote judgments, trials, disputes, and also the turning points in diseases.

[224] See footnote above.

[225] **BD**: That is, with people considered to be part of his household.

[226] *Epimeignumi.* That is, he will consort, or have intercourse.

[227] Based on Rhetorius Ch. 65.

4 If Saturn and Mercury mark the Hour while Jupiter is setting, they make stupid, careless and unintelligent people.

5 If Venus is enclosed[228] by Saturn and Mars in a single sign, and squared by the Moon and Mercury, it makes those who are possessed and inspired by a god, with divine frenzy.

6 The Moon marking the Hour and Saturn culminating, while Mercury is setting, makes those suffering from partial paralysis, as well as deranged persons.

7 The Moon, Mars, and Mercury chancing to be pivotal, apart from Jupiter and Venus, make robbers, thieves, and those who force doors.[229] **8** Moreover if Saturn, being in the underground, looks upon them, it makes grave-robbers.

9 If Mars and Mercury, chancing to be in the setting pivot, <and> if looked upon by the Moon by diameter or square, they make robbers and murderous men who are crucified or hurled down from a precipice.

10 Mars and Mercury happening to be pivotal, and within the same degrees, apart from the aspect of benefics, make liars, false accusers, forgers, and perjurers. **11** If Saturn and the Moon are looking upon them, they make dirty persons, sorcerers, and those who call up the dead; the Moon being full, bodily flowing away from Saturn, makes crippled[230] persons and those driven by [divine] fury,[231] and sometimes also blind men. **12** Waning, and bodily flowing away from Mars, [the Moon] makes the same things.

13 If Mars marks the Hour, and Jupiter is setting within the same degrees, while the other stars are averted, it makes those inspired by a god.

14 If Saturn, opposing the Moon, manages her, the native will be inspired by a god, an epileptic; if the triplicity rulers of the light of the sect chance to be in diameter, and are seen by malefics, they make epileptics, especially when the Hour-marker or its ruler is seen by Saturn or Mars.

15 Mercury,[232] being averted from the Hour-marker and the Moon, always makes epileptics; if a malefic looks on as well, it makes those who are possessed by a demon.

---

[228] That is, "besieged" (*emperiechētai*).

[229] That is, burglars.

[230] *Apoplēktos*. **EG**: Also, struck by apoplexy, paralyzed, or struck dumb.

[231] *Mainomenos*. Also, simply "madmen".

[232] **EG**: This sentence is similar to *Tet.* III.14.

16 The Moon having her bond at her fullness,[233] makes those possessed and inspired by a god, or those who prophesy; if Mars looks upon her as well, it makes those possessed by a demon or with divine frenzy.

17 If the ruler of the Lot of Fortune, or of Spirit, in the ninth or third, chance to be opposed by malefics, they make those who utter oracular pronouncements, rave mad, or make prognostications.

18 The[234] Moon, having either her new or full phase, seen by Saturn,[235] and apart from Venus and Jupiter, makes those who are taken by demons; [also] being full, and seen only by Mars, especially in Sagittarius and Pisces.

19 <If the Moon is with the malefics but without the benefics, the illnesses are latent but incurable; but>[236] if Jupiter looks upon her, it gives healing by physicians, diets, or drugs; and Venus,[237] through oracles and the assistance of the gods.

20 Mars or Saturn in the underground [makes] those taken by demons or terrified[238] by phantoms; if Venus is also there, it makes those inspired by a god, or those who make utterances.

21 Saturn or Mars being on the Lot of Spirit, or opposing it, apart from Jupiter and Venus, make men raving mad or ecstatics; and think the same things in the case of Full or New Moons.

22 The ruler of the Lot of Spirit opposing it, makes those indiscreet of counsel, with contrary opinions, boastful, and insolent persons.

Chapter 22: On robbers[239]

1 The[240] Moon, Mars and Mercury, when they are pivotal and apart from Jupiter and Venus, indicate robbers or thieves; but if Saturn, by grave robbers.

---

[233] *Syndesmos.* **EG**: That is, being full while on the Node.

[234] **BD**: This is very similar to *Tet.* III.14.

[235] **BD**: But Ptolemy is probably right that she should be a New Moon with Saturn, to parallel the Full Moon with Mars.

[236] **BD**: Adding with the sense of Ptolemy.

[237] Reading for "the Moon," with Ptolemy.

[238] *Phoberizomenos.* **EG**: Cumont (p. 194 n. 1), argues that this should rather be "inspired" (*phoibazomenos*), in line with Valens, *Anth.* II.37. **BD**: But surely Mars and Saturn indicate fear, so we have let this stand.

[239] Edited from **W**, f. 68v.

2 Saturn, Mars and Mercury chancing to be on the setting pivot, looked upon by the Moon by a diameter or square in tropical signs, indicate drunkards.

3 Mars and Mercury within the same degrees, show deceit.

4 The triplicity rulers of the light of the sect, opposing each other or seen by malefics, indicate deceit.

Chapter 23: On death[241]

1 The Lot of death: from the Moon to the eighth place, and the same from the Hour-marker. **2** Where the Lot falls, if you find malefics either squaring or opposing the place of the Lot, say that he has died.

3 The ruler of the bound of the setting pivot being under the rays, means death. **4** The bound lord of the setting point, when it is a malefic, and is seen by another malefic, while averted from the benefics, indicates death.

5 Mercury, as bound lord of the setting pivot, and having its longest distance [from the Sun], with the malefics witnessing, shows death. **6** Understand the same also with Venus, when she is separated from the Sun by her longest distance.

7 The ruler of the Lot of Fortune being under the rays, surrounded or witnessed by malefics, means death.

8 The Moon, full, decimated by Mars, while the benefics <do not> bear witness, indicates death.

9 The malefics inspecting the lights from above,[242] apart from the testimony of benefics, mean death.

10 The Moon in the underground pivot, with Mars, apart from Jupiter and Venus, shows death.

11 Mercury opposed to the Moon, not looked upon by benefics,[243] means death.

---

[240] **BD:** This sentence resembles Rhetorius Ch. 88.

[241] Edited from **W**, f. 69r. This chapter is based on statements in Rhetorius Ch. 77, which however often differs in key details.

[242] *Kathyperterountōn.* That is, "overcoming."

[243] **BD:** Or rather, looked at by malefics.

Chapter 24: The Lot of the noxious place,[244] from Saturn till Mars (or alternately, from Mercury)[245]

1 This Lot, corrupted by malefics, harms every inception, and causes to fail. **2** The Moon decreasing in light, separating from Mars, or—being full—from Saturn, indicates that the inception is not good.

3 The rulers of the New Moon,[246] when averted from the places [of the luminaries], or opposing them, makes [the effects] hard to accomplish, and shows the inceptions to be contradictory.

4 The Sun, when he does not look upon the Lot of Fortune, or its ruler, indicates the failure of the inception.

5 The lords of the bounds <of the luminaries>, badly placed in relation to both lights, or under the rays, show the abasement of the inception.

6 It is indeed necessary to examine as well in every inception the preceding phase of the Moon, and the one it is about to make, as well as their rulers, and what kind of position they hold, since the places of the phases indicate the attempt, but the rulers, the completion.

Chapter 25: On the connections and separations of the Moon[247]

1 The Moon having moved from <*missing*>[248] towards the Sun, scatters wealth, especially when in a sign of a malefic.

2 From Jupiter towards Venus, it indicates some well-born person deprived of what is his own, particularly when she is waning. **3** Having advanced from Jupiter towards Mercury, increasing in light, it means good things; decreasing, evil things. **4** From Jupiter towards Saturn, waxing, it

---

[244] That is, the Lot of chronic illness.

[245] Edited from **W**, f. 69v. Sentences **1-5** are based on Rhetorius Ch. 78; the suggestion of Mercury seems to be Theophilus's own. It is projected from the Ascendant and reversed by night. Sentence **6** is based on Rhetorius Ch. 79.

[246] *Synodopansēlēnos.* **EG:** As tricky as the word may seem (supposedly indicating both Full and New Moons), following Rhetorius (*CCAG* VIII.4, p. 199) it seems to indicate only the conjunction. Besides, Parisinus Gr. 2425 (see *CCAG*) has "syzygy" instead.

[247] Edited from **W**, f. 70r. **BD:** Much of this material is well reflected in Firmicus Maternus, *Mathesis* IV.9-14 (Holden's Ch. IV.3a-f). Cf. also *Labors* Ch. 4.

[248] **BD:** It is hard to know what configuration this is: we would expect Saturn, but the Saturn-Sun combination does not indicate this in Firmicus Maternus.

shows anxieties from strangers; waning, cowards, captives, and humble-spirited people.

5 The Moon waxing, moving from Mars towards the Sun, shows someone in want, and short-lived. **6** Towards Venus, waxing, it indicates an adulterer and licentious person; waning, someone who does nothing. **7** Towards Mercury, waxing, some renowned general; waning, someone found guilty and making no progress. **8** Towards Saturn, waxing, someone who does not make any progress, and sloth; waning, epileptic, or bending.[249] **9** Towards Jupiter, waxing, a famous general; waning, those with lung disease and suffering from many things.

10 The Moon moving from the Sun towards Venus, waxing, shows barrenness; towards Mercury, a perjurer and someone prone to fall. **11** Toward Saturn, those who scatter wealth. **12** Towards Jupiter, waxing, some orphan.

13 The Moon waxing, moving from Venus to Mercury, shows those in charge of women; waning, some <lacuna> or procurer, or eunuch.

14 The Moon moving from Mercury to Mars shows liars and cheats. **15** When increasing in light and moving to the Sun, forgers; towards Venus, waxing, some perfumer or musician; towards Jupiter, waxing, in masculine signs, it is good as a whole; towards Saturn, waxing, it shows those faltering in speech, and stammering.

16 The Moon moving from Saturn towards Mars, waxing, shows those who do harm, and short-lived. **17** Towards the Sun, spirit-possessed; towards Venus, someone licentious; towards Mercury, a teacher and someone who knows;[250] waning, someone having an impediment in his speech, or vain.[251]

18 The Moon in the house of Mars shows someone prone to quick action.

19 The Moon on the Hour-marker indicates widows; setting, living abroad, suffering hardship.

---

[249] *Koilos.* **BD:** This probably means a "hunchback," as in Firmicus.
[250] **EG:** This especially means the future.
[251] Reading *kouphon* for *kophon*.

Chapter 26: After how long will the influences take place[252]

1 In every inception one should observe the ruler of the bound which marks the Hour, what kind of placement it has: that is to say, whether it is pivotal, post-ascending the pivots, or declining from them; whether in the hemisphere under or above the earth; whether a morning [star] or evening [star]; under the rays, or stationary; whether it exchanges a bound with its sign ruler, and whether the latter is useful or prejudicial, and if [it is] of the contrary sect. **2** Also, which stars are bearing witness to it, and if it is configured with the lights.

3 In relation to these things, a clear judgment can be made: for when it is pivotal, out of the rays of the Sun, when it marks the Hour or culminates, the inception will accomplish its effects immediately. **4** But if it chances to be in the post-ascensions from these pivots, when the former exchanges a figure with other stars, the effects will take place ([and] in a similar way, when it happens to be in the setting or underground pivot). **5** But if it descends from the setting, coming to the fifth place, it becomes slower [to show the effects]. **6** And if in the declines, [it will be] after many years, according to the natural period of the star.

ꙮ　ꙮ　ꙮ

7 *Otherwise.* Take the interval of degrees from the Moon of the inception till the bound of the ruler of the Hour-marker, and if you find that interval to be less than 180°, release[253] that interval from the degree of the Sun. **8** But if the number of degrees exceeds 180°, begin the releasing from the degree opposite the Sun. **9** Where the number leaves off, see the ruler of that bound, which position it holds, and based upon that, declare concerning the time of the fulfillment of the influences. **10** If the number leaves off in a bound belonging to the same ruler of the bound of the Hour-marker, the effects will be accomplished in those days.

---

[252] Edited from **W**, f. 71r-71v.
[253] **BD:** Or rather, "project."

Chapter 27: On knowing whether he lives or has died[254]

1 From the Hour-marker and its ruler, and from the pre-ascension of the Hour-marker. **2** If the ruler of the Hour-marker is in the twelfth, in the bounds of malefics or with malefics, or harmed by a figure of a malefic, both lights being maltreated, together with the Lot of Fortune, or their rulers, say that such man has died.

3 *Another way.* The ruler of the preceding New Moon, when averted from the Hour-marker or from the place of the New Moon, or witnessed by malefics, it means death.

4 *Another way.* The Lot of Fortune with malefics, chancing to be underground, the benefics being averted, indicates death. **5** Similarly when in the twelfth or sixth place.

6 *Another way.* Examine the tenth and its pre-ascension, also whether the lights are with the Lot of Fortune or with its ruler. **7** Also observe whether they are pivotal or declining from the pivots; also whether all or at least most of them are in the bounds of malefics, or are cast a diameter or square [from them]; [and] whether their twelfth-parts fall in the bounds of malefics. **8** In relation to them, it is appropriate to examine the bound ruler of the preceding New Moon, as well as from which star the Moon is separating, and where she was three days before. **9** Once more, should these together be declining from the pivots, say that he is dead. **10** But[255] if you find the opposite conditions to what has been said, say that he is not dead.

Chapter 28: On poisoning[256]

1 When Mercury is maltreated (says Theophilus), it indicates poisoning, theft and perjury; if Venus is conjointly injured as well, [it means] witchcraft[257] by a woman, such as potions to enchant,[258] charms of hatred, and such-like. **2** Moreover, if the maltreatment is found on pivots, these things will become more difficult: if on the Hour-marker or Midheaven, more evi-

---

[254] From **W**, f. 71v; **E**, f. 346v. See also *OVI* Ch. 8.7 (Version 1) which is virtually identical.

[255] **EG:** This last sentence only appears in **E**.

[256] Edited in *CCAG* XI.1 (p. 263), from **B** f. 111v. **EG:** *Pharmakeia* indicates poisoning, or the use of drugs to influence other persons (as in some descriptions of witchcraft).

[257] *Pharmakeia.*

[258] *Philtra.* **EG:** That is, philtres or potions to enchant or seduce.

dent and conspicuous; in the setting or underground, hidden and unseen. **3** In the post-ascensions, vigorous and long-lasting. **4** In the declines, quickly dissolving and becoming extinguished.

Chapter 29: In order to know whether a letter is true or false, whether it was written cunningly, brought by \<a slave\> or a free man[259]

1 When Capricorn or Gemini mark the Hour, or else when the Sun is in this sign, the malefics being there or bearing witness, and the Moon is maltreated, do not trust the letters, for they lie.

2 In the same way, when the Moon is found in Taurus or Leo, or the Hour-marker is averted from the benefics, a slave brought the letter.

3 When the benefics are decimating or configured with the lights, or with the Hour-marker, the letter is true and certain.

Chapter 30: What does the inquiry indicate?[260]

1 When the lights are declining and unconnected from the Hour-marker, and the pivots are divided by the malefic[261] stars,[262] the enquiry is not about a man but about beasts, and which of these, [is] according to the nature of the signs and the combined peculiar qualities of the co-rising stars.[263]

2 *Otherwise.* Search for the preceding syzygy, and the star ruling it, and the lights of the inception: for if all of the places of the inception, the most authoritative ones, or most of them, chance to be unconnected from the place of the syzygy, the matter signified is a beast.

---

[259] Based on **W**, f. 72v; **B**, f. 141r.

[260] Edited from **A** f. 43r, and **B** f. 141r. This whole chapter is based on *Tet.* III.8 (Robbins pp. 261-63). This is an instance of thought-interpretation But in Ptolemy these are *natal* indications showing that the native is animal-like (or perhaps what we would now call having birth defects). For sentence **1**, see also Heph. III.3, which also applies some of these natal considerations to inception charts.

[261] **B**: "benefic."

[262] **BD**: To my mind this should be understood as the malefics being *distributed throughout* the pivots, i.e., that they are in the various pivots. But Theophilus is following the language of Ptolemy.

[263] Here ends **B**.

3 *Otherwise.* The lights found in four-footed or bestial signs, while the malefic stars are on the pivots: it is a beast. **4** When the remaining [stars] are not bearing witness to the lights, it means either a tamed or a wild beast; but if the benefics are also bearing witness, they show dogs, cats, or similar animals. **5** Mercury bearing witness: birds, swine, oxen, goats, or the like. **6** If the lights are found in signs of human shape while the remaining stars are in the same situation, and the benefic stars do not bear witness to any of the said places, they show hermaphrodites and deaf-mutes.[264] **7** If Mercury is corrupted as well, it shows mute and toothless individuals.

Chapter 31: About what kind of man [is it asked]?[265]

1 Mercury marking the Hour[266] and configured with the Moon,[267] means a scribe or a teacher, trader, banker, soothsayer or astrologer. **2** If Saturn himself is also bearing witness, it indicates a priest or interpreter of dreams, or a frequenter of temples. **3** If Jupiter bears witness it means a public speaker, notary, or some man associated with important individuals.

4 Venus marking the Hour or configured with the Moon (she being in Mercurial places) indicates a seller of ointments, oil or wine, or a perfumer or trader in scents and medicines. **5** When Saturn is bearing witness as well, it means a druggist,[268] or a similar person. **6** If Jupiter is also witnessing, an athlete or winner in sport games, or some man managing women.[269]

7 Mars[270] marking the Hour and configured with the Sun (being in places of Saturn) indicates a cook, moulder, cauterizer, smith. **8** When the Sun is not configured, and the Moon is in Saturnian places, it indicates a shipbuilder, carpenter, farmer, or splitter of wood. **9** If Saturn is configured with it as well, a drawer of water, some keeper of [exotic] animals[271] or an embalmer.

---

[264] *Harpok<ra>tiakous.*

[265] Edited from **A** f. 43r, and **B** 141r. This chapter is based on *Tet.* IV.4 (Robbins pp. 383-89), which discusses a *native's* profession and action.

[266] **BD**: *Tet.* does not specify being in the Hour-marker.

[267] **BD**: The configuration with the Moon is not listed in Ptolemy.

[268] Also, "poisoner."

[269] **BD**: In Ptolemy, this is a man whose advancement is due to women; in Theophilus, this sounds like a pimp.

[270] **B** ends here.

[271] *Zōotrophos.*

10 If Jupiter is also configured and well-placed, it means a soldier or military commander.

11 *Otherwise.* Venus and Mercury marking the Hour and configured with <the Moon> (she being in their bounds), mean a player of musical instruments, a musician, a worker in the theatre,[272] an actor, a dealer in slaves, a dancer, weaver, painter, or sculptor of men. **12** But if Saturn bears witness to them, it indicates a merchant of female finery. **13** If Jupiter bears witness, it means a lawyer, or a public fiscal officer.

14 *Otherwise.* Mars and Mercury marking the Hour indicate an armorer, a maker of sacred monuments, physician, wrestler, or some adulterer or forger. **15** If Saturn bears witness to him, it indicates a murderer, burglar, <*lacuna*>, or sneak-thief. **16** If Jupiter bears witness to them, it indicates a lover of arms, fond of fighting, someone energetic, fearsome, or skillful.

17 Venus and Mars marking the Hour, <dominating>[273] the disposition, indicate a dyer, perfumer, a worker in tin, lead, gold and silver, fond of <*lacuna*>.[274] **18** If Saturn is configured to them, it means the robbery of the dead, a mourner, [or] a piper at funerals. **19** If Jupiter is bearing witness as well, <*lacuna*>,[275] [bearing] some sacred <instruments>,[276] a supervisor of women, or <*lacuna*>.[277]

20 If they are in signs of human shape <*text breaks off*> ...

---

[272] *Thymelikos.* **EG**: This can be understood both as an actor or a musician.

[273] **BD**: Tentatively filling in a lacuna, with *Tet.*

[274] **BD**: Ptolemy has druggists and doctors.

[275] **BD**: Ptolemy has the frequenters of temples and interpreters of omens.

[276] **BD**: Filling a lacuna with *Tet.*

[277] **BD**: Ptolemy has matchmakers and the interpreters of marriages (?).

ON VARIOUS INCEPTIONS

[THE FIRST HOUSE]

Chapter 1.1: On tropical signs[1]

1 When the tropical signs mark the Hour, do not undertake a journey, for it will be difficult, slow and with no good. **2** Friends will turn enemies, and then again will become friends. **3** One ought to plant [trees], but do not lay foundations. **4** Do give earnest-money. **5** Those who are laid up in bed in the tropical signs will rise up [from bed], <or> dissolve the illness, in seven days. **6** If on the day of taking to bed it moves from tropical to fixed signs, this will bring on death. **7** One ought not depart [for] nor go on a military campaign. **8** Should someone flee, [his] seizing will take place thus: so long as the Moon is in the same sign, you will discover him quickly; but if she goes past the tropical signs, being found in one of a different kind, he will perish. **9** If someone makes a promise [to pay something], it will not be paid in full. **10** Dreams are false, physicians do not heal, the sea[2] does not help, or another one completes the task. **11** It is of no use for women to get started on the warp. **12** If someone has fled from the country, he will return, for one should not start any certain matter in tropical signs.

Chapter 1.2: On bicorporeal <signs>[3]

1 When the bicorporeal signs mark the Hour, never go to the market-place, for the business has deceit, and it lies exposed to illness and other [evils]. **2** The weddings that take place in bicorporeal signs turn into adultery, and much trouble and distress are increased for such couples. **3** If someone flees and is laid hold of in bicorporeal signs, he will be a runaway

---

[1] Edited in Heeg, p. 63, from material attributed to Orpheus. **BD**: This material bears the further title, "From the twelve-place [circle] of Orpheus concerning inceptions," indicating (as Heeg points out on p. 62) that Theophilus must have had access to Orphic texts.

[2] *Hygra*. **EG**: The adjective *hygros* means "moist" or "damp," but this is most likely taken in its metonymic meaning, "sea."

[3] Edited in Heeg, pp. 64-65, from material attributed to Orpheus. **BD**: This material bears the further title, "From the twelve-place [circle] of Orpheus concerning inceptions," indicating (as Heeg points out on p. 62) that Theophilus must have had access to Orphic texts.

again. **4** Should someone promise to give payment, he will not give as he said. **5** Favors and gifts will be beautiful. **6** You can intend to apply yourself to planting and birds. **7** Taking to bed brings fever once more, and the sickness is a recurrent one; the illnesses are doubled in either good or evil. **8** It is favorable to start a journey. **9** If anyone dies in bicorporeal signs, another one is about to die also; and <if> anyone falls ill, another one will also fall ill <in> his house. **10** There is victory in bicorporeal signs, though soon the evil things <*lacuna*>, for they will be doubled. **11** Teachers and physicians learn well in bicorporeal signs.

Chapter 1.3: On fixed <signs>[4]

1 When the fixed signs mark the Hour, acquisitions and purchases are secure. **2** In fixed signs one ought to take a wife and [take control of] her affairs. **3** It is[5] useful to undertake an art or work, for intentions are fulfilled. **4** The thief will easily be found, and it is safe to travel abroad. **5** He who becomes an enemy will not become a friend again. **6** Judgments [of disease] are certain, for either they bring death, or the length of the illness, or else the sickness is dissolved in seven days. **7** Imprisonment in fixed signs is bad, for he who has been provoked to anger will not change his mind. **8** Should anyone ask for money, it will not be given to him. **9** One ought to start with words and music in fixed signs. **10** One who borrows will hardly give back what is due. **11** It is good to be taught to write, <and> also to make friends: tropical signs produce changes and bring struggles among them. **12** In the same way too, when the Moon passes through the said signs, it shows the things that the Hour-marker indicated.

---

[4] Edited in Heeg, pp. 65-66, from material attributed to Orpheus. **BD**: This material bears the further title, "From the twelve-place [circle] of Orpheus concerning inceptions," indicating (as Heeg points out on p. 62) that Theophilus must have had access to Orphic texts.
[5] **EG:** The Greek text has "not" here which, as already noted by Cumont (who decided to put it in brackets), does not make any sense.

Chapter 1.4: The images[6] of the signs

Comment by Dykes. No source information is available for this chapter.

Chapter 1.5: On New and Full Moons[7]

1 Let conjunctions[8] and Full Moons not be observed by malefics.

2 The Full Moon should not fall into the ecliptical places.[9]

3 New and Full Moons should not be opposed nor squared by malefics, for they depress and corrupt the inceptions: in general, the situation is difficult.

4 Do not let the lords of the Full Moons and conjunctions occupy the Bad Daimōn,[10] for they carry away from the land and the fatherland; they even cause poverty.

5 When the malefics are looking from above[11] they also take away by violence; well-placed, they grant the privilege of the front seats,[12] as well as [a good] reputation.[13]

6 If the lords of the conjunctions and Full Moons fall into bad places, they foster confidence for those who borrow money, and destroy those who lend their own; when in fixed signs, [this is] especially in the fatherland; in bicorporeal ones, from those of the same kin; in tropical ones, from foreigners.

7 Let[14] the rulers of the Hour-marker and of the Moon not oppose one another, for if so, they cause death away from the fatherland; and if malefics are observing there will also be violent death.[15]

---

[6] **EG**: Or, "likenesses."

[7] Edited it *CCAG* I (pp. 137-38), from **L** f. 68.

[8] That is, of the Sun and Moon, here and below.

[9] That is, the Nodes. **BD**: But *Carmen* V.6, **3** refers to the Moon actually being eclipsed.

[10] That is, the twelfth. **EG**: Here a marginal scholion reads: "Because the rulers of the conjunctions <and> Full Moons, when in the Bad Daimōn, cause migration and need; but if the malefics are seeing, they also take away by violence." "Take away" seems to refer to death.

[11] This refers to overcoming.

[12] *Proedria.* **EG**: This is a metaphor for respectful treatment, from the practice of granting front-row seats to important or favored people.

[13] *Doxa.*

[14] See Rhetorius Ch. 77 (Holden p. 128).

Chapter 1.6: On inceptions[16]

1 In each inception one must consider the sign in which the Moon turns out to be, as well as the conjunction that takes place each month: whether it chances to be in sign of the inception itself, or in the squares or diameters of the sign of the Moon. 2 For should the conjunction take place in such a figure, with the witnessing of the malefic stars, declare the inception most unfavorable, especially if the malefic star does not have a relation of such a kind in the inception; but if in some way the conjunction happens to be with benefic stars, or on the isosceles lines[17] relative to[18] the conjunction, or the sign of the Moon, say that the inception is good, particularly if it has some rulership relation to the nativity. 3 However, if the conjunction takes place on the same figures in relation to the sign of the Moon while one of the malefic stars conjointly exerts a baleful aspect[19] to the nativity, it will work plenty of evils.

4 Work out these things the same way when the sign of the Full Moon[20] is configured, and [if] this sign is in turn configured with that of the nativity, while a malefic is present, it brings about all the worst evils. 5 But if a benefic star becomes the deliverer[21] it also means good things. 6 In a similar way we must study all the phases of the Moon in every inception, for they have great power on the general activities that take place at the time (that is, in each and every season, like sowing and harvesting).[22]

---

[15] **EG:** Here a marginal scholion reads: "For the lords of the Hour-marker and of the Moon, when opposing each other, cause death abroad; should the malefics also see, they cause violent death."

[16] From **L**, f. 69r; also **W**, f. 84r.

[17] *En tais kata isoskelēs grammais.* **BD/EG:** We believe this means "in the trine" of the previous Sun-Moon conjunction.

[18] **EG:** Reading *pro* with **L** would yield *"before"* the conjunction; but **W** reads *pros*, "in relation to," "relative to," or "on the side of" the conjunction. Either way the sentence is unclear.

[19] *Katopteuō.*

[20] **W:** "the sign that obeys the Full Moon."

[21] Or, "savior" (*sōtēr*). **EG:** This does not seem to be a technical term, but just that the benefic does save or deliver from problems.

[22] **BD:** Theophilus is speaking of the mundane effects, which will rarely affect most people's inceptions; but he was working for generals who had to know about things like crop yields and supplies on campaign.

7 When[23] the conjunction takes place in Libra while both malefic stars are on it, in the second phase, the heliacal rising said to take place in Leo, the sowed seeds will disappear under the earth, Mars being a cause of winds and droughts, as well as rust in corn; Saturn, on the other hand, of chilling and an attack of worms on the earth at the time of sowing. **8** When these are absent, and Jupiter and Venus come to be at the retreat from the conjunction (which is the second sign, called second rising),[24] either being in, or bearing witness to the sign, the sowed seeds will then thrive and prosper, giving plenty of fruits, especially if Mercury also happens to be on the conjunction or in the following sign. **9** Indeed, the above-mentioned are on the whole the effective and powerful places and configurations that lead to either corruption or favorable effects.

10 Petosiris, in the same book,[25] says that this is how one must consider the preceding conjunction, as well as its separation: with which star, or by which star these places are seen, and to which star such a sign [belongs], for many things contribute to the accomplishment of the effects, both to exalt or depress the matters of the nativity. **11** The same things can be said about the Full Moon. **12** Examine with which star it takes place, or by which it is witnessed, and with these thoughts in mind declare further on the matters concerning the second quarter and gibbous phases. **13** As has been written before about the second quarter and the second gibbous [phase], one should examine closely with great care and keep watch on these figures.[26]

14 In addition,[27] it is also necessary to closely study the inceptions when the Moon is in the seasonable[28] or ecliptic[29] signs—that is, where the As-

---

[23] This paragraph seems to be loosely related to *Tet.* II.8 (Robbins pp. 179-81). **BD:** As with so many paraphrases of Ptolemy, it reads awkwardly.

[24] *Phōsphorēsis*, or the drawing away from the Sun by 15°, which is a helical rising.

[25] **BD:** This may be ultimately from the original Nechepsō-Petosiris book.

[26] **EG:** Here ends W. The rest of the chapter is only found in Laurentianus 38.34.

[27] **BD:** This paragraph seems to be loosely based on what became *Carmen* V.44, on prices and selling. There, *Carmen* mentions both the Nodes and the signs of northern and southern declination. This is ambiguous because these are two *different* circles: (1) the lunar circle which intersects at the Nodes but is farthest away in latitude at the so-called "bendings," and (2) the zodiac itself, which intersects at Aries and Libra but is farthest away in declination at the solstitial signs of Cancer and Capricorn. As the paragraph continues, *Carmen* is more interested in declination and speed, and leaves the Nodes behind. In a similar way, Theophilus (1) mentions signs that are "seasonable" or appropriate (*kairikos*) as well as signs on the ecliptic—these could be the equinoctial and solstitial signs; but then he (2) mentions the Nodes and the bendings. So Theophilus is keeping the ambiguity alive

cending Node is, or in its squares or diameter. **15** When in these, the matter is dissolved or given up, and the activities do not bear fruit, and nothing comes to perfection at all. **16** However, if in some way something is put for sale or purchased, the buyer will rob, defraud, or despoil the seller of the item, or even escape, especially if one of the malefic stars is on the same degree, or looks upon or bears witness to the Moon. **17** But should a benefic star be with the Moon, or testify to it, the inception in such a configuration will be in the middle.

Chapter 1.7: Otherwise, on inceptions [of travel][30]

1 The matter on inceptions is grasped from the square figures of the Moon: that is, when the squares appear favorable and when they do not. **2** Consider carefully the sign to which the Moon is coming, that it does not come to the square where a benefic or evil planet has previously been, since should it be a benefic star, what comes to pass will be moderate.

2 As[31] regards the signs related to waters, the sea, and sailing, we must observe that the matters concerning the Moon in no way chance to be taking away,[32] so that, not only is she not approached by both malefic stars (thus being corrupted), but also those signs which are resembling,[33] since these inceptions are difficult, not only for those sailing, but also because the ship itself will be destroyed together with those men.

---

but makes it worse by making it seem as though the Lunar circle is the *same* as the other signs. Furthermore, unlike *Carmen* he adds material about the malefics and benefics. For a different version that is more thorough and closer to *Carmen*, see excerpt #7 in Appendix A below.

[28] *Kairikos.* See footnote above.

[29] Related to the eclipses.

[30] From **L** f. 70r, and **W** f. 85v.

[31] **BD**: Demetrius (see Schmidt 1995 [*Sages*] p. 64) has two paragraphs here on the signs pertaining to sailing, and indeed **4-21** are based on him; but this sentence does not clearly reflect Demetrius.

[32] *Aphairetikos.* **BD**: Meaning unclear; this resembles the Arabic use of نقص ("decrease"), indicating some kind of corruption or damage to the Moon.

[33] *Empherēs.* "answering to," or "resembling." Meaning unclear.

3 But if the Moon alone chances to be maltreated, the signs related to sailing and water being testified to by benefic stars, the ship will not be completely destroyed together with all the men.[34]

[Travel, according to Demetrius][35]

4 The Moon being cast a square by Saturn, Mercury being on another square:[36] he will suffer penalty, censure or treachery on account of a decision or court judgment.

5 The Moon[37] with Mercury, and Jupiter squaring, will cause travelling abroad or intense[38] activity, and in foreign lands he will have slaves who will become prominent.

6 The Moon[39] with Mercury, while Saturn[40] casts a diameter, causes wounds, unpleasantness, and ambush by enemies, as well as destruction, consumption, and impediments in foreign lands; sometimes he will also be captive, sick, and slandered.

7 The Moon being in Aries,[41] Mars in it, and Mercury looking upon it: he will return, allied in arms. **8** If the two stars are harmed, he will depart by force and violently: but [that is] when the stars that are with her are in ecliptical signs,[42] retrograde, under the rays of the Sun, or in the decline of the Midheaven.[43]

9 <The Moon in Gemini and Saturn in Sagittarius means animals will be harmed; but if Saturn is in Virgo, they will have weakness and harm in the body.>[44]

---

[34] **L** adds: "or some will be saved, and the ship will be completely destroyed."

[35] For **4-21**, see Schmidt 1995 (*Sages*, pp. 64-66), from *CCAG* VIII.3, pp. 98-99.

[36] **EG:** A marginal scholion remarks: "that is, when Saturn squares the Moon, and is in turn opposed by Mercury."

[37] Cf. also *Carmen* V.23, **20**, which has nothing about slaves. Demetrius says that he will befriend a superior persion.

[38] *Oxupragia*. **EG:** This translation is somewhat speculative, as it is not in the lexicon.

[39] Cf. *Carmen* V.23, **14**. But notice

[40] Reading with Demetrius for "Mars."

[41] Reading with Demetrius for "Virgo."

[42] I.e., where the lunar Nodes are.

[43] **EG:** A blank space now appears here in **W**, before beginning with **10**, but **L** continues uninterrupted with **10**.

[44] **BD:** Adding with the sense of Demetrius.

10 And [if] the Moon [is] with Mercury, and Venus by triangle is looking upon her,[45] it means going backwards because of winds.[46]

11 The[47] Moon in each sign, while moving with her lesser speed, indicates that the voyage will be very slow.

12 The Moon[48] being with Saturn hinders the travelers and makes their expedition extremely slow.

13 If[49] Mars looks upon the Moon in Sagittarius, there will be disturbances along the way for the one journeying abroad, and he will even be hurt.

14 The main point of all that has been said on the current subject: If someone travels abroad, look at the Hour-marker, for it is related to the matter of being abroad, on account of being a sign that means one's own place of origin. **15** And also look at the setting, which will in turn indicate matters related to foreign lands. **16** Proceed to divide the interval of the path, that is, of the journey abroad, from the Hour-marker up to the setting pivot, and thus declare concerning the journey: if benefic stars see the signs from the Hour-marker until the setting, he will travel well; but if malefic stars, contrariwise. **17** Similarly, if benefic stars are in the first signs, or in the middle ones, and malefic stars are located in the last ones of the series, declare accordingly.

18 Know about the journey as a whole [by] dividing the interval by signs, from the setting up to the Hour-marker, considering in a similar way the sign of the Moon, taken from the phase of the conjunction until the Full Moon, thus showing the departure; but taking from the Full Moon up to the conjunction will show the return.

19 The Moon in Aries[50] moves quickly along the sign, so he will return. **20** If in Libra, it is prejudicial.[51] **21** In Aries,[52] someone will come to the city,

---

[45] **BD:** I have slightly altered the wording (changing "are looking" to "is looking") with Demetrius, because the manuscripts omitted **9** and so flowed uncertainly into **10**.

[46] *Palindromēsis hupo anemōn.* **BD:** That is, being driven back by winds (Demetrius).

[47] **BD:** This sentence is not in Demetrius; but note that when the Moon is slow she is sometimes said to be "like" the motion of Saturn (see the next sentence).

[48] Cf. also *Carmen* V.23, **13**.

[49] Cf. also *Carmen* V.23, **16**.

[50] Reading with Demetrius for "Virgo."

[51] Or, "inconvenient" (*asumphoros*).

[52] **BD:** Demetrius has a lacuna here. Since **19** already had Aries, it cannot be that; but I believe that this might be Virgo, since the text here has confused Aries and Virgo twice. However, Demetrius says that *if* the traveler meets with a prominent person, the traveler

and [one] who acts with the aid of prominent people will quickly accomplish his matters.

Chapter 1.8: The influence of the ascending and descending Nodes[53]

1 If the Ascending Node comes to be with Jupiter and the Sun in the Hour-marker of the enquiry, [they being] high and mounting to the north of the ecliptic, the inception means a king or a great ruler, and his long endurance and longevity, as well as prosperity. **2** If the Ascending Node comes to be with the Moon, on the Midheaven or Hour-marker, while the malefic[54] stars are declining but the benefic ones are in productive places, it indicates that there will be profits and much wealth, as well as a great beginning; [it is] the opposite of this when malefic stars are in productive places and the benefic ones are declining: there will be destruction of the afforded things.

3 Now, if the Descending Node comes to be with the Moon and Jupiter in the declines, the setting point, or the underground pivot, they take away what the seven stars give; but if the Moon chances to be in some way included in this configuration in opposition to the Sun, by direct reasoning those expected to partake of this misfortune will die. **4** But should benefic stars be on pivots, say that the inception will be about some who have returned.

5 If[55] the Ascending Node happens to be 90°[56] mounting to the north, say that the inception is well-reputed and glorious; and from 91°[57] up to 180° high and descending southward, the Moon being with it on the same degrees while the benefic stars are declining, then it indicates moderate repute. **6** From 180° up to 270°, the inception is low and worthless. **7** From 271° up to 360°, from its lowest it begins to mount higher: the Moon being on those

---

will be slain; so perhaps this is something else entirely, like Capricorn or Scorpio (ruled by Saturn and Mars).

[53] From **L**, f. 70v; also **W** f. 87r.

[54] **L** reads: "benefic."

[55] **BD**: This paragraph seems to refers to the right ascension of the Node, or perhaps its longitude *as considered* in terms of declination. For when the Node is between 0° Aries and 0° Cancer, it approaches the greatest northern declination; between Cancer and Libra, it is in northern but a lower declination; between Libra and Capricorn it is in the lowest declination; and between Capricorn and Aries it rises again.

[56] **BD**: Reading for "60," since Theophilus is evidently dividing the ecliptic or equator into four quarters.

[57] **BD**: Reading for "61"; see previous footnote.

same degrees, judge that there will eventually be ascension and progress in the matters signified by the inception.

8 If the Descending Node comes to Jupiter it partially harms the inception, but if Saturn as well, it gets even more depreciated; though if in opposition to the places of benefics, it will neither harm nor help.

Chapter 1.9: On the manner of the inception[58]

1 From the Hour-marker we shall accordingly understand the manner of the inception, as well as from the stars being on it, and those bearing witness to its ruler, and to its bound lord. **2** Let us consider their co-mixture in detail:

3 Saturn: those in the innermost part,[59] envious, talkative, mean-souled, opinionated and self-willed, especially related to secret affairs or those connected with the Mysteries. **4** Also, he grants benefits from those who have retired.

5 Jupiter causes lucky occurrences, plenty of welfare, and very fine weather; also, loving one's friends, pious and revered matters, as well as those related to archons and rulers.

6 Mars: those [who are] audacious and reckless, venturesome, and quick to anger. **7** As regards activities, he is profitable and quick.

8 Venus: purgative and medicinal, affectionate, orderly, loving the Muses.

9 Mercury: the intellectual, the common, and what is easy to deal with; also, that which is well-ordered, matters related to the household, or what is easy to procure.[60]

10 And from them and their co-mixture is seen what kind of character of manner the inception has.

---

[58] From **L**, f. 71r; also **W**, f. 88r.
[59] *Moixos.* **EG**: Generally, in the temples.
[60] *Euporistos.* **EG**: Mainly as regards one's sustenance.

Chapter 1.10: On the lights[61]

1 In every inception, if the Sun chances to be in a masculine sign, or the Moon in a feminine one, the inception and its character is a good combination.[62] **2** Now if [it is] contrariwise, it will be incongruous, inconvenient, anomalous, and bereft of great activity. **3** If both lights are in feminine signs, the matter is deprived of strength and inefficient, and its character unreliable and fickle. **4** But, if not only the lights but also the sign marking the Hour happens to be feminine, and [is] looked upon by them, the whole matter of the inception is turned completely feminine.

5 It is also necessary that the stars bearing witness also see the lights, for if no star is configured with them, or is in its own[63] house or exaltation, the matters of the inception will be untempered. **6** But when configured, or when the lights look at them, the benefics hurling their rays to them, or besieging or decimating them, then the inception will be great and much talked about. **7** But if [it is the] malefic stars, the opposite: the matter of the inception will be inferior, fallacious, and subject to slander.

8 If the lights chance to be pivotal, being either in the Hour-marker or the Midheaven, and the benefics post-ascend them, the matter of the inception will be judged royal and pertaining to rulership, and likewise with profitable results. **9** If the malefics, contrariwise: difficult and worthless. **9** Now, should they[64] be spear-bearers to the lights, and these see each other, the matter of the inception will be declared greater, of the highest repute, and most royal.

Chapter 1.11: On the Sun in the inception[65]

1 For the brilliancy of the inception, and people of high authority, and sometimes regarding royal affairs, we must take the Sun: let him be well-placed in every inception. **2** Therefore, if he is in a productive place (especially the Hour-marker or Midheaven), or even much better, in his own place, or his own sect, witnessed, besieged or decimated by benefic stars,

---

[61] From **L**, f. 71r; also **W**, f. 88r. **BD:** Much of this chapter resembles *Tet.* IV.3 (Robbins pp. 377*ff*), on status.

[62] *Eukratos*, lit. "well-tempered" or "of a good mixture."

[63] That is, the star bearing witness.

[64] **BD:** I take this to be the benefics.

[65] From **L**, f. 71v; also **W**, f. 89r.

especially in the tenth place, the most brilliant office and glory will follow; and when culminating he indicates loftiness as well as a great deal of superiority and the eminence of affairs. **3** However, he is difficult when he is besieged, decimated by malefic stars, or attached[66] to a malefic, when it dissolves the brilliancy of the inception.

4 When the lights are in the same place, the inception will foster no reflection or good judgment, nor any intense activity. **5** Now, if, while being with each other, they are opposed or squared by malefic stars while no benefic is watching, they lead to subordination and experiencing abasement or terrible weaknesses. **6** And if the Sun marks the Hour, understand it in relation to the evil or favorable figures of the Sun, dealt with above.[67]

7 The Moon setting when a malefic is present, means subjection and scornfulness. **8** The Sun setting is difficult for beloved ones and brethren; it also causes sickness in hidden places, especially when a malefic is bearing witness, except when he sets together with an evening Mercury: for in this case this it renders the inception favorable and harmless.

Chapter 1.12: On the Moon in the inception[68]

1 It is appropriate to take a look at which star the Moon is about to connect with, or adhere to, and, in the sign next to her, with which star she casts a figure (since that sign will rule the undertaking of the inception, and will show the leading features).

2 When the Moon is void of course, and is not about to connect with any star, it reveals that the inception is void and its matter hard to come by.

3 If the Moon connects with a malefic, or is taken from [one] malefic towards another, it makes the inception difficult and dangerous; but when the Moon connects with a benefic star, say the opposite. **4** If the Moon moves from a malefic to the connection or adherence[69] with a benefic, the occurrence will go from a most difficult beginning to an easier and more comfortable situation, according to the quality of the star (that is to say, of

---

[66] *Kollōmenos*, lit. "glued." **BD**: In Hellenistic astrology, this is a bodily conjunction within 3°.

[67] **BD**: That is, in **2** above, but using malefic stars instead of benefics.

[68] From **L**, f. 71v; also **W** f. 89v.

[69] That is, an aspect or conjunction within 3°, respectively.

that from which she separates). **5** [It is] the opposite when it moves from a benefic towards a malefic star.

6 One should also look at their ruler and bound lord, for if it is productive,[70] eastern, and seen by benefic stars, it does not leave the inception without significance; though when it is unproductive, setting, placed in its depression, or wronged by[71] a malefic star, say the opposite.

7 See as well its twelfth-part, that no malefic oversees it.[72] **8** Similarly, see the condition of the sign decimating the inception,[73] as well as by which stars it is seen, and in what kind of figure its ruler happens to be, since if the Moon is in that sign there will be a healthy development of the matter, and the whole outline of the inception can thus be observed—that is, in relation to the testimony of the stars.

9 Mars opposing or squaring the Moon, or being together with her, or when the Moon connects with[74] Mars, or – in her waning phase – she connects with, opposes, or squares Saturn, especially on pivots, is bad for everything: such as, when her first quarter and the Full Moon are harmed by Mars, it shows that the inception will come into misfortune, loss and banishment. **10** In the same say, when her second quarter and her conjunction with the Sun is harmed by Saturn, especially on the Midheaven, the inception in this condition will fall asunder. **11** However, then the Moon connects with the Hour-marker, the judgment will be the opposite.

12 The inception is good when the Moon is in her own exaltation, increasing in light, in sect, and her twelfth-part chances to be in a good bound. **13** This is excellent in a nocturnal inception, on the Hour-marker, on the Midheaven or their post-ascensions, for these conditions render the inception brilliant. **14** In diurnal inceptions [she is best], in the underground and setting pivots.

15 One should also compare the rulers of the signs where the New Moons take place, and the ruler of the Moon, whether they chance to be of the same sect, and by which stars they are witnessed: since from all these in combination, we judge what the enquiry will be.

---

[70] *Chrematizon.* **BD**: That is, in one of the busy or profitable places.

[71] *Adikoumenos.*

[72] *Epopteuō.* **BD**: This may mean overcoming, particularly decimation.

[73] **BD**: This must be the tenth sign.

[74] *Sunaptō*, here and below.

16 We should also observe where the assembly[75] with the Sun takes place, for if the ruler of those bounds chance to be with the Moon in this inception, pivotal or being productive as an eastern star, the inception will be considered distinguished and notable; but if on the Hour-marker as well, even more so. **17** Moreover, should a benefic star bear witness, [it is] much better; and if it is of the same sect, it could not be better—and the judgment will be made according to the nature of the star and its co-presence. **18** If the ruler of the bounds of the conjunction is found to be congenial with that of the inception, both productive[76] and in testimony to each other, the inception is most remarkable. **19** And if the place of the conjunction is found to be corrupted in the inception, or if the ruler of the bounds of the conjunction is in its depression, or overpowered[77] by malefic stars, or setting, or in unproductive places, it means that the inception is most worthless and fruitless.

Chapter 1.13: Examination of the mixture of the stars: what matters someone wishes to inquire about[78]

1 If someone approaches to ask while the royal trigons mark the Hour, and the Sun or Jupiter is culminating, the Sun having spear-bearers, the inquiry is about a king.

2 But if Mars and Jupiter mark the Hour, or else culminate, and signs of a different type mark the Hour, it is about satraps and generals.

3 If Saturn and Jupiter are well placed and busy,[79] [the inquiry is] about the management of royal matters, guardianship, and wealth; though if they are badly placed, it is about some evil matters.

4 Venus and Jupiter moving harmoniously, and having good dealings: [it is] on sacred matters and religious worship, as well as on rulership, glory, pleasure, and marriage.

---

[75] *Sunodos.*

[76] **BD:** That is, in one of the busy or profitable places.

[77] *Katischuō.* **BD:** This is probably overcoming.

[78] From Parisinus Gr. 1991, f. 74; also **L** f. 72v; see also **B** f. 141v. **BD:** This chapter is on the subject of thought-interpretation, casting a chart to determine what a client is thinking about. See especially my *Search of the Heart.*

[79] *Chrematizontōn.*

5 Venus and Mercury being harmoniously placed, and having good dealings with each other: [it is] on female affairs and the character of a woman, as well as sexual pleasures.

6 Jupiter and Mercury configured with each other and with good dealings: [it is] about an enquiry on royal matters, and the abuse of trust by dominant and authoritative persons.

7 Saturn and Mercury configured[80] and in good dealings: [it is] on widowhood, childlessness, and barrenness; also on words about people connecting with each other.[81]

8 Saturn and Jupiter configured and overlooking the Moon, while Mars bears witness: [it is] on ill language from people of the household, and intercourse.

9 Mars and Venus in the same place, or else in square or diameter to each other: [it is] on unseemly intertwining,[82] adultery, and such blameworthy things; and especially with Mercury bearing witness, the love of boys as well.

10 Saturn and Mercury in combination: [it is] on foreknowledge and divination, as well as on images of certain arcane matters, mysteries, and instruction; with Mars bearing witness, on the art of divination as well.

11 Saturn and Mars being harmoniously placed: on farming and such things; but their mixture being of a heterogeneous nature, when the combinations given are of different sorts, it is necessary to judge, as said before, the squares and diameters cast to each other (but especially malefics that oppose them) as harmonious.

12 For the mixture, one must compare the natures of the signs and the qualities of the rulers, and even also the benefic which is in its prime, that is, on the Hour Marker or on the Midheaven, [since their being pivotal and] the malefics in post-ascensions leads to the failure of the matters of these inquirers. **13** [It is] contrariwise when the malefics become pivotal and the benefics post-ascend, whence it is necessary to closely and accurately watch their places and times.

14 For the examination of the mixture, one must consider the nature of the signs and the quality of the ruling stars, and which is the most powerful of the benefics (that is, that one in the Hour Marker or Midheaven). **15** The malefics post-ascending cause the failure of the matters enquired upon, and

---

[80] **B** omits from here through "configured" in the next sentence.

[81] *Epiplokē*. **EG**: This could be either sexual or social intercourse.

[82] *Sumplokē*. **EG**: This mainly refers to sexual intercourse.

[it is] contrariwise when malefics come to the pivots and benefics post-ascend. **16** From these one can conveniently make accurate judgments about places and time. **17** And as regards this mixture, it is especially appropriate, first of all, to observe the star which most powerfully rules the inception, and is the strongest to deliver its gifts. **18** And in addition to the strengths of the stars, [one should also examine] those bearing witness, for – once observed – they sway the force[83] of the inception.

19 Then we should examine the Midheaven, as well as its ruler and the stars bearing witness to it: we shall thus learn about the result of the action, and also the manner of the outcome. **20** For when a benefic is on or witnessing the Midheaven, the effects of the question will be accomplished in a favorable and easy manner; but if a malefic has full authority over the Midheaven or its lord, the action will accomplish its effects badly, or it will be completely without effects. **21** In general, Saturn corrupting the Midheaven (either when brought to it, being in diameter to it, or decimating it) freezes the action or else it makes it blameworthy, and does not let it reach completion; Mars causes the same things: accusations, punishments, and he fosters plots. **22** But if the ruler of the Midheaven is under the rays, in the place of the Bad Daimōn, or in its own depression, the inquirers will be led astray from their pursuits, or their progress becomes dull. **23** So long as no one bears witness to the Midheaven, its ruler is rendered ineffectual, and the inquirer will become unsuccessful. **24** Those having in the question the rulers of the Midheaven and the Hour Marker, as well as the Moon, badly placed as regards the arrangement of the inception, such actions that they may undertake will turn out to be useless. **25** But if a malefic is on the Midheaven in an alien house, or out of sect, bearing witness to the Midheaven or its rulers, it will cause punishments and blames. **26** However, Mars being badly placed [also brings] anarchies; and looking upon [the Midheaven], he damages severely and greatly because he heightens and stimulates the activity, being by nature an energetic star. **27** But if the Moon connects with the rulers of the Midheaven, the inception being productive and friendly as regards sect, the matter will turn out to be one of good fortune and remarkable. **28** Moreover, if the ruler of the Lot of Fortune or of the Midheaven, post-ascends the Midheaven, the action is found to be even more energetic, except that it will have a late fulfillment. **29** And if no star is on the Midheaven nor on its post-

---

[83] *Energeia.*

ascension, nor on the Hour-marker, nor on the Lot of Fortune, nor even looking upon those places, these [inceptions become] passive and wavering.

Chapter 1.14: On what someone wishes to ask about

Comment by Dykes. No source information is given for this chapter, but note the similarity of its title to the first part of the previous chapter, Ch. 1.13.

Chapter 1.15: On the recurrence of the stars[84]

1 The star of Mercury returns to his [place] after 116 days,[85] and the star of Venus, after 584.[86]

2 The[87] star of Saturn makes its great return after 265 days (the orbital period[88] 59, rising 256); the star of Jupiter, at 427 days (the orbital period 46, rising, 361). **3** The star of Mars, at 284 days (the orbital period 151, rising 136).

Chapter 1.16: About the manner of the inquirer[89]

1 Look at the sign of the Hour-marker and its rulers. **2** For if there are benefics as well as malefics (and if those in it chance to be well), we say that his way of life is good. **3** But should they be badly placed, then [it is] very bad, and especially when the conjunction is in the same sign in which the question was generated. **4** When it is asked in either of the two squares from the Hour-marker, or when a conjunction is made, or diameter, not being looked upon by any benefic star, but on the contrary by a malefic, the things said above will be worse, and the evil things will be stronger.

---

[84] From Parisinus Gr. 1991, f. 75v.
[85] Reading for 176. **BD:** This is the number of days in Mercury's synodic cycle.
[86] **BD:** This is the number of days in Venus's synodic cycle.
[87] **BD:** I do not understand the meaning of the following numbers.
[88] *Peridromos.*
[89] From Parisinus Gr. 1991, f. 75r; also **L**, f. 73v.

5 Moreover, if the star distributing the highest depressions[90] chances to be in square to them, thus also will there be evil things, if they chance to be in the indecent signs.

Chapter 1.17: Concerning [his] manner, in another way[91]

1 The inception for this kind of matter will turn out to be stronger when the Moon comes to both trigons or both squares from the Hour-marker, for it imposes an end on the matters of the inception, especially when the benefic stars lie on the same figures. **2** But if a malefic is simultaneously on a pivot in the squares of the Moon, the completion of effects will experience an interruption.[92] **3** And the effects will be accomplished (though with delay), if the Moon passes through the declines, and when she moves to the squares, in the presence of benefics.

Chapter 1.18: What we are asked about[93]

1 If Saturn, marking the Hour, makes a western sextile to Jupiter (he himself being western or achronycal), the man about whom we are asked is an old one, a eunuch, or a childless man; but if he is eastern, it indicates a sluggish man, maltreated, evil, and weak.

2 And if Jupiter is on the Hour-marker, and well configured with the Moon, this will be a ruler or commander, or even a king; but if the Moon or the Sun do not bear witness to him, he will be a good man without evil. **3** Observe the same when the Sun is on the Hour-marker or on the Midheaven.

4 The Moon and Venus, about women and female matters.

---

[90] *Hypsēlotata tapeinōmata*, meaning unclear. **BD:** This could have something to do with the superior planets having their falls in the movable signs: Saturn in Aries, Jupiter in Capricorn, Mars in Cancer, and even the Sun in Libra. So, Theophilus could be referring to the planets which rule those very signs: for example, if the Moon (who rules the sign of Mars's fall) is squaring Mars.

[91] From Parisinus Gr. 1991, f. 75v; also **L** f. 73v.

[92] *Ekkopē*. Lit. "cutting out".

[93] From Parisinus Gr. 1991, f. 75v; also **L**, f. 73v.

5 Mars, one from another tribe or a soldier; in a place of Saturn, a slave or a subordinate.

Chapter 1.19: Of what kind is the inception[94]

1 One should investigate the rising Hour-marker, those on it, and the ruling wandering stars[95] as well as the combined nature of the co-rising stars: you will thus know of what quality the inception is. **2** Those which are morning risers and make a phase, magnify. **3** Stationary: at first intense and harsh, but when going forward and once again moving ahead, moderate. **4** At the second station, it is weakest. **5** Setting [under the rays] again, completely inglorious. **6** Thus, when bringing everything into account, and deciding upon the matter of inceptions and their influence, it is appropriate to make inferences about its deduced inherent qualities from its strength.

Chapter 1.20: What is the nature of the inception[96]

1 We should guess the nature of the inception from a combined research, and the measure of its nature, from the strength of the ruling stars. **2** For when they are rising[97] or pivotal, they indicate the nature of the inception to be authoritative; when setting or declining, more deficient. **3** And when they are decimated by benefics, glorious and useful; if by malefics, depressed and inglorious, and prone to fall. **4** And indeed the general fulfillment of the effects is seen from the eastern and western disposition of the stars.

Chapter 1.21: On inceptional distribution[98]

1 We[99] certainly infer bodily occurrences, as well as life abroad, from the Hour-marker; also the quality of its nature.[100] **2** From the Lot of Fortune,

---

[94] From **L** f. 74r; also Parisinus Gr. 1991, f. 75v-76r; also see **W** f. 91v.

[95] **EG**: Or, "the rulers of the wandering stars"; to this **L** adds: "and in the same way as the Moon, as she moves through the signs."

[96] From **L**, f. 74r; also **W**, f. 92r; and Parisinus Gr. 1991, f. 76.

[97] *Anatolikoi*. **BD**: This must mean rising out of the rays, or simply being outside of them; likewise setting indicates already being under the rays or going under them.

[98] From **L**, ff. 74 r-v; **W** f. 92v.

progress [as regards wealth] and ill fortune. **3** From the Moon, the passions and concerns of the soul. **4** From the Sun, the things related to glory and reputation. **5** From the Midheaven, actions and activities, as well as the remaining pastimes. **6** From the second place, things desired. **7** From the setting, oppositions and enemies. **8** From the underground, the end of matters, whether it is favorable or the contrary.

9 The completion of effects is taken from the natural, combined, and peculiar quality of the dominant planets (which could be either productive or noxious), as well as from the familiarity or antipathy with the ruling place. **10** How long it will take for the effects to take place is strongly indicated by the change of the configuration of the dominant stars of the noxious places, and their transit towards their own places; or from the phases of the Sun and the Moon in relation to the noxious signs.

Chapter 1.22: Making conjectures about the inception[101]

1 The[102] peculiar nature and shape of the signs and of their rulers, as well as the places in which they chance to be, also the wandering stars co-rising with the luminaries and the pivots—all these are weighed[103] together in the inception. **2** Even the connections and separations from the luminaries and from the rulers of the matters, as well as their figures: from all these together we estimate the events resulting from the inception.

3 When the lords of the inception are in the north,[104] they cause an increase in the intensity of the inception; in the south, a loosening. **4** Having an arrangement on the east, they indicate the younger;[105] towards the Midheaven above the earth, sacred and royal matters as well as middle age;

---

[99] **BD**: Sentences **1-5** are based on Ptolemy, *Tet.* IV.10 (Robbins p. 449), who lists these as *natal* points to distribute.

[100] **BD**: Theophilus probably means the quality of *life* at any given time.

[101] From **L**, ff. 74v; **W** f. 93r.

[102] This entire chapter is based on *Tet.* II.7-II.8, which however concerns eclipses, and not the luminaries individually.

[103] *Paralambanontai*, lit. "taken together to be compared."

[104] **BD**: I take this to be northern and southern ecliptical latitude.

[105] *Neōteros*. Also, "sudden and unexpected events."

towards the setting pivot, some legal matters and changes, as well as old age and those who have departed.

5 Configured as evening stars with respect to the Sun, and as morning stars in relation to the Moon, they cause the matters of the inception to decrease. **6** When they are opposed[106] they also do so, but moderately. **7** Configured as morning stars with respect to the Sun, and evening stars in relation to the Moon, the inception will bear its results completely.

8 When favorably placed (or the opposite), the effects of the matters of the inception are accomplished accordingly:[107] and this is apprehended from the peculiar quality of its nature, and of the productive nature of its ruling stars and their mixture with one another, as well as the places which they happen to move into. **9** For indeed the Sun and the Moon are, in some way, the leading stars of the inception, and these are the causes of the rest [of the planets] and of the whole of the activity, as well as of the rulership of the stars; and even of the strength or weakness of the predominating stars. **10** The comprehensive observation of those which take the lordship shows the quality of the effects accomplished.

11 In a similar way, if any of the wandering stars chances to be on its own place of the zodiac, it is observed according to its familiar strength, exactly like from their natures and qualities, and not as the familiarities of the stars happen to be.[108] **12** And again, because in their combination, it is necessary to consider not only the mixture of the wandering stars with one another, but also that of those who share in the same nature, be they fixed stars or places of the zodiac.

---

[106] **BD:** I take this to mean opposed to the Sun or Moon.

[107] **BD:** That is, the goodness or badness of the configuration dictates the goodness or badness of the event (from Ptolemy).

[108] **BD:** This sentence, adapted awkwardly from *Tet.* II.8 (Robbins p. 179), means that anything similar to the planet's nature will reinforce its indication: e.g. Venus, a Venusian fixed star, and a Venusian sign, will all reinforce Venusian significations.

Chapter 1.23: On the strength of the accomplished effects of the stars and signs[109]

1 The completion of the effects occurs particularly indeed, according to the familiar nature of each one of the stars, and of the nature of the twelfth-parts. **2** One must proceed to make a judgment by combining their strengths all together according to their configurations, the changes in the signs, as well as the phases with respect to the Sun, and fittingly understanding the combination in their activities: mixing the partaking natures, and the peculiar nature of the accomplished effects, which are many-colored.

3 One ought also to observe closely how familiar those stars are, which take on the lordship of the accomplished effects, in relation to the force of its character, for it gives clear indications of the influences. **4** The benefics being there, and in familiarity with the inception, and not decimated by any other of the opposite sect, they then work out their help according to their own nature. **5** But when they (so to speak), do not share in familiarity, or are decimated by those opposing them, they hardly help. **6** Being in a harmful combination, and taking on the rulership of the accomplished effects, if indeed they chance to be in familiarity with the inception, they harm less. **7** But if they do not have the rulership of the matters, let them not be decimated by those having familiarity with it; the malefic which is more vehement in its mixture will be the one carrying out the completion of effects.

8 *Another way*: In general terms, this is how one must always study the completion of effects from the peculiar nature of the signs. **9** Whether there is more or less of increases or relaxation in intensity, is taken from the nature of the house rulers among the stars, and the figures with respect to the Sun and the Moon: not only the conjunctions and Full Moons, but also the half-Moons, as the Moon as a whole rules the specific character as regards the completion of effects.

10 *Another way*: The Moon empty in course, and not connecting with any of the stars in the same sign in which she is, and not witnessed thereafter by benefics, shows an empty inception.

11 *Another way*: The ruler of the Hour-marker and of the Midheaven, and of the second place, being in favorable places and witnessed by benefics, be-

---

[109] From **L**, f. 75r; also **W** f. 94. **BD:** This chapter is redolent of Ptolemy's style, especially the constant use of "familiarity," but at present I cannot seem to find it.

ing on pivots or post-ascensions, indicates good fortune and welfare; in the declines, imprudence and inaction. **12** The measure of the doing well or inaction of the inception is known from the first star entering the Moon's place or the Hour-marker.

Chapter 1.24: On the star ruling the inception[110]

1 Now if the star ruling the inception is found in the setting sign, or in the underground pivot, or in the post-ascension of the Hour-marker, or in the sign that has already set, or its ruler is in the places of the Moon, opposed by the star of the inception or by its ruler, the inception will be disturbing and wavering, and more harmful than helpful. **2** This is especially true when the malefics are co-present or witnessing.

3 If in some way the star or its ruler chances to be in the place of the Bad Daimōn, or in the third place from the Hour-marker, it causes punishments and loss of riches; but if it falls into the right-hand trigon of the Midheaven (or in the place of Bad Fortune),[111] or in the right-hand squares of the Midheaven, or in the right-hand trigons of the Hour-marker, and its ruler is present, the inception will be favorable by reason of the agreement of the leading two pivots (that is, the Hour-marker and the Midheaven), except at the beginning of the inception, when there will be a little trouble; but later it will be straightened out.

4 It is also necessary to consider in all inceptions the stars opposing, now the exaltations, now the depressions,[112] together with its rulers, as well as their arrangement, and this way proceed to make a judgment on the matters at hand.

---

[110] From **L**, f. 76r; also **W** f. 96v.

[111] That is, the sixth.

[112] *Hupsēlotapeinōma*. **EG**: Or more colloquially, "now high, now low"; nevertheless the meaning is unclear.

Chapter 1.25: Of what kind is the inception[113]

1 It is necessary to consider the Moon in inceptions.

2 When she chances to fall into the Nodal points of either the south or the northern extreme of her orbit,[114] it contributes to the more varied and the slower; when in her bond,[115] to the quicker and more practical.

3 But on the east while the luminaries increase their light, [it contributes to] the more evident and high in repute, as well as the steadier. **4** In the decreasing of the lights, as well as their concealments, to the slower and more sluggish, as well as the dimmer and the more insignificant.

5 Also, the Sun is softened in inceptions when he chances to be on the pious places,[116] [since] it contributes to higher repute, the more just, and decent; but in the impious signs, to the more depressed, unintelligible, and the more unpleasant to live with, as well as things hard to succeed in.

Chapter 1.26: Whether the matter is helpful or harmful[117]

1 Let us consider the peculiar characteristic of the Hour-marker and of the star therein, or of the star looking upon it, and its signification[118] from the transit of the ruling stars to each figure, phase, station, or to the familiar places.

Chapter 1.27: Concerning the character and strength of the inception[119]

1 One must consider the quality of each of the stars in every inception based upon the peculiar characteristic of their nature, and even from the surrounding twelfth-parts, as well as from its configuration relative to the

---

[113] From **L**, f. 76r; also **W** f. 97r.

[114] **BD/EG**: That is, her greatest ecliptical latitude, sometimes called the "bendings."

[115] **BD/EG**: That is, her Node.

[116] **BD**: Here, as with Ch. 1.29, this sounds like perhaps the signs of exaltation and fall; but in Ch. 5.4, the "eight" pious places sound like the angles and succeedents.

[117] From **L**, ff. 76r-v; also **W** f. 97v.

[118] *Episēmasia*. **EG**: That is, the symptoms or changes brought about by weather or illness.

[119] From **L**, f. 76v; also **W** f. 98r.

Sun and the pivots. **2** And according to how it has turned out for us using all of these ways, their strength [is] first, from their being risers [out of the rays] and in direct motion as regards their own movement.[120] **3** [And it is also] from their relationship with the horizon: for, on the Midheaven or post-ascending the Midheaven, they are especially powerful, [but] secondly when they are on the horizon itself, or post-ascending it especially, or else under the opposite meridian, or simply configured with the rising place: [in] this way they are not weak.

Chapter 1.28: On inceptions, in plain language[121]

1 It is necessary to consider the rulers and their own places, as well as the signs, [and] the stars bearing witness: and from this you will concisely learn the significations and the time of their fulfillment, whether soon or slow. **2** It is even appropriate to observe also the rulers of the matters, as we have already said above, so that they do not fall into the sign opposite the Moon, and malefics are not in it, or in a square or diameter; or that the lord of the sign be declining or retrograde, or setting, or disconnected from the Hour-marker, or from the Moon.

2 From all of these things you will learn about the inception, except that in diurnal inceptions it is appropriate to make the stars of the diurnal sect productive; but in nocturnal inceptions the stars are productive when in places of their own sect: for then they provide an inception which is not bad.

3 Similarly when they are in their own trigons, or occupy their own houses.

4 On the pivots, they are more powerful: the strongest pivots are the Hour-marker and the Midheaven.

5 A bad star in its own place or exaltation, when productive, will have the strength of a benefic.

6 It is also helpful to recognize the combinations of all the stars and signs, and so declare about the inception, for it is never appropriate to express one's ideas about the inception in relation to only one notion of a star. **7** For indeed one must consider from the Hour-marker, present events; from the Midheaven, events happening after a short time; from the setting pivot,

---

[120] **EG: L** adds: "for then they are especially strong, even when retrograde."
[121] From **L**, f. 76v; also **W** ff. 98r-v.

events that take place more slowly; from the underground, the realities[122] and the result: for also in relation to this figure, the inception must be considered altogether.

9 Now, if the whole arrangement is seen to be underground, analyze the first star ascending towards the east, what kind it is, what its placement is, and by which stars it is witnessed, for such star will rule the inception. **10** And when a benefic is indeed on the Midheaven it promotes growth in the matters of the inception, especially when they are of the sect; and a malefic standing out of sect, or not having a relation, is a cause of falling.

ᏚᏅ   ᏚᏅ   ᏓᏅ

11 *Otherwise*: In every inception one must observe the bound ruler of the previous conjunction, how it is placed, as well as Fortune and its lord, and its bound ruler, how it stands with respect to the Sun and before which ruler it rises; [it is better with] the malefics being averse and the benefics rising before Fortune.

ᏚᏅ   ᏚᏅ   ᏓᏅ

12 *Otherwise*: The stars on pivots foster events, both those present and those sure to occur in the future (whether good or bad). **13** The stars on post-ascensions provide events slower to occur. **14** Now indeed, the benefics being on pivots, with the malefics post-ascending, the beginnings of the matters are successful, but the events that follow, and those expected to occur, will be difficult and a cause of falling; similarly when the malefics are on pivots, with the benefics post-ascending, at first the things will be worn with toil, but the things thereafter will be favorable, and show the quality and nature of the stars.

15 And the malefics post-ascending increase enemies; in a similar way the benefics bring plenty of friends.

16 And the malefics declining will liberate from harm most quickly, but the benefics bring good deeds.

17 And being in the fixed signs, [they are] immutable in their effects; in bicorporeal signs, easily changing.

---

[122] *Huparxeis*.

18 And when they are stationary they are definitely most powerful in their activities; when they are retrograde or running back again,[123] they become irregular and unstable as regards their activities.

19 And being under the rays they become weak altogether.

20 The eastern star is propitious, only if it is productive[124] and rises in the east: they make the activities more vigorous and successful. **21** When they are evening [stars][125] they become slower. **22** But they are the strongest if they are in an eastern eclipse.[126]

23 But the diurnal morning [stars],[127] and the nocturnal evening [ones],[128] become causes of abundance and activities.

24 And if the benefics move from the rising towards the setting, quickly say that the beginnings will be favorable; but if from the setting, say the contrary. **25** You should understand in the same manner concerning the malefics.

26 Also even in the pre-setting[129] (that is, the eighth place), the benefics which are there bring about no good; the malefics cause moderate harm.

27 *Otherwise*: When the malefic stars are out of sect and productive[130] in the inceptions, they diminish the good deeds. **28** When they are indeed in their own places and in sect, in relation to [what is] efficacious, they bring help among harmful, insecure, and malignant conditions. **29** But when out of sect and productive,[131] they become even stronger in their harmful condition.

30 Whichever rulers of the inception are unproductive, under the rays, or in their depressions, they are rendered weak.

31 *Otherwise*:[132] In general, the squares and diameters of the malefics, as well as their presence together, with respect to the luminaries and the Hour-

---

[123] *Palindromountes.*

[124] **BD**: That is, in a busy or advantageous or good place.

[125] *Hesperia.*

[126] *Anatolikē kathairesis.* **BD**: To my mind this sounds like being in the heart of the Sun.

[127] *Hēmerinos heōias.*

[128] *Nukterinos hesperias.*

[129] *Produsis.*

[130] **BD**: Again, in the busy, advantageous, or good places.

[131] **BD:** I believe this means that they are still in their own places as just mentioned in **28**, else this would contradict **27**.

[132] For this sentence, cf. *Carmen* IV.4, **7-8**.

marker, the benefics being corrupted, are difficult, especially when they decimate; the trigons are free from harm and more moderate.

Chapter 1.29: A synopsis by means of tables[133]

1 If you wish to do research in a most abridged way, operate thusly, as
with a small table of every ruler and star common to each type, upon examination of which, if you find those stars that chance to become rulers in
pious[134] signs, then their quality becomes eminent; on the other hand should
they be found in their depression signs, then the matters will be abased in
relation to everything you search for.

Chapter 1.30: General instructions[135]

1 From a universal standpoint, the benefics do not always give good gifts,
nor the malefics evil ones, [but it is rather] according to the nature of the
signs, their arrangement, and rulers: the events will be fulfilled in this manner.

---

[133] From **L**, f. 77v; also **W** f. 101r. **EG:** By a "table," Theophilus is referring to a simple or
abridged way of analyzing the planets.

[134] **EG/BD:** Here, Theophilus seems to mean the exalted signs, especially since this is opposed to the signs of depression; however, in Ch. 5.4 he speaks of the "eight" pious signs,
which sounds like the angles and succeedents.

[135] From **L**, f. 77v; also **W** f. 80v.

[THE SECOND HOUSE]

Chapter 2.1: The second heading
of the twelve manners of inceptions[136]

1 The[137] ruler of the second place, when found to be in bad places, and observed by malefics, indicates the bad prospects of the inception.

2 *Otherwise:*[138] The Moon being taken to the second place, increasing in her lights and adding in numbers, as well as being configured with the Sun, Mars being averse, and her ruler and that of the second place being well placed, the matters of such inception are rendered glorious and remarkable. **3** If the Moon is subtracting in her lights and numbers, and observed by benefics, the result of the inception will not have balance nor do well at first.

4 *Otherwise:* A benefic being on the second place indicates favorable things to be expected; though the malefics being there show sluggishness and the inaction of the things inquired about them.

5 But should the lord of the Lot of Fortune, happen to be in the second place or on the Hour-marker, with benefics, it indicate good things; but if malefics, they prepare bad things. **6** Saturn being on the place, and ruling the Lot or the Midheaven,[139] causes forgetfulness about riches. **7** Mars ruling the Hour-marker and the Lot of Fortune brings punishments and accidents; if the second place is also the house of Venus, it brings harm from women. **8** The Sun being in the second place, ruling the Lot of Fortune or the Hour-marker, indicates a most depressed inception. **9** Venus being in the second place, ruling the Lot or the Hour-marker, eastern, indicates profits coming from humid places; if western, from sacred places. **10** Mercury being under the rays and passing through the second place indicates a lack of activity in the inception; [but] if eastern, quick activity, and it indicates profit from commerce. **11** The Moon being in the second place, Saturn on the Hour-marker, shows idleness and sluggishness.

12 If[140] a malefic looks upon the second place by square or diameter, being together with the lord of the second place, it indicates the fall of livelihood and death. **13** With a second place Venus, the punishment will

---

[136] From **L**, f. 77v; also **W** f. 101r.

[137] Cf. *Carmen* I.29, **14**.

[138] For this paragraph, cf. *Carmen* I.29, **15-16**.

[139] **BD**: So reads the text, but this should probably be "Hour-marker."

[140] For this paragraph, cf. *Carmen* I.29, **4-11**.

come from women. **14** But if Mercury, for the sake of activities, calculations, inheritances, and letters. **15** [If] the star of Jupiter, the harm will come from important people or public matters. **16** If the star of Mars, say that the harm will be from matters related to soldiers, war, battle, burning, theft, or robbery. **17** Though if the star of Saturn, say that the harm will come from old people, a slave, or a manumitted slave. **18** If the Sun, say that the harm will be from the father or the family.

19 If the Ascending Node chances to fall into the second place, with one of the benefics or one of the luminaries, it shows things related to the amassing of much wealth. **20** If the Descending Node were found in this place, it would cause punishments and vexatious prosecution. **21** But if a malefic were together with it, or bore witness to it, it would give indications for acquisition and profit. **22** And the lord of the preceding conjunction or Full Moon chancing to be in this place, causes the loss of riches.

Chapter 2.2: On buying[141]

1 Let[142] us assume that the Moon is the matter;[143] the star from which the Moon has flowed away, the one who sells or makes a promise; and that which it connects with, the buyer. **2** If the Moon flows away from a benefic and is taken towards a malefic, the giver will give badly, or will not give at all, or will sell badly; the taker or buyer will be appropriately[144] and badly forsaken.[145]

---

[141] From **L** f. 78v; also **W**, f. 109v. This chapter is reflected in *Carmen* V.9, **1-3** (which however is much clearer there).

[142] For this chapter, cf. *Carmen* V.10, **1-4**.

[143] **BD**: That is, the commodity or thing being traded.

[144] *Sumphorōs*.

[145] **BD**: The idea here (expressed poorly by Theophilus) is that benefics show good will and success for the party with whom they are associated; malefics show the contrary. So if the Moon is separating from a benefic and applying to a malefic, then something goes wrong with the sale because the malefic is where the management of the matter winds up, and the buyer ends up being unhappy.

Chapter 2.3: On the finding of lost objects[146]

1 Let[147] the Hour-marker be the object lost; the Midheaven, the one who has lost it; the setting, the one who has stolen it; the underground, where it will be carried.

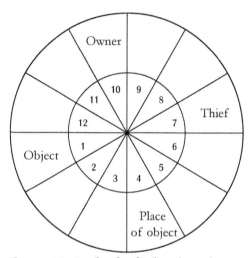

Figure 17: Angles for finding lost objects

2 If[148] a benefic star looks upon the Hour-marker, the lost object will be saved; if [upon] the Midheaven, it will be found; similarly when it is on the setting pivot.

3 Look[149] at the Moon, in which sign she is, in the bounds of which star, and you will find the object lost. **4** When the Moon is in the bounds of Saturn, the lost things will be rotten, ancient, and not worthy a word from anyone about them. **5** But if Jupiter, it is money, or a garment, or even great and noble things. **6** If Venus, things concerning the world of women, or such things. **7** If Mars, some new things, and also things as if worked with fire. **8** If Mercury, books, or money, or some commercial matters.

---

[146] From **L**, f. 78v; also **W** f. 110r.
[147] Cf. *Carmen* V.36, **20**.
[148] Cf. *Carmen* V.36, **21**.
[149] For this paragraph, cf. *Carmen* V.36, **44-56**.

9 If[150] the Moon were at the beginning of the sign, and she has[151] moved from one place to another, say that the lost object is within the house.

Chapter 2.4: On [legal] judgments[152]

1 The Hour-marker will be the accuser, the setting the accused, the Mid-heaven the judge, the underground the decision about to be made.

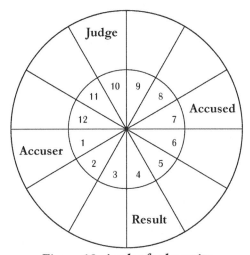

Figure 18: Angles for lawsuits

2 If Saturn is on the Hour-marker, the accuser will be of bad repute. **3** But if Mars, daring and causing fear, inflexible, having a single mind.[153] **4** If Jupiter, glorious and just, as well as well-established and not disturbed. **5** If Venus, he will be gluttonous, consuming and seeking to consume other things and accuse. **6** If Mercury, meticulous, instructed, and moved by a spirit.

---

[150] Cf. *Carmen* V.36, **43**, which however says that if the Moon is at the end of a sign, it *will* be transferred to another place.

[151] Perhaps this should read, "has *not*" (see previous footnote).

[152] From **L**, f. 79r; also **W** f. 110v. **BD**: This chapter seems to be drawn broadly from *Carmen* V.34, but see also *Labors* Ch. 28, in which Theophilus has adapted this material on lawsuits for war.

[153] **EG**: Following **W** (*monachou*). **L** reads *monomachou* ("of a single battle," or "gladiator").

7 If Saturn is on the Midheaven, he is a bad judge; if Mars, reckless and hot-headed; if Jupiter, just and pious; if Venus, virtuous; if Mercury, meticulous and precise as to one's rights.

8 If Saturn is setting, the accused will be wrong; if Mars, it will be bad for the accused; if Jupiter sets, the accused will be honest.

9 If Saturn is in the underground pivot, the accused will be judged dishonest; if Mars, he will suffer illegal treatment; if Jupiter, he will be judged honest; if Venus, the judge will be summoned to court, but will judge falsely; if Mercury, the judge will be persuaded with money.

10 Also observe closely the signs, and the bounds of the stars, as well as the twelfth-parts, proceeding similarly, and declaring thusly.

Chapter 2.7: On runaways[154]

1 He who escapes in tropical or bicorporeal signs, while the Moon marks the Hour, occupying the same degree, the rulers being on the same degrees, will make a return, and especially if a malefic is looking from above. **2** But when a benefic is witnessing, he will not return.

3 However, if a malefic chances to be in the squares or diameter[155] of the Moon, or the Moon is about to connect with a malefic while a benefic does not bear witness, he will be caught around those days when the Moon moves towards the corruption of the malefic, and he is never let go unpunished, thus undergoing calamities when he is exposed.

4 And if the corruption, both of the Moon, and of the Hour-marker, becomes powerful, a benefic not bearing witness [to any of them], there will be danger for them in the escape, and they will be destroyed.

5 They are hard to bring back when a benefic *does*[156] bear witness to the corrupting places; and if a malefic is not decimating any of them, the benefics being in the fixed signs, they become hard to find, assisted by the influence of the benefics. **6** [But] if [the benefics] fall in tropical and bicorporeal signs, and they bear witness, it will so happen that they will return, but they will not be injured.

---

[154] From **L**, f. 79r; also **W**, f. 111r. For sentences **1-6**, cf. *Carmen* V.37, **38-43**.
[155] **EG:** Reading with *Carmen* for the symbol of Cancer (which looks similar).
[156] **BD:** Omitting "not," with *Carmen*.

7 Being[157] on the Hour-marker, the Moon looking from above, causes them to be easy to find.

Chapter 2.6: On thieves[158]

1 The thieves,[159] in the same manner, escape notice of their guilt[160] as long as the benefics assist; but with the malefics looking from above, they will be taken.

2 The[161] discovery of the lost things is something we also need to find out about.

3 When the Moon and her place moves away from a corrupted figure,[162] [the thief goes] towards perdition; up to a benefic, he will repent.

Chapter 2.7: On those we inquire about: whether they are friends or enemies[163]

1 It is necessary to observe closely the sympathies and antipathies from the lords of the Hour-marker and its diameter,[164] as well as their arrangement. **2** For when they are configured with each other by trigon or hexagon, they have sympathy; by diameter or square, they lack sympathy.

---

[157] **BD:** This sentence seems to be missing something, and may derive from *Carmen* V.37, **44**, which simply says that if the Sun looked at both the Ascendant and the Moon, the master will bring back the runaway and the stolen property.

[158] From **L**, f. 79v; also **W** f. 111v.

[159] Cf. *Carmen* V.37, **38-39** and **42**, and Ch. 2.5 above, **1-2.** .

[160] **EG:** That is, no one will know they are guilty.

[161] Cf. broadly *Carmen* V.36, **1-19**.

[162] This must be "towards" a malefic, as with *Carmen* V.37, **39-40**, and Ch. 2.5 above, **3**.

[163] From **L**, f. 79v; also **W** f. 112r. See also Ch. 8.1, which is virtually identical.

[164] **BD:** That is, the seventh.

Chapter 2.8: An inception [on] whether a matter is true or false[165]

1 The fixed signs on the Hour-marker, and their rulers in fixed signs as well, together with the Sun and the Moon, indicate truth.

2 Another way: The luminaries and the Hour-marker, together with their lords, being in bounds of benefics, indicate truth.

3 The benefics occupying the pivots, and [the stars] that bear witness to the luminaries, and the lights themselves, indicate truth.

4 The benefics bearing witness to each other and to the luminaries, apart from the harm of the malefics, indicate truth.

5 The signs of straight ascension on the Hour-marker, and containing their own rulers, or the luminaries, indicate truth.

6 Mercury as a morning riser,[166] out of the rays of the Sun, and being in productive[167] places, not corrupted by Saturn and Mars, means truth.

7 The Lot of Fortune and its lord being well-placed and not harmed by malefics, indicate truth.

8 The signs and stars not having these conditions, but lying opposite to these, always show that the matter about which it is inquired has deceit and imposture. **9** Because of this, one must turn one's attention to all these things, or rather, to the nature of the signs and their twelfth-parts, and in this way declare concerning the inception.

---

[165] From **L**, f. 79v; also **W** f. 104r.

[166] *Heōios anatolikos.*

[167] *Chrēmatistikos.* **BD**: That is, the busy or advantageous or good places.

[THE THIRD HOUSE]

Chapter 3.1: The third heading of the twelve manners of inception[168]

1 The Moon ruling the Hour-marker and the Lot of Fortune, and being in the third place with a star of the sect, increasing in light and adding in numbers, indicates many good things from the beginning, as well as authority. 2 But if she were found together with the Sun in this place, or in conjunction, there will be abundance coming from sacred places. 3 However, should Saturn be present in the place of the Moon, there will be much harm. 4 But if Jupiter were with it in the same place, it indicates much wealth. 5 Though if Mars is with the Moon in the third place, it means quick action, and riches obtained from wrongdoing. 6 Venus conjoining with the Moon in the third place indicates power and wealth. 7 Mercury being with the Moon, and having a relation to the Lot of Fortune and the Hour-marker, indicates that there will be wealth from speech and thought.[169]

8 The Moon in the third place fosters living abroad. 9 The lord of the third place being well placed and witnessed by benefics, means friendship with great men. 10 The malefics in this place cause harm from friends, as well as dangers in foreign countries. 11 The lords of the fifth place, and those of the eleventh, being side-by-side in the third place, bring profit from living abroad and from friendship. 12 The lord of the seventh place being in this place, indicates foreign marriage.

13 If the third place is in Cancer or Leo, and the benefics bear witness, they indicate good luck. 14 In the same way, also in Sagittarius and Pisces. 15 If the third place is found in Aries or Scorpio, witnessed by Mars and Venus, they show adultery for the lover, in the same way as in Taurus and Libra. 16 If the third place is found in Gemini or Virgo, while Mars looks on, such [people] will suffer many evils, and will be severely punished by friends. 17 The Ascending Node being in the third place, the luminaries bearing witness together with benefics: it indicates that there will be much help from

---

[168] From L, f. 78r; also W f. 103r. BD: This chapter originally appeared in the list of contents as part of the second house, as Ch. 2.2; but since it is clearly part of the third house, I have moved it here.

[169] *Epinoia*. EG: This can also mean "deceit."

friends; if the Descending Node chances to be in the third place, he will have harm coming from friends.

[THE FOURTH HOUSE]

Chapter 4.1: The fourth heading of the twelve manners of divisions of the inceptions[170]

1 The fourth manner of inceptions indicates the work of the astrologer in relation to the witnessing of the stars. **2** For when the benefics are assisting the place,[171] it means approval and good repute for the astrologer; if the malefics, condemnation and blame.

---

[170] From **L**, f. 79v; also **W** 104r. **BD:** This chapter was originally listed in the table of contents as part of the second house, as Ch. 2.9. But because it is clearly labeled as a fourth-house topic, I have moved it here.

[171] **BD:** My guess is that this is the fourth place or IC, and does indicate the astrologer. Normally we think of the astrologer as being indicated by the seventh, but a good rationale for the fourth is the fact that the astrologer's *reputation* is part of the *result* of the inception: if the result of the question or inception turns out to be correct, the astrologer's reputation benefits; if not, it is harmed.

[THE FIFTH HOUSE]

Chapter 5.1: The fifth heading of the twelve manners of inceptions[172]

1 Observe closely the two luminaries and the Hour-marker. **2** When for instance either two [of these] places, or three, and the 30° of these,[173] comprise bicorporeal, or tropical, or prolific signs, with any witnessing from benefics, as well as the co-presence of these, [and] should the rulers (I say) in the same way be in double or tropical signs, and the Lot of Fortune or its ruler were found in the most authoritative places of the inception, or the stars were found in those places by twos,[174] and if either all or most of them were involved in this figure, say that the woman about whom it is asked, is pregnant.

Chapter 5.2a: On masculine or feminine births, or about those in the womb[175]

1 If we wish to know about male or female births, we need to examine the Hour-marker, the luminaries, their rulers, their bounds, and their 30°.[176] **2** If all or most of them were made masculine, we shall say that the baby in the womb is a male; if they were made feminine, then female.

Chapter 5.2b: Whether the inception is eminent or not[177]

1 Indeed, in inceptions, the sign of the Lot of Fortune should not escape notice either, as well as the sign following it, and even the third one.[178] **2** And

---

[172] From **L**, f. 80r; also **W** f. 104v. **BD:** The Arabic version of this material is found in al-Rijāl, *Skilled* I.42.

[173] **BD:** Meaning unclear. The Arabic version "the shares of their twelfth-parts."

[174] *Ana duo.* **EG:** This might mean something like "each of the two most authoritative places." **BD:** The Arabic version says "two planets of these ones greater in testimony."

[175] From **L**, f. 80r; also **W** f. 112r.

[176] **BD:** Again, meaning unclear.

[177] From **L**, f. 80r; also **W** f. 105r.

[178] **BD:** At first glance this looks like the first, second, and third from Fortune; but it is also possible that this is an angular triad from Fortune: i.e., Fortune itself and the signs on either side.

if the benefics were in those places or looking upon them, the beginning, middle, and end of the inception will then be glorious.

3 But if benefics were in or bore witness to the first one, while malefics were found in the second, the beginning will be honored, and the middle difficult.

4 Now, if the first sign becomes corrupted and the good ones occupy the second one, the first things indicated by this inception will be difficult, the second, glorious.

5 [It is] likewise in relation to the matters of the third sign; and you will have the proposal of the whole inception.

Chapter 5.3: When we are asked whether someone will be highly esteemed in his desired pursuits or not[179]

1 Examine those stars that obtain the rulership of the Lot of Fortune: what kind of arrangement and strength they have, the stars configured with them or decimating them, or else whether they chance to be of its sect. **2** For when they (I mean, the stars that obtain the rulership of the Lot of Fortune) are in strength, they more quickly bring about good things, particularly when they happen to be witnessed by the luminaries in familiarity. **4** But if the stars of the opposite sect decimate the familiar places, or when they follow them, they cause the diminution of the matters, as well as poverty, and a failure to grasp the general opportunity provided by the approach to the pivots or post-ascensions of those stars that afford the cause.

Chapter 5.4: Otherwise, whether a woman is pregnant[180]

1 [Proceed] this way. **2** It is known from two places, the place at the summit and the ruler of the bound perpendicular to it:[181] for this itself will be

---

[179] From **L**, f. 80r; also **W** f. 112r. For this chapter, cf. Ptolemy, *Tet.* IV.2 (Robbins p. 375).

[180] From **L**, f. 80v; also **W** f. 112v. Because **11-12** and **13** are most likely from Petosiris, and the earlier sentences have some unusual poetic phrases and terms, that whole paragraph might be based on Nechepsō-Petosiris or some compilation containing their views. As for this chapter, it is reflected in al-Rijāl, *Skilled* I.42.

the ruler, provided that the lord of the bounds is well placed. **3** But if it is not, the stars on the place at the summit, or in the underground pivot diametrical to the Midheaven pivot, lying on the same degrees, or those lying on the Hour-marker, or the post-ascension of the Hour-marker, or on the setting pivot, or in the eighth place, while none of the malefics come to be opposed to them, and one of these places (or most of them), are in such condition, indicate that the woman carries a baby in her womb.

4 *Otherwise*: Know[182] this that concerns the stars in every inquiry of such a kind, that one of them is productive of children and the regulator of the pregnancy, and [is] is of the nature of the place that Jupiter occupies. **5** If you find this [place] and its triplicity rulers in the eight pious signs,[183] out of the rays of the Sun, then there is pregnancy. **6** And if the rulers were mostly in the place above the top, it will be even better. **7** And if the rulers of the Moon, or the Moon itself, chance to be in fertile signs, there is pregnancy. **8** But when Jupiter and its rulers happen to be in the undisciplined[184] signs, and particularly when the Sun is under the setting pivot, the ruler of the bound of the Midheaven falling out of the pivots and being in the declines, it is found that there is no pregnancy.

9 *Otherwise*: If you found some of the rulers of the Midheaven with the Sun being busy,[185] and having the right of speaking first,[186] witnessed by benefics, there is pregnancy. **10** If there is not such a figure, there is no pregnancy.

11 *Otherwise*:[187] It is necessary to examine Jupiter and Venus, as well as Mercury: if these are maltreated by Saturn and Mars, say that there is no pregnancy. **12** And if the Moon is corrupted, [then] without any doubt there

---

[181] **BD:** But what exactly would this be? See **8** below, which uses the bound of the Midheaven itself, and makes more sense.

[182] This paragraph may be based broadly on *Carmen* II.8-II.9, but the unusual poetic nature of some of the language here suggests it was taken from some other didactic poem.

[183] **BD:** This might simply mean the angular and succeedent places, of which there are indeed eight. But see Ch. 1.29, which opposes the pious signs to the signs of "depression," which sounds like the signs of exaltation and fall.

[184] *Ataktos.* **BD:** If we are correct about the "pious" signs being the angles and succeedents, this probably means the cadent or declining places. This is how the Arabic version reads it.

[185] That is, being in the good or advantageous or busy places.

[186] *Protologia.* **EG:** This seems to mean that they have the authority to be significators.

[187] Sentence **11** represents the view of Petosiris, according to Valens (*Anth.* III.39). But since Valens reports **12** later in his next paragraph, **12** (and probably the rest of the paragraph) is also from Petosiris.

is no pregnancy. **13** If [Jupiter, Venus, and Mercury] are on pivots, and <not> corrupted,[188] they indicate pregnancy. **14** Again, when the Moon is making a loosing of her bonds[189] and connecting with malefics, say that with such loosing, there will be no pregnancy.

15 Otherwise: The Lot of children [is taken] from Jupiter up to Saturn, and the same from the Hour-marker. **16** If there is a benefic opposing or in square to this Lot, there is pregnancy.[190] **17** If there is not any star in the aforesaid places, then there is no pregnancy.

Chapter 5.5: Whether the baby is masculine or feminine[191]

1 If[192] the Sun comes to a square of the Lot of children (and the diameter), in a masculine sign, it is a boy; if the Moon is in a feminine sign, then it is a girl.

2 *Otherwise*:[193] The fifth place from the Hour-marker being feminine, and its ruler being in a feminine sign, it is a girl. **3** But if masculine, and the sign of its ruler being masculine, it is a boy.

4 *Otherwise*: It is necessary to take a look at the degrees of the Hour-marker, and those of the luminary of the sect,[194] and observe whether they are the bounds of a masculine or feminine star—or, whether the Hour-marker has a masculine or feminine star [in it]. **5** For the stars that foster feminine births are Saturn, Venus, and the Moon; masculine, Jupiter, the Sun, and Mars.[195] **6** <And if Mercury was eastern, it indicates males, while if he were western it indicates females.>[196]

---

[188] **BD:** Adding with *Skilled* I.42. Now, Valens (*ibid.*) says that if the *malefics* are on the Midheaven or IC, there are *no* children. So perhaps Theophilus decided to put this in a positive way.

[189] **BD:** This probably means that she is just leaving the conjunction or opposition of the Sun.

[190] **W** ends here.

[191] From **L**, f. 81r; also **W** f. 114r.

[192] Cf. *Carmen* II.10, **4**.

[193] Cf. *Carmen* II.13.

[194] **BD:** In *Skilled* I.46, this is the planet which distributes children—and this is stated in *Carmen* to be the triplicity lord of Jupiter. So I suspect that that is the realmeaning here.

[195] **BD:** For a discussion of this passage, see the Introduction, Section 2.

[196] **BD:** Adding with *Skilled* and al-Qasrani.

7 *Otherwise*: Aside from the masculine or feminine character of the Hour-marker and of the lights, the eastern and morning figures of Mars and also Venus contribute to masculine births; setting and evening [configurations], to feminine births.

[THE SIXTH HOUSE]

Chapter 6.1: The six headings of the twelve inceptions[197]

1 Establish the pivots just like in a nativity, and the positions of the stars, [and see] what kind of arrangements they have in the inception, assigning the Hour-marker to the sick one, the setting to the place where the ailing one takes to bed, and the illness itself, of what kind it is; and the Midheaven to the physician, the underground, the end of the illness. **2** In the same way also, the Moon indicates what the illness is, and of what kind its cause is.[198]

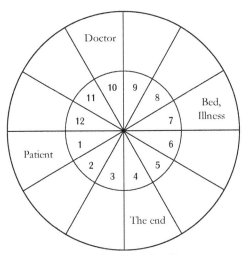

Figure 19: Angles for illness

3 And when the Hour-marker is seen by the malefics, and the setting by benefics, it indicates that the illness will be slow to heal, and the weakness will persist.

---

[197] From **L**, f. 81r; also **W** f. 105v. **BD:** In this chapter, sentences **1** matches an alternative way of assigning angles which is found in one of the Dorotheus *Fragments* (V.41, 1-41, **1-4**). The way found in *Carmen* and *Fragment* V.41, 36-68, **1-4** is to put the doctor in the Ascendant and the patient on the Midheaven. However, the rest of the chapter does not really match the rest of the passage in *Carmen* **33-39**. So this might reflect something from another author, or perhaps one of many Dorotheus-inspired variations which were available to Theophilus.

[198] Cf. *Carmen* V.30.

4 But if the Midheaven gets maltreated, it will happen that the physician is a bad one, and there will be complaints about him.

5 The underground being seen by malefics is an unambiguous indicator of dangers for the sick one; if benefics, it indicates salvation.

6 You must observe which star has produced the illness: that is to say, the closest star that comes to the setting a few days before the illness, or when a star under the rays [is] in square or opposition to the Moon itself. **7** Also observe when this figure changes: for instance, towards morning rising, and the rest of the configurations, so that you know when the sick one will recover his health.

8 One must bring a physician to the sick one when the Moon is in signs of straight ascension, and in single signs,[199] connecting with benefics, or when Mercury is also in bounds of benefics, and in a similar way with the Sun. **9** When it concerns illnesses in the eyes, and the arrival of the physician, let it not be when the Moon is on one of her bonds.[200]

Chapter 6.2: Otherwise, on the sick[201]

1 When it comes to the subject of the sick, one must observe the Hour-marker and the Moon, as well as their rulers and their twelfth-parts. **2** From the stars looking from above, and the conjunction of the Moon, you will see whether they will be dangerous, insignificant, or light to bear: for when only the benefics are witnessing, the release from the illness is quick, and it indicates a lack of danger. **3** Mars on the other hand [indicates] courage, roughness, and a tendency to fall; Saturn, long-lasting and dangerous [illnesses]. **4** And the Hour-marker of the illness, as well as its lord, means the breath of life. **5** The Moon [indicates] the body: if it is corrupted, the body will be correspondingly harmed.

6 But if the Hour-marker or its lord, or Fortune, are both corrupted together, and no benefic looks from above, the danger becomes manifest. **7** The sign in which the Hour-marker or the Moon, or their diameters are, will determine the nature of the illness: declare that there is danger in the part of the body with which the sign has dealings.

---

[199] *Aplous.* **EG**: That is, not double.

[200] **BD**: That is, the conjunction or opposition of the Sun.

[201] From **L**, f. 81r; also **P** f. 2.

8 Sickness will be known from the beholding of the aforesaid stars, for the symptoms and the loosening are figured in relation to the course of the Moon. **9** Whence, on the third day the signs from which she changes her position, moving on to another figure, bring on a crisis;[202] on the fourth day, [it brings on a crisis] when she comes to the hexagon, at the beginnings of the sign, separated from the degree from which she started by the thirtieth part; and on the seventh day, when she makes a square to the place from which she started; and on the ninth day when she sets;[203] on the fourteenth day, after she has come to the diameter from the place where she started her course, she has passed through two quarters of seven days, and comes into another square; twenty, when by three weeks the Moon comes to decimate herself. **10** These, in passing through such figures, remain without danger, and become long-lasting. **11** But if indeed, having moved from a figure to another one, she is looked upon by a malefic, or the Moon comes to be in the bounds of a malefic, the sickness will be prolonged.

12 If the <Hour-marker>[204] is not seen by a malefic, there is a loosening [of the illness]. **13** But if the closest and first which is about to make a figure to Jupiter, takes a malefic, being the next about [to also contact] a benefic, as it slips away from the first, the danger will be alleviated, as long as the Moon is also about to make a figure with benefics.

14 If the sickness appears to be long-lasting, one must observe (once the taking to one's bed has occurred), the star responsible for the corruption: that is, when it will be about to make an exit. **15** And when a benefic moves towards the figure of the taking-to-bed, make your judgment at this time.

---

[202] **BD:** This could be the source of the Moon's position at 40° which is recommended in *Carmen* V.42, **18**, but which is not supported by the Dorotheus *Fragments*. For if the Moon moves about 12°-13° per day, then after three days she will have traveled almost 40°.

[203] **BD:** This is the trine from her original position.

[204] **EG:** Although this is a lacuna, it appears to be the first part of the symbol for the Ascendant. Unfortunately, this is a complicated sentence that seems to be missing something, so it is hard to understand anyway.

Chapter 6.3: Another [chapter] on taking to one's bed, when we know the birth

Comment by Dykes. This chapter has two versions, the most complete of which comes first. This is a method mentioned in *Carmen* V.42, **46-49**, but which (as Eduardo Gramaglia points out) also appears in Valens (*Anth.* III.8). The version in *Carmen* assumes that the native's *gestation* is one of seven or ninth months, and this dictates whether one will divide by seven or nine. But as both Valens and the versions here show, one must first determine whether the "critical" or "climacteric" period is one of "the seventh" or "the ninth." *Anth.* III.8 gives the instructions for finding a crisis of the seventh, but unfortunately the instructions for the ninth are incomplete.

[Version 1: *L, f. 81v*]

1 If the critical period chances to be divisible by nine, take the count from the day he was born, up to the day in which he took to bed,[205] and after counting those days, subtract groups of nine. **2** And if it leaves off in the ninth,[206] he will invariably die. **3** If in the middle of the nine,[207] he will be saved.

4 But if it chances [to leave off] in the critical period resulting from the division by seven, count the same way from the Moon: a convulsive abatement will follow around its waning phase. **5** When she looses her bond,[208] see that the place that has dealings with the place of the body under treatment is not the rising degree, or the sign that the Moon occupies, or the places opposing them. **6** Besides, a malefic should not be in the Hour Marker, or conjoining the Moon herself, or opposing her, or on pivots, while the Moon is post-ascending without the testimony of benefics: for if so, the concurring conditions will be difficult to manage with medical treatments.

---

[205] **BD**: In *Carmen* V.42, **46-49**, Dorotheus likewise counts the days between the native's birth and the day he got sick. But in *Anth.* III.8, one counts from the day of the heliacal rising of Sirius to the birthday. This makes sense in that the method there is attributed to Nechepsō.

[206] That is, with no remainder.

[207] That is, with a remainder.

[208] That is, when separating from the conjunction or opposition of the Moon.

7 If the Moon is not in tropical or bicorporeal signs, or on the Hour Marker, and if benefics bear testimony, the ailing conditions will not be repeated.

[Version 2: Laurentianus 28.13, f. 237r]

1 If the critical period chances to be divisible by nine, take the count from the day he was born, up to the day in which he took to bed, and after counting those days, divide by nine. **2** And if the outcome is nine, he will invariably die. **3** If less than nine, he will be saved.

4 But if it chances to be in the division divisible by seven, divide the summed-up days by seven in the same way, and you will find what you search according to the same reasoning.

[THE SEVENTH HOUSE]

Chapter 7.1: The seventh heading of the twelve manners of inceptions: on childless hermaphrodites, and which of them is barren[209]

1 Take the man from the Hour-marker, and the woman from the setting, and take a look at the nature of the fifth and eleventh signs from the Hour-marker, as well as the stars looking from above. **2** See also whether the fifth sign or its lord is maltreated: then say that the man is barren. **3** If the eleventh place and its lord are similarly corrupted, say that the woman is barren.

4 In the same way, take the Sun and Mars for the man, and the Moon and Venus for the woman. **5** Of these, the corrupted ones indicate the one who is barren.

Chapter 7.2: On bad luck[210]

1 Take a look at the stars that indicate the matter, whether they chance to be in familiar places and the sect. **2** If they are not in such a condition, they are uncertain, with no progress, and incomplete.

---

[209] From **L**, f. 82v; also **W** f. 106r. **BD**: The *CCAG* sources treat this as two separate chapter headings, but it is only a single chapter; therefore we have numbered this solely as 7.1.

[210] From **E**, f. 126v.

[THE EIGHTH HOUSE]

Chapter 8.1: Whether the one about whom we ask is a friend or an enemy[211]

1 It is necessary to examine the sympathies and antipathies from the rulers of the Hour-marker and the place opposite to it, and from their positions. **2** For when they are configured with each other, the trigons are sympathetic, and the diameters and squares uncongenial.

Chapters 8.2-8.5

Comment by Dykes. No source material is provided for these chapters:

Chapter 8.2: Another [chapter], on the short-lived[212]

Chapter 8.3: Another [chapter], on the releasing of the rays of a malefic[213]

Chapter 8.4: Another [chapter], on the triplicity lords of the Hour-marker[214]

Chapter 8.5: Another [chapter], on the triplicity lord of the underground[215]

Chapter 8.6: On the ill-fed[216] degrees by signs, when the Moon comes to them[217]

Comment by Dykes. The degrees below are listed as *ordinal* numbers, as can be seen in the case of Libra. So, "1" means "the first degree," namely 0° -

---

[211] From **W**, f. 112r; also Marcianus Gr. 334, f. 38r. **BD**: The *CCAG* sources list this as Ch. 8.2, but their 8.1 is only a title for the eighth house, with no content or topic; therefore, we have renumbered this as the first chapter. See also Ch. 2.8, which is virtually identical.

[212] But do see *Carmen* I.4, I.7, and I.9.

[213] But do see the chart examples in *Carmen* III.1 and III.2.

[214] But do see *Carmen* I.4 and I.7.

[215] But do see *Carmen* IV.3, **17-20**.

[216] *Atrophōn.* **BD**: I find this to be an unusual term, but the idea is one of illness and wasting away.

[217] From **E**, f. 126v.

59', and "30" means "the thirtieth degree," namely 29° 00' - 29° 59'. However, I do not know the source of these degrees nor exactly what they are meant to show.

Aries	1, 11, 12, 15, 20, 21, 25, 28
Taurus	11, 15, 21, 23, 27
Gemini	4, 10, 15, 21, 23, 27
Cancer	1, 3, 15, 18, 21, 25, 28
Leo	7, 8, 11, 12, 17, 20, 24, 26
Virgo	11, 15, 17, 19, 22, 23, 25
Libra	8, 10, 12, 13, 20, 28, 30
Scorpio	5, 8, 12, 14, 20, 24, 26
Sagittarius	5, 9, 13, 14, 21, 24
Capricorn	5, 10, 12, 20, 26
Aquarius	6, 9, 14, 15, 24, 27
Pisces	4, 7, 8, 14, 18, 21, 24, 26

Chapter 8.7: On knowing whether someone lives or has died[218]

[Version 1: E, f. 346v; also A, f. 42r-v:]

1 From the lord of the Hour-marker, and the Hour Marker itself, and from the lords of the pre-ascension of the Hour-marker.[219] **2** When [the lord of the Hour-marker][220] is in the twelfth, or in bounds of a malefic, or with it, he is harmed by the malefic, [and], in addition to this figure, when the lights themselves are corrupted, together with the Lot of Fortune, and their rulers, say that such a man has died.

3 *Another way*: The ruler of the preceding syzygy being in aversion to the Hour-marker or to the place of the syzygy, witnessed by malefics, means death.

---

[218] This is found in two versions (see below), but see also *Apotel.* Ch. 27, which is virtually identical (and which is based in part on the same passage in **E**).

[219] That is, the twelfth.

[220] **BD**: Reading with *Apotel.* Ch. 27.

4 *Another way*: The Lot of Fortune chancing to be together with malefics, while the malefics are in aversion, indicates death; similarly when in the twelfth place.[221]

5 *Another way*: Look at the four pivots, and their pre-ascensions, as well as the lights, with the Lot of Fortune, and their rulers. **6** And [see] whether most of them are in pivots or have declined from the pivots, whether most of them are in bounds of malefics, and have a diameter or square cast [onto them] by them, or else their twelfth-parts have fallen into bounds of malefics. **7** One should besides examine the bound ruler of the preceding syzygy, as well as from which star the Moon is flowing away, and where it was three days before. **8** And should these have declined [all] together, declare that he is dead. **9** But if the above-said conditions are the opposite, say that he is not dead.

*[Version 2: **B**, f. 112r:]*[222]

1 It is known from the ruler of the Hour-marker itself, and the rulers of the pre-ascension of the Hour-marker.

2 < ... > the 15 [degrees], and their pre-ascensions, as well as the lights, together with the Lot of Fortune, and their rulers.

6 If they are in pivots, most of them, or they turn out to be in bounds of <mal>efics, or are carried over under the rays, or cast a square to ... and their twelfth-parts have fallen into bounds of malefics, to < ... >

7-8 ... similarly, the first syzygy in their bounds, it is necessary to observe from which star the Moon has flowed away, and three days before, and ... and if none are declining, say that the Moon also < ... >.

9 But if those mentioned above are in the opposite condition, say that he will not die.

Chapter 8.8: Otherwise, on those who are dead

Comment by Dykes. No source information is available for this chapter.

---

[221] **BD:** *Apotel.* adds "the sixth."
[222] The sentence numbers here are aligned with the fuller version above.

[THE NINTH HOUSE]

Chapter 9.1: On being abroad[223]

*[Version 1: From **B**, f. 112v]*

1 If someone asks you about this matter, search from the Hour-marker and from the ninth place, from the Moon, as well as from their lords. **2** If the lord of the Hour-marker, that of the ninth place, or the Moon herself, is found in the twelfth place and about to move into the Hour Marker, it shows that the one travelling abroad will depart quickly at that time, especially if also the Hour-marker is found to be the Moon's own house or exaltation.

3 In the same way, when the lord of the Hour-marker or of the ninth place is found to be retrograde, it indicates that the one travelling abroad will return.

4 If Mercury is found to be moving towards the Hour-marker or connecting with the lord of the Hour-marker, it shows that those in his house will receive a letter about him, either from that one, or from another. **5** Mercury flows away from benefics, it shows that the letter includes a good explanation; but if contrariwise it flows from malefics, it indicates the opposite.

6 If the benefics are found on the Hour-marker, or in the ninth place, or in the twelfth, it indicates a favorable return; if malefics are found there, the opposite.

*[Version 2: From **E**, f. 130r]*

On being abroad, whether he will return quickly

1 Let the inquirer on the matter of travelling abroad investigate the Hour-marker. **2** If the lord of it approaches the post-ascending pivot, being close to it, expect the traveler to return quickly: [take] the degrees in between as days, months or years: then, these things are certain, when the lord of the place bears witness to it.

2 Or rather, on being abroad: it is necessary to look at the lord of the seventh sign, whether it approaches the pivot.

---

[223] **BD:** This is listed as Ch. 9.2 in the *CCAG* sources, but only because on the previous page of **B** (f. 112r) a chapter heading for 9.1 appears, without any content or other title. So, we have renumbered the chapters so as to make this the first chapter.

3 Some take a look at the lord of the second place: if it were found to be post-ascending the pivot, especially when retrograde, while no malefic is looking, they say that he will depart.

Chapter 9.2: Otherwise, on being abroad and returning

Comment by Dykes. No source material is available for this chapter.

Chapter 9.3: Another [chapter] on living abroad[224]

1 If[225] you wish to learn about the matter of prolonged living abroad, examine the Sun and the diameter of the Sun, as well as his square, and what star is decimating it, and what is approaching them. **2** If Venus or Jupiter are near them, know that his return will be without harm; but if the malefics come to those places, or the Moon is taken from their opposition, as soon as someone begins his journey abroad it will become difficult and hard to bear. **3** When a benefic does not come near the Sun and the Moon and a malefic connects with the Moon, he will return to his country, but <after> fleeing and having submitted to vexation and dangers. **4** If Mars were found [to be] towards the leading sign, and Saturn towards the following one, [with] the Moon in the middle and Jupiter not looking from above,[226] it would make the misfortunes greater, terrible and difficult; if she were seen by Jupiter, the grief will be lighter.

5 The[227] second sign from the Hour-marker indicates the return, and prolonged living abroad, as well as that from which none returns. **6** Examine indeed its ruler: should it be found retrograde, his journey will become empty and be in no wise effective. **7** If it stands still and is favorably taken towards the front,[228] the one having lived abroad for long will return happily to his home. **8** If the ruler of the second place itself were found on the pivot

---

[224] Edited from **E**, f. 130v; and **B** f. 112v.

[225] For this paragraph, cf. *Carmen* V.23, **1-6**.

[226] **BD:** This seems to mean that the Moon is besieged by sign.

[227] For this paragraph, cf. *Carmen* V.23, **7-13**. But Theophilus reads closer to Sahl here.

[228] **EG:** That is, after being stationary, the planet begins to add in degrees, thus moving forward, or towards "the front."

of the Hour-marker or of the Midheaven, <it will be successful; if in the setting pivot>,[229] he will become sick. **9** If it were found on the underground pivot, it indicates death. **10** If the Moon were found underground, together with Saturn, it means loss and long-lasting lingering abroad.

Chapter 9.4: On the lord of the ninth place

Comment by Dykes: No source for this chapter is given in the *CCAG*.

Chapter 9.5: On returning from living abroad[230]

1 If you are asked about living abroad, whether someone returns or not, or if he lives or has died, and in how many days or months he will return, examine the Hour-marker. **2** If it is looked at from above[231] by benefics, or they are in it, on the same degree, he will return on that very day, or will at least begin his journey on that day. **3** But if there are both malefic and benefics looking from above, he will not return from that journey willingly.[232] **4** If a benefic is on the Hour-marker, and a benefic looks upon it, he will return after 15 days. **5** And if a benefic is rising[233] and a malefic is setting, he will not return until 30 days. **6** And if benefics are on the setting pivot while malefics look upon them, he will return within 3 months. **7** If a malefic is in the fourth while other malefic looks upon it, he will not return.

8 If a malefic is on the Hour-marker and a benefic looks upon it from the seventh, he will begin his journey abroad on that very day; and if malefics look upon it, he will return within 15 days. **9** If malefics are located in the fifth place from the Hour-marker, the staying abroad will be frustrated, bringing him need and restraint, and will force him to stay in foreign lands until his death. **10** If a malefic is on the Hour-marker while another malefic is looking upon it, such a man will die abroad. **11** Now, should a malefic be on

---

[229] Adding with Sahl's version of this question, and the sense of *Carmen*.

[230] Edited from Martianus Gr. 334, f. 146v.

[231] *Epitheōreō*, here and below. **BD:** But this can also be understood simply as "looked upon" or "contemplated," as we often put it. In this case it may mean being overcoming by a superior aspect.

[232] *Ekonti.*

[233] **BD/EG:** This seems to mean rising in the east, and setting in the west, not a relation to the Sun's rays.

the Midheaven and another malefic is looking upon it, the one travelling abroad will perish. **12** If a malefic is on the Midheaven, looked at from above by another malefic, he will not die on this travel.

Chapter 9.6: When we are asked about vows[234]

Comment by Dykes. No source material is available for this chapter, but do see Heph. III.8.

Chapter 9.7: For the setting up of the cauldron[235]

1 If you go on a military campaign under the command of a king or a general, for the setting up of the cauldrons, tents, and quarters for the line of battle of the war, or for movement from [one] place to another, let the Moon not be corrupted, and increasing in light and according to the measurement of her numbers, as well as high and ascending (that is to say, mounting north), and witnessed by Jupiter and Venus or in contact with them, and not seen by Saturn or Mars: since when she is seen by Saturn it causes the movement to be extremely slow, by Mars it leads to war and danger.

Chapter 9.8: On migration from one place to another[236]

1 If[237] someone enquires about moving to another place,[238] and which [place] is better, [whether] this or that one, take a look at the lord of the

---

[234] **EG**: This can include wishes, prayers, curses, etc. (*euchē*).

[235] Edited from **L** f. 171v, and Laurentianus 28.13, f. 216v. For this chapter, cf. *Carmen* V.7. **EG**: The word for "cauldron" is *kortina* (not found in the Greek lexicon), which I take to be a transliteration of the Latin *cortina*, used for cauldrons in open spaces. It may refer to the cauldrons that were set up in the encampment for boiling lead, pitch, and oil, which were generally suspended over simple stone fireplaces. They could be used for pouring white-hot liquids onto the enemy.

[236] Edited from **E**, f. 255r.

[237] For **1-2**, cf. generally *Carmen* V.14, **1-3**.

[238] **EG**: That is, settling in a foreign land.

Hour-marker, the Moon, and the ruler of the hour; and the one of them that is pivotal, that will prevail as the indicator.[239] **2** So consider the indicator itself: and if it flows away from an infortune and applies to a benefic star, the change of place will be beneficial; but should it separate from a benefic star and apply to a malefic one, it would show that the change to foreign lands will be unfortunate.[240]

3 And if the indicator does not make either a separation or connection, see whether it is placed towards the end of a sign, and is about to pass from one sign into another. **4** If it has greater power in that sign in which it is (like when it is in house, exaltation, bound, trigon, or face), being weak in the sign to which it is about to move, it shows that it will be better for the enquirer to remain where he is. **5** However, if it will be more powerful in the second sign, then he had better change residence. **6** And if the indicator is found at the beginning of a sign, and it has greater strength in the sign towards which it is heading, it shows that it is good to move. **7** And if the indicator has strength in the sign in which it is, and is unfortunate in the sign to which it is about to change, then it is better for him to settle where he already resides.

Chapter 9.9: On letters[241]

1 See the Moon and Mercury, which show the matter on all things written, and rolls of papyrus. **2** For the Moon also shows what is written on a roll of papyrus: if these [two] see the benefic stars, the text is good [news], if malefic, evil. **3** Also see the connections and flowings-away of the Moon: if she flows away from benefic stars, the text is good [news]; if from infortunes, bad. **4** But should the Moon be deprived from either a separation from, or application to, any star, it shows [something in the] middle: neither good nor evil.

---

[239] *Talel*, here and throughout the chapter. **BD:** This is a Greek transliteration of the Arabic دليل or *dalīl*, "indicator" or "significator." It suggests that the current version of this chapter was not Theophilus's own Greek but came through an Arabic intermediary; or perhaps he himself adapted it from an original Arabic source.

[240] **EG:** Reading for *kreittōn* ("better"). **BD:** If the current version of this sentence did come from an Arabic source, the adjective might have been أنحس ("more unfortunate, worse"), which was misread as أحسن ("better").

[241] Edited from Marcianus 335, f. 301r. This entire chapter (or its source) seems to be the source of 'Umar's chapter on the same topic, from his book of questions: see *The Book of the Nine Judges*, §5.60.

5 If the Moon connects with an unfortunate star, it shows bad things. **6** But in the same way as when she applies to a benefic star it shows good things, it has the same meaning when she is declining from the Hour-marker and connects with a benefic star. **7** But if the star which the Moon contacts is in between the ruler of the Hour-marker and that of the Midheaven,[242] or even better, when it applies to the ruler of the Midheaven, this being benefic, then it shows that the written things are good [news], or dealing with royal affairs or matters of high repute, and of good deeds. **8** However, if a malefic star is received by the ruler of the Hour-marker and of the Moon, like when seeing it from its house, exaltation, or bound, it similarly indicates matters about kings or rulers, but also unrighteous deeds.

9 And if the application of the Moon, or her separation, is by means of a square, diameter, or a conjunction, it shows that the written things are true, especially if she is received among them. **10** If she is not received, it also shows that it is true, though also that there is petty controversy. **11** If from a trigon or hexagon, it causes joy and merriment. **12** And whether it is received or is not, in the same way look at the Moon: if she sees a benefic star, the letter is true; if a malefic one, a lie.

---

[242] **BD**: In *Judges*, this is clearly a transfer or collection of light.

[THE TENTH HOUSE]

Chapter 10.1: On the proposal of a ruler

Comment by Dykes. This chapter is found in **B**, f. 113r, but is identical to *Labors* Ch. 25, and so the reader is referred there.

Chapter 10.2: Whether this comes to pass

Comment by Dykes. Unfortunately, we cannot find this passage. The citation in *CCAG* VIII.1, p. 124 refers to Florence, Magliabech 7, f. 149, but this is in the middle of a commentary on Ptolemy's method of finding the longevity releaser (which extends for pages before and after this). Perhaps in the future we will be able to locate it.

Chapter 10.3: Whether the matter comes to pass or not, and whether it is imminent or delayed[243]

1 Above all, it is necessary to examine the culminating sign and its rulers: and if they are pivotal, the matter takes place on the spot. **2** But if those rulers fall in the post-ascensions of the pivot of the Midheaven, the matter will come into being after some time, especially if they are in the hemisphere under the earth, and make a figure with the Sun. **3** When declining from the Midheaven, they indicate that the matter has already taken place. **4** If they are in the third, sixth, ninth, and twelfth place, and they do not make a figure with the lights, they indicate that the matter will not take place.

Chapter 10.4: On the place pertaining to action

Comment by Dykes: This chapter is one of several which were partly preserved in **B**, as mentioned in *CCAG* VIII.1, p. 125 n. 1. But this particular chapter has been erased from the manuscript by someone, leaving only its title.

---

[243] Edited from Laurentianus 28.13, ff. 216v-217r.

APPENDIX A: ARABIC PASSAGES OF THEOPHILUS

In this Appendix I translate 14 sets of Arabic passages which explicitly cite Theophilus, usually on topics *not* found in the Greek works in this volume.[1] For example, al-Rijāl's *Skilled* I.42 contains a passage attributed to Theophilus, and whose sentences match *On Various Inceptions* Chs. 5.1 and 5.4—but because they do not add anything to our understanding of Theophilus, I have not included them here. But *Skilled* I.43 is not reflected in the Greek manuscripts, so I have included it. But in other cases I found other authors' use of known passages from Theophilus interesting. Of this material:

- Six passages (#1, 9-12, 13) are straightforward natal delineations, usually (but not always) based on Dorotheus. This gives evidence of a separate natal work not yet identified.
- Two passages (#5-6) are inceptions or questions, which are either from a separate work, or more likely were originally part of the incomplete tenth house material of *OVI*.
- One passage (#2) is an inception or question, which is probably based on otherwise unknown natal material on sterility.
- Three passages (#4, 7-8) are inceptions based on Dorothean inceptions. But they are sometimes much fuller than what is found in *OVI* or *Carmen*, which suggests the existence of a separate work on questions or inceptions.
- One passage (#3) is a question also found largely in *OVI*, but I include it here because it gives more insight into the use of Saturn as a female planet. For more on this, see my Introduction, Section 2.
- One passage (#14) is a set of inceptions also largely found in *OVI* and *Labors*, but I include it here as an example of how some Arabic writers understood (or misunderstood) Theophilus.

So, six passages indicate that Theophilus wrote a separate natal work, and six passages (or perhaps only four) suggest some other work on inceptions or questions. Pingree claims (without specific cites) that numerous passages in one of Māshā'allāh's works on questions also draw on Theophilus,[2] but

---

[1] Another source Sezgin mentions but does not explain precisely (p. 50), is evidently in the Danishgah Library (Iran), by a man named Baihaqī, *Collections*.

[2] Pingree 1997, pp. 128-29.

until I translate these for my forthcoming Māshā'allāh volume, I cannot be sure.

Following are the manuscripts used for al-Rijāl:

- **B**: London, British Library Add. 23399.
- **N**: Istanbul, Nuruosmaniye 2766.
- **1485**: *De iudiciis astrorum* (Venice: Erhard Ratdolt, 1485).

As for Sahl's *Book on Nativities*:

- **M**: Teheran, Majlis 6484.
- **E** is Madrid, Escorial 1636.

Please note that the sentence numbering for the Abū Ma'shar and al-Rijāl passages reflect only the sentences in the Theophilus section, *not* where they fall within the chapter as a whole. These sentences will be renumbered for future translations.

1. Abū Ma'shar, *Great Introduction* VIII.4

Fifth house, Lot of children:[3]

1 The Lot of children, according to what Hermes and all of [his] predecessors claimed, is taken by day from Jupiter to Saturn (and by night the contrary), and on top of it is added the degrees of the Ascendant, and it is cast out from the Ascendant, so where it reaches, there is the Lot of children. **2** And this Lot coincides with the Lot of life.

3 So as for by night, the Lot of children and the Lot of siblings coincide in one place.

4 And Theophilus claimed that the Lot of children is taken by day *and* by night from Jupiter to Saturn; but the first Lot which Hermes and all of [his] predecessors claims, is more appropriate.

---

[3] See Lemay, Vol. 3, p. 630.

Fifth house, Lot of male children:[4]

1 Since the Moon indicates childhood and the young age, and Jupiter indicates coming-to-be and development and creation,[5] and male children, they calculated the Lot of male children from those two, and they said: the Lot of male children is taken by day and night from the Moon to Jupiter, and on top of it is added the degrees of the Ascendant, and it is cast out from the Ascendant.

2 And some of the Persians said that the Lot of male children is taken by day from the Moon to Saturn (and by night the contrary), and it is cast out from the Ascendant.

3 And Theophilus claimed that it is taken by day and night from the Moon to Saturn, and cast out from the Ascendant.

4 And some of the Persians as well as Theophilus said that these two Lots which they mentioned should be turned to for help with the good fortune of the native, just as the Lot of Fortune is turned to; and they are certainly right that to this Lot belongs the indication of good fortune, even though the correct [way] of extracting the Lot of male children is the one which Hermes mentioned.

Fifth house, Lot, of female children:[6]

1 Since the Moon has the indication of childhood and feminization, and to Venus belongs the indication of coldness and moisture, and female children, Hermes said the Lot of female children is taken by day and night from the Moon to Venus, and on top of it is added the degrees of the Ascendant, and it is cast out from the Ascendant.

2 And Theophilus said it is taken by day from the Moon to Venus, and by night the contrary, and cast it out from the Ascendant.

3 But what Hermes said is more correct, because both of the two planets are nocturnal, and the Moon's indication by day and night over female children is stronger than that of Venus—so one ought to begin with [the Moon].

---

[4] See Lemay, Vol. 3, pp. 630-31.

[5] Or, "character" (الخلق).

[6] See Lemay, Vol. 3, p. 631.

Sixth house, Lot of slaves:[7]

1 Hermes and the ancients said that the Lot of slaves is taken by day and night from Mercury to the Moon, and is cast out from the Ascendant, so where it terminates, there is this Lot. **2** And if this Lot and its lord were made fortunate, he will gain good from slaves; and if they were made unfortunate he will get what is detestable from them. **3** And if the Lot was excellent in condition, and its lord bad in condition, the good will be granted to him from slaves, [but] then after that harm will be granted (and if it was the contrary, then it is to the contrary). **4** And if this Lot was in a sign of many children, then he will have many servants, attendants, followers, and an entourage; and it was the contrary, then it is to the contrary.

5 And Theophilus said this Lot is taken to the contrary by night.

6 And Zādānfarrūkh [al-Andarzaghar] and others besides him claimed that the Lot of slaves is taken by day from Mercury to the Lot of Fortune, and by night the contrary, and it is cast out from the Ascendant. **7** But the first one which Hermes mentioned, is more appropriate.

2. Al-Rijāl, *Skilled* I.43: Whether the pregnancy will be completed or not[8]

1 And Theophilus said: If the Moon was full and[9] she conjoins with Mars or connects with him, it indicates a miscarriage and the death of the woman.

2 And likewise, if Mars looked to Venus, and she is in his places (especially Scorpio), it indicates miscarriage.

3 And if you found the infortunes in the tenth from Venus, elevated over her, and especially if they were looking from the stake of the earth,[10] it indicates the corruption of the fetus by the woman.

4 The misfortune of the Lot of Fortune or its lord, from a square or opposition, without the aspect of the fortunes, is an indicator of the corruption of the fetus in the belly of the woman.

---

[7] See Lemay, Vol. 3, p. 632.
[8] Edited from **B** (slide 46R) and **N** (slide 45R).
[9] Reading for "or."
[10] N reads, "of the Ascendant."

3. Al-Rijāl, *Skilled* I.46: If the fetus is male or female

1 And[11] Theophilus said: If you found the Sun in the squares[12] of the Lot of children[13] or its opposition, in a male sign, then it is male; and if it was the Moon, in a female sign from that position, then it is female.

2 And[14] call for testimony from the lord of the bound of the Ascendant and the lord of the bound of the planet indicating the distribution of children.[15] **3** For if the [lords of] the two bounds were two male planets, then it is male; and if the two planets were female, then it is female.

4 And the planets indicating males are the Sun, Jupiter, and Mars;[16] and [those indicating] females are Venus, Saturn,[17] and the Moon. **5** And If Mercury was eastern, he indicates males, while if he was western, he indicates females.

6 And[18] in the matter of Saturn and Mars, I say that the majority of the ancients differed on this statement about them, so they made Saturn be male and Mars female, and in that they saw evidence for each one.

---

[11] Cf. *OVI* Ch. 5.5, **1**, drawn from *Carmen* II.10, **4**.

[12] Reading with **N**, for "degrees."

[13] Reading with *OVI* Ch. 5.5, **1** (and *Carmen*), for "luminaries."

[14] For this paragraph, cf. *OVI* Ch. 5.2a.

[15] This is the triplicity lord of Jupiter, as stated in *Carmen* II.9, **7**; but see also *Carmen* II.9, **11**.

[16] Reading with **N** and *OVI* for **B**'s "Saturn."

[17] Reading with **N** and *OVI* for **B**'s "Mars."

[18] This statement is now al-Rijāl's own.

4. Al-Rijāl, *Skilled* III.17: On imprisonment[19]

1 And Theophilus[20] said, concerning the matter of the imprisoned: If the Ascendant was Aries or Scorpio, and Mars in one of the stakes of the Ascendant, and the Moon connecting with one of the fortunes, and Mars looks at that fortune or at another fortune, then report the quickness of the imprisoned person's liberation. **2** And the time in it will be upon Mars's coming to that fortune by his body, or it will be days in accordance with what is between them both, in degrees.

3 Now if the Ascendant was Taurus, then it indicates the long time of the confinement; but if the fortunes looked at Venus or at the Moon, they indicate liberation, by the command of God (be He exalted!). **4** And if the infortunes looked at them, they indicate ruin; while if there was equally an aspect from the infortunes and the fortunes to Venus, then that side which the Moon looks at will win, being greater and stronger than the other. **5** Now if the Lot of Fortune was made unfortunate along with the subversion of the Moon and Venus, it indicates the ruin of the imprisoned person in his confinement. **6** And if the imprisonment on that day was because of assets [someone] seeks in it, all of it will be extracted [from him] after hardship afflicting him, and adversity inflicted upon him. **7** And state likewise about Libra, except that it is easier in indication, and less in the length of the confinement.

8 And if the Ascendant was Gemini or Virgo, and Mercury is made fortunate, and the Moon is like that or[21] transfers the good fortune of a fortune to

---

[19] Edited from **B** slides 128L-130r, and **N** slides 113R-114R. In this chapter, Theophilus seems to have reorganized *Carmen* V.28 along different lines. First, instead of treating each sign individually if the Moon is in them, he arranges them by their lords, and attributes them to the Ascendant; he then combines these statements with Dorotheus's about what each planet means with the Moon. Then he creatively mixes and matches the rest of the chapter, concerning other planetary combinations. The special contribution here is to offer a form of timing: either the real-time transit of one planet to another, or the number of the degrees between them, converted into days or years. For a different version of this, see *Labors* Chs 22a-22b.

[20] After the name of Theophilus, the manuscripts contain one or two words. **B** has أصطفن, which could be pronounced "Astafan," i.e. "Stephen." **N** has عن أضطفر \ أضطغر, which would be "from" Astafan, but I believe this probably was originally بن, "son of." Now, Theophilus was the son of Thomas, not Stephen; but the protégé of Theophilus *was* named Stephen. So I conjecture that this passage may have been reported by Stephen, perhaps in Arabic, about what Theophilus wrote.

[21] For the rest of this sentence, cf. *Carmen* V.28, **15**.

Mercury, then report his safety and the quickness of his liberation; while if he was made unfortunate (and especially by Mars), without the aspect of a fortune, it indicates his ruin after rough circumstances afflict him. **9** Now if Jupiter looked at him, or he was in one of his stakes, and he had an allotment in that stake, it indicates the long time of his confinement, without emergency or beating or loss—then he will be freed from it. **10** And the time of his liberation will be when Mercury comes to Jupiter by his body, and conjoins with him. **11** Now[22] if the Moon was made fortunate by Jupiter as well, it reduces the time, and that is at *her* coming to him before Mercury does: for liberation will be hoped for him at [that] time. **12** Now if that is delayed, he will certainly not miss out on having his situation change, being liberated, and being made easier—and it will remain like that whenever she conjoins with him or comes to him, up to [the time when] Mercury comes to him, so that [Mercury] will attend to his release after her, by the command of God. **13** And indeed this situation will <not>[23] take place if an infortune looked at Mercury, so it undermines him; but as for if [Mercury] is free of the infortunes and is also made unfortunate, and the Moon likewise, then [the man's] leaving will be hoped for at the assembly of the Moon with Jupiter, the first time, if God wills (be He exalted!).

14 And if the Ascendant was Cancer, then judge for the Moon and the lord of her house concerning the quickness of the release and its slowness, by means of what you see of their condition, in good fortune and misfortune.

15 And if the Ascendant was the Sun, then understand the condition of the Sun and Moon together, in good fortune and subversion: for if you found them both corrupted by Saturn, falling away from Jupiter, then that man will be imprisoned because of a man of elevated rank. **16** And if one of them was mixed with Jupiter or Venus from a strong, excellent places, having a claim in it, and Jupiter is looking at Leo, it indicates that he will be rescued and liberated, and he will not remain except for the amount of degrees which are between the Moon and Jupiter by connection, in days. **17** Now if there was a completed connection, then when she comes to him and conjoins with him, it indicates liberation, if God wills.

18 And if the Ascendant was Sagittarius or Pisces, and Jupiter is in a stake (or not a stake, provided that he is safe from the infortunes), and the Moon

---

[22] Again, for the first part of this sentence, cf. *Carmen* V.28, **15**.
[23] Adding with 1485.

likewise, then it will be all right for him in his confinement, and for his assets, and he will see what he loves from his confinement, and respect in his position. **19** And if he [or the Moon] mixed with an infortune or with both infortunes together, then look at the stronger of the two, whichever it was: for [the judgment will be] based on it—but due to the place of the infortunes, there is no escape from the altering of the matter of the imprisoned person to [one of] hardship, even though its affair will not be powerful due to the place of Jupiter and the goodness of his indication.

20 And if the Ascendant was Capricorn <or Aquarius>,[24] and Saturn in one of the stakes of the Ascendant, looking at it from a trine, and [the fortunes][25] look at Saturn and the Moon, then it will repel powerful hardship from him as well as much adversity, even though his confinement will last a long time due to the place of Saturn. **21** And his period will be years, according to the amount of what is between the Moon and Saturn in degrees of connection.

22 And[26] when Jupiter is free of the infortunes, while at the same time mixing with the Moon, it indicates powerful delight reaching the imprisoned person in his confinement, and the quickness of his liberation. **22** And the time in it is days, according to the amount of what is between the degree of the Ascendant and Jupiter.

23 And[27] when the Moon happens to be in the lower region of the circle (and it is what is between the Midheaven up to the stake of the earth), and Mars in the higher region of it (and it is what is between the stake of the earth up to the stake of the Midheaven), and he is looking at the Moon from a stake, it indicates the quickness of the imprisoned person's departure from his confinement—through death. **24** Now if the Moon occurred in the higher region, and Jupiter inspects her from a stake, and Mars looks at her from a trine, it indicates the liberation of the imprisoned person from his confinement, and his rescue, without loss or trouble.

25 And if the Moon conjoined with Saturn in the fourth or the tenth, it indicates the long time of the confinement, and harm in assets and his body—unless Jupiter looks at her from a stake in which he has a claim. **26**

---

[24] Added by Dykes.
[25] Adding with the sense of 1485.
[26] For this sentence, cf. *Carmen* V.28, **14**.
[27] For this paragraph, cf. *Carmen* V.28, **26-28**.

Now[28] if Jupiter and Saturn looked at the fourth stake (or the tenth) from a powerful position, and they both participated in the aspect, then understand the condition of the Moon: for[29] if you found her with Saturn, it indicates the flight of the imprisoned person from his confinement, and the shattering of his chains, even though fear will attach to him as well as injustice[30]—but it will not get victory over him due to the aspect of Jupiter from his position, and his strength in it.

5. Al-Rijāl, *Skilled* III.22: On the length of the rulership and lives of those in authority[31]

1 And Theophilus son of Thomas said: if the one in charge took charge by day, then look at the Sun and the Ascendant: for if the fortunes looked at them, and [the Sun] is in the Ascendant, tenth, or eleventh, and the lord of his bound or his house is in an excellent place, and likewise the lord of the Ascendant, and the Ascendant is a fixed sign, and the Sun in its triplicity,[32] and in the Midheaven is a fortune, then his period [in office] will last a long time, in goodness and health. **2** And when the Sun was in the Ascendant, tenth, or eleventh, or in the seventh or eighth, and the lord of his bound is looking at him, then [that lord] is the governor. **3** And if it does not look at him, then [take] the lord of the house, exaltation, or triplicity: and if it looks at him, then it is the governor (and the meaning of that is the "house-master"). **4** Now if the house-master was in a stake, it indicates its lesser

---

[28] For this sentence, cf. *Carmen* V.28, **24** and **29**. Note that in *Carmen's* **24**, Saturn and Jupiter are looking at *the Moon* from a trine, which could easily be the "powerful position" here; but in **29**, Jupiter is looking at the Moon (who is with Saturn) *from* the tenth—that is, the tenth from her, overcoming her—or *from* the fourth sign from her, viz. the inferior square.

[29] For this statement about Saturn, cf. *Carmen* V.28, **17**.

[30] Reading ظلام for كلام ("speech").

[31] I have simplified the title of this long chapter. Edited from **B** (slides 137R-L) and **N** (slides 119L-120L). It is a source of Sahl, *Questions* Ch. 10, **79-119**.

[32] The Sun could not be there if he was in the places just mentioned; perhaps this is a separate condition, or the Sun is in the trine (triplicity) of the lord of the Ascendant. 1485 reads as though the *Sun* is in the fixed sign, with no mention of a triplicity or trine. Likewise Sahl (*ibid.*, **81**) only says that the Sun is in "an excellent place" from the Ascendant, and also that the Sun is in the fixed sign.

years, and if it was in the eleventh or fifth, it is [also] like that; and if it was in the third or ninth, it indicates months according to its lesser years; and in the sixth or twelfth, it is less than that.

5 And when a fortune looks at the Sun[33] from a trine or sextile, or conjoins with him, in an excellent place, then add months to the time period according to the number of [the fortune's] lesser years. **6** Now if an infortune looks at him from a square or opposition, it subtracts months from him in accordance with [the infortune's] lesser years. **7** And you work in this topic just as you work with the releaser and the house-master, and their increases.[34]

8 And when the infortunes look at the Ascendant, and the Sun is in a bad place, the one in charge will not cease to be in fear, hardship, and trouble. **9** And if Mars was in the tenth and the Sun in the Ascendant, and it is a convertible sign, then the people of his work will be in conflict with him, and flee from him many times, until he hides himself, and his end will [end] towards his ruin.

10 And if Jupiter was in the Midheaven, in an excellent place, it indicates his elevation and his increase, and his renown will spread far, and [it indicates] the abundance of his accumulation of assets.

11 And when the governorship was by night, then work with the Moon equally as you worked with the Sun.

12 And when Mercury was in the Midheaven with Jupiter,[35] then he will govern [the man's] affair with gentleness, insight, and patience, and his name and renown will be spread far and wide due to that, and he will increase in his work, and especially if the Moon looked from a left square.[36] **13**

---

[33] See the footnote to **7**.

[34] This sentence shows that there is some ambiguity in how Theophilus is adapting natal material to the inception of someone taking power. First, **7** confirms that he is indeed adapting from natal material. But according to that logic, while the Sun may be the longevity releaser, it is only the *house-master* which grants a specific amount of years (just as described in **4**), and likewise the additions and subtractions from the fortunes and infortunes should affect the years which the house-master is able to grant. But in **6** we see Theophilus suddenly speak of planets looking at the *Sun*. I believe that he does this because while he is using the releaser method in relation to the Sun, the Sun is *also* his proxy for "authority" (just like the Moon in nocturnal charts, below). So Theophilus has introduced a confusion because he has not properly figured out how to distinguish his significator of authority from the house-master for longevity.

[35] Probably in accordance with the conditions in **10**.

[36] This probably *her* left square (overcoming Mercury and Jupiter).

Now if the Sun was with them both in the tenth, without an aspect from Mars and Saturn, his renown will extend far, and his lifespan will be long, and he will vanquish all others.[37] **14** And Jupiter indicates likewise if he was with the Moon, in the house of one of them, in the Midheaven, and Venus in an excellent position.

15 And when the two fortunes are in the tenth, it indicates the goodness of his work, and his customs; and in the fourth [it indicates] his safety and good health.

16 And if the Sun was in the eighth or sixth, and the lord of the Ascendant a fortune (and it is in [the Ascendant] or in the tenth), it indicates the uprightness of the matter of the one in charge—in his soul and his body—while it will be feared that the one who put him in charge[38] is ruined.

17 And if the lord of the Ascendant was in the sixth or twelfth, and the Moon and the lord of her house in a bad position, and Mars in the Midheaven or in the Ascendant (and Mercury with him), it indicates an abundance of conflict, and that his enemy will vanquish him, and his work will not be completed.

18 And if the Tail was in the Ascendant, and the lord of the Ascendant in a bad position, and Saturn and Mars in one of the stakes, and the Moon made unfortunate, then due to that he will have assistance from the underclass, undermining his command, and he will not cease to be sad, until he leaves.

19 And if the lord of the fourth was in the Ascendant or in the tenth, or in any of the excellent places, cleansed of the infortunes, and the lord of the house of the Moon is like that [also], it indicates the length of his stay in his work, and the agreeableness of his reputation in it.

6. Al-Rijāl, *Skilled* III.22: On the length of the rulership and lives of those in authority[39]

1 And Theophilus said: If the time of the governorship of the one in charge is not[40] known, and then you were asked about his condition in his

---

[37] Lit., "the remaining," "what remains."
[38] Or, "who assisted him" (**N**). This seems to mean that he killed or harmed his predecessor or one who aided him into power.
[39] I have simplified the title. Edited from **B** (slide 140R-L).

remaining or his withdrawal, then look: for if you found a fortune in the Ascendant, and its lord in an excellent place, and the lord of the Midheaven in a strong place, cleansed of the infortunes, it indicates the goodness of his condition, and the length of his stay. **2** And likewise if they were both in fixed signs, in a stake or in the fifth, or in the eleventh, cleansed of the aspect of the infortunes, his stay will be long and his condition good.

3 And if there was an infortune in the Ascendant, and its lord falling, and the lord of the Midheaven in a bad place, it will hasten his departure, and especially if Mars was in the Midheaven, in a convertible sign. **4** And if the lord of the Ascendant or the lord of the tenth was in the sixth or in the twelfth, then judge the withdrawal of his command—unless Jupiter is going eastern, in the Ascendant or the tenth, for then his removal will be slowed down. **5** And if the lord of the Ascendant is in the seventh, and the lord of the tenth in the ninth, and Mars in the eleventh, then his departure is already near and the evil is coming close to him. **6** Now if it was Saturn instead of Mars in the eleventh then it is likewise, but [there will be] delay in it, because in every matter Saturn indicates delay.

7 And if Jupiter was in the Midheaven and the lord of the Midheaven in the Ascendant, and it is a fortune, and the lord of the Ascendant is a fortune and it is in the eleventh, and the stakes safe from the infortunes, and the Sun in an excellent place, then judge his stability in his work, and the goodness of his condition, and the long length of his life, and especially if the Ascendant was a fixed sign—for that is stronger and firmer.

8 And if you found the lord of the Midheaven and the lord of the bound of the degree of the Midheaven both made fortunate, and the Moon inclining with them both, in a position in which she has a claim and strength,[41] in a sign having two bodies, then state that he will be strong in his work, and will increase and be firm in it—and if he had already departed from it, he will return to it.[42]

---

[40] 1485 omits this "not." The difference is important, because if it should not be there and so the time is known, then this is an event chart or inception; but if it should be there and so the time is *not* known, then this is a question.

[41] Omitting what seems to be a redundant repetition of much of the first part of this sentence.

[42] At this point in al-Rijāl, two more questions are introduced on this topic, but I am not confident that they are still from Theophilus.

7. Al-Rijāl, *Skilled* VII.11.1: On buying and selling[43]

1 And Theophilus said: If you wanted the purchase of something, then let the Lot of Fortune be in one of the two houses of Jupiter, connected with him or with Venus; and indeed, the better choice in it belongs to Jupiter. **2** And if you wanted its sale, then let the Moon be in her exaltation or in her triplicity, falling away from the infortunes, they not looking at her, withdrawing from[44] the fortunes: for that will be completed according to what he desires in it.

3 And if you wanted to buy something cheaply, then enter into that when the Moon is in the second square of the Sun, in a declining[45] sign, and she is reducing in glow and calculation, with Mercury, and they are both safe from the infortunes. **4** Now if she does not happen to conjoin with Mercury, then let Mercury be safe from the infortunes.

5 And when the Moon is in the first square of the Sun and he buys something, he will be granted its [true] value in it, which he wants; and every work he begins in it will proceed according to truthfulness and fairness. **6** Now if Jupiter looked at the Moon while she is in this position from the Sun, in what he sells *or* buys there will be uprightness and fairness.

7 And if the Moon went past this [first] square up to the opposition, it is harsher in appropriateness for one selling[46] something, or an inception in [something], or seeking a lawsuit.[47]

8 And if she flowed away from the opposition up to the second square of the Sun, then it is more excellent for one buying.

9 And if she passed this square up to the assembly with him, then [it is good] for one who wanted to buy something secretly or in a hidden way, with no one knowing about it—and especially if a fortune looked at her.

---

[43] Edited from **B** slide 290r, and **N** slide 242L. For this chapter, cf. *Carmen* V.44, *OVI* Ch. 1.6, **14-16**, and the excerpt from the original *Pentateuch* in Heph. III.16.

[44] This is spelled as though it is the Moon, but a lot depends on what Theophilus believes that the fortunes do for prices. Some traditional astrologers viewed fortunes as producing more goods, leading to lower prices; others, that they made something valuable and so led to high prices.

[45] ناقص. This is not the usual word for a falling or cadent place, but like *OVI* Ch. 1.6, **14-16** (and *Carmen*) it may be a reference to declinations.

[46] This should be "buying," with *Carmen* and the *Pentateuch*, quoted in Heph. III.16, **14-17**.

[47] For lawsuits, cf. *Carmen* V.6, **8**.

10 And if the Moon was in the two western quadrants (and they are from the tenth up to the seventh, and the opposite of that), and the lord of the Ascendant is subtracting in course, and the lord of the Midheaven safe from unfortunate things, it is more excellent in what he buys cheaply.

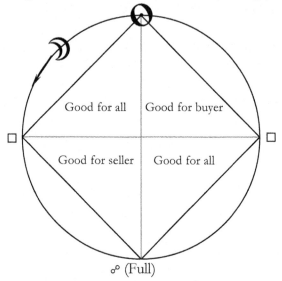

Figure 20: Phases of Moon for buying (Carmen V.44, 48)[48]

8. Al-Rijāl, *Skilled* VII.20.3: On building the foundations of estates and houses[49]

1 And Theophilus said about the ancients who spoke about this: When you wanted to build a home for yourself or for your descendants after you, then make the Moon fit, as well as the Ascendant and its lord, and the Lot of Fortune: for they are more confirmed in the indication of capital, the good, and benefit.

2 And make Mercury fit as well, and strive to have Mars falling away from all of that, if you have control over that. **3** Now if that could not be, then make Venus be strong, in an excellent place from the Ascendant of the building, and her power over Mars from his trine or sextile, or in a stake elevated

---

[48] I have relied on Heph. III.16's quotation of the entire passage from the Dorotheus poem to help clarify this.

[49] Edited from **B** (slide 292L) and **N** (slide 245L).

over him. **4** And [let] Saturn be falling away from them both[50] as you are able, for Mars will scarcely corrupt anything with them, because he always has love [when] with her (and with the Moon) when seeing her from friendship, while Saturn is full of harm with Venus when he partners with her in anything, and looks at her with strength from a position in which he has a claim.

5 And[51] let the Moon be increasing in light and course, and Jupiter and Venus in her conjunction, trine, or square, and Saturn and Mars be falling away from her, for Saturn indicates misfortune in building and organizing, and the long time of the work, and labor in it, while Mars indicates its demolition and burning.[52]

9. Sahl, *Nativities* Ch. 2.11: The statement of Theophilus on good fortune and assets

1 If[53] you found both of the two lords of the triplicity of the luminary to be strong,[54] they indicate high rank from the beginning of his life to its end. **2** And if one of the two was strong and the other weak, his benefit will be in the time of the strong one of them, and his baseness in the time of the one of them [that is falling]. **3** And if they were both falling, they indicate baseness from the beginning of his life to its end. **4** And the aspect of the fortunes and infortunes increases in that and subtracts from that, and the partnering lord of the triplicity supports them both in their elevation, through its strength (if it was strong), and brings [them] down (if it was a falling [place]). **5** And if the lord of the triplicity was under the rays, then it has no strength.

6 And if the luminaries testified to a planet in its own house, then it is an indication of good fortune.

---

[50] That is, Venus and the Moon.

[51] For this paragraph, see *Carmen* V.7 (all).

[52] Following this sentence, al-Rijāl says that Theophilus matches the statements of an unknown Khurzādah (or similar name), in the rest of "the" election (**B**) or the "elections" (**N**). But until my edition of al-Rijāl comes out, it will be hard to know what this means.

[53] For this paragraph, cf. *Carmen* I.24, 3-8.

[54] By "strong," Theophilus might mean simply being "angular" or "pivotal" or "advancing," since he contrasts this in the next sentence with "falling," the usual term for being cadent. But since there are many ways to be "strong," and since this work for falling also has general connotations of being base, we might consider other conditions as well.

7 And[55] every planet which is strong indicates assistance by reason of its essence. 8 If Jupiter was strong, it indicates wealth by reason of the powerful. 9 And if it was Venus, then in relation to women. 10 And if it was Mercury, then by reason of writing and commerce.

11 And[56] if there was a fortune in the eleventh, it indicates the acquisition of assets.

12 And[57] if the lord of the house of assets was a fortune, strong, not made unfortunate, it indicates riches and rank. 13 And if it was like that [but] in the aspect of an infortune, perhaps he will encounter tribulation; but if with that it was falling, he will not leave [that] tribulation until he dies. 14 And if it was falling [but] not made unfortunate, then [it indicates] what is middling of assets; and if it was the reverse, then reverse it.

15 And[58] when you find the lord of the house of assets strong, in good order, and the Moon strong, increasing in her calculation and her glow, trining the Sun, it indicates what is most powerful of leadership and wealth. 16 And if the Moon was like that [but] decreasing in her calculation and her glow, it indicates decrease in that.

17 And[59] if the lord of the Lot of assets was a fortune, in its own house, exaltation, or bound, and the Lot made fortunate,[60] it indicates riches; and if it was the reverse, then reverse it. 18 And if it was eastern it will be preferable, and if it was western [but] arising within seven days, it indicates wealth without rank. 19 And if it and the Lot were both eastern, it indicates its duration and his good living.

10. Sahl, *Nativities* Ch. 3.2: On [the] abundance and scarcity [of siblings]

32 Theophilus said: If you found the lord of the house of siblings in a sign of many children, [and] a fortune looking at it, and the infortunes were fall-

---

[55] For this paragraph, cf. *Carmen* I.28, **24.**

[56] This is probably based on *Carmen* I.28, **30.**

[57] This paragraph bears a similarity to *Carmen* I.28, **25-26** (which is on the Lot of assets, not the second place). However, it is much better explained than *Carmen*, which again suggests that Theophilus's version of Dorotheus was more thorough.

[58] For this paragraph, cf. *Carmen* I.29, **15-16.**

[59] For this paragraph, cf. *Carmen* I.29, **20-22** and **24.**

[60] Reading for "a fortune."

ing <away from it> or one of them looked by means of a weak aspect, then his brothers and sisters will be many, and children will be born to their mother based on what you see of the position of the lord of the house of siblings and the number of fortunes with it which assist it, and the position of the Moon. **33** So, speak about their scarcity and abundance in accordance with that, from the amount named for it.[61] **34** And if you found the lord of the house of siblings in a sign of few children, and you found one of the infortunes assembled with the lord of the house of siblings from a powerful position, and you found the fortunes weak in aspect, and you found the Moon made unfortunate by that infortune which made the house of siblings unfortunate by its influence over it, then judge that the child[62] has already been separated from its parents. **35** Except that if you find the house of siblings made fortunate by one of the fortunes and you find power for that fortune in its position, then you say that a child will be born to his father after him <*unclear*> survive.[63]

36 And if you found the lord of the house of siblings in the twelfth, and you found Mars inspecting it from the stakes, with the strength of Mars and his claims in the position he is in, it introduces hardship and wounds upon him from his siblings, or grief from the Sultan, or intense quarrels.

11. Sahl, *Nativities* Ch. 3.4: The benefit of the siblings[64]

7 The[65] statement of Theophilus on this. **8** He said: Look at the harmony of the Lot of Fortune with the lord of the house of siblings and to the Lot of

---

[61] This is awkward, but means the number of significators listed, and the number of planets involved.

[62] **E** reads, "the native" or "the one born," but in context this must refer to one of the siblings.

[63] Reading with **M**. **E** reads "a child... <*uncertain*> the powerful."

[64] This section is rather difficult in the Arabic, due to spelling differences and mismatches in the dotting of letters between the two manuscripts. My sense is that either Theophilus was very difficult for the original Arabic translator, or the source text was in poor condition. For example, in **10** the text repeats the phrase "and the Moon inspects" for both the fortunes and the Lot of Fortune, whereas normally it would say it once and then list both of the objects in a row. Or in **12**, Sahl has both good and bad things happening at the beginning of the lifespan, when we would expect them to happen at different times.

[65] For this paragraph, cf. *Carmen* I.23, **36-37**.

siblings, and the falling away of the infortunes from them: for that is what indicates that intense love and friendship and good will be bestowed upon him from his siblings.

9 And if you found the Moon assembled with the lord of the Lot of Fortune, or inspecting it with a connection, and it[66] is made fortunate, cleansed of the infortunes, then the native will be higher than his siblings, and he will overpower them, and they will seek his favor, and he will give preference to[67] them. **10** And if you found the Lot of Fortune made unfortunate, while you found the Lot of siblings and the house of siblings made fortunate, then the native will be in need of his fraternal relations, and he will seek their favor, and they will be higher than him: and he will not cease to rely on them[68] in his livelihood—unless you find the Moon inspecting the Lot of Fortune and the Moon inspecting the fortunes: for in that case, you will say that the native's livelihood will be taken away from him due to the corruption of the Lot of Fortune, but some of his circumstances in his livelihood will be good without his siblings, and he will disengage from them due to the goodness of the Moon with the fortune which helps her.

11 Now[69] if you wanted to know in which of the times of his lifespan that will be, whether its beginning or its end, then look first at the Moon and at the lord of the house of the native's assets:[70] for if you found them both made fortunate, then say that the goodness of his livelihood will be at the end of his lifetime.

12 Then, look at the Lot of Fortune, and due to the place of its misfortune it will indicate his suffering and the scarcity of his leadership; and what he encounters of the good will be at the beginning[71] of [his] lifespan, and that is due to the situation of the Lot of Fortune's misfortune at the beginning of his lifespan. **13** Then, see by which of the two infortunes the Lot of

---

[66] This is probably the lord of the Lot and not the Moon.

[67] Reading in Form II so as to avoid the redundance of "be higher than" (Form I).

[68] Reading with the sense of the previous sentence, for what seems to be "he will not cease to act with them" (lit., "be in their actions").

[69] At this point Theophilus turns to the *native's* livelihood and assets, presumably because he wants to know if and when the native will have to rely on his siblings.

[70] E has the house of his assets itself, not its lord.

[71] The timing in **11-12** does not make much sense to me. Sentence **11** says that if the Moon and lord of the second are in a good condition, then it will take time to develop and will only manifest later; but if they were in a poor condition would they likewise only show misfortune later? Likewise, **12** says that if the Lot is unfortunate, that will also only manifest later; so if it were good, would it manifest later or earlier? Something may be missing here.

Fortune is made unfortunate: for if it was Mars, from [a situation of] power, and the fortunes fell away from him, then report that he will not cease to be miserable in his livelihood, subordinate to people of corruption and robbers and immoral living. **14** And if the infortune was Saturn, in his power, then he will become one of the underclass, and pimps, and porters, and what is like that of contemptible works, and he will remain in that [condition] (based on what you see of the Lot of Fortune) unless [that planet] manages the house of [the native's] assets.

15 And the good fortune of the Moon (which I explained to you) truly puts his condition in order after that corruption, [and] then he will rise out of these actions based on what you see of the position of the Moon and her condition, and the position of the infortunes relative to the house of his assets.

12. Sahl, *Nativities* Ch. 4.1: Introduction [to the topic of parents]

6 And Theophilus said: Look at the Lot of exaltation, and it is that you take by day from the degree of the Sun to the degree of his exaltation, and it is cast out from the Ascendant, and where it terminates, that is the degree of Exaltation; and by night from the degree of the Moon to the degree of her exaltation, and projected from the Ascendant, and where it terminates, that is the degree of Exaltation.

7 So, look at the lord of the bound of this degree: now if it was Saturn and he was under the rays,[72] and you found Mercury connecting with Saturn, and you found the Moon made unfortunate by one of the two infortunes, and there was misfortune upon her from the position of the fall of the Sun (and that is that the misfortune of the Moon is from the first degree of Libra to 19°, which is the fall of the Sun), or you found her made unfortunate as well from her own fall, or the fall of Saturn (who is the lord of the bound of the degree), then know that the mother has certainly committed a deed of wickedness in this birth, and this native is not of his father, and he will do works which will humiliate him if he was noble in his lineage and deeds.

---

[72] I believe Theophilus uses Saturn because he is one of the natural significators of the father, and being under the rays suggest a hidden or unknown father.

8 Now if Jupiter was the lord of the bound of Exaltation, and the Moon was inspecting Jupiter, and the Sun was like that with Jupiter, inspecting him, then the native belongs to his father. **9** And if the Moon and Mercury were both made unfortunate, and Saturn was under the rays, then know that the mother has certainly committed a deed of wickedness in that birth. **10** Now if one of these three was cleansed of the infortunes, then know that the child is legitimate but the mother has committed an act of wickedness.

11 And if the Lot of exaltation was in the bound of a planet, then that planet is called the lord of the Lot of exaltation: and if it was made unfortunate, and Mercury and the Moon were both made unfortunate by whichever of the two infortunes it was, then the native is from another father; and God is more knowledgeable.

13. Sahl, *Nativities* Ch. 6.2: On chronic illness of the eyesight

34 And[73] Theophilus said: Know that the harm of Mars is worse than the harm of Saturn, and the worst is [if] the luminary[74] is in the seventh and the infortunes follow it, and it is in the stake of the Moon;[75] and more unfortunate for that is if it is at the fullness of the Moon. **35** Now[76] if Jupiter looked at the Sun from [the Sun's] own place,[77] his eyesight will not wholly disappear, but a little bit will remain. **36** And if Saturn and Mars met together above Jupiter[78] from the stakes, with an aspect and connection, so the position of the Sun and Moon is weakened, then all of his eyesight will disappear.

37 And[79] if the Moon was with Saturn in Sagittarius, then that will afflict him in two places: one of them is his eye, and the other in the <*uncertain*>[80] of the archer; and likewise, if she looked at Saturn from a square or opposition, judge the scarcity of the eyesight.

---

[73] For this sentence, cf. *Carmen* IV.2, **25** and **27-28**.

[74] Theophilus seems to mean the Sun, because the next sentence presents a mitigating condition.

[75] In *Carmen* IV.2, **28**, this is Mars opposing the Moon ("from the seventh"), so he would indeed be in her whole-sign angle.

[76] For this sentence, cf. *Carmen* IV.2, **26**.

[77] This would have to be Leo.

[78] This must mean they are decimating him.

[79] Cf. *Carmen* IV.2, **33-34**.

[80] The MSS seem to read an undotted: بصسب. There seems to be some confusion between the anatomy of Sagittarius and the anatomy of the body.

38 Now[81] if the nativity was by night and the Moon is made unfortunate by Saturn instead of the Sun, it is the left side and the left eye, and the left hand, and <*uncertain*>[82] the chronic illness will afflict him in it, and [the treatments] will not benefit in his chronic illness, until he dies with his chronic illness—if the one in charge of the misfortune was Saturn.

39 And[83] if the Moon was made unfortunate from a square or opposition,[84] it indicates cataracts or an ailment in the eye; now if an infortune looked in addition,[85] then he will be blind. **40** Now if with that the Moon was full, then that is above[86] cataracts but below blindness. **41** And if the infortunes looked at her from a square or opposition, and the fortunes looked at her as well, there will be cataracts of both eyes, and a powerful dimness [of vision] will happen to him in his eyes, and that is because the Moon is unfortunate along with the misfortune of the two stakes, so that what I mentioned will afflict him in both eyes, but he will not be blind: for if something of the fortunes looked at her, then that chronic illness will be benefited by the treatments and remedies, and the chronic illness of the eyes will not be complete, and his eyes will change at times to fitness and times to corruption due to the aspect of the infortunes and fortunes.

43 And[87] if the luminaries are corrupted in the Ascendant or the opposite, it indicates harm in the eye, and likewise if the luminaries were in one of these two places and the infortunes rise after them.

44 And[88] if the Moon was full, replete in [her] glow, and she connects with an infortune in a stake, it will harm his eyesight. **45** And if a fortune looked at her, [*illegible*].[89]

---

[81] Cf. *Carmen* IV.2, **40-41**.

[82] M seems to read, "and his sickliness will afflict him in" the chronic illness, but the word for sickliness could also be the word above for cataracts. E has a few more words but they are illegible.

[83] For **39-40**, cf. *Carmen* IV.2, **43** and **51**.

[84] But this is *only* if she is also on one of the fixed stars or clusters which indicate harm to the eyesight (see below).

[85] Perhaps Theophilus means that the *other* infortune is looking, along with the one which makes her unfortunate.

[86] That is, "more than" or "worse than."

[87] Cf. *Carmen* IV.2, **24** and **27**.

[88] Compare **44-45** with **40-41** above.

46 If the Moon was replete in [her] glow, and she is in the Ascendant and has testimony (or the nativity was by night), and Mars was with her in the sign, connecting with her, it indicates the disappearance of the native's eyesight. **47** And if,[90] along with what I mentioned, the twelfth-part of the Moon was with Mars, that chronic illness will afflict him in his childhood or from that year.[91]

[The degrees of chronic illness and blindness, from Dorotheus]

48 And[92] if you found the Moon in the degrees of chronic illness in the signs, and the infortunes looked at her and their bound, <it indicates> a defect of the eyesight generally, or in the rest of the body: because in the signs are positions which if the Moon is made unfortunate in them, or the lord of the Ascendant, it indicates the corruption of the eye; and that is:

49 If the Moon was in Leo, having already passed half [of it] until she completes 18°, and that is around the mane of the Lion, which is called *al-Dafārah*.[93]

50 And in Scorpio, in the eighth, ninth, and tenth degree, and in 23, and it is the forehead of the Scorpion.

51 And in Sagittarius, from 6° to 9°, and that is the place of the arrow.

52 And in Aquarius, the tenth, eighteenth, and nineteenth, and that is due to the place of the rope which is in it.

53 And in Capricorn, from 26° to 29°, and that is because of the spines.

54 And in Taurus, from 6° to 10°, because of the position of the Pleiades.

---

[89] About seven words in **M** are largely erased due to water damage, and **E** is largely illegible for this half of the page. But see **41** above, which basically says that a fortune will make the harm or ailment less.

[90] For this sentence, cf. *Carmen* IV.2, **42**.

[91] Lit., "from his year" or "from her year." This suggests that perhaps the illness will begin after the lesser years of either the Moon or Mars.

[92] For **48-57**, see *Carmen* IV.2, **43-51**.

[93] M spells this as الّدوارة (E is illegible), "the rotation." However, as *al-dafārah* or *al-dhafārah*, it means something like "the stinking." However, Kunitzsch and Smart 2006 (p. 41) say that this name is *al-Dafīrah* (الضّفيرة), "the lock of hair," an error for Coma Berenices in Cancer. At any rate, this is still the mane of Leo.

55 And in Cancer, the ninth degree to the fifteenth, and that is due to the place of the cloud.[94]

56 If[95] you found the Moon in something of these signs, decreasing in glow, made unfortunate from hostility, then the eyesight will be chronically afflicted. **57** And if she was increasing in glow, full, there will be water in his eyesight, and <uncertain> and [what] resembles that like <uncertain>, and his eyesight will not be obscured.

58 Now if Mars likewise testified by conjunction or an aspect of hostility, it indicates an abcess or burning by fire, or a blow from a group of people. **59** And if Saturn was the one testifying, he will have the action of coldness along with that, and an abundance of eating.

14. Sahl, *On Times* Ch. 8: On the Times of War

2 From[96] the statement of Theophilus: if you wanted to know the time in which fighting will happen, then look ([in] the hour [when] you were asked), at the luminaries. **3** For if they were opposite[97] each other, they speed up the fighting.

4 And[98] if there were 20° between the Moon and the degree of the connection, they slow down the fighting. **5** And if the Moon was with any of the planets in her own house, the fighting will be quick,[99] and especially if the Sun was looking at her.

6 And[100] if the twelfth-part of the Moon was in the Ascendant or Midheaven,[101] or the place of the Sun or the lord of his house, or with a planet which has just arisen,[102] that indicates the quickness of the fighting.

---

[94] That is, the cloudy cluster Praesepe.

[95] For this paragraph, cf. *Carmen* IV.2, **50-51**.

[96] For this paragraph, cf. *Labors* Ch. 14, **1-2**. Sahl restates this more fully and accurately in **7-9** below. Broadly speaking, sentences **2-9** are from *Labors* Ch. 14, and ultimately from *Carmen* V.36, **1-6**.

[97] This should be "trine": see **7-9** below.

[98] For this paragraph, cf. *Labors* Ch. 14, **3-4**. For this sentence, *Labors* has only 8°, but the point is that she is not actively making a connection yet.

[99] Or perhaps, "hastened" (عَاجَلَ).

[100] See *Labors* Ch. 14, **5**.

[101] **E:** "the tenth."

7 And[103] he[104] also said: If you wanted to know the time of this fighting and when it will be concluded, then look at the luminaries. **8** For if they looked at each other from the trine,[105] and they both looked at the Ascendant, the fighting will be concluded quickly; and if they were looking [at each other] from the square, the fighting will not be concluded quickly, and the fighting will go on, and they will shift from place to place, and especially [at] the beginning. **9** And if they were looking from the opposition, the fighting will not be concluded quickly.

10 And[106] if the Lot of Fortune was in the Midheaven, the fighting will be concluded in the quarters.

11 And[107] if the Sun at the question was in the square of the Ascendant or the square of the Moon, then indeed the cessation of the fighting is also in the quarters. **12** And if the Sun at the question was looking at what I mentioned from the opposition, the cessation of the fighting will be in the oppositions; and from the trine, in the triplicities. **13** And that is when Jupiter and the Moon both come to be looking at the Ascendant, in just the way that the Sun was looking at the question.[108]

14 And[109] look also at the Lot of religion[110] and at the planet which was with Mars or in his quarter.[111] **15** And if they were fortunes it will be over quickly; and if they were infortunes, the war will remain firm and intensify and be long. **16** And if the fortunes were mixed up with the lord of the Lot,

---

[102] This must mean, "arisen from out of the Sun's rays."

[103] For ths paragraph, see *Labors* Ch. 14, **1-2**.

[104] E reads, "And *Hermes* said." But this is clearly Theophilus (*Labors* Ch. 14, **1**).

[105] **B** adds the sextile, but both **E** and *Labors* omit it.

[106] Cf. *Labors* Ch. 2, **23**, which says instead that the war will be ended *quickly*. But the broader point is related to **11-12** below: whatever the relation between the Sun and Moon when the fighting starts, it will also stop when they recur in them. So for this sentence, if the Lot of Fortune is in the tenth sign, then by definition the Sun and Moon must be square to each other (in a lunar quarter): so, the fighting will end at some other lunar quarter.

[107] For **11-12**, cf. *Labors* Ch. 12, **38-39**, which is ultimately based on *Carmen* V.23, **1-3**.

[108] This must refer to the transiting Jupiter and Moon, aspecting the Ascendant of the question chart.

[109] For this paragraph, cf. broadly *Labors* Ch. 37, **1**.

[110] الدّين, although in Hermann's version (*Search* Ch. II.5.3) he reads "Fortune." To me the Lot of Spirit makes more sense, but I could understand the Lot of Fortune. But consider also the Lot of expedition, described in *Labors* Ch. 23.

[111] That is, square.

one of the two sides will not hesitate to leave off and flee, based on what you see of the position of the fortune from the lord of the Lot.[112]

---

[112] E omits "the lord of."

BIBLIOGRAPHY:

Abū Maʿshar al-Balkhi, *Liber Introductorii Maioris ad Scientiam Iudiciorum Astrorum*, ed. Richard Lemay (Naples: Istituto Universitario Orientale, 1995)

Al-Nadīm, Muhammad b. Ishaq, trans. and ed. Bayard Dodge, *The Fihrist of al-Nadīm: A Tenth-Century Survey of Muslim Culture* (New York and London: Columbia University Press, 1970)

Al-Rijāl, ʿAli, *De Iudiciis Astrorum* (Venice: Erhard Ratdolt, 1485)

Bidez, J. and F. Cumont eds., *Les Mages Hellénisés: Zoroastre, Ostanes, et Hystaspe D'après la Tradition Grecque* (Paris: Société d'Éditions "Les Belles Lettres," 1938).

Burnett, Charles, and Ahmed al-Hamdi, "Zādānfarrūkh al-Andarzaghar on Anniversary Horoscopes," in *Zeitschrift für Geschichte der Abrabisch-Islamischen Wissenschaften* vol. 7, 1991/92, pp. 294-400.

Burnett, Charles, and David Pingree eds., *The Liber Aristotilis of Hugo of Santalla* (London: The Warburg Institute, 1997)

Catalogus Codicum Astrologorum Graecorum [CCAG], Vols. I-XII (Brussels: Henri Lamertin 1898-1936)

Dorotheus of Sidon, trans. Benjamin Dykes, *Carmen Astrologicum: The ʿUmar al-Tabarī Translation* (Minneapolis, MN: The Cazimi Press, 2017)

Dykes, Benjamin trans. and ed., *The Book of the Nine Judges* (Minneapolis, MN: The Cazimi Press, 2011)

Dykes, Benjamin, trans. and ed., *Astrology of the World I: The Ptolemaic Inheritance* (Minneapolis, MN: The Cazimi Press, 2013)

Dykes, Benjamin, trans. and ed., *Astrology of the World II: Revolutions & History* (Minneapolis, MN: The Cazimi Press, 2014)

Dykes, Benjamin, trans. and ed., *The Astrology of Sahl b. Bishr* Vol. 1 (Minneapolis, MN: The Cazimi Press, 2017)

Evans, James, *The History and Practice of Ancient Astronomy* (New York and Oxford: Oxford University Press, 1998)

Halleux, Robert and Jacques Schamp eds., *Les Lapidaires Grecs* (Paris: Société d'Edition "Les Belles Lettres," 1985)

Hephaistio of Thebes, *Apotelesmaticorum Libri Tres*, ed. David Pingree, vols. I-II (Leipzig: Teubner Verlagsgesellschaft, 1973)

Hephaistio of Thebes, *Apotelesmatics* vols. I-II, trans. and ed. Robert H. Schmidt (Cumberland, MD: The Golden Hind Press, 1994 and 1998)

Hephaistion of Thebes, trans. Eduardo Gramaglia and ed. Benjamin Dykes, *Apotelesmatics Book III: On Inceptions* (Minneapolis, MN: The Cazimi Press, 2013)

Hermann of Carinthia, Benjamin Dykes trans. and ed., *The Search of the Heart* (Minneapolis, MN: The Cazimi Press, 2011)

Hoyland, Robert G., *Seeing Islam as Others Saw It: A Survey and Evaluation of Christian, Jewish and Zoroastrian Writings on Early Islam* (Princeton, NJ: The Darwin Press, Inc., 1997)

Hoyland, Robert G., *Theophilus of Edessa's Chronicle and the Circulation of Historical Knowledge in Late Antiquity and Early Islam* (Liverpool: Liverpool University Press, 2011)

Hugo of Santalla, *Liber Aristotilis* (published by Dykes as *The Book of Aristotle*), in Dykes, trans. and ed., *Persian Nativities I* (Minneapolis, MN: The Cazimi Press, 2009)

Ibn Khaldun, trans. Franz Rosenthal, *The Muqaddimah: An Introduction to History* (Princeton: Princeton University Press, 1980)

Kunitsch, Paul, trans. and ed., "Liber de Stellis Beibeniis," in *Hermetis Trismegisti: Astrologica et Divinatoria* (Turnhout: Brepols Publishers, 2001).

Kunitzsch, Paul and Tim Smart, *A Dictionary of Modern Star Names* (Cambridge, MA: New Track Media, 2006)

Ludwich, Arthurus, *Maximi et Ammonis Carminum de Actionum Auspiciis Reliquiae* (Leipzig: B. G. Teubner, 1877)

MacBean, Alexander, *A Dictionary of Ancient Geography* (London: G. Robinson and T. Cadell, 1773)

Magdalino, Paul and Maria Mavroudi eds., *The Occult Sciences in Byzantium* (Geneva: La Pomme d'or, 2006)

Maternus, Firmicus, *Mathesis*, trans. and ed. James H. Holden (Tempe, AZ: American Federation of Astrologers, Inc., 2011)

Maternus, Julius Firmicus, Matheseos Libri VIII [Mathesis] (Stuttgard: B.G. Teubner, 1968)

Morell, Thomas, *Lexicon Graeco-prosodiacum* (London: T. Cadell *et al.*, 1824)

Paulus Alexandrinus, *Late Classical Astrology: Paulus Alexandrinus and Olympiodorus*, trans. Dorian Gieseler Greenbaum, ed. Robert Hand (Reston, VA: ARHAT Publications, 2001)

Pingree, David (1963a), "Astronomy and Astrology in India and Iran," *Isis* vol. 54/2 (1963), pp. 229-46.

Pingree, David (1963b), "The Indian Iconography of the Decans and Horas," in *Journal of the Warburg and Courtauld Institutes*, vol. 26, No. 3/4 (1963), pp. 223-54.

Pingree, David, "The Indian and Pseudo-Indian Passages in Greek and Latin Astronomical and Astrological Texts," in *Viator* vol. VII (1976), pp. 141-95.

Pingree, David, trans. and ed., *The Yavanajātaka of Sphujidhvaja* vols. I-II (Cambridge, MA and London: Harvard University Press, 1978)

Pingree, David, "Māshā'allāh: Greek, Pahlavi, Arabic and Latin Astrology," in Ahmad Hasnawi et al. eds., *Perspectives arabes et médiévales sur la tradition scientifique et philosophique grecque* (Paris: Peeters and Institut du Mond Arabe, 1997), pp. 123-36.

Pingree, David, "Classical and Byzantine Astrology in Sassanian Persia," in *Dumbarton Oaks Papers*, Vol. 43 (1989), pp. 227-39.

Pingree, David, "From Alexandria to Baghdād to Byzantium: The Transmission of Astrology," in *International Journal of the Classical Tradition*, Vol. 8, No. 1, Summer 2001, pp. 3-37.

Pingree, David, "The Ṣābians of Ḥarrān and the Classical Tradition," in *International Journal of the Classical Tradition*, Vol. 9, No. 1, Summer 2002, pp. 8-35.

Pingree, David, "A Greek Ephemeris for 796: the Work of Stephanus the Philosopher?" in *Centaurus* vol. 45 (2003), pp. 79-82.

Pingree, David, "Sasanian Astrology in Byzantium," *La Persia E Bisanzio* (Rome: Accademia Nazionale dei Lincei, 2004), pp. 539-53.

Pingree, David, "The Byzantine Translations of Māshā'allāh on Interrogational Astrology," in Magdalino 2006, pp. 231-43.

Principe, Lawrence M., *The Secrets of Alchemy* (Chicago and London: University of Chicago Press, 2013)

Ptolemy, Claudius, *The Geography*, trans. Edward Luther Stevenson (Dover Publications: 1932)

Ptolemy, Claudius, *Tetrabiblos*, trans. F.E. Robbins (Cambridge and London: Harvard University Press, 1940)

Ptolemy, Claudius, ed. Wolfgang Hübner, *Apotelesmatika* (Stuttgart and Leipzig: B. G. Teubner, 1998)

Rhetorius of Egypt, *Astrological Compendium*, trans. and ed. James H. Holden (Tempe, AZ: American Federation of Astrologers, Inc., 2009)

Riess, Ernst, "Nechepsonis et Petosiridis Fragmenta Magica," in *Zeitschrift für das classische Alterthum*, vol. 6, Suppl. 1, pp. 325-94.

Schmidt, Robert H., trans. and ed. *Definitions and Foundations* (Cumberland, MD: The Golden Hind Press, 2009)

Schmidt, Robert trans. and Robert Hand ed., *Dorotheus, Orpheus, Anubio, & Pseudo-Valens: Teachings on Transits* (Berkeley Springs, WV: The Golden Hind Press, 1995)

Schmidt, Robert, *The Astrological Record of the Early Sages in Greek* (Berkeley Springs, WV: The Golden Hind Press, 1995)

Sezgin, Fuat, *Geschichte des Arabischen Schrifttums* vol. 7 (Leiden: E.J. Brill, 1979)

Valens, Vettius, *Anthologies*, trans. Mark Riley (unpublished; circulated publicly as a PDF)

Valens, Vettius, ed. David Pingree, *Vettii Valentis Antiocheni Anthologiarum Libri Novem* (Leipzig: Teubner Verlagsgesellschaft, 1986)

Valens, Vettius, *The Anthology*, vols. I-VII, ed. Robert Hand, trans. Robert Schmidt (Berkeley Springs, WV: The Golden Hind Press, 1993-2001)

Varāhamihira, ed. David Pingree, *Brhadyātrā* (Government of Tamil Nadu, 1972)

Vescovini, Graziella Federici, "La Versio Latina Degli *Excerpta de Secretis Albumasar di Sadan*," in Archives d'Histoire Doctrinale et Litteraire du Moyen Age, Vol. 65 (1998), pp. 273-330.

GLOSSARY

This glossary is an expanded version of the one in my 2010 *Introductions to Traditional Astrology* (*ITA*), with the addition of other terms from my translations since then. After most definitions is a reference to sections and Appendices of *ITA* (including my introduction to it) for further reading—for the most part, they do *not* refer to passages in this book (and if so, are labeled as such). It is continuously updated as translations continue and more knowledge of the Latin, Greek, and Arabic authors becomes known.

- **Absent from** (Ar. غائب عن). Equivalent to **aversion**.
- **Accident** (Lat. *accidens*, Ar. حادث). An event which "befalls" or "happens" to someone, though not necessarily something bad.
- **Adding in course.** See **Course**.
- **Advancing, advancement** (Ar. إقبال, مقبل, زائد; Lat. *accedens*). When a planet is in an **angle** or **succeedent** (sometimes ambiguous as to **whole sign** or **quadrant division**), preferably moving clockwise by diurnal motion towards one of the angular axes or **stakes**. The opposite of **retreating** and **withdrawing**. See III.3 and the Introduction §6.
- **Advantageous places.** One of two schemes of **houses** which indicate affairs/planets which are more busy or good in the context of the chart (III.4). The seven-place scheme according to Timaeus and reported in *Carmen* includes only certain signs which **look at** the **Ascendant** by **whole-sign**, and suggests that these places are advantageous for the *native* because they look at the Ascendant. The eight-place scheme according to Nechepso (III.4) lists all of the **angular** and **succeedent** places, suggesting places which are stimulating and advantageous for a planet *in itself*.
- **Ages of man.** Ptolemy's division of a typical human life span into periods ruled by planets as **time lords**. See VII.3.
- **Agreeing signs.** Groups of signs which share some kind of harmonious quality. See I.9.5-6.
- *Alcochoden.* Latin transliteration for *kadkhudhāh*, the **House-master**.
- **Alien** (Lat. *alienus*, Ar. غريب). See **Peregrine**.
- *Almuten.* A Latin transliteration for *mubtazz*: see **Victor**.
- **Angles, succeedents, cadents.** A division of houses into three groups which show how powerfully and directly a planet acts. The angles are the 1st, 10th, 7th and 4th houses; the succeedents are the 2nd, 11th, 8th and 5th; the

cadents are the 12th, 9th, 6th and 3rd (but see **cadent** below). But the exact regions in question will depend upon whether and how one uses **whole-sign** and **quadrant houses**, especially since traditional texts refer to an angle or pivot (Gr. *kentron*, Ar. وتد) as either (1) equivalent to the **whole-sign** angles from the **Ascendant**, or (2) the degrees of the **Ascendant-Midheaven** axes themselves, or (3) **quadrant houses** (and their associated strengths) as measured from the degrees of the axes. See I.12-13 and III.3-4, and the Introduction §6.

- **Antiscia** (sing. *antiscion*), "throwing shadows." Refers to a degree mirrored across an axis drawn from 0° Capricorn to 0° Cancer. For example, 10° Cancer has 20° Gemini as its antiscion. See I.9.2.
- **Apogee (of eccentric/deferent).** The point on a planet's **deferent circle** that is farthest away from the earth; as seen from earth, it points to some degree of the zodiac. See II.0-1.
- **Apsides, apsidal line.** In geocentric astronomy, the line passing through the center of the earth, which points at one end to the **apogee** of a planet's **deferent**, and at the other end to its **perigee**.
- **Applying, application.** When a planet is in a state of **connection**, moving so as to make the connection exact. Planets **assembled** together or in **look at** by sign and not yet connected by the relevant degrees, are only "wanting" to be connected.
- **Arisings.** See **Ascensions**.
- **Ascendant.** Usually the entire rising sign, but often specified as the exact rising degree. In **quadrant houses**, a space following the exact rising degree up to the cusp of the 2nd house.
- **Ascensions.** Degrees on the celestial equator, measured in terms of how many degrees pass the meridian as an entire sign or **bound** (or other spans of zodiacal degrees) passes across the horizon. They are often used in the predictive technique of ascensional times, as an approximation for **directions**. See Appendix E.
- **Aspect.** For the verb, see **look at**. As a noun, it is a **configuration** between two things (such as two planets or a planet and a sign): see **sextile**, **trine**, **square**, and **opposition**. See also **Connection** and **Assembly**
- **Assembly.** When two or more planets are in the same sign, and more intensely if within 15°. (It is occasionally used in Arabic to indicate the

conjunction of the Sun and Moon at the New Moon, but the more common word for that is **meeting**). See III.5.

- **Aversion.** Being in the second, sixth, eighth, or twelfth sign from a place. For instance, a planet in Gemini is in the twelfth from, and therefore in aversion to, Cancer. Such places are in aversion because they cannot **look at** it by the classical scheme of aspects. See III.6.1.
- *Azamene.* Equivalent to **Chronic illness.**
- **Bad ones.** See **Benefic/malefic.**
- **Barring.** See **Blocking.**
- **Bearing** (Lat. *habitudo*). Hugo's term for any of the many possible planetary conditions and relationships. These may be found in III and IV.
- **Benefic/malefic.** A division of the planets into groups that cause or signify typically "good" things (Jupiter, Venus, usually the Sun and Moon) or "bad" things (Mars, Saturn). Mercury is considered variable. See V.9.
- **Benevolents.** See **Benefic/malefic.**
- **Besieging.** Equivalent to **Enclosure.**
- **Bicorporeal signs.** Equivalent to "common" signs. See **Quadruplicity.**
- **Blocking** (sometimes called "prohibition"). When a planet bars another planet from completing a **connection**, either through its own body or ray. See III.14.
- **Bodyguarding.** See **Spearbearing.**
- **Bounds.** Unequal divisions of the zodiac in each sign, each bound being ruled by one of the five non-**luminaries**. Sometimes called "terms," they are one of the five classical **dignities**. See VII.4.
- **Bright, smoky, empty, dark degrees.** Certain degrees of the zodiac said to affect how conspicuous or obscure the significations of planets or the Ascendant are. See VII.7.
- **Burned up** (or "combust," Lat. *combustus*). Normally, when a planet is between about 1° and 7.5° away from the Sun. See II.9-10, and **In the heart.**
- **Burnt path** (Lat. *via combusta*). A span of degrees in Libra and Scorpio in which a planet (especially the Moon) is considered to be harmed or less able to effect its significations. Some astrologers identify it as between 15° Libra and 15° Scorpio; others between the exact degree of the **fall** of the Sun in 19° Libra and the exact degree of the fall of the Moon in 3° Scorpio. See IV.3.

- *Bust*. Certain hours measured from the New Moon, in which it is considered favorable or unfavorable to undertake an action or perform an **election**. See VIII.4.
- **Busy places**. Equivalent to the **Advantageous places.**
- **Cadent** (Lat. *cadens*, "falling"; Ar. ساقط). This is used in two ways: a planet or place may be cadent from the **angles** (being in the 3rd, 6th, 9th, or 12th), or else cadent from the **Ascendant** (namely, in **aversion** to it, being in the 12th, 8th, 6th, or 2nd). See I.12, III.4, and III.6.1.
- **Cardinal.** Equivalent to "movable" signs. See **Quadruplicity.**
- **Cazimi**: see **In the heart**.
- **Celestial equator**. The projection of earth's equator out into the universe, forming one of the three principal celestial coordinate systems.
- **Centers of the Moon**. Also called the "posts" or "foundations" of the Moon. Angular distances between the Sun and Moon throughout the lunar month, indicating possible times of weather changes and rain. See *AW1*.
- **Choleric**. See **Humor.**
- **Chronic illness (degrees of)**. Degrees which are especially said to indicate chronic illness, due to their association with certain fixed stars. See VII.10.
- **Cleansed** (Ar. نقيّ, Lat. *mundus*). Ideally, when a planet in **aversion** to the **malefics** (but perhaps some would consider a **sextile** or **trine** acceptable?).
- **Clothed**. Equivalent to one planet being in an **assembly** or **aspect/regard** with another, and therefore partaking in (being "clothed in") the other planet's characteristics.
- **Collection**. When two planets **aspecting** each other but not in an applying **connection**, each apply to a third planet. See III.12.
- **Combust**. See **Burned up.**
- **Commanding/obeying**. A division of the signs into those which command or obey each other (used sometimes in **synastry**). See I.9.
- **Common signs**. See **Quadruplicity.**
- **Complexion**. Primarily, a mixture of elements and their qualities so as to indicate or produce some effect. Secondarily it refers to planetary combinations, following the naturalistic theory that planets have elemental qualities with causal power, which can interact with each other.

- **Confer**. See **Handing over**.
- **Configuration**. A geometrical relationship between signs, which allows things to **look at** each other or **connect**.
- **Configured**. To be in an **aspect** by **whole-sign**, though not necessarily **connecting** by degree.
- **Conjunction (of planets)**. See **Assembly** and **Connection**.
- **Conjunction/prevention**. The position of the New (conjunction) or Full (prevention) Moon most immediately prior to a **nativity** or other chart. For the prevention, some astrologers use the degree of the Moon, others the degree of the luminary which was above the earth at the time of the prevention. See VIII.1.2.
- **Connection**. When a planet applies to another planet (by body in the same sign, or by ray in **configured** signs), within a particular number of degrees up to exactness. See III.7.
- **Conquer** (Lat. *vinco*). Normally, the equivalent of being a **victor**, which comes from the same Latin verb.
- **Convertible** (منقلب). Equivalent to the movable signs. See **Quadruplicity**. But sometimes planets (especially Mercury) are called convertible because their **gender** is affected by their placement in the chart.
- **Convey**. See **Handing over**.
- **Corruption**. Normally, the harming of a planet (see IV.3-4), such as being in a **square** with a **malefic** planet. But sometimes, equivalent to **Detriment**.
- **Counsel** (Lat. *consilium*). See **Management**.
- **Course, increasing/decreasing in**. For practical purposes, this means a planet is quicker than average in motion. But in geometric astronomy, it refers to what **sector** of the **deferent** the center of a planet's **epicycle** is. (The planet's position within the four sectors of the epicycle itself will also affect its apparent speed.) In the two sectors that are closest to the planet's **perigee**, the planet will apparently be moving faster; in the two sectors closest to the **apogee**, it will apparently be moving slower. See II.0-1.
- **Crooked/straight**. A division of the signs into those which rise quickly and are more parallel to the horizon (crooked), and those which arise more slowly and closer to a right angle from the horizon (straight or direct). In the northern hemisphere, the signs from Capricorn to Gemini are crooked (but in the southern one, straight); those from Cancer to Sagittarius are straight (but in the southern one, crooked).

- **Crossing over**. When a planet begins to **separate** from an exact **connection**. See III.7-8.
- **Cutting of light**. Three ways in which a **connection** is prevented: either by **obstruction** from the following sign, **escape** within the same sign, or by **barring**. See III.23.
- *Darījān*. An alternative **face** system attributed to the Indians. See VII.6.
- **Decan**. Equivalent to **face**.
- **Decimation**. A form of **overcoming**, specifically from the superior **square** (i.e., the tenth sign from something else).
- **Declination**. The equivalent on the celestial **equator**, of geographical latitude. The signs of northern declination (Aries through Virgo) stretch northward of the **ecliptic**, while those of southern declination (Libra through Pisces) stretch southward.
- **Decline, declining** (Gr. *apoklima*, Ar. حدر, سقط). Equivalent to **cadence** by whole sign, but perhaps in some Arabic texts referring rather to cadence by **quadrant house** divisions.
- **Decreasing in number**. See **Increasing/decreasing in number**.
- **Deferent**. The large circle off-center or **eccentric** to the earth, on which a planet's system rotates, or at least its **epicycle**. See II.0-1.
- **Descension**. Equivalent to **fall**.
- **Detriment** (Lat. *detrimentum*, Ar. وبال ["corruption, unhealthiness"] or ضدّ ["the opposite"]). The sign opposite a planet's **domicile**. Libra is the detriment of Mars. See I.6 and I.8.
- **Dexter**. "Right": see **Right/left**.
- **Diameter**. Equivalent to **Opposition**.
- **Dignity** (Lat. "worthiness"; Ar. حظّ, "good fortune, allotment, share"). Any of five ways of assigning rulership or responsibility to a planet (or sometimes, to a **Node**) over some portion of the zodiac. They are often listed in the following order: **domicile, exaltation, triplicity, bound, face/decan**. Each dignity has its own meaning and effect and use, and two of them have opposites: the opposite of domicile is **detriment**, the opposite of exaltation is **fall**. See I.3, I.4, I.6-7, VII.4 for the assignments; I.8 for some descriptive analogies; VIII.2.1 and VIII.2.2f for some predictive uses of domiciles and bounds.
- **Directions**. A predictive technique which is more precise than using **ascensions**, and defined by Ptolemy in terms of proportional semi-arcs.

There is some confusion in how directing works, because of the difference between the astronomical method of directions and how astrologers look at charts. Astronomically, a point in the chart (the significator) is considered as stationary, and other planets and their **connections** by degree (or even the **bounds**) are sent forth (promittors) as though the heavens keep turning by **primary motion**, until they come to the significator. The degrees between the significator and promittor are converted into years of life. But when looking at the chart, it seems as though the significator is being **released** counterclockwise in the order of signs, so that it **distributes** through the bounds or comes to the bodies or connections of promittors. Direction by **ascensions** takes the latter perspective, though the result is the same. Some later astrologers allow the distance between a significator/releaser and the promittor to be measured in either direction, yielding "converse" directions in addition to the classical "direct" directions. See VIII.2.2, Appendix E, and Gansten.

- **Disregard.** Equivalent to **Separation.**
- **Distribution.** The **direction** of a **releaser** (often the degree of the **Ascendant**) through the **bounds.** The bound **lord** of the distribution is the "distributor," and any body or ray which the **releaser** encounters is the "**partner.**" See VIII.2.2f, and *PN3.*
- **Distributor.** The **bound lord** of a **directed releaser.** See **Distribution.**
- **Diurnal.** See **Sect.**
- **Division** (Ar. قسمة). In the context of **house** theory, it refers to any **quadrant house** system, as these are derived by dividing each of the the **quarters** by three. Synonymous with houses by **equation,** and opposed to houses by **number.**
- **Domain.** A **sect** and **gender**-based planetary condition. See III.2.
- **Domicile.** One of the five **dignities.** A sign of the zodiac, insofar as it is owned or managed by one of the planets. For example, Aries is the domicile of Mars, and so Mars is its domicile **lord.** See I.6.
- **Doryphory** (Gr. *doruphoria*). Equivalent to **Bodyguarding.**
- **Double-bodied.** Equivalent to the common signs. See **Quadruplicity.**
- **Dragon:** see **Node.**
- **Drawn back** (Lat. *reductus*). Equivalent to being **cadent** from an **angle.**
- **Dodecametorion.** Equivalent to **Twelfth-part.**
- *Duodecima.* Equivalent to **Twelfth-part.**
- *Dastūriyyah* (Ar. دستوريّة). Equivalent to **Spearbearing.**

- **East** (Lat. *oriens*). The Ascendant: normally the rising sign, but sometimes the degree of the Ascendant itself.
- **Eastern/western (by quadrant).** When a planet is in one any of the **quadrants** as defined by the axial degrees. The eastern quadrants are between the degrees of the **Ascendant** and **Midheaven**, and between those of the **Descendant** and *Imum Caeli*. The western quadrants are between the degrees of the Midheaven and Descendant, and between those of the *Imum Caeli* and the Ascendant.
- **Eastern/western (of the Sun).** A position relative to the Sun, often called "oriental" or "occidental," respectively. These terms are used in two major ways: (1) when a planet is in a position to rise before the Sun by being in an early degree (eastern) or is in a position to set after the Sun by being in a later degree (western). But in ancient languages, these words also refer mean "arising" or "setting/sinking," on an analogy with the Sun rising and setting: so sometimes they refer to (2) a planet arising out of, or sinking under, the **Sun's rays**, no matter what side of the Sun it is on (in some of my translations I call this "pertaining to arising" and "pertaining to sinking"). Astrological authors do not always clarify what sense is meant, and different astronomers and astrologers have different definitions for exactly what positions count as being eastern or western. See II.10.
- **Eccentric.** As an adjective, it describes circles that are "off-center" to the earth; it is also a synonym for the **deferent circle**, the larger circle in a planetary model (which is likewise eccentric or off-center).
- **Ecliptic.** The path defined by the Sun's motion through the zodiac, defined as having 0º ecliptical latitude. In tropical astrology, the ecliptic (and therefore the zodiacal signs) begins at the intersection of the ecliptic and the celestial equator.
- **Election** (lit. "choice"). The deliberate choosing of an appropriate time to undertake an action, or determining when to avoid an action; but astrologers normally refer to the chart of the time itself as an election.
- **Element.** One of the four basic qualities. fire, air, water, earth) describing how matter and energy operate, and used to describe the significations and operations of planets and signs. They are usually described by pairs of four other basic qualities (hot, cold, wet, dry). For example, Aries is a fiery sign, and hot and dry; Mercury is typically treated as cold and dry (earthy). See I.3, I.7, and Book V.

- **Emptiness of the course.** Medievally, when a planet does not complete a **connection** for as long as it is in its current sign. In Hellenistic astrology, when a planet does not complete a connection within the next 30°. See III.9.
- **Enclosure.** When a planet has the rays or bodies of the **malefics** (or alternatively, the **benefics**) on either side of it, by degree or sign. See IV.4.2.
- **Epicycle.** A circle on the **deferent**, on which a planet turns. See II.0-1.
- **Equant.** In Ptolemaic astronomy, a mathematical point in outer space from which measurements are made. At the equant, planetary motion is seen as virtually constant and unchanging in speed. See II.0-1.
- **Equation.** (1) In astronomical theory, a correction that is added to the **mean motion/position** of a planet, in order to convert its idealized position to its **true motion/position**. Equations are found in a table of equations calculated individually for each planet. (2) In **house** theory, it refers to any **quadrant house** system, where house divisions are derived by exact calculation or equation (Ar. التّسويّة); synonymous with house division by **division**, and **whole-sign** houses by **number**.
- **Equation of the center (planetary theory).** The angular difference between where the center of a planet's **epicycle** is, as seen from the **equant** (also known as its **mean position**), and its **true position** as seen from earth.
- **Equation of the center (solar theory).** The angular difference between the **mean Sun** (where we expect it to be) and the **true Sun** (where we observe it to be).
- **Equator (celestial).** The projection of the earth's equator into space, forming a great circle. Its equivalent of latitude is called **declination**, while its equivalent of longitude is called **right ascension** (and is measured from the beginning of Aries, from the intersection of it and the **ecliptic**).
- **Escape.** When a planet wants to **connect** with a second one, but the second one moves into the next sign before it is completed, and the first planet makes a **connection** with a different, unrelated one instead. See III.22.
- **Essence** (Lat. *substantia*). Deriving ultimately from Aristotelian philosophy, the fundamental nature or character of a planet or sign, which allows it to indicate or cause certain phenomena (such as the essence of Mars being responsible for indicating fire, iron, war, *etc.*). This word has often been translated as "substance," which is a less accurate term.

- **Essential/accidental.** A common way of distinguishing a planet's conditions, usually according to **dignity** (essential, I.2) and some other condition such as its **configurations** or **connections** (accidental). See IV.1-5 for many accidental conditions.
- **Exaltation.** One of the five **dignities**. A sign in which a planet (or sometimes, a **Node**) signifies its matter in a particularly authoritative and refined way. The exaltation is sometimes identified with a particular degree in that sign. See I.6.
- **Excellent place** (Ar. مكان جيّد). Includes several of the **advantageous places**, among which the Ascendant, Midheaven, and eleventh are consistently mentioned. (These may be the only excellent places.)
- **Face.** One of the five **dignities**. The zodiac is divided into 36 faces of 10° each, starting with the beginning of Aries. See I.5.
- **Facing.** A relationship between a planet and a **luminary**, if their respective signs are configured at the same distance as their **domiciles** are. For example, Leo (ruled by the Sun) is two signs to the **right** of Libra (ruled by Venus). When Venus is **western** and two signs away from wherever the Sun is, she will be in the facing of the Sun. See II.11.
- **Fall** (Gr. *hupsōma*, Ar. هبوط, Lat. *casus, descensio*). The sign opposite a planet's **exaltation**; sometimes called "descension." See I.6.
- **Falling** (Lat. *cadens*, Ar. ساقط). Refers to being **cadent**, but sometimes ambiguous as to whether dynamically by **quadrant division** or by **whole sign** (which is also called **declining**).
- **Falling away from** (Ar. سقط عن). Equivalent to **aversion**.
- **Familiar** (Lat. *familiaris*). A hard-to-define term which suggests a sense of belonging and close relationship. (1) Sometimes it is contrasted with being **peregrine**, suggesting that a familiar planet is one which is a **lord** over a degree or **place** (that is, it has a **dignity** in it): for a dignity suggests belonging. (2) At other times, it refers to a familiar **configuration** or **connection** (and probably the **sextile** or **trine** in particular): all of the family houses in a chart have a **whole-sign** aspect to the **Ascendant**.
- *Fardār.* See *Firdāriyyah*.
- **Feminine.** See **Gender**.
- **Feral** (Ar. وحشيّ, Lat. *feralis*). Equivalent to **Wildness**.
- **Figure.** One of several polygons implied by a **configuration**. For example, a planet in Aries and one in Capricorn do not actually form a **square**, but

they imply one because Aries and Capricorn, together with Libra and Cancer, form a square amongst themselves. See III.8.

- *Firdāriyyah* (Ar. فرداريّة). A **time lord** method in which planets rule different periods of life, with each period broken down into sub-periods (there are also mundane versions). See VII.1.
- **Firm**. In terms of signs, the **fixed** signs: see **Quadruplicity**. For houses, equivalent to the **Angles**.
- **Fixed**. See **Quadruplicity**.
- **Fixing** (Gr. *pēxis*). See **Root**.
- **Foreign** (Lat. *extraneus*). Usually equivalent to **Peregrine**.
- **Fortunate**. Normally, a planet whose condition is made better by one of the **bearings** described in IV.
- **Fortunes**. See **Benefic/malefic**.
- **Foundations of the Moon**. See **Centers of the Moon**.
- **Free** (Ar. نزيه, Lat. *liber*). Sometimes, being **cleansed** of the **malefics**; at other times, being out of the **Sun's rays**.
- **Gender**. The division of signs, degrees, planets and hours into masculine and feminine groups. See I.3, V.10, V.14, VII.8.
- **Generosity and benefits**. Favorable relationships between signs and planets, as defined in III.26.
- **Good ones**. See **Benefic/malefic**.
- **Good places**. Equivalent to **Advantageous places**.
- **Governor** (Ar. مستولي). A planet which has preeminence or rulership over some topic or indication (such as the governor over an eclipse); normally, it is a kind of **victor**.
- **Greater, middle, lesser years**. See **Planetary years**.
- *Halb* (Ar. حلب). Probably Pahlavi for **sect**, but normally describes a rejoicing condition: see III.2.
- **Handing over** (دفع إلى) What a planet making an **applying connection** does to the one **receiving** it. See III.15-18.
- *Hayyiz*. (Ar. حيّز). Arabic for **domain**, normally a gender-intensified condition of *halb*; but sometimes seems to refer to **sect**. See III.2.
- **Hexagon**. Equivalent to **Sextile**.
- *Hīlāj* (Ar. هيلاج, from the Pahlavi for "releaser"). Equivalent to **releaser**.
- **Hold onto**. Hugo's synonym for a planet being in or **transiting** a **sign**.
- **Horary astrology**. A late historical designation for **questions**.
- **Hour-marker**. Equivalent to **Ascendant**.

- **Hours (planetary).** The assigning of rulership over hours of the day and night to planets. The hours of daylight (and night, respectively) are divided by 12, and each period is ruled first by the planet ruling that day, then the rest in descending planetary order. For example, on Sunday the Sun rules the first planetary "hour" from daybreak, then Venus, then Mercury, the Moon, Saturn, and so on. See V.13.
- **House.** A twelve-fold spatial division of a chart, in which each house signifies one or more areas of life. Two basic schemes are (1) **whole-sign** houses, in which the **signs** are equivalent to the houses, and (2) **quadrant houses**. But in the context of dignities and rulerships, "house" is the equivalent of **domicile.**
- **House-master.** Often called the *alcochoden* in Latin, from the Ar. transliteration *kadkhudhāh* (from the Pahlavi. One of the lords of the longevity **releaser**, preferably the **bound lord**. See VIII.1.3. But the Greek equivalent of this word (*oikodespotēs*, "house-master") is used in various ways in Hellenistic Greek texts, sometimes indicating the **lord** of a **domicile**, at other times the same longevity planet just mentioned, and at other times a kind of **victor** over the whole **nativity**.
- **Humor.** Any one of four fluids in the body (according to traditional medicine), the balance between which determines one's health and **temperament** (outlook and energy level). Choler or yellow bile is associated with fire and the choleric temperament; blood is associated with air and the sanguine temperament; phlegm is associated with water and the phlegmatic temperament; black bile is associated with earth and the melancholic temperament. See I.3.
- *Hyleg.* See *Hīlāj.*
- **IC.** See *Imum Caeli.*
- *Imum Caeli* (Lat. "lowest part of heaven"). The degree of the zodiac on which the lower half of the meridian circle falls; in **quadrant house** systems, it marks the beginning of the fourth **house**.
- **In the heart.** Often called *cazimi* in English texts, from the Ar. كصيمي. A planet is in the heart of the Sun when it is either in the same degree as the Sun (according to Sahl b. Bishr and Rhetorius), or within 16' of longitude from him. See II.9.
- **Increasing/decreasing in calculation.** A planet is increasing in calculation when its **equation** is added to the **mean motion/position**, because

the **true motion/position** is farther ahead in the zodiac than the mean one. It is decreasing in calculation when the equation is subtracted. See *Compilation* IV.3, **6**.

- **Increasing/decreasing in number.** When the daily speed of a planet (or at least the speed of the center of its **epicycle**) is seen to speed up (or slow down). When moving from its **perigee** to its **apogee**, it slows down or decreases in number, because it is moving farther away from the earth; when moving from the apogee to the perigee, it speeds up or increases in number because it is coming closer to the earth.
- **Indicator.** A degree which is supposed to indicate the approximate position of the degree of the natal **Ascendant**, in cases where the time of birth is uncertain. See VIII.1.2.
- **Inferior.** The planets lower than the Sun: Venus, Mercury, Moon.
- **Infortunes.** See **Benefic/malefic.**
- *ʾIttiṣāl* (Ar. اتّصال). Equivalent to **Connection.**
- **Joys.** Places in which the planets are said to "rejoice" in acting or signifying their natures. Joys by house are found in I.16; by sign in I.10.7.
- *Jārbakhtār* (Ar. جاربختار, from the Pahlavi for "distributor of time"). Equivalent to **Distributor;** see **Distribution.**
- *Kadkhudhāh*, an Arabic transliteration from the Pahlavi for the **House-master**, often called the *alcochoden* in Latin transliteration.
- *Kardaja* (Ar. كردجة, from Sanskrit *kramajyā*). An interval used in the rows of astronomical tables such as in the *Almagest*. Each row begins with a value (called an "argument"), and one reads across to find the corresponding value used to correct such things as planetary positions. The increment or interval between each argument is a *kardaja*. A single table may use different increments based on theoretical considerations, levels of accuracy needed, *etc.* Some books of tables defined the *kardajas* in terms of sine functions. According to al-Hāshimī (1981, p. 143), the lower **sectors** of a planet's epicycle (closer to the earth, where it is retrograde) are the "fast" *kardajas*. But this probably also refers to the lower sectors of the eccentric or deferent circle, closer to a planet's **perigee.**
- *Kasmīmī* (Ar. كصميمي). See **In the heart.**
- **Kingdom.** Equivalent to **exaltation.**
- **Largesse and recompense.** A reciprocal relation in which one planet is rescued from being in its own **fall** or a **well**, and then returns the favor when the other planet is in its fall or well. See III.24.

- **Leader** (Lat. *dux*). Equivalent to a **significator** for some topic. The Arabic word for "significator" means to indicate something by pointing the way toward something: thus the significator for a topic or matter "leads" the astrologer to some answer. Used by some less popular Latin translators (such as Hugo of Santalla and Hermann of Carinthia).
- **Linger in** (Lat. *commoror*). Hugo's synonym for a planet being in or **transiting** through a **sign**.
- **Lodging-place** (Lat. *hospitium*). Hugo's synonym for a **house**, particularly the **sign** which occupies a house.
- **Look at** (Lat. *aspicio*, Ar. نظر). Two things may look at each other if they are in signs which are **configured** or in **aspect** to each other by a **sextile**, **square**, **trine**, or **opposition**. See III.6 and **Whole signs**. A **connection** by degrees or orbs is a much more intense aspect. Places and planets which cannot see or look at each other, are in **aversion**.
- **Look down upon** (Ar. أشرف). Synonym for **overcoming**, and in particular **decimation**.
- **Lord of the year**. The **domicile lord** of a **profection**. The Sun and Moon are not allowed to be primary lords of the year, according to Persian doctrine. See VIII.2.1 and VIII.3.2, and Appendix F.
- **Lord**. A designation for the planet which has a particular **dignity**, but when used alone it usually means the **domicile** lord. For example, Mars is the lord of Aries.
- **Lord of the question**. In questions, the lord of the **house** of the **quaesited** matter. But sometimes, it refers to the client or **querent** whose question it is.
- **Lord of the year**. In mundane ingress charts, the planet that is the **victor** over the chart, indicating the general meanings of the year.
- **Lot**. Sometimes called "Parts." A place (often treated as equivalent to an entire sign) expressing a ratio derived from the position of three other parts of a chart. Normally, the distance between two places is measured in zodiacal order from one to the other, and this distance is projected forward from some other place (usually the Ascendant): where the counting stops, is the Lot. Lots are used both interpretively and predictively. See Book VI.
- **Lucky/unlucky**. See **Benefic/malefic**.
- **Luminary**. The Sun or Moon.

- **Malefic.** See **Benefic/malefic.**
- **Malevolents.** See **Benefic/malefic.**
- **Management** (Ar. تدبير). A generic term referring to how a planet "manages" a topic by signifying it. Typically, planets "hand over" and "accept" management to and from each other, simply by **applying** to one another. See III.18.
- **Marking the Hour.** Equivalent to being in or on the **Ascendant.**
- **Masculine.** See **Gender.**
- **Maximum equation (solar theory).** The greatest angular amount of the **equation of the center,** which occurs when the **mean Sun** is perpendicular to the **apsidal line.**
- **Mean motion/position.** The motion or position of a planet as measured from the **equant,** namely assuming a constant rate of speed. To be contrasted with **True motion/position.**
- **Mean Sun.** A fictitious point which revolves around the earth in exactly one year, in a line parallel with the **true Sun.** The mean Sun represents where we would expect the Sun to be, if it traveled in a perfect circle around the earth. It coincides with the true Sun at the Sun's **apogee** and **perigee.**
- **Meeting** (Ar. اجتماع). The conjunction of the Sun and Moon at the New Moon, which makes it a **connection** by body.
- **Melancholic.** See **Humor.**
- **Midheaven.** Either the tenth sign from the **Ascendant,** or the zodiacal degree on which the celestial meridian falls.
- **Minister.** A synonym for **Governor.**
- **Movable signs.** See **Quadruplicity.**
- *Mubtazz* (Ar. مبتزّ). See **Victor.**
- **Mutable signs.** Equivalent to "common" signs. See **Quadruplicity.**
- *Namūdār.* (Ar. نمودار) Equivalent to **Indicator.**
- **Native.** The person whose birth chart it is.
- **Nativity.** Technically, a birth itself, but used by astrologers to describe the chart cast for the moment of a birth.
- **Ninth-parts.** Divisions of each sign into 9 equal parts of 3º 20' apiece, each ruled by a planet. Used predictively by some astrologers as part of the suite of **revolution** techniques. See VII.5.
- **Nobility.** Equivalent to **exaltation.**
- **Nocturnal.** See **Sect.**

- **Node.** The point on the ecliptic where a planet passes into northward latitude (its North Node or Head of the Dragon) or into southern latitude (its South Node or Tail of the Dragon). Normally only the Moon's Nodes are considered. See II.5 and V.8.
- **Northern/southern.** Either planets in northern or southern latitude in the zodiac (relative to the ecliptic), or in northern or southern declination relative to the celestial equator. See I.10.1.
- **Not-reception.** When an **applying** planet is in the **fall** of the planet being applied to.
- **Number** (Ar. عدد). In the context of **house** theory, it refers to **whole-sign** houses (namely, by assigning the house numbers by counting to each sign); it is opposed to **quadrant houses** (by **division** or **equation**). For its use in calculating planetary positions, see **Increasing/decreasing in number**.
- **Oblique ascensions.** The **ascensions** used in making predictions by ascensional times or primary **directions**.
- **Obstruction.** When one planet is moving towards a second (wanting to be **connected** to it), but a third one in a later degrees goes **retrograde**, connects with the second one, and then with the first one. See III.21.
- **Occidental.** See **Eastern/western**.
- **Opening of the portals/doors.** Times of likely weather changes and rain, determined by certain **transits**. See VIII.3.4, and *AW1*.
- **Opposition.** A **configuration** or **aspect** either by **whole sign** or degree, in which the signs have a 180° relation to each other: for example, a planet in Aries is opposed to one in Libra.
- **Optimal place** (Lat. *optimus*). See **Excellent place**.
- **Orbs/bodies.** Called "orb" by the Latins, and "body" (جرم) by Arabic astrologers. A space of power or influence on each side of a planet's body or position, used to determine the intensity of interaction between different planets. See II.6.
- **Oriental.** See **Eastern/western**.
- **Overcoming.** When a planet is in the eleventh, tenth, or ninth sign from another planet (i.e., in a superior **sextile**, **square**, or **trine**), though being in the tenth sign is considered a more dominant or even domineering position. See IV.4.1 and *PN3*'s Introduction, §15.

- **Own light**. This refers either to (1) a planet being a member of the **sect** of the chart (see V.9), or (2) a planet being out of the **Sun's rays** and not yet **connected** to another planet, so that it shines on its own without being **clothed** in another's influence (see II.9).
- **Part**. See **Lot**.
- **Partner**. The body or ray of any planet which a **directed releaser** encounters while being **distributed** through the **bounds**. But in some translations from Arabic, any of the **lords** of a place.
- **Peregrine** (Lat. *peregrinus*, Ar. غريب), lit. "a stranger." When a planet is not in one of its five **dignities**. See I.9.
- **Perigee (of eccentric/deferent)**. The point on a planet's **deferent circle** that is closest to the earth; as seen from earth, it points to some degree of the zodiac. It is opposite the **apogee**. See II.0-1.
- **Perverse** (Lat. *perversus*). Hugo's occasional term for (1) **malefic** planets, and (2) **places** in **aversion** to the **Ascendant** by **whole-sign**: definitely the twelfth and sixth, probably the eighth, and possibly the second.
- **Phlegmatic**. See **Humor**.
- **Pitted degrees**. Equivalent to **Welled degrees**.
- **Pivot**. Equivalent to **Angle**.
- **Place**. Equivalent to a **house**, and more often (and more anciently) a **whole-sign** house, namely a **sign**.
- **Planetary years**. Periods of years which the planets signify according to various conditions. See VII.2.
- **Portion** (Lat. *pars, portio*; Ar. جزء). Normally equivalent to a degree, but sometimes to the **bound** in which a degree falls.
- **Possess**. Hugo's synonym for a planet being in or **transiting** a **sign**.
- **Post** (Ar. مركز). A **stake** or **angle**. (The Arabic verb is virtually equivalent to Ar. *watada*, used for a stake.) Sometimes translated as **center**, as in the centers of the Moon.
- **Post-ascension**. Equivalent to **succeedent**. See **Angle**.
- **Posts of the Moon**. See **Centers of the Moon**.
- **Pre-ascension**. Equivalent to **cadent**. See **Angle**.
- **Prevention**. See **Conjunction/prevention**.
- **Primary directions**. See **Directions**.
- **Primary motion**. The clockwise or east-to-west motion of the heavens.
- **Profection** (Lat. *profectio*, "advancement, setting out"). A predictive technique in which some part of a chart (usually the **Ascendant**) is ad-

vanced either by an entire sign or in 30° increments for each year of life. See VIII.2.1 and VIII.3.2, and the sources in Appendix F.

- **Prohibition**. Equivalent to **Blocking**.
- **Promittor** (lit., something "sent forward"). A point which is **directed** to a **significator**, or to which a significator is **released** or directed (depending on how one views the mechanics of directions).
- **Pushing**. See **Handing over**.
- *Qāsim/qismah* (Ar. قاسم, قسمة) See **distributor** and **distribution**.
- **Quadrant**. A division of the heavens into four parts, defined by the circles of the horizon and meridian, also known as the axes of the **Ascendant-Descendant**, and **Midheaven-IC**.
- **Quadrant houses**. A division of the heavens into twelve spaces which overlap the **whole signs**, and are assigned to topics of life and ways of measuring strength (such as Porphyry, Alchabitius Semi-Arc, or Regiomontanus houses). For example, if the Midheaven fell into the eleventh sign, the space between the Midheaven and the Ascendant would be divided into sections that overlap and are not coincident with the signs. See I.12 and the Introduction §6.
- **Quadruplicity.** A "fourfold" group of signs indicating certain shared patterns of behavior. The movable (or cardinal or convertible) signs are those through which new states of being are quickly formed (including the seasons): Aries, Cancer, Libra, Capricorn. The fixed (sometimes "firm") signs are those through which matters are fixed and lasting in their character: Taurus, Leo, Scorpio, Aquarius. The common (or mutable or bicorporeal) signs are those which make a transition and partake both of quick change and fixed qualities: Gemini, Virgo, Sagittarius, Pisces. See I.10.5.
- **Quaesited/quesited**. In **horary** astrology, the matter asked about.
- **Querent**. In **horary** astrology, the person asking the question (or the person on behalf of whom one asks).
- **Questions**. The branch of astrology dealing with inquiries about individual matters, for which a chart is cast.
- **Reception**. What one planet does when another planet **hands over** or **applies** to it, and especially when they are related by **dignity** or by a **trine** or **sextile** from an **agreeing** sign of various types. For example, if the

Moon applies to Mars, Mars will accept or receive her application. See III.15-18 and III.25.

- **Reflection.** When two planets are in **aversion** to each other, but a third planet either **collects** or **transfers** their light. If it collects, it reflects the light elsewhere. See III.13.
- **Refrenation.** See **Revoking**.
- **Regard.** Equivalent to **looking at** or an **aspect**.
- **Releaser.** The point which is the focus of a **direction**. In determining longevity, it is the one among a standard set of possible points which has certain qualifications (see VIII.1.3). In annual predictions one either directs or **distributes** the longevity releaser, or any one of a number of points for particular topics, or else the degree of the **Ascendant** as a default releaser. Many astrologers direct the degree of the Ascendant of the **revolution** chart itself as a releaser.
- **Remote** (Lat. *remotus*, prob. a translation of Ar. زائل). Equivalent to **cadent**: see **Angle**. But see also *Judges* §7.73, where al-Tabarī (or Hugo) distinguishes being **cadent** from being **remote**, probably translating the Ar. زائل and ساقط (**withdrawing** and **falling**).
- **Render.** When a planet **hands over** to another planet or place.
- **Retreating** (Ar. إدبار). When a planet is in a **cadent** place (but it is unclear whether this is by **whole sign** or **quadrant divisions**); see also **withdrawing**. The opposite of **advancing**. See III.4 and the Introduction §6, and **Angle**.
- **Retrograde.** When a planet seems to move backwards or clockwise relative to the signs and fixed stars. See II.8 and II.10.
- **Return, Solar/Lunar.** Equivalent to **Revolution**.
- **Returning.** What a **burned up** or **retrograde** planet does when another planet **hands over** to it. See III.19.
- **Revoking.** When a planet making an applying **connection** stations and turns **retrograde**, not completing the connection. See III.20.
- **Revolution.** Sometimes called the "cycle" or "transfer" or "change-over" of a year. Technically, the **transiting** position of planets and the **Ascendant** at the moment the Sun returns to a particular place in the zodiac: in the case of nativities, when he returns to his exact natal position; in mundane astrology, usually when he makes his ingress into 0° Aries. But the revolution is also understood to involve an entire suite of predictive techniques, including **distribution**, **profections**, and *firdāriyyah*. See PN3.

- **Right ascensions.** Degrees on the celestial **equator** (its equivalent of geographical longitude), particularly those which move across the meridian when calculating arcs for **ascensions** and **directions**.
- **Right/left.** Right (or "dexter") degrees and **configurations** or **aspects** are those earlier in the zodiac relative to a planet or sign, up to the **opposition**; left (or "sinister") degrees and configurations are those later in the zodiac. For example, if a planet is in Capricorn, its right aspects will be towards Scorpio, Libra, and Virgo; its left aspects will be towards Pisces, Aries, and Taurus. See III.6.
- **Root** (Gr. *pēxis*, Lat. *radix*, Ar. أصل). A chart used as a basis for another chart; a root particularly describes something considered to have concrete being of its own. For example, a **nativity** acts as a root for an **election**, so that when planning an election one must make it harmonize with the nativity.
- **Safe.** When a planet is not being harmed, particularly by an **assembly** or **square** or **opposition** with the **malefics**. See **Cleansed**.
- **Sālkhuday / sālkhudāh** (Ar. سالخداه \ سالخدى, from Pahlavi, "lord of the year"). Equivalent to the **lord of the year**.
- **Sanguine.** See **Humor**.
- **Scorched.** See **Burned up**.
- **Secondary motion.** The counter-clockwise motion of planets forward in the zodiac.
- **Sect** (Gr. *hairēsis*). A division of charts, planets, and signs into "diurnal/day" and "nocturnal/night." Charts are diurnal if the Sun is above the horizon, else they are nocturnal. Planets are divided into sects as shown in V.11. Masculine signs (Aries, Gemini, *etc.*) are diurnal, the feminine signs (Taurus, Cancer, *etc.*) are nocturnal.
- **Sector** (Ar. نطاق). A division of the **deferent** circle or **epicycle** into four parts, used to determine the position, speed, visibility, and other features of a planet. See II.0-1.
- **See.** See **look at**.
- **Seeing, hearing, listening signs.** A way of associating signs similar to **commanding/obeying**. See Paul of Alexandria's version in the two figures attached to I.9.6.
- **Separation.** When planets have completed a **connection** by **assembly** or **aspect**, and move away from one another. See III.8.

- **Sextile.** A **configuration** or **aspect** either by **whole sign** or degree, in which the signs have a 60° relation to each other: for example, Aries and Gemini.
- **Share** (Ar. حظ). Often equivalent to **dignity**, but also to **sect.**
- **Shift.** (1) Equivalent to **sect** (Ar. *nawbah*), referring not only to the alternation between day and night, but also to the period of night or day itself. The Sun is the lord of the diurnal shift or sect, and the Moon is the lord of the nocturnal shift or sect. (2) In mundane astrology, it refers to the shift (Ar. *intiqāl*) of the Saturn-Jupiter conjunctions from one **triplicity** to another about every 200 (tropical zodiac) or 220 (sidereal zodiac) years.
- **Sign.** One of the twelve 30° divisions of the **ecliptic**, named after the constellations which they used to be roughly congruent to. In tropical astrology, the signs start from the intersection of the ecliptic with the celestial equator (the position of the Sun at the equinoxes). In sidereal astrology, the signs begin from some other point identified according to other principles.
- **Significator.** Either (1) a planet or point in a chart which indicates or signifies something for a topic (either through its own character, or house position, or rulerships, *etc.*), or (2) the point which is **released** in primary **directions**.
- **Significator of the king.** In mundane ingress charts, the **victor** planet which indicates the king or government.
- **Sinister.** "Left": see **Right/left.**
- **Slavery.** Equivalent to **fall.**
- **Sovereignty** (Lat. *regnum*). Equivalent to **Exaltation.**
- **Spearbearing.** Planetary relationships in which some planet protects another, used in determining social eminence and prosperity. See III.28.
- **Square.** A **configuration** or **aspect** either by **whole sign** or degree, in which the signs have a 90° relation to each other: for example, Aries and Cancer.
- **Stake.** Equivalent to **Angle.**
- **Sublunar world.** The world of the four **elements** below the sphere of the Moon, in classical cosmology.
- **Substance** (Lat. *substantia*). Sometimes, indicating the real **essence** of a planet or sign. But often it refers to financial assets (perhaps because coins are physical objects indicating real value).
- **Succeedent.** See **Angle.**

- **Sun's rays** (or Sun's beams). In earlier astrology, equivalent to a regularized distance of 15° away from the Sun, so that a planet under the rays is not visible at dawn or dusk. But a later distinction was made between being **burned up** (about 1° - 7.5° away from the Sun) and merely being under the rays (about 7.5° - 15° away).
- **Superior**. The planets higher than the Sun: Saturn, Jupiter, Mars.
- **Supremacy** (Lat. *regnum*). Hugo's word for **Exaltation**, sometimes used in translations by Dykes instead of the slightly more accurate **Sovereignty**.
- **Synastry**. The comparison of two or more charts to determine compatibility, usually in romantic relationships or friendships. See *BA* Appendix C for a discussion and references for friendship, and *BA* III.7.11 and III.12.7.
- *Tasyir* (Ar. تسيير, "dispatching, sending out"). Equivalent to primary **directions**.
- **Temperament**. The particular mixture (sometimes, "complexion") of **elements** or **humors** which determines a person's or planet's typical behavior, outlook, and energy level.
- **Testimony**. From Arabic astrology onwards, a little-defined term which can mean (1) the planets which have **dignity** in a place or degree, or (2) the number of dignities a planet has in its own place (or as compared with other planets), or (3) a planet's **assembly** or **aspect** to a place of interest, or (4) generally *any* way in which planets may make themselves relevant to the inquiry at hand. For example, a planet which is the **exalted** lord of the **Ascendant** but also **looks at** it, maby be said to present two testimonies supporting its relevance to an inquiry about the Ascendant.
- **Tetragon**. Equivalent to **Square.**
- **Thought-interpretation**. The practice of identifying a theme or topic in a **querent's** mind, often using a **victor**, before answering the specific **question**. See *Search*.
- **Time lord**. A planet ruling over some period of time according to one of the classical predictive techniques. For example, the **lord of the year** is the time lord over a **profection**.
- **Transfer** (Ar. نقل) When one planet **separates** from one planet, and **connects** to another. See III.11. Not to be confused with a **shift** of triplicities in Saturn-Jupiter conjunctions, or the annual **revolutions**, either mundane or natal.

- **Transit**. The passing of one planet across another planet or point (by body or **aspect** by exact degree), or through a particular sign (even in a **whole-sign** relation to some point of interest). In traditional astrology, not every transit is significant; for example, transits of **time lords** or of planets in the **whole-sign angles** of a **profection** might be preferred to others. See VIII.2.4 and *PN3*.
- **Translation**. Equivalent to **Transfer**.
- **Traverse** (Lat. *discurro*). Hugo's synonym for a planet being in or **transiting** through a **sign**.
- **Trigon**. Equivalent to **Trine**.
- **Trine**. A **configuration** or **aspect** either by **whole sign** or degree, in which the signs have a 120° relation to each other: for example, Aries and Leo.
- **True motion/position**. The motion or position of a planet as measured from the earth, once its **mean motion/position** has been adjusted or corrected by various types of **equations**.
- **True Sun**. The zodiacal position of the Sun as seen from the earth.
- **Turn** (Ar. دور). A predictive technique in which responsibilities for being a **time lord** rotates between different planets. See VIII.2.3 for one use of the turn, and *AW2* for an explanation of the mundane Turns. But it can occasionally refer more generally to how the planets may equally play a certain *role* in a chart: for example, if the lord of the Ascendant is Saturn, it means X; but if Jupiter, Y; but if Mars, Z; and so on. It may also refer to methods in which cycles through the planets, assigning them roles as **time lords**.
- **Turned away**. Equivalent to **Aversion**.
- **Turning signs**. For Hugo of Santalla, equivalent to the movable signs: see **Quadruplicity**. But *tropicus* more specifically refers to the tropical signs Cancer and Capricorn, in which the Sun turns back from its most extreme declinations.
- **Twelfth-parts**. Signs of the zodiac defined by 2.5° divisions of other signs. For example, the twelfth-part of 4° Gemini is Cancer. See IV.6.
- **Two-parted signs**. Equivalent to the double-bodied or common signs: see **Quadruplicity**.
- **Under the rays**. When a planet is between approximately 7.5° and 15° from the Sun, and not visible either when rising before the Sun or setting

after him. Some astrologers distinguish the distances for individual planets (which is more astronomically accurate). See II.10.

- **Unfortunate**. Normally, when a planet's condition is made more difficult through one of the **bearings** in IV.
- **Unlucky**. See **Benefic/malefic**.
- **Upright** (Ar. قائم). Describes the axis of the MC-IC, when it falls into the tenth and fourth signs, rather than the eleventh-fifth, or ninth-third.
- *Via combusta*. See **Burnt path**.
- **Victor** (Ar. مبتزّ). A planet or point identified as the most authoritative over a particular topic or **house** (I.18), or for a chart as a whole (VIII.1.4). See also *Search*. Dykes distinguishes procedures that find the most author-itative and powerful planet ruling one or more places (a victor "over" places) or the member of a list of candidates which fulfills certain criteria (a victor "among" places).
- **Void in course**. Equivalent to **Emptiness of the course**.
- **Well**. A degree in which a planet is said to be more obscure in its operation. See VII.9.
- **Western**. See **Eastern/western**.
- **Whole signs**. The oldest system of assigning house topics and **aspects**. The entire sign on the horizon (the **Ascendant**) is the first house, the en-tire second sign is the second house, and so on. Likewise, aspects are considered first of all according to signs: planets in Aries look at Gemini as a whole, even if aspects by exact degree are more intense. See I.12, III.6, and the Introduction §6.
- **Wildness** (Ar. وحشيّة, Lat. *feralitas*). When a planet is not **looked at** by any other planet, for as long as it is in its current sign. See III.10.
- **Withdrawing**. In some Latin translations (*recedens*), equivalent to one planet **separating** from another. But in Arabic (زائل), a withdrawing plan-et is dynamically **cadent**, moving by diurnal motion away from the degree of the axes or **stakes**—a near-synonym of **retreating**, and the opposite of **advancing**.
- *Zij*. The Arabic for a Persian word meaning a set of astronomical tables for calculating planetary positions and other things. Ptolemy's *Almagest* can be considered a *zij*.

INDEX

In this index I have included numerous astrological concepts as well as interpretive topics, but they are handled somewhat differently. By an "astrological concept," I mean something of general applicability, like "retrograde" or "exaltation": since these can be scattered throughout any kind of passage or discussion, I have flagged each instance of them. But by an "interpretive topic," I mean things like "weather": since these often have their own section or chapter titles which begin more lengthy, focused discussions, I usually flag only a chapter title or the first paragraph, and leave it to the reader to explore the rest. For this reason a concept like "pivots" may have many entries, but each mention in the text might be brief; likewise a lengthy topic like "weather" might have fewer entries but span several pages.

'Abbāsid Caliphate ... 1, 5-6, 10-13, 17-18, 101

'Abdallah b. 'Ali 11

Above/under the earth. 53-54, 57, 59-60, 77, 79-81, 94, 99, 119, 126, 213, 222, 237, 276

Abū Ma'shar 6, 16, 278

Abū Muslim 10, 101

Agapius, Bishop of Manbij 11

al-Andarzaghar 3, 6, 36-42, 280

al-Dāmaghānī 39

al-Jabbār 13-14, 19

al-Mahdī (Caliph) ... 3, 5, 13-19, 21, 28, 33

al-Mansūr (Caliph) ... 12-13, 19, 101

al-Nadīm 1, 7, 9

al-Qasrānī 30-31

al-Qiftī 5

al-Rijāl, 'Ali (Haly Abenragel).. 16, 30, 32, 42, 89, 256-57, 277-78, 280-82, 285, 287-91

al-Saffāh (Caliph) 10-11

al-Tabarī, 'Umar ... 12, 16, 42, 274, 324

Anonymous of 379 .... 26, 29

Antiochus 75, 84

Aristotle 3, 9, 154

Aspect delineations..68, 70, 72, 74

Aversion ... 79, 85, 129-30, 193, 195, 196, 207-11, 214-15, 228, 252

Baghdad ... 1, 3, 5-6, 12-13, 15, 17-18, 21, 33-34, 41, 124

Bar Hebraeus, Gregory . 5-6, 9, 15

Besieging (planets) ... 75, 97, 208, 228

Bible 26, 35, 150-54

Bizīdaj 40-42

Boll, Emilie 29

Bonatti, Guido 19

Book of Aristotle 3, 26, 37-42

Bounds ... 59, 74-75, 108, 127-28, 147-48, 154-59, 194-95, 210-11, 213-14, 217, 231, 243, 248,

250, 252, 256-59, 262-63, 268-69, 281, 288, 295-96

Burned path (*via combusta*)......84

Burnett, Charles 37, 39-40

Chaldeans 154

Chorography 110

Comets 106, 152

Critical days 263

Critodemus 8, 22, 124

Ctesiphon 21

Cumont, Franz ... 5, 29, 41, 112, 116, 209, 219

Decans .. .82-83, 160, 162-77, 181

Demetrius 224

Deucalion (son of Theophilus).7, 17-19, 25, 34, 49, 149

Dionysius of Tellmahre 11

Distributions 236

Dorotheus of Sidon ... 1-2, 4, 7, 14-16, 20-23, 29-32, 35, 38, 42-44, 51, 60, 76, 78, 85, 89-91, 93, 99, 108, 112, 124, 131, 261, 263-64, 277, 282, 290, 292, 298

   Pentateuch ... 42-44, 85, 91, 289

Easternness/westernness 10, 31, 43, 53, 60, 62, 74, 84, 90, 100, 104-05, 109, 125, 129, 131-33, 135-36, 138, 142, 145, 148, 164, 169, 184, 197, 202, 230-31, 235-36, 244, 246, 259-60, 281, 288, 292

Eclipses ... 10, 106, 146, 147, 160-63, 220, 223, 237

Egyptians ... 21, 123, 126, 140, 154, 160, 162

Exaltation, fall ... 59, 63, 91, 104-05, 139, 194, 197, 201, 203-04, 228, 230-31, 233, 235, 240-42, 244-45, 258, 270, 274, 275, 285, 289, 292, 295

Firmicus Maternus. .8, 25, 211-12

Fixed stars ... 26-29, 33-35, 41, 51, 123-24, 192, 194, 236, 238, 297-98

Galen 9

Harrān 3-4, 6, 11

Heilen, Stephan 8

Hephaistion of Thebes ... 4, 8, 25, 30, 40, 42-44, 51, 81, 89

Heraclius (Emperor) 16

Hermann of Carinthia 30, 300

Hermes ... 26, 49, 110, 152, 278-80, 300

Hishām (Caliph) 9

Holden, James ... 7, 28, 40-41, 85, 193-95, 197-04, 211, 220

Homer 9

House-master (*kadukhudah*) 108, 131, 285-86

Houses in war 104, 215

Hunain b. Ishaq 9

Ibn Khaldun 5-6, 8, 12, 16, 18, 21

Ill-fed degrees 267

In the heart (*cazimi*) 164-66, 168, 172-74, 176-77

Indians, Indian astrology 4, 12, 19

Ingresses

   in inceptions 274

   mundane ... 2, 17, 21-24, 33, 108, 123, 125, 128, 130,

133-36, 138, 140, 142, 146, 155

Jesus.. 152

Julianus of Laodikaia ... 35,   74, 103, 105, 107

Juste, David................................38

Kankah the Indian.......................12

Khurāsān 10, 12-13, 18, 33

Khurzādah (unknown astrologer) 291

Light, increasing/decreasing ...53, 58, 63-64, 67, 73, 80, 89, 139, 211, 212, 230, 253, 273, 291

Lord (ruler) of month 138, 140

Lord (ruler) of year.................. 131

Lot............................21-22, 51, 204

of assets............................43, 292

of building.........................95-96

of children .. 198, 259, 278, 281

of corruption or chronic illness 136

of death 210

of exaltation 295-96

of expedition...................91, 300

of female children 279

of Fortune ... 22-24, 53, 84, 92, 95, 97, 99-101, 128, 146, 187-89, 194-95, 198, 201-04, 209, 210, 211, 214, 233, 234, 236, 246, 252-53, 256-57, 268-69, 279-80, 282, 289-90, 293-95, 300

of life...................................... 278

of male children 279

of marriage 198, 200

of religion 300

of siblings............................. 294

of slaves................................ 280

of Spirit 209, 300

of the king........ 22, 141-42, 145

of the month ... 22, 25, 141-42, 145

of the noxious place or chronic illness................................. 211

of the populace.............22, 146

of victory.............................. 101

of war..............................84, 101

Royal.......... 22-23, 125, 128-30

Manethō 40

Margiana...............................13, 50

Mars in war ... 74, 85, 92, 101-03, 111

Marwān II (Caliph) 9-11

Māshā'allāh ... 3, 7, 12-13, 16, 17, 36-39, 41, 277

Mercury in war......................... 104

Merv 10, 13

Michael the Syrian 11

Moon

connections   and   separations 65-66, 79, 85, 94, 97, 211, 229

days of 97, 194

Morning/evening stars..30,   66-67, 84, 86-87, 89-90, 114, 126, 132, 138, 148, 155-60, 164, 178-85, 196, 213, 229, 236, 238, 244, 252, 260, 262

Moses 150

Mu'āwiya (Caliph)......................5

Nawbakht the Persian 12

Nechepsō ... 2, 21, 24-25, 134, 140, 144, 222, 257, 264

Nodes ... 95, 102, 108-09, 111, 147, 195-96, 198-205, 209,

220, 222-24, 226-27, 241, 247, 253-54

Number, adding/subtracting..55, 77, 90, 105, 139, 145, 201, 204, 246, 253

Obert, Charles 32

Olympiodorus........................... 152

Orpheus...................... 218-19, 305

Overcoming/decimation 53, 56, 58, 60, 70-72, 89, 105, 129, 210, 215, 220, 228, 230-31, 233, 250, 257, 271-72, 285, 286, 296

Pamprepius...................................29

Paul of Alexandria 152

Petosiris......21, 144, 222, 257, 258

Pingree, David..1-9, 13, 16-17, 20, 25, 27-28, 30, 33-40, 42, 45, 101, 103, 105, 107, 121, 124, 277

Pivots, post-ascensions, declines 42, 44, 52, 55-57, 60, 62-63, 65-67, 69, 72, 86, 92, 96-97, 101, 104-05, 108, 110, 113, 123-30, 134, 137, 187-91, 196, 207-09, 213-16, 226, 228, 230-33, 235-37, 240, 242-43, 252, 257-58, 261, 264, 268-71, 274-76, 289, 291

Planets
    animals................................... 187
    in angles.... 55-57, 59-60, 62-63
    in the houses........ 195, 197-204
    metals.................................... 186
    vegetation............................. 186

Plato 3, 153-154

Praxidicus.................................. 101

pre-ascensions........................... 269

Precession........................27-29, 41

Ptolemy, Claudius ... 2, 7-8, 16, 18, 22, 25, 27, 29-30, 32, 35, 79, 106, 123, 125-26, 191, 209, 215-17, 222, 237-39, 257, 276

Qabalah 32

Reception................................... 275

Releaser (*hyleg*) ... 108-09, 126-27, 131, 276, 286

Retrogradation...54, 77, 80, 93, 106-07, 122, 151, 204, 224, 242, 244, 270-71

Rhetorius of Egypt..2-4, 6-8, 16-17, 20, 25-29, 33-41, 85, 103, 105, 107, 187, 193-95, 197-207, 210-11, 220

Sahl b. Bishr...4, 13, 19-20, 26, 31-32, 39-43, 54, 84, 87, 271-72, 278, 285, 291-93, 295-96, 299

Sasanian Persians1, 4-5, 7, 9-10, 18

Saturn as feminine.......................30

Schmidt, Robert... 30, 65-66, 68, 75, 84, 91, 116, 119-120, 137, 223-224

Sect... 22, 24, 32, 54-55, 57-58, 63, 66, 88, 89, 104, 107, 110, 126, 128, 130-31, 136, 194, 196, 201, 206, 208, 210, 213, 228, 230-31, 233, 239, 242-44, 253, 257, 259, 266, 279, 286

Serapio 84

Signs
 bicorporeal...51, 55-56, 58, 60, 62, 78-79, 104, 111, 148, 218-20, 243, 250, 256, 265
 crooked and straight..........252
 fixed...43, 51, 78, 104, 107, 111, 118, 218-20, 243, 250, 252, 285, 288
 masculine/feminine...54, 56-57, 59, 60-61, 65, 69-70, 73, 99, 110-11, 118, 126, 196, 212, 228, 256, 259-60
 tropical...51, 56, 58, 60-62, 64-65, 71, 78, 104, 109, 111, 148, 197, 200, 210, 218-20, 250, 256, 265
 types of land...................82, 185
Spear-bearing....86, 228, 231, 238
Stations...79, 104, 115, 125, 129-30, 155, 166-67, 170-71, 173, 178-79, 184, 197, 202, 213, 236, 241, 244, 271
Stephanus (associate of Theophilus)...3, 16-17, 19, 34, 36, 41, 282
Sundbādh.................................101
Theophanes.................................11
Theophilus of Edessa...1-45, 49-51, 53-56, 58, 60, 65-66, 74-75, 78-80, 83-84, 86, 89-90, 92, 96, 99-100, 106, 108-10, 112, 122-23, 126-27, 131-35, 140-41, 149, 152-54, 192-93, 200, 211, 214-16, 218-19, 221-22, 226, 235, 237, 245, 247, 249, 259, 261, 271, 274, 277-82, 285-97, 299-300

Thought-interpretation...30, 215, 231
Timocharis......................7, 22, 124
Transits, transiting...23-25, 60, 64-65, 66, 82, 108, 125, 129, 133, 138, 140, 142, 144-46, 163, 164-77, 179-84, 237, 241, 282, 300
Triplicity lords...93, 125, 128-31, 194, 208, 210, 258, 291
Twelfth-parts...35, 75, 82, 84, 196, 203, 206-07, 214, 230, 239, 241, 250, 252, 256, 262, 269, 298-99
'Umayyad Caliphate..1, 5-6, 9-12, 18, 40
Under/out of the rays...43, 58, 60, 62, 66, 73, 75, 89-90, 93, 95, 100, 104, 114, 122, 125-27, 131-32, 135-36, 138, 141, 147-48, 154-60, 164-85, 194-95, 200-01, 203-04, 210-11, 213, 224, 233, 236, 242, 244, 246, 252, 258, 262, 269, 291, 295, 296
Valens, Vettius.8, 22, 24, 124, 140, 209, 258-59, 264
Varāhamihira.................................4
Void/empty in course...95, 99, 229, 239
Weather...154, 156-60, 162-63, 169, 173, 177, 181
Yavanajātaka..........................4, 32
Yazdijird III.................................1
Yazīd III (Caliph).......................11
Zāb, river and battle.............10-11
Zarādusht/Zoroaster...26, 101, 112

CPSIA information can be obtained
at www.ICGtesting.com
Printed in the USA
BVOW09s0306010817
490718BV00005B/99/P